DEMOCRAT AND DIPLOMAT

Democrat and Diplomat

THE LIFE OF WILLIAM E. DODD

Robert Dallek

OXFORD
UNIVERSITY PRESS

Oxford University Press is a department of the
University of Oxford. It furthers the University's objective
of excellence in research, scholarship, and education
by publishing worldwide.

Oxford   New York
Auckland   Cape Town   Dar es Salaam   Hong Kong   Karachi
Kuala Lumpur   Madrid   Melbourne   Mexico City   Nairobi
New Delhi   Shanghai   Taipei   Toronto

With offices in
Argentina   Austria   Brazil   Chile   Czech Republic   France   Greece
Guatemala   Hungary   Italy   Japan   Poland   Portugal   Singapore
South Korea   Switzerland   Thailand   Turkey   Ukraine   Vietnam

Library of Congress Catalogue Card Number: 68-29717
ISBN: 978-0-19-993172-9

1 3 5 7 9 8 6 4 2

Printed in the United States of America
on acid-free paper

For My Parents and Geraldine

Contents

Preface to the Paperback Edition

IN 1968, WHEN I first published my biography of William E. Dodd, *Democrat and Diplomat*, Dodd, who had gained prominence in the 1930s as American Ambassador to Nazi Germany, had been lost from view. My book, which had been my doctoral thesis, brought Dodd back into focus as a Jeffersonian democrat whose shrewd judgments on Nazi horrors had deepened Franklin Roosevelt's concerns about Hitler's threat to democracies everywhere and international peace.

The book provided a window into the tensions between FDR's White House and the conservative State Department professionals, who believed that Dodd's antagonism to the Nazis compromised his ability to gather information on them and impoverished his reports on conditions in Germany. Roosevelt, by contrast, valued Dodd's view of Nazi intentions as a useful barometer of where Europe was heading and what would serve America's national interest. The president and his undiplomatic ambassador were more astute than the State Department's overly cautious experts, who put diplomatic correctness above political astuteness.

By the time my book was published, Dodd's view of the Nazis seemed almost redundant. The horrors of World War II, including the unthinkable crimes of the Holocaust, dwarfed the early insights of an ambassador, who, in a time of isolationism, was a small voice with little public impact. But it influenced the president, whose resolve to run against the popular current of detachment from world affairs made a great difference in getting the country prepared for its essential part in the war.

In 2011, when Erik Larson published *In the Garden of Beasts: Love, Terror, and an American Family in Hitler's Berlin*, readers were ready to reengage with 1930s Germany. But Larson wasn't just any author; he had established himself as a successful popular writer with a 2003 bestseller, *The Devil in the White City*. As important, his reconstruction of Berlin under the Nazis, Dodd's ambassadorship, and his daughter Martha's intimate relations with Nazis and Soviet agents, as well as her life as a spy for the Russians, gives his book the feel of a novel. His rendering of events put me in mind of the observation that truth can be stranger than fiction. It also reminded me of Philip Roth's assertion that it is difficult to be a fiction writer in America since the reality often outdoes the novelist's imagination.

I was grateful that Larson's book gave me the chance to revisit my four-decades-old book and republish it at a time when, judging from Larson's success in reaching a very wide audience, readers might like to learn more about Dodd as a historian and ambassador. Larson's book focuses on Dodd's first year and a half in Berlin, though he does include brief closing chapters about the end of his ambassadorship and the two years after he returned to the United States, where he lectured about the Nazi threat and the importance of defeating Germany in the war that erupted in September 1939, some six months before he died. My more detailed account of Dodd after 1934 may fill in the outlines of Larson's discussion of this period in Dodd's ambassadorship and life.

While Larson's volume devotes far more attention to Martha Dodd than I provided, this new paperback edition of my book gives me a chance to add a chapter to her story. In the fall of 1968, my wife and I traveled to Europe, where, among other things, I hoped to meet Mrs. Stern (Martha Dodd married a New York investment broker named Alfred Stern in 1938). She and I had been in touch about my book. She had given me permission to quote from her father's papers in the Library of Congress. She was in Prague, where she and her husband had taken up residence in 1957. They fled the United States for Mexico in 1953 after they were accused of espionage and lived there for four years before moving to Czechoslovakia. The FBI apparently had a substantial body of evidence linking them to Soviet agents in the United States. When I first wrote to her, she urged me to run our correspondence through her attorney in New York. Since I had nothing to hide and assumed that our correspondence would be read by U.S. government agents, I insisted on writing her directly.

During our trip to Europe, which began in London and continued through Paris and Berlin, I asked at the U.S. embassies and consulate about traveling to Czechoslovakia. Because Soviet troops had occupied Prague to repress what was described as the Prague Spring under Alexander Dubcek, we were advised not to go to Prague. In Berlin, however, a consulate official thought it would be no problem.

American journalists were in the city, as well as U.S. diplomats, and he saw no reason that we couldn't go as tourists. The chance to see Prague in the midst of a historical struggle for freedom and to meet the then-legendary Martha Dodd overcame our anxieties about the risk of entering a politically volatile world.

It turned out to be a memorable adventure. As we crossed the border into Czechoslovakia, the border guard genially noted that Dallek is a Czech name. "Would I be called to service in the Czech Army?" I half-jokingly said to my wife.

Although an October-gray overcast—part seasonal rains and part coal-burning smog—greeted us in Prague, we could quickly recognize why so many visitors praised the central city's attractive squares and the spires of the storied Charles University. The Europa Hotel, where we stayed, was a throwback to the elegant 1920s, with large, high-ceilinged rooms and bathrooms down the hall appointed with large tubs and lacking anything resembling a modern shower. The restaurants spoke volumes about the austere life under a Communist regime. Meat dishes were measured out in kilograms surrounded by abundant potatoes—a diet high in starch and low in protein.

My goal of meeting Martha Dodd was put to the test the day after our arrival. Joe Alex Morris, the *Los Angeles Times* correspondent covering Eastern Europe, whom I met in the hotel bar, told me that Mrs. Stern had not been seen since Soviet troops had occupied the city. I promised to report back to him if I located her. My search began with a streetcar ride to a name and an address on the envelopes she used to correspond with me. The apartment residence in a somewhat shabby neighborhood proved to be that of Martha Dodd's secretary, a middle-aged woman who greeted our inquiries for Mrs. Stern with suspicion. She hesitantly invited us in after some explanation of who I was. Over tea, she initially explained that Mrs. Stern was out of the city. When would she return? I asked. She didn't know, or so she said. But after more conversation, she explained in a hushed voice, perhaps fearful that our conversation was being recorded, that Mrs. Stern, fearing the Soviets would accuse her of being a CIA agent and instigator of the Czech rebellion, had fled to Havana, Cuba.

I was not totally surprised. Morris had told me that Martha Dodd was a kind of fish out of water in Prague: she moved around in a chauffeured limousine and was notable for her expensive, fashionable clothes that one associated more with society ladies in Paris than with a devoted supporter of a Communist regime. Although happy to have her on their side, her Soviet contacts never saw her as anything but a somewhat unreliable dissenter from accepted American ideas. One Soviet assessment of her reads: "She considers herself a Communist and claims to accept the party's program. In reality [she] is a typical representative of American bohemia, a sexually decayed woman ready to sleep with any handsome man."[1] No doubt, some in the Soviet intelligence hierarchy saw her as a possible double agent, living in Prague but really a subversive force advancing U.S. interests.

I never met her. In 1976, after the Justice Department dropped the charges against the Sterns, citing the unavailability of witnesses and the statute of limitations, Martha declared her intention to travel to London. We renewed our correspondence and made a plan to meet in England, where I expected to be in the summer for some research on Franklin Roosevelt's foreign policy leadership. But she never made the trip to London, explaining that family illness had changed her plans.

I am grateful to Erik Larson for having so skillfully reconstructed the Dodd history, which reminds people not only of how astute Dodd was in Berlin but also—and more important—of how delusional the Nazis and millions of Germans were. As the German philosopher Friedrich Nietzsche said, "Convictions are more dangerous enemies of truth than lies."

Robert Dallek
Washington, D.C.
January 2012

Preface to the Original

WILLIAM EDWARD DODD was an important American whose life and many public activities influenced major American developments. The author of significant histories, biographies, and essays, an architect of Chicago's great university and history department, a brilliant lecturer and inspiration to two generations of students, a tireless fighter for progressive advance, and Franklin Roosevelt's ambassador to Nazi Germany for four and a half years, Dodd helped fashion American attitudes and affairs in the first forty years of the twentieth century.

Dodd's life also has something important to tell us about the nineteenth-century American in a twentieth-century world. Faithful to an America of yeomen farmers, small towns, and popular control, Dodd is an example of the Jeffersonian democrat who found it difficult to understand the problems generated by an urban, industrial society. Stated another way, Dodd's life is evidence of the fact that nineteenth-century beliefs were a source of difficulty and confusion in dealing with twentieth-century affairs.

At the same time, Dodd's life shows that Jeffersonian values remained a source of strength and understanding in a radically different era. Indeed, it is partly the argument of this book that Dodd's effectiveness as an educator, historian, reformer, and diplomat derived in good measure from his Jeffersonian beliefs. Hence, if the flexibility and modernity of some twentieth-century Jeffersonians seems, in the words of one writer, to be "an inviting enigma," it is my hope that this study of Dodd will take us part of the way toward solving this riddle.

Since more than a third of this volume deals with Dodd's ambassadorship, I should like to add a prefatory word about that section of the book. When I began this work on Dodd, it was primarily out of an interest in his diplomatic career or, more specifically, out of a desire to understand why someone as perceptive about Nazism as Dodd should have a reputation as a poor diplomat. In answering this question, I concluded not only that Dodd was a far more successful ambassador than we have been inclined to think but also that his diplomatic career tells us a great deal about the nature of effective diplomacy in Nazi Germany. Since Dodd's ambassadorship was at the center of German-American relations, this study should also contribute to our growing knowledge of diplomatic conduct in Berlin and Washington in the prewar years.

In the course of this study, I have had the aid and advice of many people. The staffs of the Manuscript Division of the Library of Congress, the Franklin D. Roosevelt Library, the Historical Division of the Department of State, and the University of Chicago Library all eased my way through the many manuscripts I had to consult for this work, and I wish to express my sincere appreciation for their help. Mrs. Martha Dodd Stern kindly granted me permission to quote from her father's papers and saved me from a number of errors through a careful reading of the manuscript. The Academic Senate of the University of California at Los Angeles and the President's Office of the University provided me with research funds and released time that significantly hastened the completion of my work.

Three of my former teachers and colleagues at Columbia University gave an initial version of this manuscript the benefit of their wise counsel. Fritz Stern suggested numerous revisions and additions, which helped make this a far more complete and penetrating study than it otherwise would have been. The same was true for William E. Leuchtenburg, whose kind attention to my work at a particularly trying moment made more difference than he might have guessed. My largest obligation belongs to Richard Hofstadter. His help and friendship have been a call to generosity and balanced scholarship, which I hope mark the pages of this book and all I may do in my career.

A number of other friends and colleagues have placed me in their debt with a variety of helpful suggestions and corrections. They are Fred L. Israel, Larry Kincaid, Lawrence W. Levine, James McLachlan, Walter P. Metzger, and Hans Rogger. To this list I would like to add the name of Richard Weiss with a special note of thanks for friendship and counsel that have served me in this work and much else. In the closing stages of my research and writing, I was spared countless library chores by Beverly Bollinger, Nancy Hollander, and Gary May. The manuscript was entirely and ably typed by Claire Pirone.

This note of acknowledgment would not be complete without an expression of appreciation to my wife, Geraldine R. Dallek, whose help and encouragement made her a partner in this book as in all else.

R.D.

DEMOCRAT AND DIPLOMAT

I

A Race of Settlers and Farmers

WILLIAM EDWARD HEARD about it often as a boy. The Dodds had come through the Civil War better than most. The slaves were gone, of course, but they had been few in number and certainly fewer than those lost by planters in the Deep South. There was some property damage toward the end when the Sherman Yankees ruthlessly searched the old Dodd place in Clayton on their way from Goldsboro to Raleigh. But it could have been worse. The year's food supply had been salvaged, hidden in a great hollow log, and the horses had been saved when secreted in a dark huckleberry swamp. Yet even their loss would not have been so bad. Harry Durham, after all, the nearest neighbor, had lost members of his family in the war, and local "fire-eaters" had given up the fight at the end of a Yankee rope.[1]

The Dodds had almost always come through better than most, and they had been in North Carolina for over a hundred years. The family, as near as the boy and later the man could place it, was of Scottish or English ancestry with New World origins in the 1740s.[2] The first to come across apparently was a David Dodd, a farmer who settled among the Highland Scots in eastern North Carolina's Cape Fear Valley. But although the Cape Fear Scots spoke little English, wore the kilt, and opposed the War of Revolution against king and country, David Dodd rose to major of militia, membership in the General Assembly, and a part in the North Carolina constitutional convention of 1776. David's sons, however, William, Reuben, and Dempsey, were never so illustrious. They were still men William Edward could be proud of nevertheless. "A race of…settlers…[and] farmers,"[3] they moved north from the Cape Fear Valley into Johnston County, acquired land, prospered in diversified farming, bought a few slaves, and passed the fruits of their toil on to their sons.

The next two generations of Dodds, William's grandfather and father, were less fortunate; the rush of affairs played havoc with their private lives. John Dodd, the grandfather, had done well enough. In the 1840s he established his family and inheritance of slaves on a cotton farm in Clayton, thirty-nine miles southeast of Raleigh. There he gained respect as a yeoman farmer—one of North Carolina's few holders of ten or fewer slaves. But the Civil War saw to that distinction and left John Dodd with little to provide his sons. The oldest boy, John Daniel, had subsistence at home until his twentieth year in 1867. But then, eager to marry his neighbor's daughter, Eveline Creech, he moved to Raleigh to earn a stake. Finding work as a custodian at North Carolina's Hospital for the Insane, he remained in the capital for more than a year. Upon his return in December 1868, he married "the Creech girl" and took up farming on a piece of Creech property outside of Clayton. That Stanford and Martha Creech had land enough to spare for their oldest daughter and first son-in-law was probably unusual in the southern United States in 1868. The Creeches, much like the earlier Dodds, were solid North Carolina citizens with a bit more than most.[4]

The newlyweds, with help from relatives and friends, in a matter of days constructed a four-room frame house on their property and settled directly into their fathers' ways, habits traditionally assuring lives of middle-class success. The ingredients were long hours, hard work, cotton crops for cash, and wheat, corn, oats, beans, hay, potatoes, and peas for livestock and table. The first year of marriage gave John and Eveline Dodd all they could ask. Crops were good, cotton went for 25 cents a pound, and, best of all, there was a son, William Edward, born in his father's house on October 21, 1869.

For the boy growing up in the 1870s and '80s there was much talk of politics and the Old South. From his father, a firm believer in "white democracy," William Edward learned about the war and northern wrongs—radical reconstruction, carpetbag governors, and Republican tariffs were objects of almost daily scorn. Only a strong Democratic party, his father often said, could remedy the southern plight. His mother, by contrast, spoke chiefly of the old days, of slavery and the slave family at her father's home. "Though…given…a Negro girl, Mary Lee by name, for a personal servant when…quite young, [Eveline Dodd] always spoke of slavery as a terrible thing. She even said the slaveholders were wholly to blame for the great civil conflict…." It was an opinion William rarely heard. Eager to know more, he asked family friends and neighbors about such things and kept written records of what they said.[5] The pervading influence of his early years was that of his parents' efforts to sustain the heritage of yeoman success: work in the fields, crops and livestock, younger brothers and sisters, new rooms in the frame house; in past years it had all added up to accomplishment and a decent standard of life. The experience of the 1870s and '80s, however, taught the father and especially the son that tradition did not square with current facts.

In the two decades after the war, the North Carolina farmer in particular and the southern farmer in general suffered a severe economic eclipse. Whereas manufacturing, transportation, and banking prospered in the postwar years, farmers—tenants and small landholders alike—found it increasingly difficult to make ends meet. Returns on their produce dropped steadily, while prices on manufactures, fertilizer, cotton bagging, farm machinery, and other essentials did not decline as much or at all. A cycle of falling prices, increasing costs, crop-liens, and mortgages drove tenants into "peonage" and owners into tenancy. The "sturdy" yeoman of prewar years was now the picture of frustration and despair.[6]

Clayton, North Carolina, a farming community of some two to three hundred families did not escape the turmoil of the day. "Every year of my boyhood," William Edward later recalled, "the price of cotton, the one market commodity of the county, fell lower and lower, and all the articles we bought, clothing, shoes, furniture and the like sold at rising prices.... There was little wealth of any sort, not three old time pleasure carriages still in use; and all the pre-war aristocrats were on the same social level as their former small-farmer neighbors." "My...acquaintances and kindred were poor people...," he recalled. "...All worked in the fields with their own hands from sun to sun. The...merchants and their clerks were the only exceptions to this general rule. The daughters of the Hornes and...of the McCullen family were the only people I ever knew who drove or rode on summer evenings for their health or pleasure."

By the time William Edward was eleven his father's fortunes had declined to near bankruptcy. In 1880, like so many other southern farmers, he was producing more cotton than ever before, but the cruel cycle of prices and costs had driven him to borrow and mortgage his land. Only easy credit terms supplied by his wife's uncles, Sam and Ashley Horne, local supply or dry-goods merchants, allowed the family to retain its home.[7]

Small wonder a Mississippi man declared agriculture the world's "basest fraud." Small wonder William Edward and his brothers sought an avenue of escape from the farm. Not that William shirked household duties and chores or rebelled against field work with one's "own hands." As a matter of fact, he was his father's most diligent son. In a family of seven children competing for recognition from parents burdened with financial woes, the surest path to approval was through obedience and hard work—the two traits William Edward most consistently exhibited at school.

Enjoined to work hard at everything he did, William earned a reputation as Clayton's most studious boy in and out of class. "Monk Dodd," his schoolmates razzed, had no time for fun: foot races, baseball, raid the melon patch, round the neighborhood pond were games he never played. Apparently finding the rewards of study more gratifying than any to be gained on the farm, William soon exhausted the resources of Clayton's "five-months-a-year free school." Offered only the "fundamentals of learning"—reading, writing, geography, grammar, and arithmetic—in a crowded classroom with a single teacher, William persuaded his great-uncle Sam Horne sometime in the 1880s to pay the "moderate" costs of attendance at Professor E. G. Beckwith's "Utopia Institute," the "best school Clayton ever had." In the company of less burdened teachers and excellent students like John White, the minister's son, and his cousin Herman Horne, William excelled at his studies even more than before. Consequently, when Professor Beckwith was called to teach mathematics at Wake Forest College in December 1888, William was invited to join a Miss Ellington in temporarily running the school. In June, at the end of the term, however, Professor Beckwith closed the "Institute" and left William to return to work on his father's nearly impoverished farm. But more eager now than ever for instruction in the "higher courses," William laid plans for a military career. Believing himself unprepared for a four-year military college, he decided upon a year's further study in a "fine" private academy. Winning his father's consent and his uncle's support for the plan, he left Clayton in September on the first long journey of his life, one hundred and twenty-five miles to the Oak Ridge Military Institute in the north central section of the state.[8]

Almost twenty when he arrived at Oak Ridge, William was older than most of the boys whom Professors J. Allen and Martin Holt, the proprietors of the school, aimed "to inspire with a combination of lofty ideals and interest in scholarship." A natural leader to the younger boys, William at once took first rank in the class, distinguishing himself as cadet and student. Encouraged by his immediate success, he solicited and won support in the spring for an application to the United States Military Academy at West Point from "eleven North Carolinians, including a sheriff, a clerk of court, two doctors, two state senators, and Josephus Daniels," the Raleigh newspaper editor. Though endorsed as a young man "no service nor exposure can daunt," as "apt, practical, ambitious, and determined," and as having a "conscientious sense of duty," William won only an alternate's appointment. He next thought of the exclusive state university at Chapel Hill. While admission to the University of North Carolina might force some revision in his plan, it seemed a small price to pay for attendance at an institution which was in fact beyond his reach. In 1890 William's social position and previous education tacitly barred him from admission. Such a policy was common to southern state universities maintaining a tradition of exclusiveness dating back to ante-bellum days. His rejection, however, did not discourage him unduly, especially when Professor Holt notified him that he was to have his diploma in June with high honors in English and history. His best course of action, Holt advised, was to replenish his now exhausted funds with a job as principal of Glen Alpine's only public school and to wait out some final word from West Point.[9]

Glen Alpine, a community of five hundred in western North Carolina, was hardly William's idea of a place to settle down; even final news in the summer of 1890 of rejection from West Point could not persuade him of that. Besides, there were other prospects. A friend at Oak Ridge had told him about "President John M. McBryde," the new and energetic head of the Virginia Agricultural and Mechanical College, some one hundred and fifty miles away. The school had "great teachers" and funds from the federal land grant act for deserving students. It was in fact just what William wished. Winning admission to the spring term with a small grant to see him through the year, he set out from Glen Alpine in January on "the long and marvelous railroad journey over the Blue Ridge to Knoxville, up the famous Tennessee and Virginia valleys" to the "wonderful mountain campus at Blacksburg." There William was led, baggage and all, across the snow-covered grounds to meet President John McBryde, the "distinguished aristocrat of South Carolina," who spoke to him not of hard work and studies, but "of skating, sledding, horsemanship and sports." "It surprised me," William recalled. "But he was kindly nevertheless and soon had me classified...."

If William at first thought President McBryde and his nine staff members frivolous, he soon changed his mind. The Virginia Agricultural and Mechanical College, or Polytechnic Institute, as it became known in 1896, was chiefly a military college with rules and regulations strictly applied. Every one of the one hundred and thirty-five students dressed in the "college uniform of dark blue blouse, gray trousers and forage cap" in which he marched to classes and meals morning, noon, and night. The strict schedule of discipline extended to three field drills a week, room inspections, and off-campus passes. Even class hours were no exception: Commandant of Cadets Lt. J. A. Harman taught geometry and calculus in the best West Point fashion: students sat with backs straight, stomachs in, chins out, and eyes ahead while cadet Dodd demonstrated mathematical proofs at the blackboard.

William's four and one half years at the V.A.M.C. worked a profound change in his plans. Within a year the attractions of military drill and course work had worn thin and the whole system of discipline became a burden to his body and mind. Apparently other students suffered from the same sense of boredom and oppression, for they went to great lengths to manufacture diversions and pranks. Sending a roommate's belongings to a girl friend was a common practice, as well as sham duels in which unsuspecting freshmen were led to believe they had accidentally killed an opponent. One year students painted the President's cow and hoisted a professor's carriage to the top of his house. William had little use for such pranks and in fact resigned his lieutenancy in the cadet corps in his last year when a prankster went unpunished for dousing him with a water bucket during an inspection tour. There were milder, more constructive diversions, however, such as the introduction of baseball and football in 1892 and the organization of a dance club in October 1893. But again William had neither aptitude nor appetite for games and dances; almost twenty-two when he arrived at the college, his sights were fixed on more serious things, especially the intellectual and social opportunities never before opened to him.[10]

Of the seven programs of study leading to the Bachelor of Science degree in 1891, William chose the broadest one, V.A.M.C.'s version of liberal arts, "general science." In his four and one half years at the college he mastered the intricacies of French, German, Latin, English, history, chemistry, botany, physics, mathematics, and mechanics, subjects either totally or partly new to him. His greatest interest, however, was in the English, history, and political economy courses taught by "the most stimulating instructor at school," Professor Edward Sheib. Thrilled with his discovery of the classics and a talent for writing, in the spring of 1892 William and a classmate sparked a revival of the campus literary magazine which had not been published in three years.

His initial interest in *The Gray Jacket* was as a forum for intense religious feelings he had come to hold during his first year in Virginia. While having had some religious training at home, he did not develop a strong interest in formal religion until 1892–93. He "deported himself as 'an active and consecrated Christian and Baptist'"; he "attended church and prayer meeting regularly, and…he taught a girls' class at Sunday school." He joined the Y.M.C.A. and contributed a monthly column about the association to *The Gray Jacket*. "Why not everyone join the Young Men's Christian Association?" he asked his fellow students. "It will encourage and foster the principles of true manhood. It will aid you in carrying out what your parents wish you to carry out. Yes, every laudable ambition will receive an impetus….If an evil influence is exerted, the student…often makes a wreck of his life….In youth carelessness, thoughtlessness, or idleness, is often the beginning of a worthless existence….The very dawn of such a life is in the neglect of religious service."[11] Religion was the helpmate of ambition.

Although William became president of his college Y.M.C.A. in 1894 and represented it at a national assembly in Northfield, Massachusetts, his interest in literature, history, and current affairs had by then exceeded his concern with formal religion. He gave up his association column in 1894 to become *The Gray Jacket*'s literary editor; and he contributed essays on "Walter Scott," "Dean Swift," and "Abuses of the English Language," for which he won the college essayist's medal. He helped elect Fred W. Simpson, his best friend, president of the senior class, and he contributed several essays to *The Gray Jacket* on the causes and remedies of southern poverty and distress. The desire for riches, "the worship of Mammon," the sacrifice of independence and honor, the neglect of tradition and education, the failure to "appreciate her great men," and the decline of the small farm had all, in William's estimate, driven the South "toward the bottom of America's honor list." Schools, libraries, and the celebration of the "great Southern past" would help reverse the trend. But only the return to the small farm, cultivated by independent, sturdy yeomen could uplift the South and restore it to its vaunted place in the Union. Revive old values, he told his schoolmates. "We are our own masters if we give not ourselves to other powers." A nation's, a section's greatness derives not from "money, population, climate or situation," but from the "uprightness" and "self-reliance" of her citizenry. However determined he had been to escape his father's farm, William's attraction to the southern yeoman farmer lasted all his life.[12]

With his shift in interest from religion to writing and current affairs, William decided by his senior year in 1895 that his tastes and talents best suited him for a career in journalism. His model for this life's venture was Josephus Daniels, editor from 1885 to 1895 of the Raleigh *State Chronicle* and the Raleigh *North Carolinian*. As a progressive, but staunch Democrat, Daniels favorably impressed young Dodd with his crusades for prohibition and public education and his campaigns against the American Tobacco trust and the Republican party. What particularly attracted William was Daniels' willingness to be a reformer in the Democratic camp. At a time when thousands of North Carolina farmers showed themselves more loyal to the Populist Alliance than to the old Democracy (the Democratic party), William admired Daniels' efforts to make his paper "the bridge on which both Alliance and non-Alliance Democrats might march to victory." Loyalty to his party and his image of it as an instrument for reform was to be a hallmark of Dodd's life. "Will has been a Democrat from the day he was born and he'll die one," his father once boasted.[13]

If Daniels' example and William's talents inclined him toward journalism, other considerations seemed to bar the way. Only the most "extensive and varied ... acquirements," Fred Simpson explained, would permit him "to excel" in this profession. Besides, where did he intend to find a job? Without an answer to this question, William decided to alter his immediate plans. He took work as Clayton's public school teacher in the summer of 1895 and accepted an offer from President McBryde to return in the fall to the V.A.M.C. as a graduate instructor in history for a two-year term.

William found several reasons to return to Blacksburg. Above all, he liked it there, though Blacksburg itself held few attractions; in 1895 it was still "a mere village" located eight miles off the main railway line. The pace and tempo of the campus, however, refreshed and excited him as nothing ever had before. Under President McBryde, the school was undergoing a dramatic change. In William's four years alone, the student body and staff had increased almost three-fold, while in McBryde's entire sixteen-year term student enrollments reached a high of 728, and sixty-seven new buildings transformed the grounds. Moreover, McBryde turned an industrial school granting certificates in practical agriculture and mechanics into a four-year college awarding undergraduate and graduate degrees. But beyond all this, William's return to Blacksburg promised him further association with Professor Sheib in an individual program of study toward an advanced degree.

William never regretted returning, for his second stay in Blacksburg proved to be more enjoyable than the first. For the first time he lived off-campus—a privilege denied undergraduates—and escaped all military routine. He shared rooms with other graduate students in a local minister's home and took meals each night at Slade's Inn, the favorite village spot. He joined the Society of Bachelors, or Bachelor Club, and passed happy evenings debating the topics of the day—free silver, populism, tariffs, and trusts. He prepared classes in sophomore history and read widely in preparation for a general science master's exam. Most important of all, though, with the help of Professor Sheib, he finally settled on a career.[14]

Believing William an extraordinary student and a potentially brilliant teacher, Sheib urged him to pursue a Ph.D. in history and an academic life. Nearly twenty-eight in the spring of 1897, William did not wait to make up his mind. With seven hundred and fifty dollars in savings, he announced his intention to begin full-time work at Harvard or Yale in the fall term. But Sheib advised him to go abroad. Having earned his doctorate in the psychology of education at the University of Leipzig in 1885, Sheib urged him to take a German Ph.D. Graduate study in America, Sheib explained, was but an imitation of the original. Germany was still "the fountainhead of historical scholarship," and many of America's prominent historians, including Henry Adams, Herbert Baxter Adams, and John W. Burgess, had studied there for a time. Moreover, if he went to Leipzig, he would soon find himself in the company of Karl Lamprecht, the famous advocate of the "collective psychological," or cultural, approach to history.[15]

For all Sheib's encouragement, William nevertheless had great doubts. For one, he feared his departure might jeopardize a budding romance with Jessie Battle, a Clayton girl attending North Carolina's Salem College. Secondly, in 1897 it was no longer common for Americans to seek their historical training abroad. In fact, of twelve professional historians teaching in the South in that year, only one had earned his Ph.D. in Europe, with the majority having studied at Johns Hopkins University in Baltimore. Moreover, William anticipated expenses of up to two thousand dollars over the next two years, and his application for a correspondent's job with *Men,* the international journal of the Y.M.C.A., had come to naught. If he chose to go, the money would have to come from his uncle Sam Horne. Determined at least to try, William bicycled in late May from Blacksburg to Raleigh to tell his uncle the plan. Something of an early North Carolina industrialist, an immensely energetic and wealthy man with "credit...up to tens of thousands of dollars" and holdings in the Raleigh Commercial National Bank and the Careleigh Phosphate Works, Horne proved even more generous than William hoped. He agreed to lend him fifteen hundred dollars in exchange for an unendorsed promissory note with unlimited time to pay. Journeying on to Clayton to bid his family and friends good-bye, William encountered there many "a skeptical...glance. Everybody in Clayton wondered whether they would ever see me again," he recalled. "Ashley Horne...had a few years before taken an ocean trip to New York....A terrific storm overtook him on the return journey; and he often spoke of the terrors....His experience did not add to the cheer of my proposed ocean voyage."

Despite such misgivings, William's return to Clayton only stiffened his resolve to go. The sight of his father's meager farm and news of Herman Horne's admission to graduate study at Harvard encouraged his desire to get on with his career. With "all" his "earthly possessions...a big, new trunk and a bicycle in the [ship's] baggage car," he "...set out in early June via Norfolk for the great unknown."[16]

II

The Leipzig Adventure

ALTHOUGH HE REFUSED to be deterred by "family doubts," William sailed from New York on June 7, 1897, with considerable anxiety about the wisdom of his venture. His first weeks in Europe only added to his qualms. No sooner did he arrive in Leipzig than he barely escaped a fatal accident. "Unacquainted with the traffic rules of a great city," he narrowly missed a collision with a street car. "But for the sudden halting of the car," he remembered, "…[he] might never have entered the university." Moving off to find living quarters, he discovered what he believed to be a comfortable but modest room near the Johannis Kirche in the university quarter. But a week's stay proved his judgment on the pension unsound. The church's "everlasting bells" rang out every hour of the day and night and "a pushy Deutsches Mädchen [was] always trying to attract [his] attention." His first encounters at the university were even more distressing. Attending the lectures of the prominent historians, Karl Lamprecht and Erich Marcks, he found it almost impossible to follow what they said. His whole reason for coming seemed jeopardized by a language bar.[1] Other, more distant concerns weighed on William as well. He could not forget that his father and family continued to live poorly on their meager farm while he had borrowed "a huge sum" to come abroad to pursue what might well prove to be an unsatisfactory course. At times he felt himself unworthy and in consequence begged reassurance from his cousin and friends. "You think a great deal of this place [Clayton] and people," Herman Horne wrote him at the beginning of August, "and

I can assure you in return that you are beloved here. Everybody has a good word for you." "You say you would like to know what your classmates' thoughts were as regards you and your studies while at Blacksburg," Fred Simpson replied. "They are mine," he wrote without elaborating, "and I think they are natural ones." Such encouragement somewhat eased his mind, but he continued to wrestle with self-doubts. When Jessie Battle announced six months later that she could no longer be anything more than a friend, William assumed that her decision rested upon "a previous judgment" that he was "unworthy." "Jessie is not your enemy," the reliable Horne now wrote. "She is a good friend who thinks very much of you." But William could not believe it; indeed, he decided for a time that no woman could think much of him, or at least he feared this enough to demand assurances from Horne of its falsity.[2]

If such misgivings particularly plagued him in these months, it was characteristic of William to spare no effort to ensure his success. He soon took daily German lessons from "a most conscientious teacher" and added to his hour sessions by regular conversations with a German friend. He moved to a satisfactory apartment at 12 Johannisallee, twenty minutes from the university and fifteen minutes from a boarding house popular with his new-found American friends. Fearing that too close association with his countrymen would preclude any facility with German, he limited his English conversation to their evening dinner meeting once a day.

By November, when university work began "in earnest," he was feeling settled in. The German language no longer defeated him, and he went daily to hear lectures by Lamprecht and Marcks. His comprehension was now so good, in fact, that he attended lectures in philosophy and read German novels "as an occasional relief from history—especially the then popular charming story writer, Heinrich Seidel."

At the beginning of his Christmas holiday in mid-December, he even felt himself ready for a two weeks' tour. He bicycled south to Dresden...., where for the first time he heard one of Wagner's operas. On Christmas Day he traveled slowly down the Elbe to Meissen, "a fascinating old town.... For a young Carolina-Virginian," it was a visit "rich in suggestion and instruction."[3] Like Washington Irving earlier in the century, William found himself in "the shadowy grandeurs of the past."[4]

By the time William returned to Leipzig he had begun to feel that his whole experience was rather heady stuff. But it was more than his accomplished German and firsthand glimpses of the past which exalted him. Like so many other American students in Germany in those and earlier days, he was infected by the condition of *Lernfreiheit,* the freedom to come and go as he pleased. When news came in February of Jessie Battle's rejection, for example, he launched a "mild revolt against his puritan upbringing," learning to drink beer, and cultivating his recently acquired taste for opera with attendance at Leipzig performances in the company of an English girl known about the university as a coquette. Not long after, at Easter time 1898, he went off to Weimar with Johann Hoffmann, his closest German friend. Tramping about the city, Hoffmann proudly discoursed on "the great men who had studied at Luther's famous boys' school" and showed William through Goethe's home. Unlike Henry Adams, who thought Weimar "a nice, funny little pumpernickel" where "they bore you to death...with Goethe and Schiller," William pronounced it "the 18th century German Athens."[5]

What helped make William's excursions and life in Leipzig so enjoyable during these months was his growing confidence that he would earn his Ph.D. By April 1898, barely ten months after coming to Germany, he had already completed what he felt to be a substantial course of lectures and readings toward his degree. To prepare for his only required test, final oral examinations in modern European history, education, and philosophy, he attended as many as twenty lectures a week to hear Wilhelm Wundt on educational and experimental psychology, Überweg-Heinze on modern philosophy, Karl Lamprecht on German cultural history, and Erich Marcks on the recent history of the French and German states.[6]

Of the four, William easily found Lamprecht the most stimulating. The directing spirit of Leipzig's modern history faculty and "a man of prodigious vanity," Lamprecht was the most controversial German historian of his day. "If the value of an historian were measured by the noise which his name makes in the world," one contemporary wrote, "Lamprecht would be one of the great ones." When William came to Leipzig in 1897, Lamprecht had only recently won his reputation; between 1891 and 1895 he published the first six volumes of his *Deutsche Geschichte* which, in his own words, "accomplished a revolution in history." "The important milestones in the development of historiography," he boasted, "are Voltaire, [Ernst] Bernheim, and I." Lecturing to 350 students a semester on the nature of this "revolution," Lamprecht argued that history was a science which could uncover the "immanent laws" contributing to the development of "the German consciousness" or "national folksoul." Comparing himself to Leopold von Ranke and his school of "purely political historians" who thought to understand history through the study of individuals, Lamprecht insisted that historical truth could only be achieved through the study of conditions and the "collective or social psychological." His *kulturgeschichtliche Methode* would do no less than "establish a science of history, based upon sociological laws."[7]

Though Lamprecht's estimate of his contributions far exceeded that of contemporary and subsequent historians,[8] he nevertheless exercised an "immense influence" over Leipzig students and attracted almost one hundred budding scholars each year to his seminars in *Kulturgeschichte.* There were so many students demanding training with Lamprecht that in April 1898 William found himself unable to enroll in the "great" man's seminar; and since none of Lamprecht's colleagues and assistants shared his enthusiasm for *Kulturgeschichte,* William was compelled to study political history in a seminar with Marcks. Despite the difference in subjects and emphasis, Marcks, like Lamprecht and all German historians of the time, viewed his seminar as a workshop of scientific practice in which students learned the method of their discipline and undertook their own research.[9]

As it turned out, Marcks' seminar was all William could have asked. There were at least three highly intelligent German students who contributed greatly to their discussions and debates. Along with Otto Hoetzsch, Arnold Meyer, and Heinrich Laube, all of whom later won national reputations for their work, William scrutinized the volumes of Ranke, Theodore Mommsen, Heinrich von Treitschke and Heinrich von Sybel. With "much objectivity and little partisan or patriotic pleading," they "idolized" Ranke's "character and work," pronounced Mommsen's *Romische Geschichte* not "quite disinterested and objective," declared Treitschke the "foremost of historical propagandists," and "reworked" von Sybel's *Begrundung des Deutschen Reiches* "at many points." They "studied most critically the problem of responsibility for the outbreak of the Franco-Prussian War," and frankly acknowledged "that for once in history a German diplomat—Bismarck—had outwitted the French." Marcks himself guided all their work, and in contrast with Lamprecht, urged them to consider the historical importance of individual men. Having only recently completed studies of Admiral Coligny, Kaiser William II, and England's Queen Elizabeth, Marcks pronounced biography and history practically one and the same. Greatly impressed with Marcks's ideas and approach to history, William decided at the close of their seminar in August to meet the thesis requirement for his degree with a study in political biography. It was in fact the first of several such works he would write during his career.[10]

If Marcks's influence helped determine the kind of work William would do both in the short and long run, there were far more personal factors at work in determining what the content of that scholarship should be.[11] When he came to Leipzig in the summer of 1897, Dodd found himself for the first time in his life compelled to defend what he liked to call his "instinctive attraction to the Jeffersonian faith." Given the uncertainties of his early years—uncertainties which plagued him all his life—and given the attractive descriptions, indeed celebrations, of his yeomen ancestors and his father's efforts to follow their ways, it is not surprising that William took Thomas Jefferson and the Jeffersonian tradition as a firm model of conduct. "I have a sneaking suspicion," he once wrote Carl Becker, "that you are as much of an eighteenth century man as I am...." Further, having lived almost exclusively among farmers and their offspring in the upper South, he never knew anyone to dispute the essential virtue of that section's traditional ways. But his two earliest and closest American acquaintances in Leipzig, Vernon L. Kellogg and Elliott H. Goodwin, soon put his ideas to the test. Kellogg, a Kansas Republican who later became a famous entomologist and Herbert Hoover's friend and aide, repeatedly pronounced the South and all its traditional habits guilty of the Civil War. Kellogg "gave me as a sort of hint and parting shot," William later recalled, "a copy of [the] Bigelow [*sic*] papers. I then was all-too-Southern, he too Northern." Goodwin, a Massachusetts Republican and the grandnephew of Harvard's President Charles W. Eliot, contrasted southern poverty with northern wealth as an argument for the Republican party, industrialism, and imperial expansion.[12]

In answer to Goodwin, who despite their differences became a lifelong friend, William argued that such ideas promoted inequality of condition, undemocratic attitudes, and an urge toward war, exactly the conditions William detected in the Germany of that day. In lectures, he told Goodwin, his professors praised the conservatism of the American Supreme Court and Constitution. In his seminar, his fellow students joyously celebrated the victory of "a real German and an aristocrat" over a Social Democratic candidate for the Reichstag—a professor widely known for his pacifism and social work not unlike that of Jane Addams. In his pension, Fräulein Zobel, his landlady, repeatedly closed off heated discussions with the remark that "it 'Ist streng verboten' to talk that way about the Kaiser." Everywhere he turned there was warlike talk: Johann Hoffmann "loved…to expatiate about his crazy hero [Friedrich Nietzsche]: 'Supermen,' 'the will to power,'…'Macht,' 'conquest,' 'der Tag,'…'war,' [and] 'world conflict.'" "'How helpless would the United States be if invaded by a great German army?'" Hoffmann once asked. Wilhelm Wundt drove English students from his lectures with verbal sallies against Britain's challenge to German empire. Lamprecht announced the death of Bismarck with trembling voice and fled the lecture hall in tears. German students organized protest rallies against the admission of foreigners to their universities and particularly singled out Slavic and Jewish students for abuse. Germans questioned his opposition to the Spanish-American war and announced that "Germany too would one day have her place in the sun." Such attitudes might be fine for Germans, William lectured Goodwin, but they had no place in the United States.[13]

What particularly disturbed Dodd in all this was the fact that Goodwin's ideas and "German attitudes" seemed already to have fixed themselves firmly in American minds. Moreover the "seedbed" and "planting ground" of American democracy, the Old South, by contrast, was in sharp eclipse: William himself had fled the "ancestral home," and even his father in the fall of 1897 had abandoned his farm and land; Sam and Ashley Horne purchased it as a site for a "huge" cotton manufacturing plant. Why were Jefferson's democracy—the best possible social and political system contrived by man—and the South—the great Jeffersonian base—so much on the wane? William decided to make the answers to these questions the chief object of his historical work. He would begin with the origins of the Democratic party in a study on Jefferson's return to politics in 1796.[14]

That William's distance from source materials in the United States might prove a bar to his thesis seems never to have occurred to him or to Marcks, who gave full approval to his plan. For all the talk in the 1890s in German universities of scientific investigation and thorough research, Ph.D. candidates in history found themselves able to satisfy thesis requirements with essays of fewer than one hundred pages researched almost exclusively in printed sources. The test, of course, was whether the student contributed something new, but even then, judging from William's experience, the research he undertook was something less than rigorous.[15]

Traveling to London in August 1898 to consult American state papers in the British Museum, William gathered sufficient material in only six weeks' time to tell adequately his "Jefferson-Hamilton story." This excluded weekends given over to travel and fun. One weekend he "loitered about Stratford-on-Avon trying to understand the miracle of William Shakespeare...." From Stratford he walked first to Warwick to see "the wondrous reminders of Medieval England," and then to Kenilworth to view the remains of the ancient castle in and around which the novelist, Walter Scott, laid one of his classic scenes. It was "one of the most delightful and stimulating weekends of...[his] life." Though the pressure of work prevented him from traveling more widely, he came away from England in the autumn with a deep appreciation of that country's tradition and life.

After several weeks of work on his thesis in Leipzig, he set out during his Christmas holidays to study "certain American state papers" in Berlin which had escaped him in London. But stopping at Wittenburg on the way "to meditate upon the scene and reminders of Martin Luther," he found that "the old church, the door on which the 95 theses had been nailed, and the miraculous medieval nooks and crannies in the little city made history seem even more real than before." More enthusiastic about touring than about research, he spent much of his time in Berlin "walking about the city, visiting the gold deposit at Spandau," "the wonderful tombs of the Hohenzollerns" at Charlottenburg, and "the famous museum of war materials and conquered flags...[near] the Wilhelmplatz" where he caught a glimpse of "Kaiser Wilhelm II being greeted by a group of Prussian officers."[16]

Despite these and other distractions, William's thesis suffered not in the least. During the next seven months, he worked continuously on the "little book," reaching conclusions about the origins of the Democratic party which still have validity to this day. In contrast with the conventional notion that Jefferson spent his time after retiring from Washington's cabinet in organizing or directing an opposition party, William emphasized Jefferson's great reluctance to return to politics and the pressure which his friends put upon him to do so. As a later historian put it: "Jefferson did not create a party: a wide-spread popular movement recognized and claimed him as its leader."[17] When William presented the thesis to Marcks, the "Gelehrter" offered some sharp criticism of his written German, but made only one substantive complaint; he believed Dodd had been too critical of George Washington.

With his thesis accepted, William rushed toward the completion of his degree. In a three-hour session at the beginning of August in *die Halle,* as the German students called the examination room, William passed his final examination *cum laude.* A few days later he was again at work on the dissertation, reading carefully Marcks's brief comments on the margin. After satisfying all Marcks's complaints, he found a printer who, in line with university regulations, agreed to publish one hundred copies for less than one hundred dollars. With the manuscript in the printer's hands and several weeks to wait, he decided upon a final fling, a tour to Frankfurt and "thence through Switzerland over the St. Gothard Pass to Northern Italy and return."

Despite the exhilaration of his travels and the prospect of his Ph.D., William returned to Leipzig in a gloomy mood. During his two years in Germany he had continually worried about his chances of landing a teaching job. With "no dream of being located in the North," with no university connections in the South, and only German letters to recommend him, he correctly assumed that he would be hard pressed to find a spot. But whatever else may have changed during his time in Germany, William was as determined as ever to earn success. To be sure, his qualms about winning a post occasionally shook his resolve, leading him in the fall of 1899 to consider the possibility of taking up a consular career; but there was still the gratifying encouragement of his cousin Herman Horne, who now urged him to understand that he would surely find a job in the States.

Once having decided to seek a post at home, William made a direct line for Raleigh. Arriving at his father's home in early November, he took out little time for social calls, going right to the business of finding a job. In two months' time, with the help of Josephus Daniels, who endorsed him as "a young man of...keen historical insight and an excellent literary style," William found himself a nominee for three attractive jobs. President Charles W. Dabney of the University of Tennessee negotiated with him "a little on a proposed salary of $600 a year....But the offer was not...made." The trustees of the Greenville (South Carolina) College for Women considered him for the presidency of their school, but again no offer was forthcoming. Most disappointing of all was his failure to win an opening at Chapel Hill, where Daniels had so many friends. "My training was for a professorship of history," Dodd complained. "Only nobody wished my services!"[18]

Whatever his distress, William's problems in locating a job served chiefly to encourage his interest in writing and lecturing. Convinced that professional recognition and a position would come primarily on the strength of his written and spoken word, he published two articles in November on German militarism in Daniels' Raleigh *News and Observer,* and he lectured at North Carolina Agricultural and Mechanical College, Durham's Trinity College, and the Virginia Polytechnic Institute in December and January on the Protestant Reformation in Germany, "European Schools of History Today," and "Glimpses of Politics and Men One Hundred Years Ago." At the same time he began research on a biography of Nathaniel Macon, "third speaker of the National House of Representatives and one of the co-workers of Thomas Jefferson."

Through such a study, Dodd hoped to expand on his Leipzig thesis and explore the rise and spread of Jefferson's democracy in greater detail over a longer period of time. Beginning his work with newspaper files and documents on early North Carolina history in the state library, he soon discovered that he had few personal manuscripts to go on. To help remedy this, he undertook a visit in the spring to Warren County, the "broken and bankrupt region where Macon had lived and where slavery had flourished on a grand scale." Standing in May 1900 by the "huge pile of rock" that marked Macon's final resting place, he wondered at the lack of any "indication" of who or what Macon had been. Visiting "the unique 18 x 20 foot house in which the famous democrat of aristocratic family . . . lived all the later decades of his life," and sensing "as never before the traditions and behavior" of this old South, he determined to reconstruct for posterity a word portrait of this man and his times. "History," he recalled, "had its grip upon me as I returned to Raleigh."[19]

If history had its grip upon him, there was also much in his work which could be related to current affairs. Having called his study to the attention of Josephus Daniels, Dodd won an acknowledgment from the editor that his biography might give the nation and the South a portrait of a "model statesman." Daniels, in fact, was sufficiently convinced of the currency of Dodd's work to promise help with its publication and to ask Dodd to bring his historical knowledge to bear against President John C. Kilgo of Trinity College, a Republican defender of North Carolina's tobacco trust. Wishing to answer Kilgo's attack on Jefferson as "an infidel, . . . a demagogue and a leveller," Daniels directed Dodd to construct an article for the *News and Observer* proving the "Virginian" a Christian and a democrat.[20]

Daniels' encouragement and his own eagerness to establish his professional standing inclined him to rush the Macon book, but shortly after coming home William found himself "enthralled" by another interest. Renewing his acquaintance with Martha Johns, a friend of Jessie Battle's at the Salem Female College, and an occasional correspondent during the Leipzig days, William was soon strongly attached. Although she was six and a half years his junior, a member of a "unique" Auburn family, formerly owners of many slaves and still counted as "wealthier and more aristocratic" than Clayton folks, Martha Johns reciprocated his feeling. His "reputation as a hard and venturesome student," he was convinced, "gave me a welcome that made my visits delightful." As the spring of 1900 came on, they drew closer together, but with "no income and no position," he "delayed the momentous question."

His decision to defer a proposal until he could find a job actually served as a boon to his work. Still convinced that a position would have to come to him on the basis of his post-doctoral achievements, he traveled to Washington at the end of May to study secondary works at the Library of Congress which, aside from James Schouler's multi-volume *History of the United States under the Constitution,* were not available to him in Virginia. After reading Henry Adams on Jefferson and "a mass of correspondence" held by Justice A. B. Hagner of the District of Columbia Supreme Court, his thesis "no longer looked good" to him, and he "never glanced over its pages again."[21]

Despite his growing disregard for his Leipzig work, it served in combination with his current studies to win him a professorship. In mid-August, toward the end of his stay in Washington, he met the Reverend James Hammond, pastor of the city's Southern Methodist Church. A graduate of Randolph-Macon College in Ashland, Virginia, Hammond expressed the opinion that "a biographer of Nathaniel Macon might be a suitable professor of history in a college named for Randolph and Macon." Though "of the same opinion," William left Washington with nothing more said. His return to Raleigh, however, was brightened by an invitation from the president of the college to visit the campus "'as soon as possible.' 'Since it' was about the last possible chance that year," William permitted "no delay." He traveled to Ashland, which impressed him as a "beautiful little town," where he met Robert Emory Blackwell, the senior member of the faculty. A Leipzig student in 1878–79, Blackwell at once formed a favorable impression of the young man. Although he asked no letter of recommendation, he contracted with William for a trial year.

Despite a number of reservations about the institution, the appointment enormously elated Dodd. He "noticed a more considerate and respectful attitude" among his relatives and friends, and he "pinched" himself to see if he "were the same person. To be a professor at Randolph-Macon," he believed, "made a difference!"—though apparently not enough to allow him to marry. With a salary of only $900 and "a debt of $1500 hanging over" him, he and Martha Johns decided to bide their time. While he had hopes of securing his position and retiring a part of his debt during the year, his primary satisfaction at that moment came from the knowledge that "after all the Leipzig adventure might not...have been a blunder."[22]

III

Scientific History

FOR ALL HIS high hopes, a month's residence in Ashland, Virginia, was enough to put Dodd back in the doldrums. Ashland, he quickly discovered, though only sixteen miles north of Richmond, was neither a Leipzig nor a Raleigh. A typical Virginia rural community with no telephones, electric lights, running water, or paved streets, it housed twelve hundred residents in old, unpainted homes with huge fields for vegetables and livestock. Founded originally as a health resort, it became a way station for the Richmond, Fredericksburg and Potomac Railroad in 1866. When Dodd arrived there in September 1900, it was known chiefly as a training ground for Methodist ministers and as a center for Methodist revival meetings. The community, according to one resident, was so puritanical that "cards, dances, the theater, and even a little claret in lemonade spelled sin." One organizer of harmless card parties was condemned to "do penance under the devil's watchful eye."

The college itself was by Dodd's standards more a "small Sahara...than an intellectual oasis" in a cultural desert. Founded in Boydon, Virginia, in 1830 as the first Methodist Episcopal institution of higher learning in the United States, the college was induced by a twelve-acre land grant from the railroad to move to Ashland in 1868. By 1900 the Ashland campus was the men's division of the Randolph-Macon system, which included a women's college at Lynchburg, Virginia, and an academy in Baltimore. Despite its growth, the men's college was faltering when Dodd took up residence there in September. With eight dormitories, two office buildings, and a

nine-thousand-volume library to accommodate one hundred and thirty students
and fifteen faculty members, the school, like all private colleges in Virginia at the
time, had trouble competing with state-supported institutions offering more attractive facilities and a less expensive education. Apparently the offer of free tuition to
ministers' sons and pre-ministerial students attracted sufficient numbers of undergraduates to keep the college going. The consequence, though, was a preoccupation
with "ecclesiastical form" which drove the "more liberal" professors, including Dodd,
to distraction. The "bright and eloquent" professor of biology, for example, "who
unfolded…the entrancing interpretation of the beginnings of life suggested by
Darwin, Wallace and Huxley," only preserved his post against the intrigues of alumni
and trustees "with the right intonation at college chapel." It was not long before
Dodd was complaining about "Randolph-Macon provincialism" and predicting
that sectarianism would soon put an end to his job.[1]

Certainly as unattractive to Dodd at the outset was the work piled on him by the
college. Invited to organize and administer a department of economics and history,
Dodd found himself with an almost endless round of duties. His preparation and
teaching of courses alone was enough to exhaust the most energetic of men. In his
first semester at the college he taught fifteen hours a week in five different courses: a
rapid survey of Greek and Roman history, five meetings a week; a history of England
from 1265 to the accession of George III, three sessions a week; the French Revolution
and the Napoleonic Wars, three times a week; a history of Virginia to 1828, twice a
week; and European and American governments, two meetings a week. The spring
semester offered him no relief; there were five more courses to be taught, adding up
to ten preparations for the year.

Even if he had wished it otherwise, the demands of his work in this first year made
Dodd into something of a recluse. He lived in a small cottage facing the railroad and
rarely showed himself on campus outside of regularly scheduled class and office
hours. In appearance, he was "as plain as an old shoe," wearing side whiskers grown
during his German student days and showing little regard for current fashions. He
was so "slight in stature" and "lean of frame" that his cheekbones were the most
prominent feature on his face. His shabby appearance and preoccupation with work
quickly won him, as in earlier years, the nickname of "Monk."

If Dodd had anything good to say about the college in this first year, it has not
turned up in print. His chief concern outside of his work was to find another
job. He beseeched Josephus Daniels, his cousin Herman Horne, and his teachers
at the Virginia Polytechnic Institute to aid him in this task. He made inquiries
as near as Chapel Hill and as far away as Kansas about positions "at a dozen
other institutions, some of which could have been no more desirable than the
Ashland college."

When no other job materialized by the end of the spring term, Dodd resigned himself to going back for a second year in the hope that his "faithful performance of present duties" would ensure his "promotion to a finally satisfying place." For the time being, however, there were certain compensations at Randolph-Macon. History was already recognized by the best students at the college as an indispensable part of their education, and the trustees rewarded his achievement with a small salary increment. Fears of losing his post had decreased sufficiently to allow him and Martha Johns to announce their engagement in August 1901 and to marry on December 24, before the end of the year. All and all, as Dodd recalled, "it was a hopeful, joyous, if a little anxious, time ... I a young historian, afraid to say historian, lest I seem egotistical and not sure the job at Ashland would remain at my command.... [The] two of us, after the manner of the ages, about to set out, poor and without friends in high places, on the road" they were to travel for thirty-seven years.[2]

By the beginning of his second year at Randolph-Macon, with the groundwork already laid for his courses, Dodd found himself able to give increasing attention to his study of Nathaniel Macon. But by then his Macon book had become something of a secondary concern. His chief interest was in the development of a "scientific attitude toward history" throughout the South. While most southern history in 1901 still "bore the imprint of the sword and magnolia cult, the aroma of the lost cause ... [and] a certain provincialism of outlook," rapid progress was being made toward the collection, study, and publication of "impartial" findings in southern historical sources. The impetus for the whole undertaking had come from Herbert Baxter Adams in the 1880s at Johns Hopkins University in Baltimore. Adams trained a score or more of young southerners in historical methodology; provided a medium of publication through the establishment of the Johns Hopkins University *Studies in Historical and Political Science;* and assembled a southern collection in the university library. During the nineties the Adams experiment was repeated all over the South: John Spencer Bassett at North Carolina's Trinity College published five monographs on North Carolina history, collected books, pamphlets, newspapers, and manuscripts for his Trinity College Historical Society, and founded the society's *Historical Papers* and *The South Atlantic Quarterly* (1902) as media of publication; William P. Trent at the University of the South explored ante-bellum history in monographs and biographies and launched *The Sewanee Review;* while Franklin L. Riley turned Mississippi's university into an active center for instruction, research, and writing concerning the state's history.[3]

Despite his heavy work load, Dodd began in his first year to imitate the achievements of Bassett, Trent, and Riley in the nineties. Determined, as he put it, to help turn southern history—and North Carolina's in particular—into something other than "mere pedigree hunting and political party history with a purpose,"[4] in September 1900, less than a month after coming to the college, he organized the Randolph-Macon Historical Society for the collection and study of North Carolina and Virginia documents. "'Much valuable material is going to ruin every day in Virginia,'" he told his students, "'for the lack of proper attention.' [Once] in ransacking a courthouse garret he uncovered a half-dozen large boxes of mouse-eaten deeds, wills, letters, and legal reports, some of them dating as far back as the late seventeenth century. The clerk of court 'was astonished that he should be asked so minutely about such worthless stuff!'"[5] Instructing a handful of interested juniors and seniors in the methods of historical writing he himself had only recently learned at Leipzig, Dodd soon had the best of them writing essays and sorting documents for publication in *The John P. Branch Historical Papers,* a quarterly journal begun in June 1901 and named for a wealthy Methodist banker from Richmond who agreed to provide annual funds.[6] While pleased with this achievement in his first year at Randolph-Macon, Dodd set himself the larger goal in September 1901 of helping to raise standards in the teaching and study of history throughout the entire South. When the American Historical Association met in Washington, D.C., in December 1901, he joined John Spencer Bassett in urging the organization of a southern branch of the association to undertake the job. Winning only the organization of an ad hoc committee, which excluded him and Bassett from its work, Dodd decided to study the problem on his own. Drawing on southern college catalogues and his personal knowledge, he published a report in *The Nation* in the summer of 1902. The heart of his argument was that "there is no section of the country in which both local and national history is so little studied and so imperfectly understood." Most southern schools of higher learning, he pointed out, required of undergraduates only one course in history, and that a course giving only the outlines of general history during three class hours a week. Only two universities employed more than one instructor in history; only the University of Texas made any creditable showing in "highly specialized study in particular fields"; and only a "visionary" among undergraduates chose a speciality in history, especially when, as often occurred, a "single text constituted the whole work of the senior history class," and that text more often than not had recorded on the margins of its pages the "stock stories and jokes doled out to patient students from year to year." The chief "causes of this backwardness," as Dodd saw it, were a "sheer conservativism in favor of the classics," the accumulation of wealth by unlettered men who cared little for a liberal education for their sons, and a general demand throughout the South for teachers who thoroughly subscribed to justifications of the southern past.[7]

When Dodd's report drew angry criticism from southern "conservatives" and the research committee presented a disappointing survey at the close of the year,

Professor William A. Dunning of Columbia University organized a formal program on history teaching in the South for the New Orleans meeting of the association in December 1903. Since Bassett was scheduled to discuss southern history teaching in general, Dodd directed his attention to conditions in Virginia and the Carolinas. In the three states, he told his colleagues, there were only seventeen history teachers for five million people. Massachusetts, with but half this population, numbered "her teachers of history by the hundreds." "Without libraries, without complete sets of public documents, without the means of reaching the few would-be students of our history, productive scholarship...fails almost entirely. And what is worse," Dodd complained, "these conditions react on the industrious and ambitious teacher so that...he becomes simply a 'hired man,' a bread-winner. He soon falls into the habit of doing nothing, then he fails to keep up his connection with the outside world, his life winds up in failure, and the South is little improved by his having lived."[8]

Dodd was determined not to let this happen to him. At his first meeting of the American Historical Association in December 1901 he introduced himself to some of the leading members of the profession, including Charles Francis Adams, Jr., Albert Bushnell Hart, and Frederick Jackson Turner. At the same meeting he joined Bassett, George P. Garrison of Texas, Bernard C. Steiner of Johns Hopkins, and Lyon G. Tyler of William and Mary in a formal discussion of southern history, giving a paper on "The Place of Nathaniel Macon in Southern History." Further, he published his first scholarly article in *The South Atlantic Quarterly* in April 1902, "North Carolina in the Revolution." Challenging the conventional notion that North Carolina had played a major role in winning the Revolutionary War, he hoped the essay would in part provide southerners, and North Carolinians in particular, with a sample of "impartial," "objective," or "scientific" history.[9]

Even more to the point was his study of Nathaniel Macon, which he completed at the beginning of 1903. The chief object of the book, he explained, was to destroy once and for all the "myth," "fancies," and "inconsistencies" about Macon and the North Carolina of his time. His method was "scientific": putting before the public previously unpublished materials and straightforward statements about "the conditions which influenced Macon," Dodd expected the fair-minded reader to draw his own conclusions. But the completed biography was so "impartial" that Dodd failed to explain his man. Refusing to discriminate between important and unimportant events in Macon's life, Dodd included everything; a fact, any fact about Macon seemed to justify its inclusion in the narrative. The consequence was a long, detailed, rambling—"comprehensive" was Dodd's word for it—catalogue of Macon and North Carolina history from the Revolution to the election of 1828.

If Dodd were "impartial" in his depiction of Macon's character, this was not the case in his discussion of larger historical issues. He was, in fact, eager to show southerners and historians around the nation that the great period in southern and national history was the one dominated by Jefferson and his "simple-lived, small farmer" supporters of the South and West. As if to have the last word with Goodwin and Kellogg, Dodd described America's history in the years from the Revolution to Andrew Jackson's election as chiefly a struggle between the democratic, nationalistic South, the true founder of the American experiment, and the undemocratic, sectionalist Northeast. It was the battle of agrarian democracy against vested interest, the clash of Jeffersonian democrats with Hamiltonian "snobs."[10]

However much of a personal statement it may have been, the publication of his Macon book in the spring of 1903 quickly established Dodd, along with Woodrow Wilson, William P. Trent, John Spencer Bassett, Edwin Mims, and William Garrott Brown, as one of the South's "liberal" or "nationalistic" historians—a trained professional eager to rise above sectional bias and integrate "the South into the national pattern of life." That northerners also shared this goal was shortly illustrated by invitations to Dodd from *The New York Times* to write for its "Saturday Review of Books" and from Professor Ellis P. Oberholtzer of the University of Pennsylvania to contribute the volume on Jefferson Davis to the American Crisis Biographies series. This did not mean, however, that northerners had only praise for Dodd's work. Contemporary critics justly complained of numerous factual errors in his work, and an excessive dependence on Schouler, both of which Dodd himself freely admitted. Moreover, later critics could also reasonably argue that "Dodd's biography was concerned more with the political history of the period…than with Macon himself," and secondly, that Dodd's themes and interpretations were less than original, or no more than a derivative statement of the esteem for Jefferson and Jeffersonian democracy current in the United States at the turn of the century.[11]

If the Macon book won Dodd a certain national standing, it also secured his position at Randolph-Macon. The college now established him in a permanent "chair," and reduced his teaching duties to nine hours a week beginning in September 1903. Furthermore, faced with the possibility of a university trying to hire him away, Robert E. Blackwell, President of the College, and Bishop James G. Cannon, Chairman of the Board of Trustees, now promised Dodd "complete freedom to speak and act on his own convictions." Actually, Dodd and his employers were not that far apart in their views. Blackwell and Cannon accepted the "New South" philosophy of sectional reconciliation, and Dodd, a conscientious Baptist, posed little threat to their religious goals for the college.

Dodd himself by the beginning of his fourth year in Ashland had settled into a comfortable routine, expecting, as he later reminded his wife, "our lives to drift there with all those earnest, prayerful Methodists." With his father-in-law's help he had purchased a handsome house with a large garden which he cultivated personally.

Since the house was on Railroad Avenue, Ashland's main street, and surrounded by pine trees and tall oaks, the Dodds had little trouble renting one or two rooms to history students. With the boarders' rent and the more than skillful housekeeping of Mrs. Dodd, the young couple lived more comfortably than some of the older and better-paid faculty members—so much so in fact that students began to speculate that the Dodds had outside means.[12]

Yet for all their expectations and comforts, in the fall of 1903 Dodd was as eager as ever to leave Ashland. As he so well understood, his ideas and attitudes toward his work were less suited to a denominational college than to one of the country's emerging universities emphasizing research and practical public service. Moreover, before October was out, Dodd was deeply distressed by the section-wide onslaught against his close friend John Spencer Bassett for having publicly taken issue with the South's handling of its "Negro problem." The demands for Bassett's removal and Dodd's outspoken support of his friend confronted Dodd with the prospect of a similar fate.[13] But when the Trinity College trustees gave Bassett a vote of confidence in December and no job offers came to Dodd from the association meeting in New Orleans, Dodd resigned himself to another year in Ashland, and the hope of future advancement through continued writing and research.

Between September and June he published in *The New York Times* five two-thousand-word reviews of historical books ranging from Guy C. Lee's popular *The True History of the Civil War* to George Otto Trevelyan's *The American Revolution*. In each case he applied the standards of "scientific" history and praised or chided the author accordingly. At the same time he edited two more issues of the *Branch Historical Papers,* published articles on "Karl Lamprecht," "Our Educational Progress" and "The United States Senate," and dispatched letters to all parts of the country for information about Jefferson Davis.[14]

When the school year came to a close in June, Dodd decided on a research trip to Washington and Richmond instead of a badly needed vacation. Despite the fact that he believed "it...for the best" and that he had "accustomed" himself to "some kinds of sacrifices," three weeks in Washington archives were all he could bear. "You must not worry so much," his wife advised. "The future will be kind to us." "I think the best thing for us to do is to...let you *rest* this summer. You know darling your health is more precious to me than all else." Returning to his Ashland home, he limited himself to reading, working in the garden, and writing two reviews for *The New York Times.*[15]

Though refreshed by a respite from the grueling pace he had sustained for over four years, the resumption of the school term in September confronted him with even heavier duties. The number of his students increased to the point where he had all he could do to assist them; *The New York Times* required him to write four reviews in three months, almost as many as he had done in the entire previous academic year; the *Branch Papers* demanded continual attention; and Karl Lamprecht arrived in Ashland from Germany to be escorted to the World Congress of Arts and Sciences in St. Louis. "I doubt that I shall ever finish the Davis," the overworked Dodd told his publisher. "Or if it should be finished, I doubt whether it will be worth publishing." The spring semester gave him little reason to change his mind. He juggled his writing commitments, contributing less copy to the *Times* while completing essays and reviews for the *Richmond Times Dispatch, South Atlantic Quarterly,* and *American Historical Review;* although he found some time for archival work in Richmond, the Davis book remained only partly researched and entirely unwritten.[16]

When the summer of 1905 came on, he was no more prepared to head South than he had been the year before. His wife, who was now pregnant with their first child, was "the bluest, loneliest mortal on earth" when he left, and his health stood in jeopardy of being "completely broken down" before his return. But he believed it absolutely essential that he go and seek out all available manuscripts in South Carolina, Alabama, and Mississippi.[17]

His trip, although it lasted better than six weeks, proved less successful than he had hoped. Outside of Alabama, Georgia, Mississippi, and South Carolina newspapers, he found little in the city library of Charleston or at the Alabama and Mississippi departments of history and archives to supplement what he had already learned in Washington and Richmond. Yet despite his inability to turn up more manuscripts and, in general, the paucity of his original sources, Dodd returned to Ashland in July determined to begin writing. As with his Leipzig thesis and his study of Macon, he could intuit the direction his book on Davis would take.[18] Davis himself, like Macon, was to be treated in the best "scientific" spirit and the most "impartial" fashion. "It is not an easy thing to think and speak dispassionately of Jefferson Davis," Dodd announced at the first. "His career recalls to the Northern man the long and agonizing struggle of 1861 to 1865; and to the Southerner, it suggests anew the separate nationality once so fondly dreamed of.... Between these extremes, it is the author's aim to steer a middle course," and "simply to relate the story of that remarkably tragic life." "I fear," as Dodd put it to Charles Francis Adams, Jr., "public opinion is still 'un-ready' for an interpretative biography." Though the book might provide less than a satisfactory portrait of Davis' character, it was to be enough for Dodd if it found a place among the "impartial" histories of the War—the War or "Irrepressible Conflict," as Dodd and most professional historians now called it, which was no longer to be blamed on the North or to "be treated as a rebellion [by the South], but rather as the great event in the history of our nation."[19]

In its broadest outlines, the book was to be an expression of the "liberal" southerners' current attitude toward all southern history. The hero was again to be Thomas Jefferson and his spirit of democratic nationalism which once had such wide acceptance in the South. The villain in the piece was to be Davis and his "ruling, monopolistic class"—the "one-twentieth of the population…who were ready for war at any time to avoid a surrender of their privileges." In 1860 it was these men, Dodd argued, with their "power of concentrated wealth, the value of lands and negroes devoted to the production of the staples—cotton, tobacco, sugar—that dominated the thought of southern men. In these princes of the plantations, the small planter saw his *beau ideal* in life; and it was, therefore, not difficult to bring such men to the support of the large masters, as it was not a rare thing for a small planter to become a great slaveholder." The Civil War was to be described as most "liberal" southern historians saw it—namely, as serving the South and the nation admirably in destroying the slave system, making possible a return to Jeffersonian values, and bringing forth once and for all "a real and vital nation."[20]

In one respect Dodd's *Davis* struck a new note. In devoting almost half his book to Davis' presidency, Dodd developed the theme that Confederate defeat could be attributed more to internal disorders and divisions than to battlefield losses or Davis' incompetency. In contrast to the prevailing idea that Davis failed the Confederacy, Dodd contended that Confederate "success was entirely within the range of possibility…but on condition of absolute (or nearly) unity among Southern leaders."[21] Dodd's conclusion helped open a discussion about Confederate rule which has not been closed yet.[22]

If Dodd had reached these conclusions about Davis and the Confederacy by the summer of 1905, he still had considerable doubts about translating them into a book. By July, when he returned from his research trip he was dead tired and wished to avoid confining himself too closely for fear he might injure his health.[23] Moreover, there were more interesting public issues now compelling his attention.

IV

Toward a Double Life

IT WAS ACTUALLY only a matter of time before Dodd became deeply involved in public affairs. From the time he returned to the United States in November 1899 to the summer of 1905 he had been greatly excited by the spirit and content of growing reform movements in all parts of the country. With a keen appreciation for current events, he recognized that widespread demands for trust and utility regulation, an income tax amendment, slum clearance, child labor laws, workmen's compensation, and an end to public vice and corruption all added up to what people were calling the progressive movement. As a man with a firsthand experience of economic deprivation, as a Jeffersonian democrat and advocate of equal opportunity, he fully endorsed the progressive programs and shared the progressives' belief that such reforms could only be achieved after the destruction of political machines and the return of popular control.

During his five-year residence in Virginia, Dodd had been particularly delighted with the success of the state's progressive forces in their battle against boss rule and corporation power. Following the pattern at work in other southern states, liberal Democrats—chiefly middle class, urban, and white—organized a reform party for the restoration of Jefferson's dream: government by middle-class citizens roughly equal in wealth and power.[1] They announced their means to this end as the defeat of regular Democrats, the acquisition of state office, the extension of popular education, and the regulation of the Chesapeake and Ohio—Virginia's—railroad trust.

The first two means to this goal had been achieved before the end of 1901. Eastern county professionals and small businessmen banded together early in 1900 to break Senator Thomas S. Martin's statewide political control. Since Martin's grip on the Democratic party, and consequently Virginia political power, rested on his ability to manipulate the Negro vote, progressive Democrats sought to disfranchise the Negro. So drastic a step, of course, required constitutional alterations, a new instrument of government barring blacks from the polls. Mounting what was then a section-wide phenomenon, a successful campaign for constitutional reform, progressive representatives convened a constitutional assembly at Richmond in June 1901. Once there, Eastern county reformers removed the only remaining barrier to their disfranchisement scheme: Western county delegates, "'more interested in economic questions' than in 'questions of suffrage,' in 'railroad domination' than in 'Negro domination,'" demanded and received a corporations commission as the price of their support. Though this agreement was for all intents and purposes a one-point bargain, it proved more durable than any dared hope; it gave Virginia progressivism a coalition and a base.

At the same time that convention delegates were attacking Martin's organization through Negro disfranchisement, other progressives were issuing a more direct challenge. Andrew Jackson Montague, state attorney general and outspoken Bryanite, supported by Richmond and Lynchburg attorneys, William Jones and Carter Glass, launched a county-by-county campaign for his party's gubernatorial nomination. Denouncing both Martin's choice for the job, Claude Swanson, and the Democratic machine, Montague demanded "popular rule" and "party nominations by direct primaries." The result of the Montague campaign was impressive: the August state party convention revealed a majority of progressive delegates and a passion for reform: Jones won adoption for a platform embodying liberal demands; Glass turned the permanent state committee into a progressive tool; while Montague gained nomination and assurance of election in the fall.

During his term of office beginning in January 1902, Montague, in Dodd's words, opened "a new era in Virginia politics with an impressive program of reform." His term as governor saw the passage of a child labor law, a corrupt political practices act, an employers' liability bill, and a temperance statute. Moreover, as Virginia's chief executive, Montague used his power and prestige to appoint a strong railroad commission, to marshal support and appropriations for improved roads, to encourage the establishment of sixteen hundred school improvement leagues and increased local appropriations, to thwart would-be lynching mobs, and to persuade the Democratic state convention of June 1904 to adopt the direct primary for party nominations.[2]

With so solid a record to run on, Montague decided in the fall of 1904 to offer a decisive challenge to the Martin machine; he announced his candidacy for Martin's Senate seat. "No real issue exists [in this primary election]," one Montague supporter wrote at the beginning of 1905, "save the destruction of the Martin machine...supported by every gambler, Sunday saloon keeper, and crook in the state."[3]

So apparently decisive a contest between progressives and politicos greatly interested Dodd. Along with hundreds of other academicians across the country, including particularly professors at the emerging universities, he experienced what one writer has called a "middle-class sense of obligation," a desire to put his expertise at the service of the state.[4]

In October 1904, therefore, a month after Montague declared himself a candidate, Dodd introduced himself to the Governor with a letter applauding his decision to run: "I do not hesitate to say to you that I trust our 'machine' may again feel the influence of your honest independence." "Relying upon volunteers and...friends to organize local political support," Montague welcomed Dodd's endorsement and invited his participation in the campaign: "I hope you will give me an opportunity of seeing you," he wrote, "and conferring with you...when you come to Richmond." Though Dodd and Montague met on more than one occasion in the next eight months, Montague asked no particular work of Dodd and in fact ignored requests from Dodd that he do so. "Command me in this good cause if I can do anything worthwhile," Dodd told the Governor in March, "...if I ever expected any position in the hands of the state, I should not venture to write so freely." But finding that Ashland and Hanover County in general were for him and that the organization of "local volunteers would arouse the politicians to buy up or otherwise secure votes that will not be cast at all," Montague decided upon a "silent campaign" for the area. It may also have been that Montague found Dodd too idealistic for his taste. It was a quality in Dodd which put off other politicians he met later in life.

Yet whatever Montague might think, Dodd decided on an active part for himself in the contest. Fired with a desire to participate in a crusade righting public wrongs and believing it "the duty of every citizen to have a share in his own government," he refused "to concur in this silent campaign." Taking the notion of public service more seriously than most of his colleagues in even northern universities, Dodd initially considered standing in the Democratic primary against the county's legislative representative, a loyal machine man; but he quickly gave up the idea as a likely waste of his time. He next suggested the organization of an "Ashland for Montague" club, but "the opinion of those present," he wrote the Governor, "was that your friends have the situation in hand." Determined to do something, he decided "to call attention to the one-sidedness of the local paper," *The Hanover Herald,* with long letters of complaint. The editor, confident of Montague's defeat, published them under eye-catching headlines: "Dr. Dodd Again Enters the Arena of Political Discussion."[5]

Hanover's "editor" in fact had it right. When confronted by the entire apparatus of the machine, Montague and the progressives suffered an overwhelming defeat: winning only 44 percent of the electorate, Montague lost by some eleven thousand votes.

Though "humiliated" by the failure of "so many others…to support" Virginia's "first real leader since the Civil War," Dodd was not discouraged by the result. "This fight has only begun," he wrote Montague soon after his defeat, "if we may judge by what has occurred in so many other states.…I, for one,…shall never cease to hold up to ridicule the winners in this fight, and I flatter myself that every boy who goes out from here [Randolph-Macon] will be…aroused to do his duty by the community and clear the state of its 'boss.'" Dodd was not alone in his hopes and intentions: other professors in America generally shared the assumption that they might have a significant impact on the thinking of their students; and other progressives around the state, including Montague, who became Dean of the University of Richmond Law School, were soon again in the field contesting Martin's political power. Dodd, himself, though returning to a full schedule of teaching and writing in the fall, including work toward the completion of his Davis volume in the next fifteen months, continued to devote considerable time and energy to "practical political work."[6]

One issue presented itself to him at once. At the close of the summer, Martin's local machine ousted Ashland's Republican postmaster, a "Mr. J. R. Fleet," "on the trumped up charge of malfeasance in office.…A combination of local Republicans with the local Democrats (manipulators of the worst sort in this state)," Dodd complained, "was made to punish the postmaster for voting independently in 1896 and 1900,…for his refusal to violate the civil service law in regard to campaign contributions" and for siding with "independent voters…[like] myself and some others who are determined to break up the 'machine' in this county."

Outraged by this latest act of "corruption," Dodd determined to fight until justice was done. After numerous conversations in Ashland and two unsuccessful appeals to the White House, he put the case before Senator Henry Cabot Lodge and Elliott Goodwin. But Lodge refused to block the appointment of Fleet's successor, a Mr. Fox, and Goodwin, now a Civil Service Commissioner, claimed no jurisdiction in the case. Another appeal to the White House, however, gained Dodd an interview with the President: Mr. Fleet is an "educated and refined gentleman," Dodd told Theodore Roosevelt. "He has been in the office for twelve years and holds the support of 95 percent of its patrons."

Having weathered a scandal in his Post Office Department just two years before, and probably eager to maintain southern progressive Republicans in office, T. R. promised to withdraw Fox's nomination and to reinstate Mr. Fleet. But the President, for whatever reasons, fulfilled only the first part of his promise and left the matter hanging there. After a year's effort, Fleet was still deprived of his job. "This state," Dodd wrote in despair, "is no more self-governing today than the Catholic Church. Thomas F. Ryan [New York financier and Chesapeake and Ohio railroad owner] is our master and he lives in New York. Thomas S. Martin is his henchman and we have powerful newspapers to defend both with none to oppose either." Dodd's description of the Virginia situation reflected what other progressives were saying about other southern states. They agreed that the "common enemy" was "the plutocracy of the Northeast, together with its agents, banks, insurance companies, public utilities, oil companies, pipelines, and railroads.... These interests," they also agreed, "were defended by southern apologists who were strongly entrenched within the old party and... controlled it through bosses and state machines." Yet, as Dodd understood, despite such difficult odds, southern progressives were waging a number of successful campaigns; the most spectacular of these was Hoke Smith's primary victory in August over the Georgia Democrats candidate for governor. In October, therefore, Dodd decided upon one final effort in Fleet's behalf. "You probably recall an interview you gave me concerning the Ashland post office...," Dodd now wrote T. R., "I see the nomination of Mr. J. R. Fleet has not been made. I venture to call your attention to the matter because news has reached me that the machinations of the local politicians have set in again...." When all he received in return was "thanks... for writing," the disappointed Dodd felt compelled to let the issue rest there.[7]

Besides, there were other matters demanding his attention. His infant son, William, Jr., was in poor health, keeping the family "on the anxious bench," and four manuscript deadlines were soon to be met: an issue of the *Branch Papers* had not yet appeared that year; a long review of John Bach McMaster's *A History of the American People* was promised for December 1; a paper on "Chief Justice Marshall and Virginia, 1813–1821" was to be read at the American Historical Association convention at the close of the year; and his *Jefferson Davis* required considerable finishing up for publication after January 1.

Though Dodd managed to drive all of his work to a conclusion in the three months after dropping "the Fleet fight," he was still unhappy with his professional standing. He believed himself worthy of a university post training "graduates," and at the association meetings in December 1906 he told Frank Hodder of Kansas and Albert Bushnell Hart of Harvard of his eagerness to leave both Randolph-Macon and the South.[8] The reason for the latter, as he explained in a letter to *The Nation* the following spring, was his impatience with business domination of southern schools.

The beginnings of such control dated from an April 1901 conference at Winston-Salem, North Carolina. Arranged by northern and southern philanthropists and professionals, the conference aimed to lift the South from its standing as the least- and worst-educated section in the country. The plan, as stated in a final report, was to give the Southland "free public schools for all [its] people, white as well as black." The goal was to be accomplished in two steps: first, propaganda campaigns financed by Robert C. Ogden and John D. Rockefeller, New York philanthropists, were to stimulate southern "public sentiment in favor of more liberal provision for universal education..." and, second, southern leaders were to convert this "sentiment" into students, teachers, books, and schools—the materials for an educated citizenry. The success of the movement was immediate and widespread: over the next ten years, 1902–12, southern school expenditures tripled, allowances per capita more than doubled, and white illiteracy fell by half. "Incalculable good," Dodd himself acknowledged in *The Nation*, "has been done. Wealthy men have been induced to contribute to the necessary funds, and southern schools and colleges have been put on a new footing; every educator of this great section...faces the future with confidence. Universal education is now popular; compulsory school laws no longer produce hideous nightmares in the minds of country legislators. Thus...a barrier to our progress has been broken down."

Dodd, however, saw a paradox in all this: the elimination of one barrier had helped produce another—a barrier to "individual and community liberty" and to Dodd's in particular. "For more than forty years," he complained in the same piece, "the South has welcomed the incoming capitalist.... Monopolies of many kinds have been freely voted by unsuspecting legislatures. The result is a newer and milder form of slavery. The beneficiaries of many concessions have wormed their way into the steering committees of the two great political parties, have found places on college boards of control, and now threaten both legislator and teacher who speak the truth about their doings.... [A] new industrial slavery...," he concluded, "is gradually taking the place of Negro Servitude." The price for business aid to education, then, or as far as Dodd could tell, was business control. What he particularly had in mind was the fact that *The South Atlantic Quarterly*—sponsored by Trinity College, one of the more heavily business-endowed colleges in the South—had "refused to publish an article from one of its regular contributors [namely, William E. Dodd]: the rejected manuscript was an arraignment of present industrial abuses in the South." Dodd had a legitimate complaint: Edwin Mims, the editor, had declined the piece on the grounds that the Trinity situation was "too delicate."[9] What is more, Dodd's complaint was not unique; there were other instances in which "well-heeled" colleges deprived business critics of free speech. But on the whole Dodd exaggerated his case; businessmen and their functionaries were hardly so capable of or so inclined toward repressive measures as Dodd seemed to think. Besides, there was little need for such efforts in the South—college and university faculties there were hardly centers of radical thought and action.

Dodd, of course, was something of an exception to the rule, though not the only one. In his advocacy of the right to engage freely in partisan activities outside the classroom, Dodd resembled other devotees of academic freedom—professors who, it is now generally understood, frequently wished a greater share of the power and respect held by American businessmen, the very people serving most often as college and university trustees.[10] Indeed, at the same time Dodd was attacking business domination of southern education, he was striking out against corporation influence in the politics of his county and state. "I have never asked for any political position," he announced in a letter to the *Hanover Herald*, "neither do I contemplate such a thing. My work is that of a teacher of history and political science, and as such I conceive it my duty to warn the community in which I live against what seems to be dangerous to the public good," Although Dodd in fact considered the elevation of academics like himself to public office a good idea, he was not being disingenuous. In his day it was a well-established, if somewhat declining, tradition of American academic life that professors cloak or conceal their ambitions, particularly if they ranged beyond the confines of university or college work.[11] "The return of Mr. [Henry T.] Wickham to the [State] Senate," Dodd explained, "...I regard as both improper and dangerous.... Wickham draws a 25,000 dollar yearly salary from the Chesapeake and Ohio.... From the people as senator he draws 300 dollars a year. As between these two masters which must he serve?... The railroads are now trying to control the state of Virginia.... 'Eternal vigilance is the price of liberty,' as well now as when Jefferson fought the opponents of popular government."[12]

Dodd's letter to the *Hanover Herald* was the opening gun in a successful six-month campaign to defeat Wickham in the Democratic primary. This time, however, unlike the 1905 contest, Dodd did considerably more than write "press releases." His candidate, Dr. Charles A. Gravatt, a physician from Caroline County with no ties to the railroad, had his fullest support. "I am practically fighting this battle alone except for the valuable help from you," Gravatt wrote him in June. "In the event of my success," the candidate announced on primary day, "...a large—perhaps the largest part of the credit—will be due to your clear dedication and active participation." Gravatt was not exaggerating. Dodd wrote speeches, arranged rallies, circulated petitions, compiled voting lists, and watched polls. The victory over the "Ryan-Martin forces" on August 28 was as much his as Gravatt's.[13]

It was, however, only a minor, local success, though Dodd took it as a harbinger of things to come, an inspiration for larger plans and victories. First on Dodd's agenda in this drive for greater accomplishments was a scheme to publish a series of letters in the Virginia newspapers pointing up machine corruption and control. He published the first of these "revelations" in the state's leading progressive journal, the *Richmond Times-Dispatch*. Its major point was that Thomas F. Ryan had hauled the Virginia delegation to the 1904 Democratic Convention in his private car. The result, Dodd asserted, was a delegation solidly for the conservative Judge Alton B. Parker. The Dodd piece, unsupported by any evidence, evoked a rash of protests and a refusal from other Virginia papers to publish his letters. Even the *Times-Dispatch* now denied him. "Ryan is so large and offensive a collection of sins," editor A. B. Williams explained, "...that it is wasting time to specialize little offenses." Finding the explanation unsatisfactory, Dodd set Williams and his fellow editors down as "afraid of the machine."

If Williams and Virginia editors in general showed themselves unreceptive to Dodd's muckraking scheme, other progressives in and out of the state praised his reform work and invited his help with their plans.[14] Former Governor Montague, for example, asked him to aid Ray Stannard Baker, the well-known progressive journalist, with his investigation of injustices visited upon Negroes in Virginia and throughout the South. Such a request must have tested Dodd's progressive faith. For, as Dodd himself admitted, he was not at all sure that he had "an intelligent and unprejudiced view of the Negro problem," or that he was "emancipated from the effects of the work of 1866 to 1876 in North Carolina," his "native state." Moreover, he was not at all sure that anything could free the Negro from his plight: "They," he had written in the previous year, "are...worse than children," and unable "to look at things from the Anglo-Saxon point of view: 1. personal purity, 2. cleanliness, 3. love of work, [and] 4. the saving of a little money for a rainy day." Yet despite his attitude toward the Negro, Dodd agreed to give Baker all the help he could. "I feel," he told Charles Francis Adams, Jr., "...the earlier we all—the nation—get down to the facts...the better for all, certainly the Negro."[15]

Even more gratifying to Dodd than the attention and respect accorded him by Montague and Baker was an invitation to dine with Theodore Roosevelt at the White House. Though the invitation came chiefly in response to an inscribed copy of Dodd's *Davis* and out of the President's desire to talk over some of the "points" raised by the book, it was further evidence of Dodd's acceptance in progressive political circles. Probably what most appealed to Roosevelt about the biography was Dodd's comparison of Jefferson Davis with contemporary industrialists and financiers in their common championship of "vested rights." It was at least the same comparison Roosevelt had drawn in a letter he had written less than two years before. But whatever T. R.'s interest in the book, Dodd gladly agreed to attend a White House luncheon on February 14. In the company of Lord and Lady Bryce, Lyman Abbott of the *Outlook,* a governor and two congressmen, Dodd enormously enjoyed the hour and a half with the President and his guests. Preserving the experience in a written memorandum, Dodd recalled the President as "blunt, quick and outspoken": he praised Dodd's study of Davis as "especially well done," declared his own writings and actions marred by numerous mistakes, and in general showed himself intelligent, perceptive, and frank about current affairs. Dodd came away deeply impressed.[16]

Less exciting, but gratifying nonetheless, was the willingness of other Virginians after the Gravatt victory to count Dodd among the progressive leaders of the state. Two days after Gravatt's election, for example, A. F. Thomas, a defeated progressive candidate from Lynchburg, urged Dodd to recognize that "the next fight will likely be in the next State Convention where I hope to meet you...." Dodd promptly replied with a suggestion for a meeting at which they could "go over the general situation" and plan a course of action.

Whether Dodd and Thomas ever had their policy-planning session is difficult to know: but it is clear that they soon agreed that the "main point" of their effort was "to get the Roanoke convention to instruct for Bryan and to send men to [the Democrats nominating convention in] Denver who are in sympathy with him." Other progressives shared the Dodd-Thomas feeling, and apparently Dodd did everything in his power to make it fact. "I write this note to thank you for the brave, manly position you have taken in the card published in the *Times-Dispatch*," a fellow progressive wrote him. "Lem Martin and John Daniel [Virginia congressmen] hope to be able to control the state convention at Roanoke and beat Bryan. I hope to have the pleasure of meeting you...[there]." "I note with pleasure that you are still an active *politician,* may I say a practical one," another note read. "When I knew you it was the theory of government alone that interested you. Now I expect to see you leading the fight at Roanoke for an 'instructed delegation.'" "We held mass meetings in Rockbridge County...," a June progress report related. "At Lexington...we voted down John Daniel as a delegate at large and gained by a good majority one resolution instructing for Wm. J. Bryan at Denver. Let us meet at Roanoke the night before and organize thoroughly before the convention meets."[17]

Dodd, however, could not attend. He was slated to teach a summer session at the University of Chicago, and professional interests were again crowding political concerns from his mind. Indeed, for all his preoccupation with progressive reform, Dodd was still primarily concerned with teaching and writing. Even at the height of the Gravatt campaign in the summer of 1907, he was rushing "during the breathing spells" to get his "overdue" life of Davis through the press and to bring out an issue of the *Branch Historical Papers* "of more than 150 pages." Moreover, in December, news of a possible opening at the University of Chicago prompted him to seek advancement to this more attractive job: "I wish you would find out," he wrote Albert Bushnell Hart, what [are] the realities of the position which [Edwin E.] Sparks leaves next year at Chicago—you know he has been elected President of the Pennsylvania State College. So far as my information goes I think the work there would suit me with the single exception that I would be grazing Rockefeller's pasture. But [Andrew C.] McLaughlin is there and...I take it that he is absolutely free....

You may refer anyone who may be interested to any well informed person in Virginia for the facts as to my standing in the South. My "Life of Jefferson Davis" which may appear any day now will show my critical attitude and perhaps a little of scholarship. Here at Randolph-Macon my classes...have always been the biggest in the college and five or six doctors, or doctor students in history at universities will show certain results.

Receiving Dodd's letter from Hart, McLaughlin talked things over with Dodd at the American Historical Association meeting in Madison, Wisconsin. Long acquainted with Dodd and his work and eager to establish a man in southern history at Chicago, McLaughlin invited him to visit the university in April to consider a formal offer.[18]

McLaughlin's proposition was "overwhelming." He suggested that Dodd come to Chicago for a trial year beginning with the summer of 1908. He was to hold the rank of associate professor at a salary of $3000; he was to teach but one course in the summer session and only two—a seminar and a lecture—during the regular year, and, best of all, he was to have the fall quarter free for his own work. If all were pleased with conditions at the close of the year, Dodd was to be made a permanent member of the faculty with a promise of promotion to full professor in three years. The excellent proposition testified to both Dodd's high standing in the profession and Chicago's great need for a southern history specialist. In its brief, fifteen-year history, the university had already become the country's major center for the graduate instruction of southern teachers. "Until the University of Chicago was opened," one journalist wrote, "Southern teachers had not been going to the great universities in large numbers....No other University has exerted such an uplifting influence over...[the South] in so short a time."

While the university impressed Dodd "as beautiful beyond comparison" and the offer as equal to his greatest hopes, he feared to say "yes": "Somehow I feel that I should not be content to work in the machine which I see so clearly here," he wrote his wife. "Besides, my knowledge and my methods might not win the approval here that they have somehow won in Virginia. The work would be higher but more under the limelight."

Saying "yes" to the offer in spite of his fears, he passed a most unhappy summer in Chicago. But it had little to do with the university. The southern high school teachers and regular Chicago students who attended his course on the history of the Old South were delighted with the work, and the presence of Francis Wayland Shepardson and Claude Van Tyne, both American historians, provided him with excellent companions. Nevertheless, his wife, who was now pregnant with their second child, was continually in his thoughts, and his accommodations at Hitchcock Hall were so uncomfortable, he wrote McLaughlin, that "sleeping…got to be so rare a commodity…that I sought out…a room in your house.…I was half-sick and needed rest and quiet.…Indeed I should have been compelled to quit my work had I not got some sleep."[19]

His return to Virginia in August, however, did not solve the problem. The quality of his accommodations at Hitchcock Hall apparently had less to do with his sleepless nights than had the deep-seated worries about the success of his work: "I see by your letter…," McLaughlin wrote in December, "that you are not feeling well.… I hope you are not taking your forthcoming duties very seriously.… There is absolutely no necessity of your getting worried about your work." But whatever McLaughlin might advise, he could not shake the fear that he would fail in his duties, and this, despite the fact that Professor H. Morse Stephens of Berkeley now also invited him to consider taking a post in his department. Actually there was nothing very extraordinary in Dodd's uneasiness. Chicago, after all, held a leading position among American universities in 1909, and anyone moving from a small denominational college to so imposing an institution might have experienced similar feelings.[20]

What was more unusual for an academician, though by no means extraordinary, was the fact that Dodd now turned again to political action for a sense of personal well-being. Indeed, if remaining at Randolph-Macon made him unhappy and if going to Chicago threatened him with failure, he could still hope for some measure of satisfaction, some feeling of achievement, from public service or reform. In September, while preparing his departure for Chicago and traveling to Raleigh and Charleston to buy library materials for Chicago's southern collection, he worked up a scheme with Frederic Bancroft, his colleague and friend, to convince college men to vote for Bryan. Their idea was to exchange letters lauding Bryan's stand on the leading issues—tariffs, trusts, and imperialism—and to send the correspondence to the Democratic Press Bureau for release to the national press. Unhappily for Bancroft and Dodd, only small portions of a few letters were ever used, and the plan to be an influence in what Dodd considered a "turning point in American history" came to naught. His personal disappointment, added to the prospect of Bryan's defeat, threw him into a mood of deep despair. "If the people fail now to elect the Nebraska leader," he wrote Charles Francis Adams, Jr., "the tendency in this part of the country will set in toward socialism." "I begin to fear," he further warned, "that in my day civil strife will come...because of the intimidation and coercion which have marked this campaign.... Have you not observed how nearly like our great slave masters of 1830–60 are our present industrial lords...?"[21] Fears about the future well-being of the nation, however, were soon eclipsed by more personal concerns. His departure for Chicago in January confronted him with the most difficult and exciting challenge of his life.

V

Somewhat of a Jeffersonian

"THE FIRST PLUNGE is the worst," John Spencer Bassett wrote Dodd in January. "After a while you get adapted to the new conditions, and a little later you come to like them."[1] In a short time Dodd was proving Bassett right. Where his six-week summer residence in Chicago had encouraged him to come back for a year, his first full quarter at the university made him decide to stay.

He found much to attract and hold him there. Located six miles south of the center of Chicago on three-quarters of a mile of parklands, and housed in Gothic buildings wearing an "air of antique dignity," the university allowed him to imagine himself either back in the country or on a European tour. The fields along the Midway Plaisance were a continual source of delight, while afternoon walks across campus grounds to classes in Cobb Lecture Hall were reminiscent of earlier strolls about German universities. Even more appealing to Dodd, though, was the sense of community with his colleagues born of common experience and rearing: many Chicago administrators and professors, like Dodd, were men of village backgrounds who "after an eye-opening sojourn on the East coast or in Europe, were set loose in an urban environment that was nonetheless close to home."

But it was not just the familiar small-town and Old World environments that drew Dodd to Chicago. The university had considerably more to recommend it: a library of almost a half million volumes with three other fine libraries—the Newberry, the Crerar, and the Chicago Public—nearby; a spirit of academic freedom permitting "no creedal restrictions," and frank "criticism of existing industrial and social conditions"; a highly serious undergraduate body more devoted to hard work than their eastern counterparts and free of such student customs as "hazing, class-fighting, face-painting, hair-cutting, kidnapping,...[and] hard drinking..."; a four-month vacation each year for research and writing with but two courses, or six to eight hours of teaching, per week in each of three quarters; an average for the entire university of only eighteen students in each class; and a graduate training center second in excellence only to Harvard and first among all American universities in numbers of doctorates conferred over the previous ten years. In sum, Chicago was "one of the liveliest, most creative academic establishments of the day."

That the university had a number of less attractive and even offensive features in 1909 was something Dodd would soon find out. But for the moment Chicago offered him something he could find almost nowhere else—a chance to join an excellent graduate history department eager for him to promote the study of the Old South.[2]

While most American universities in 1909–10 could boast of independent history departments no longer joined to departments of economics, political science, or sociology, few compared favorably in size and diversity with Chicago's. Offering courses in ancient, medieval, and modern history, the department's faculty of seven senior and three junior members claimed expertise in the American, European, English, and "Oriental" fields. The chief distinction of the department, of course, derived from the accomplishments and reputations of its faculty. Professors James H. Breasted, the Egyptologist, Andrew C. McLaughlin, the American constitutional historian, Ferdinand Schevill, the modern European specialist, and James Westfall Thompson, the medievalist, perhaps the most distinguished members of the department in 1909, played the largest role in sustaining the new but solid tradition of attracting outstanding graduate students—a tradition which included the training of thirty-one Ph.D.s in seventeen years.[3]

Dodd's decision to join the Chicago faculty in 1909 allowed the department to expand its course offerings, open a new area of graduate work, and attract yet more and better graduate students. In 1909, only Johns Hopkins and Columbia had traditions of providing excellent graduate instruction in southern history. But by that year, Herbert Baxter Adams had long since retired from Johns Hopkins, and William A. Dunning at Columbia had limited his seminars and studies to southern history after 1850. Students interested in an antebellum South were soon drawn in greatest numbers to Dodd at Chicago and Ulrich B. Phillips at Michigan.

The advantages to the department of adding Dodd to its faculty were only equal to the benefits Dodd himself derived. Appealing to his promotional and evangelical instincts, the very qualities so common to the whole Chicago enterprise, the department invited Dodd to build a southern history "factory." Promised at least a thousand dollars a year toward establishing a southern history collection in the university library, Dodd began purchasing materials at once. Records of ante-bellum southern churches preceded him to Chicago in November and December 1908, while a part of his first quarter was given over to buying newspaper files and other printed materials from Virginia collectors. His greatest accomplishment in this work was to be his acquisition of the Colonel Reuben T. Durrett Collection in 1913. Containing Kentucky and Virginia newspapers, periodicals, pamphlets, maps and government documents worth $25,000, Dodd described its value as putting "Chicago on the map for original investigation in American history." Equally important to him, however, was the opportunity to teach courses exclu-sively at the graduate level in southern and occasionally western history. In his first quarter at the university, the winter term of 1909, Dodd lectured three times a week to graduate students on the "Making of the Middle West," while meeting one afternoon a week in Cobb Lecture Hall to discuss "Problems in Southern History" with his seminar. The fact that five or six Randolph-Macon students and "many other southerners" enrolled in his courses and the fact that he immediately found himself directing a dissertation on William Branch Giles, the Virginia Congressman, put Dodd "into a frame of mind...of the teacher who is actually working among 'his own people.'"[4]

Probably nothing about the department or the university at large, however, appealed so much to Dodd as its emphasis on useful scholarship. While James Breasted and Andrew C. McLaughlin set the tone in the department with excava-tions on the Nubian Nile and government reports on the diplomatic archives of the Department of State, Dean Albion Small of the Graduate School of Arts and Literature set the mood for all the social sciences with recommendations for the "marriage of thought with action." In the comfortable surroundings of the univer-sity's Quadrangle Club and in apartments along Washington (later Blackstone) Avenue just east of the campus where he initially settled, Dodd found faculty mem-bers like Charles Merriam, the political scientist, J. Lawrence Laughlin, the economist, Robert Morss Lovett, the literature professor, and James Tufts, the phi-losopher, who shared and encouraged his enthusiasm for "useful" writing. It was in this spirit that Dodd committed himself before the end of the winter quarter to write book reviews for the Chicago *Evening Post* and one-thousand-word essays for *The South in the Building of the Nation,* a multi-volume survey of the South's con-tribution to the national life. It was also in this spirit that Dodd urged readers of *The Nation* to understand that "the firmness of real learning might be a priceless boon to us in the way of [reconciling sectional differences and] avoiding revolu-tions or wars like that of 1861."[5]

Despite Dodd's rapid adjustment to his new environment, he was not entirely sure at the close of the winter quarter in March that he wanted to remain in Chicago. With an attractive offer from Berkeley still before him, he decided to travel to the West Coast in April to compare the two schools. The two-week "journey" and "sojourn" left him more attracted to Chicago than ever before. "The great distance which I never before fully understood between Berkeley and the South," he wrote Professor H. Morse Stephens on his return, "was the one thing which even the chosen surroundings of the University of California could not counterbalance. In addition, Chicago arranges my work so that I can have four months' vacation each year...." Lastly, the experience of lecturing to Berkeley classes convinced him that his smaller Chicago groups placed less of a "strain" on his none-too-powerful voice.[6]

With the problem of remaining in Chicago put aside by the beginning of the spring quarter, Dodd quickly settled into a productive routine of teaching and writing. On Monday, Wednesday, and Friday mornings during the spring and summer months, he worked chiefly in his home at 5734 Washington Avenue preparing lectures on the history of the Old South and writing critiques of student research papers prepared for his "Problems in Southern History" and "History of Secession" seminars. Tuesdays and Thursdays by contrast were given over to reading recent books and composing his *South in the Building of the Nation* essays.[7]

In the autumn when his free quarter fell due, he began working exclusively on a one-volume history of the South, a project which was to occupy him for the next year and a half. Convinced that his story could best be told through the study of representative lives, he decided to fashion his book out of earlier lectures on Jefferson, Calhoun, and Davis, whom he considered the most important statesmen of the Old South. Writing from the "spirit of the documents" with neither footnote nor bibliographical references, his revised lectures—"my article of faith," as he came to call the book—aimed above all to explain why the South had abandoned Jefferson's democracy for Davis' philosophy of "conservative revolt."[8]

Beginning with a Jefferson essay which he believed himself "uniquely fitted" to write, Dodd described his "favorite American" as the "apostle of democracy" who came naturally to his democratic faith. "It is not difficult to see how the great principle of Jefferson's life—absolute faith in democracy—came to him," Dodd contended. "He was the product of the first West in American history; he grew up with men who ruled their country well...[and] made of a vast wilderness a smiling garden...." More important than Jefferson himself, however, was the fact, according to Dodd, that he inspired other men throughout his section and across the nation to take up the democratic faith. Destroying the "interests" "root and branch" in Virginia in 1776, Jefferson became the leader of a South-West alliance which made him

President in 1800 and gave the nation "four years...unparalleled in American history."

What this apostle of democracy stood for in Virginia, the dogma that all men are free and equal, equality before the law, popular suffrage, equal representation of equal units of population in all legislatures, abolition of negro slavery and the establishment of religious freedom—the creed of the up-country of the South before 1820—was now the national program, and Virginia became the basis and the background for the federal administration in the same way that the up-country counties in Virginia had been the basis and support of the Revolution in 1776.

But Jefferson's success and southern democracy were both short-lived. By 1810, "the leadership of this expanding, restless South," Dodd explained in his Calhoun essay, "was fast shifting from Virginia to South Carolina; and economic supremacy had already departed from the Old Dominion.... It was not unnatural then that the most powerful group in Congress in 1811 should hail from the Palmetto state...." This shift in leadership, however, at first had no important effect upon liberalism in the South; Calhoun and his fellow South Carolinians were as democratic and as nationalistic as Jefferson had been. Indeed, in 1812 Calhoun was "an ardent patriot" whose ambition was to gain the presidency through the same South-West alliance which had sustained Jefferson in his presidential years. But Calhoun's ambition and southern democracy floundered on the rock of "protection." For the South, and especially South Carolina, could not reconcile itself to high protective tariffs which the West "must favor...in order to secure to the national government the revenue to build her highways to eastern markets." Nevertheless, Calhoun persisted in his ambition: "What he was striving for during the last seventeen years of his life (1833–50) was the building of a 'solid' South which...cast into the scales of national politics, would decide all great questions in its favor. And it cannot be doubted that he expected to be elevated to the presidency as a natural result...." But this effort to "reconcile nationality with particularism" only made Calhoun "the champion of slavery and cotton, the money interests of the [lower] South [which had gained control of the section and spurned the radical faith]. From 1833 to 1850 he taught the South that property in negro slaves was more sacred than the rights and ideas so eloquently defended by his own great teacher, Jefferson. He died, the greatest reactionary of his time." Calhoun, then, "prepared the way for secession and war..., and Jefferson Davis," as Dodd had already suggested in his earlier work, "was to complete the work of Calhoun and convert the old and radical democracy of Jefferson into armies contending...for ideals and purposes absolutely foreign to the mind of the great founder."[9]

When Dodd's *Statesmen of the Old South* appeared in 1911, it at once gained the approval of other historians. Frederic Bancroft, John Spencer Bassett, William

Dunning, John H. Latané, and Charles W. Ramsdell generally agreed that it was an important work which would long have interest for historians of the Old South. At a time when southerners and northerners alike were eager to understand the whole drift of southern life and the character of the South, Dodd's book was a welcome departure from the traditional monograph on one or another aspect of the prewar South. Moreover, with the argument that ante-bellum times showed a shift in power from Virginia to South Carolina, or from Virginia's "Tidewater aristocracy" and Jeffersonian liberalism to South Carolina's cotton capitalism and political conservatism, Dodd gave his colleagues a point of departure for studying southern history which holds good to this day.[10]

In addition to its relevance for students of the Old South, though, Dodd's book had a substantial appeal for progressive historians in general. In emphasizing Jefferson's reliance on a South-West alliance to earn him the presidency as well as the clash of interests between planters and up-country farmers or Jefferson's Virginia and Calhoun's South Carolina, Dodd was helping to show that America's history was primarily the story of home-grown geographic sections or the battle between "natural economic groupings" rather than the product of Old World ideas. It is not surprising that Frederick Jackson Turner, the chief exponent of this theme, should have seen Dodd's *Statesmen* as "a bully corrective to the traditional treatment," or that Dodd should have told Turner that "in point of view and purpose I think I am not far from your own teaching. Certainly your writings have influenced me more than those of any other scholar," Dodd wrote, "and I have always been grateful to you for the direction which you gave our historical studies beginning with your paper of 1893."[11]

Dodd gave even fuller expression to this influence in a paper on "The Fight for the Northwest, 1860" which he published in the *American Historical Review* in the summer of 1911. Describing the election campaign of 1860 as a battle between the South and the East for alliance with the West, Dodd not only used Turner's notion of political sections but also invoked his image of the Northwest as a balance wheel between the sections. The paper was so persuasive and so forceful an example of progressive history that Charles Beard praised it as "the only article in...[the *Review*] that I have ever read twice or thought about afterwards....I want to take the liberty of expressing my thanks to you for your passage at arms with old-fashion American history—and your indication of how real history might be written...."[12]

Although the themes tying Dodd's essays together were to remain meaningful to historians of the Old South, the same was not true for the biographical sketches themselves. The Davis essay, of course, being no more than a summary of Dodd's earlier study, always remained in the shadow of the larger book. The Jefferson sketch had a more interesting life. Contributing to the Jefferson revival which was beginning to take on a full head of steam, the vignette was also to be of interest to later sympathetic writers on Jefferson like Vernon L. Parrington, Claude G. Bowers, and Saul K. Padover. Today, however, Dodd's celebration of Jefferson as a revolutionary "apostle of democracy," like those of Parrington and Bowers, has been eclipsed by the interpretation of the Virginian as a more complex or many-sided and sometimes unattractive man.[13] The Calhoun portrait has also given way to other, more substantial works. But this is probably less because later scholars have resolved the dilemma of whether Calhoun was a man of high principle or low expediency than because Dodd himself left the issue so unclear. Indeed, while depicting Calhoun as a man who "never ceased to long for and strive for the presidency" and whose frustrated ambition played a direct part in bringing on the Civil War, Dodd also described him as "a nationalist at heart to the day of his death" who wished not to destroy the Union but to dominate it. It may well be that Calhoun was a bit of both, but the connection of the two traits hardly emerges from Dodd's essay.[14]

Yet whatever the success of Dodd's study as a work of scholarship, it is clear that it had considerable appeal for writers on contemporary affairs. The *Outlook,* a leading progressive journal, for example, pronounced the book a "stimulating contribution to a philosophic understanding of some of the chief facts and present problems in the national life." Confirming the generally accepted progressive notion of America's history as the story of economic and sectional conflicts between democrats and "monopolists," and drawing specific analogies between the "special interests" or "magnates who exploit the resources of the country…in 1911 and their predecessors of 1861," Dodd's book impressed many readers as a "tract for the times." In this, however, Dodd's study was not unique. Like other historians around the country in that season, Dodd was now chiefly concerned with constructing a "usable past," exploiting the past "in the interests of advance," or linking "the past to current need for reforms." But more like Algie M. Simons than Charles A. Beard, who presented his findings in *An Economic Interpretation of the Constitution* after "rigorous research" and "in the spirit of the scholar with no practical political cause to defend,"[15] Dodd showed himself less interested in supplying reformers with "scientific" observations than in working directly for social action. If most "liberal" scholars, in other words, were reluctant to take part in politics outside of placing their expertise at the service of the state, Dodd never had such qualms. Indeed, by contrast, Dodd found the role of the expert, the "Wisconsin Idea," foreign to his political style and taste. Instead, he saw himself as an idealist, a committed Jeffersonian who wished to return conditions to an earlier, better time when citizens and not interests or bosses ruled the American states. Consequently, Dodd had little desire to be a scholar-expert in politics or to serve on commissions aiming to solve the problems of an urban, industrialized society. Rather, he thought in terms of joining political reformers who fought to restore the "people" to control of American political life.[16]

Soon after coming to Chicago, he found ample opportunity for such practical political work. With a population of over two million, including almost a million immigrants crowded into west side slums, with a tradition of boss rule and municipal corruption equal to almost any in the United States, with a history of long-term public utility and corporation control, the city offered outraged citizens much to contest. "Truth forever on the scaffold, wrong forever on the throne," became the motto of more than one Chicago idealist. "A half million of the people of the city are suffering," was the way Dodd put it. In response to these conditions, Chicago professors worked chiefly as expert advisers with city commissions and planning boards: President William Rainey Harper headed a Chicago commission to reform the public schools; sociology professor William I. Thomas served a city committee "scientifically" investigating widespread vice; while political scientist Charles Merriam made a study of municipal revenues for the City Club. Some Chicago professors, however, shared Dodd's inclination to precede social reform with direct political action to restore popular control.

After a short stint as an unofficial adviser on city problems, Merriam became the leading figure in this activist faculty camp. Winning election to the Chicago City Council as an independent Republican in 1909, Merriam shortly attracted nationwide attention with disclosures of wasteful, dishonest administration in City Hall. His action made him the progressives' choice for mayor in the Republican primary fight beginning in 1910.

Although a life-long Democrat with a family tradition of antagonism to Republicans dating from pre-Civil War days, Dodd saw good reason to join the Republican fray, taking a small part in Merriam's behalf. For one, party ties in the 1911 mayoralty contest were nearly meaningless—Republicans and Democrats divided into three factions each. Secondly, Merriam held the support of a formidable reform group: Jane Addams, Clarence Darrow, Harold Ickes, Graham Taylor, a host of university people and the Municipal Voters' League all contributed energetically to his campaign. Lastly, but most important in Dodd's mind, such a local coalition would help pave the way to a national reform party—a new South-West alliance for turning out Taft and bringing "a new order of things" to Washington after 1912. Actually, as far as Dodd could see, Merriam's supporters were well-nigh committed to such a scheme. After only four months in Chicago he was "certain that the Reform Republicans will... [feel] compelled to ally themselves with the progressive Democrats" in a few years.[17]

Consequently, Dodd saw it as most essential to bring other southerners around to the idea. "Do not allow Virginia, Maryland, and North Carolina to be tacked on to

New York because of any dislike of Bryan," Dodd wrote former Governor Montague in May 1909. "…What is back of Bryan is infinitely more important than he is…." "I fear the South will go with New England and public plunder…," Dodd wrote him again later in the year. "If the South should become liberal…[and] join hands with the LaFollette men of this region…a united West and South…[could] direct the Federal government for the next half hundred years!" As historical proof of the importance of the West to the South in assuring "the power of the South in the administration of the nation," Dodd sent Montague a copy of his paper "The Fight for the Northwest, 1860," with suggestions that he put it before other southerners as an argument receiving "hearty endorsements" from the professional history men.[18]

Whatever his appeals to Montague, however, Dodd had decided by the close of 1910 that the only man who could unite both sections behind a Democratic program was the newly elected southern-born Governor of New Jersey, Woodrow Wilson. "My, what an impression he is making," Dodd wrote in November. "Wilson strikes me as the man for 1912." Dodd was not alone in his observation; thousands of other Democrats around the country were shortly thinking the same thing. Wilson himself was not unaware of this trend. Indeed, at the beginning of March 1911, he met with a group of supporters in New York to discuss strategy for a nomination campaign. Although the chief conclusion emerging from the meeting was that Wilson above all needed to put himself before the people of the West, Wilson decided to launch his presidential campaign in the South. "The South is a very conservative region," Wilson said, "—just now probably the most (possibly the only) conservative section of the country." Dodd was of much the same mind. Moreover, seeing Chicago "Republicans and Independents and Democrats" as already under the Wilson spell, and feeling more at home in southern affairs, Dodd decided to spend his best energies for Wilson in the Old Dominion. Appreciating that support from a native state was almost essential in a nomination campaign, Dodd took the occasion of a research trip to Virginia in April to say words in Wilson's behalf.

Montague and Virginia liberals, however, needed no such prodding. By April 1911 they had already organized themselves into a "Democratic League" for overturning the anti-Wilson machine, and at the end of the month, Wilson himself came to Norfolk to state his own case. Moreover, as practical measures against the machine, Congressmen William Jones and Carter Glass launched primary campaigns against Senators Thomas Martin and Claude Swanson to deprive them of their seats.

But Dodd did not see this as enough. After returning to Chicago later in the month, he urged Montague to inject a measure of idealism into his campaign. "The trouble with the men who are fighting the machine," he told Montague, "is that they want office…. My idea is that you and Glass and St. George Tucker…and somebody in Norfolk (I know not who) ought to come to an understanding about what…policy, what faith you will offer to the masses of Virginians who are 'hungering and thirsting after righteousness.' If some tacit or overt understanding could be reached, I think that the progressive league could...[aid] the South...[to] face to the front at this crisis of the Nation's life...."[19]

Although telling Montague that "I know you feel the same way I do," Dodd refused to leave it at that. In June he had Charles B. Garnett of the Democratic League arrange speaking engagements for him in Louisa and Hanover counties where he discussed "The Duty of Virginia in the Present National Crisis." Addressing audiences of "farmers and country people" on July 3 and 4, Dodd repeated the familiar progressive arguments against corruption and control which Wilson himself had voiced in his recent trips to the South. Unlike Wilson, however, Dodd chose to make specific disclosures about Ryan, Martin, and a "reptile press," which at once made him the center of a controversy in the state. "Your speeches," Garnett told him, "have stirred up something of a storm." "Our opponents are making frantic efforts to discount the effect of your speeches," Jones advised, "but I do not think they have made much headway."

The sense that he had struck a telling blow against the Virginia machine, plus the fact that he believed the "regime" could now be broken "without a doubt," led Dodd to continue his work for Virginia's "liberty" even after he returned to Chicago on July 6. Publishing anti-machine letters in Virginia papers and counseling Montague on the direction of the campaign, he maintained some feeling of participation in the fight. Hence when news of a "complete" machine victory in the primaries came at the beginning of September, Dodd, like Montague, felt "disconsolate and distressed," especially since "Martin and Swanson" were now likely to "control the delegation to the National Convention." Defeat of the Wilson men in Virginia, however, should have come as no surprise to either Montague or Dodd. By September 1911 Wilson was in bad standing across the South as "an unsafe man," a proponent of socialistic schemes who "had departed from the paths of 'safe and sane' Democracy." But such a portrait of Wilson and his backers, Wilson himself understood, might yet be changed. The nomination campaign, as Dodd and Montague soon came to see, was still at its earliest stage, and of even greater solace to Dodd, the fight for the Illinois delegation was just getting under way.[20]

Whatever comfort Dodd found in this, however, was quickly vitiated by his realistic survey of Illinois politics. With the state's Democrats split into three warring factions and with none firmly in the Wilson camp, it was difficult for Dodd and other Wilson supporters to know what action to take. Perhaps in the hope of evoking some direction from Wilson, Dodd wrote him on September 9 praising his work for progress. Wilson, however, answered without reference to politics, national or otherwise. But the fact that Wilson barely knew Dodd, that he was still denying any intention of a presidential campaign, and that he did not designate William McCombs as a campaign manager to organize state support until October seems to explain Wilson's reluctance to pick up Dodd's hint. When by the beginning of December, however, it became clear that neither the conservative Roger Sullivan faction nor the progressive Carter H. Harrison and Edward F. Dunne factions would give Wilson their backing, Dodd decided what he must do.

Simultaneously with Representative Lawrence B. Stringer and "his little group of faithful Wilson men," who opened a Chicago headquarters on December 1, Dodd launched a campus "Wilson Club." Supported by Democratic and Republican faculty members at the university, and encouraged by both Stringer's group in Chicago and Wilson's information bureau in New York, Dodd made his club into a publicity office arranging speeches and distributing literature in Wilson's behalf. But such efforts, when compared with the well-organized and widespread work undertaken by the Hearst press and the Harrison-Dunne forces in support of Champ Clark, Democratic Speaker of the House, could not possibly gain Wilson a majority in the primary on April 9. At the beginning of April, therefore, in the face of what was already a "hopeless situation," McCombs beseeched the Illinois faithful to see to their precinct work: "Our reports...indicate," he wrote Dodd, "that, perhaps, our friends have been overconfident, and have not given sufficient attention to Precinct organization....You will agree with me that the most important work of the campaign consists in proper organization in each locality....This work must necessarily fall on the local workers....Confer with Governor Wilson's friends in your vicinity, looking to a plan of closer organization...." Such appeals, however, were no more effective than Wilson's "last-ditch barnstorming campaign tour...on April 5 and 6." Clark won the state primary on April 9 by a "staggering" three-to-one margin.

Although Clark's victory made him the front-runner for the Democratic nomination in the Baltimore convention, Dodd, like McCombs, assumed that "we are making a struggle which must...ultimately be successful." In this spirit, Dodd turned his attention to other states where he hoped his opinion would carry some weight. On May 10 despite presidential primary victories for Senator Oscar W. Underwood in Florida, Georgia, and Mississippi during the previous ten days, Dodd sent Wilson literature to a South Carolina friend for distribution before election day on May 15, while pressing Texas Senator Charles Culberson at the same time to do all in his power to assure Wilson's selection at the state Democratic convention on May 28. Although the Wilson movement appeared by June to have collapsed under an avalanche of Clark and Underwood votes, and although Wilson himself privately acknowledged that he had "not the least idea of being nominated," Dodd still had faith. On June 26, the day after the Democratic convention convened in Baltimore and two days before the first ballot was scanned, he led a handful of Republicans and Democrats in wiring Josephus Daniels that we "could send scores of Republicans who want to vote for Bryan or Wilson but will vote for no other man before your convention. Fight to the last and balk if the interests control. Show this to Virginia and Illinois delegations."[21]

The victory for Wilson at Baltimore came as no surprise then to Dodd; he considered it simply another step in what he now viewed as the nation's inexorable movement toward progress. Ignoring the almost insurmountable obstacles which most observers agreed Wilson had overcome, and overlooking the role of the bosses, including that of Roger Sullivan, in gaining Wilson the prize, Dodd described the victory as chiefly the work of Bryan and as "the best augury for the future of democracy we have seen in years."

It was a source of great annoyance to Dodd, then, that most of his liberal Republican friends could not agree with his estimate. With Theodore Roosevelt busily engaged by July in the formal organization of a Progressive party to oppose both Wilson and Taft, Republican progressives in and out of the university decided to abandon Wilson's candidacy to support T. R. Their attitude was probably best expressed in the *Outlook,* which had supported Wilson throughout the preconvention campaign. Though they admired Wilson no less than before, the editors said, they could not support a man whose party was boss-controlled.[22]

Actually, the split between Dodd and his Progressive friends was more fundamental. Whereas university people like Breasted, Merriam, and Small subscribed to Roosevelt's New Nationalism, with all its attendant promises of middle-class experts forging schemes of social justice and mediating conflicts at the head of the state, Dodd denounced it as undemocratic, a "government administered from above.... I prefer bad government by the people," Dodd wrote at the height of the campaign, "to good government by a great master. This is distinctly the meaning of the Roosevelt movement." Very much like Wilson in 1912, Dodd, in his own words, was "somewhat of a Jeffersonian," an opponent of extensive federal powers which might jeopardize individual freedom and equal opportunity throughout the United States.[23]

Although Dodd expressed these opinions in newspaper articles and debates in the course of the campaign, he undertook no extensive work in Wilson's behalf. Preparing a paper for the American Historical Association meetings in December, he was again concerned with professional obligations. Moreover, having "full faith in...[Wilson's] success" and having, with the exception of the Wickham fight, already done "more than I ever did before," Dodd decided to save his best efforts for post-election business, for the time when true progressives would have "a chance to say a word about what ought to be done in this country."[24]

VI

The Only Thing Worth Fighting For

WOODROW WILSON'S VICTORY at the polls on November 5, 1912, pleased Dodd more than any other public event he could remember. For the first time in his life he could think of himself as a member of the majority camp, a southern liberal Democrat whose Jeffersonian ideas would be shared by those holding national power. Even more gratifying, though, the President-elect was announcing his intention "to regenerate the Democratic Party by giving initiative and control to its progressive elements."

Taking Wilson at his word, Dodd at once thought to serve this goal in Virginia. Having been most intimately involved in that state's reform battles and having purchased a summer home in the Blue Ridge Mountains in October, a fact which, in his words, showed that his "interest in Virginia is not merely academic," he put himself forward as a man who could help the new administration arrange the state's political affairs. "I am greatly interested in the success of the Wilson administration," he wrote Josephus Daniels in December, "and I know you will have great weight with Mr. Wilson himself, so I give you the trouble of this letter.... There can be no appointment made in Virginia that will harmonize the elements there.... There is," Dodd hinted, "a dearth of good men in Virginia...." If Dodd thought to make a case for himself as a spokesman for Virginia's liberals, he received scant encouragement from Daniels, who hardly shared Dodd's estimate of Virginia affairs. The state, Daniels understood, had a large group of insurgent or progressive Democrats like

Henry St. George Tucker and Henry G. Pollard who had been fighting the Martin machine continuously for ten years. What is more, having just carried the state for Wilson and having won a number of local and statewide elections, the Virginia insurgents were in no mood to share their power and patronage with either machine men or outside supporters like Dodd.

But Dodd was not easily put off. With Wilson continuing to talk as if he would favor party liberals over machine men and specifically attacking the Martin organization in a speech at Staunton, Virginia, on December 28, Dodd assumed that the "new regime" would welcome his words of advice. Between February and April, therefore, Dodd did not hesitate to write to administration leaders about appointments and policies. "I hope you are doing what you can," one sample reads, "to prevent the appointment of Thomas Nelson Page [the prominent southern writer and candidate of the Virginia machine for a diplomatic job] to a post of importance in the new regime....I have written several letters and had a talk with my friend Josephus Daniels recently, all urging the dangers of such an appointment." "Some two weeks ago," he wrote Judge Walter Clark in April, "I took the liberty to write to President Wilson urging your appointment to the United States Circuit Court judgeship now vacant in the district...of Virginia and the Carolinas....From the moment I learned of the vacancy in February I have felt that your services on that bench would be invaluable to the country...." If such advice had any impact on Wilson, Dodd could find no evidence for it. Indeed, by the end of April, he began to believe that his suggestions for diplomatic and judicial appointments were going unnoticed, and that his warnings against the Martin "reactionists" were working no changes in Virginia. Exclusion from the councils of the new administration, however, was not unique to Dodd. By then, other progressives across the country were finding Wilson equally insensitive to their demands. In part, it was because Wilson resented direct letters of supplication and advice; but more to the point was the fact that Wilson quickly succumbed to political realities, agreeing to favor machine leaders with patronage in return for their congressional support. Senators Martin and Swanson of Virginia, for example, promised Wilson solid backing in exchange for control of their state's federal jobs.

Still, Dodd was less than soured on Wilson's regime. "I have so much faith in Woodrow Wilson and Josephus Daniels," he wrote Daniels, who had become Secretary of the Navy. "...I know you know Southern men and conditions so well that you will not allow any big slip anywhere. With all possible good wishes for your eminent success...."[1]

If Dodd was only slightly miffed at his exclusion from the Wilson circle, it was chiefly because he felt there was other—perhaps more important—reform work to be done, such as helping to make historical scholarship into an instrument of progressive advance. At the Boston meeting of the American Historical Association in December 1912, for example, Dodd joined other reform-minded historians in addressing himself to the problem of how to make the results of their work both more interesting and of greater value to the nation at large. In the spirit of James Harvey Robinson's *The New History*, Dodd and his colleagues sought ways to "turn on the past and exploit it in the interests of advance." Dodd's specific contribution to this discussion was a paper on "Profitable Fields of Investigation in American History, 1815–1865." Arguing that the ante-bellum period should no longer be viewed from the perspective of Henry Adams, Hermann von Holst, or John Bach McMaster—that is, in terms of the evolution of Old World institutions in the Northeast—Dodd urged instead a course of study which would first "treat of actual forces, social, economic, and political," and second "devote more space and more intelligent and more sympathetic attention to the needs and conditions of...the West and the South." "The principal subject which the student of this period of American history must appreciate," Dodd told his colleagues, "is the development of a dominant interest, of a dominant civilization with definite ideals...the plantation system, based on negro slavery." The remainder of Dodd's paper was chiefly given over to a discussion of "how the struggle of interests which marked the time might be illuminated by certain local and especially biographical studies." In the manner of his *Statesmen* book and in the presence of Frederick Jackson Turner, who chaired the session, Dodd implicitly urged greater attention to the "natural economic groupings" vying for power in both the Northwest and the Old South.

Despite a generally sympathetic response to his paper and the fact that he was considerably milder in his criticism of the "old order of American history" than he usually was, Dodd's essay provoked some sharp replies which put him in a fighting mood. "What is the use of long trips and Pullman fares in order to hear men talk what is not true or to witness intellectual gymnastics in which only word castles are piled up?" he asked James Shotwell in January. "If you had heard the discussion of my paper, you would have felt that most of the men had lost their powers of thought....History," he concluded indignantly, "is no completed and well labelled affair not to be opened except on the approval of high officials and very conventional gentlemen reared in the days of Leopold von Ranke."[2]

Such criticism as he met in Boston convinced Dodd that further work on behalf of the New History needed to be done. Publishing his Boston paper in the Chicago *Evening Post* "Literary Supplement" at the beginning of January, he dispatched sixty copies of the article to southern and western newspaper editors later in the month. At the same time, he reviewed Edward Channing's *History of the United States* in the *Post* as the best of the old-style American histories which, nevertheless, showed little "imagination" or a "grasp of social forces" of the time. It was a work limited above all, in Dodd's estimate, by the fact that it would little serve the public good.

In February when he traveled south for research in "neglected" southern sources, Dodd shifted his crusade for the New History from the written to the spoken word. In a Washington's Birthday speech at North Carolina's Trinity College, he announced that "there has never been a time when the call to history seemed so imperative, the call to serve and speak the truth...." "Public leaders, politicians and even preachers," he explained, "have influenced the people to believe what is not so.... We have erected a huge fabric of tradition, error and sometimes actual falsehood...."[3] Given a past which most New historians agreed was "a burden of error and wrong from which men were to be liberated," Dodd argued that it was the business of the historian to correct "almost puerile narratives" and teach young people the truth. The nature of this truth, though, was something about which Dodd and other New historians like Robinson would have disagreed. Where Robinson urged liberation from the errors of the past, or so-called absolute truths, it was in the hope of freeing men to approach the problems of the present pragmatically.[4] Dodd, by contrast, wished to see those errors of the past struck down so that Americans might yet go back to earlier Jeffersonian beliefs. If Robinson would not have agreed with Dodd's motives for striking down old falsehoods, he would certainly have subscribed to Dodd's contention that such work was "a service...on behalf of the common good.... Where can one make one's energies and abilities count for more," Dodd asked, "than in working out from the storehouses of documents...the real story of our past. To correct the misapprehensions and the partisan deceptions of other generations and thus set the serious pages of history right ought to be as big a task as an aspiring man would desire to undertake.... [For] the kind of work that is here contemplated," Dodd concluded, "...is the very salvation of the great mass of inarticulate men...."[5] It was the "kind of work" which through the rest of 1913 increasingly drew Dodd's attention from practical political affairs.

When he returned to Chicago at the beginning of March, Dodd decided to give up lecturing and book reviewing for the moment in order to concentrate on writing and editing a New American history survey. The impetus for this work dated from the Boston meeting in December where Dodd and three other prominent New historians, Carl Becker, Allen Johnson, and Frederick Paxson, agreed to contribute volumes to Houghton Mifflin's *Riverside History of the United States.* To be designed for both students and laymen and to emphasize the "whole" or "real" story of the American past, the work was to be divided into four volumes, with Dodd serving as general editor: Becker was to cover the early years down to 1783; Johnson was to study the period 1783 to 1828 in a second volume; Dodd was to write on *Expansion and Conflict,* 1828–1865; and Paxson was to close the story with a study of *The New Nation.* The entire work was to be published in 1915.[6]

Although Dodd had managed the time to draft seven of sixteen chapters by May, he found it impossible to work steadily on the book. With his usual load of seminars and lectures to give through the spring and summer quarters and with close readings to be done of partly finished dissertations on "John Slidell," "The Life of John J. Crittenden," "Mississippi and the Compromise of 1850," "The Southern Loyalists," and "The Virginia Plantation," Dodd looked forward to September when he could escape to his Virginia home for the first of three free quarters he was to enjoy during the next year and a half.[7]

When the summer session ended on August 29, therefore, Dodd immediately made for the Blue Ridge, where he settled in for a long siege of writing. It was an environment in which his work progressed rapidly. Located some fifty miles northwest of Washington within easy access of the Library of Congress, Dodd's 105-acre farm with "a rambling twelve room [stone and wood] house...built before the Revolution" sat in the Blue Ridge foothills on the upper plateau of Loudoun County—in Dodd's estimate, "the prettiest bit of country in the United States." Situated fifteen miles west of Leesburg and just outside Round Hill, a town of three hundred, his orchards and fields, like those of neighboring farmers, yielded pears, peaches, apples, grapes, corn, grain, and feed for livestock. Considerably more to him than a vacation retreat where he might engage in uninterrupted hours of study, the farm allowed Dodd to pursue a variety of tasks which refreshed his spirits and facilitated his writing. "I did much of the milking of nine cows," he described one morning's work, "fed five horses and colts, carried cream to the railroad station at six o'clock a.m and did such other work as cutting corn to fill the silo, haul lumber for buildings or repairs on the farm and rode over the country to engage a thrasher for getting my grain ready for market." "This air, or the water or the exercise or all combined," Dodd wrote McLaughlin in October, "have...wrought a change [in me] as unexpected as it is welcome...."[8]

In this environment Dodd found the energy to write steadily on a variety of subjects: a paper on Robert J. Walker, an ante-bellum southern leader, whose reputation Dodd now helped to revive; a book review of Charles Beard's *An Economic Interpretation of the Constitution,* which, though complimentary, hardly forecast the importance the work would gain; and, in a more personal vein, a long letter to Andrew McLaughlin expressing his dissatisfaction with President Harry Pratt Judson's administration of the University of Chicago: "The one thing I am constantly depressed about at Chicago," Dodd told McLaughlin, "is the failure of the University to turn its resources into research in the social sciences. There is no real understanding in the administrative mind of the University of a library.... A laboratory is understood and appreciated: the results of experiments are tangible, they affect industrial and economic life; not so in subjects like history which is now being so radically changed. Results in this field seem to alienate instead of interest the men who are the legal overlords of universities."[9]

More important than any of this, though, Dodd's residence in Virginia allowed him to complete a first draft of his *Riverside* book. Aiming above all to advance the New History, Dodd set forth his story with an almost disproportionate attention to western and southern developments in the ante-bellum period, and with greatest emphasis on sectional conflicts and shifting alliances, which rose and fell with the triumph or demise of economic groups. "The decisive motive behind the different groups in Congress at every great crisis of the period under discussion," Dodd wrote in the Preface, "was sectional advantage or even sectional aggrandizement." To understand what those advantages were, Dodd further said, one must above all consider "the greater sectional and industrial groups of 'interests' which entered into the common life of *ante-bellum* times."

Adhering to this approach in the narrative, Dodd argued that once the South came under the control of slave-holders in 1830, the section entered into a fierce competition with the "monopolists" of the East for national control. The next thirty years were marked by a South-East struggle for alliance with the Northwest. Harrison's election in 1840 was the result of an East-West agreement which collapsed when Tyler succeeded to the presidency. The year 1844 saw Polk's advancement to the highest office on the strength of a new South-West alliance which in turn fell apart within four years. Such instability grew out of the fact that the West, the home of the nation's true democrats, could trust neither the industrial East nor the plantation South. The result was a new party organized by Western leaders in 1854. "Its appeal was to the fundamental doctrine that all men are equal and that no great interest should rule the country." The new party, effecting the union of East and Northwest, declared itself opposed to slavery extension into the territories. Though defeated in 1856, chiefly by a solid southern vote for Buchanan, the party found a champion for 1860 in Abraham Lincoln, "the real friend of the poor and the dependent." Gaining the presidency and defeating the southern bid to secede, Lincoln destroyed slavery, restored the South to its former position under democratic control and forged for the first time in her history a true American nation.[10]

Such a picture of America's ante-bellum life satisfied every major requirement of the New History. Useful as a commentary on both past and current affairs, the book illustrated what every good progressive knew—namely, that "real" history was the story of economic and social groups, that change came about through conflict and that progress meant the victory of democrats over opponents of change, monopolists, or the privileged few.[11]

For most of his themes, though, Dodd took his inspiration, as in his *Statesmen* work, from Turner's *Rise of the New West, 1819–1829*; in fact, the whole book, as Dodd had outlined it in December 1913, was little more than an extension of Turner's ideas to the period immediately before the Civil War, even down to the inclusion of maps and statistical data which Dodd, like Turner, viewed as "photographs of social or economic conditions."[12]

Yet despite his considerable achievement in completing this first draft of the book by the close of the year, Dodd again found himself distracted from his writing when he returned to Chicago. Aiming nevertheless to advance his book during the next nine months, Dodd used his lectures and seminars on "The Old West," "Slavery in the Southwest," "Westward Expansion," and "Southern Influence on the Northwest" to think through some of the general themes.

To assure that he would complete the text by the close of 1914, Dodd determined to close himself off from outside demands on his time. Accordingly, he stayed away from the American Historical Association meetings in Charleston, South Carolina, at the end of 1913 and refused either to serve on the association's program committee for the coming year or to involve himself in an internal struggle for control.[13]

In addition, although he compiled a list of likely members among historians, Dodd declined invitations from John Dewey and Arthur O. Lovejoy to take some larger part in organizing the budding American Association of University Professors. But unlike one professor who turned aside an invitation to join with the remark that, "I am opposed to anything that savours of organization," Dodd saw the association as a source of possible good, and was, in fact, soon urging Dewey to use the influence of the society against arbitrary trustees. Still, committing himself to an active part in either the AAUP or the American Historical Association at this point seemed to Dodd less likely to advance the New History and progress than the completion of his text.[14]

If Dodd then assured himself the maximum amount of time for writing through the first months of 1914, he still found it impossible to finish the Riverside work until he returned to Round Hill in the fall. Plagued by "rheumatism and indigestion and lumbago" which doctors in Chicago could not cure, he found a simple remedy at the farm. Permitting himself a six-week vacation from history to milk cows, harvest maize, and make "things grow," he felt himself in "excellent physical condition" by mid-October and ready to return to the book. But the business of finishing the last three chapters and getting the whole series through the press in less than five months left him even more exhausted than before. "I am not well and the obligations which press upon me are almost unbearable," he wrote his brother in February. "The book has taken a great deal more of time and energy than was thought at first," he wrote Erich Marcks in April, "and I am rather more disposed to 'rest awhile' now than I thought I should be when the work was begun. If I ever do get back to the 'last,' as shoemakers say, I want to write a history of the Old South in three or four volumes. With the completion of that job I should be content to retire to the little farm near Washington."

But this was to be more difficult than Dodd himself imagined. For stung by differences between himself and his co-authors over editorial matters, as well as by personal attacks upon him from association "reformers," which left him accepting "it as Job took the advice of his counsellors," Dodd now had a profound reaction against both the manuscript in hand and the value of historical labors in general. Describing the *Expansion and Conflict* study as a "'miserable thing'" which others would set down as "'a poor sort of thing to have cost so much effort,'" Dodd predicted that "Southern-born men will condemn it and that Northern-born men will not be more charitable." "Still," Dodd said, "it represents several years of my best thinking and study," leaving him with the feeling that "in the field of history-writing there is no fame any more...since Gibbon. To write a good book may win one the approval of a few good friends and some others, but in ten years the best book has to be rewritten."[15]

In expressing his doubts about the Riverside volume and the value of doing any more history-writing, Dodd was also saying that he saw more important things to which he preferred to devote himself—namely, the preservation and advancement of Jeffersonian ideals. With the outbreak of the First World War in the summer of 1914 and the initiation of a preparedness campaign in America toward the end of the year, Dodd saw democracy everywhere under sharp attack. In Europe, the menace stemmed from German militarism which Dodd pronounced the "enemy of mankind." In the United States, the danger came from the old enemies of progress—"the big navy imperialists, the armor-plate monopoly, the big industrialists, and the bankers," all of whom joined to lead the preparedness campaign. "I protest that all this talk of our army and navy being out of date," he wrote Josephus Daniels in January 1915, "...is not representative of the best thought of the people I know.... Let the President stick to his high idealism. Our going into the rush for armies and navies will be following Europe afar off and confirming them in their wickedness.... At the end of the holocaust of murder our influence will count just in proportion to our faithfulness to our American ideals...." Like so many other southern and western progressives, Dodd stood convinced that America must shun European militarism in order to secure her democracy and give Europeans an example they would do well to take.

At the beginning of 1915 this was substantially what Wilson and Daniels themselves believed. And so their answers to preparationist demands were about all Dodd and other progressives could have wished. On December 8, for example, Wilson announced himself as opposed to American preparation for war as "a reversal of the whole history and character of our polity"; while at the same time Daniels declared the navy in "fine shape," and Secretary of State Bryan "adamantly opposed any plan to increase the armed forces...." This opposition to preparedness was given even stronger expression in January when the administration showed an inclination for decreases rather than increases in the military budgets for 1915.

Still, Dodd worried that such attitudes might change. For as he accurately foresaw after the Germans announced a submarine blockade of the British Isles on February 4, "if the Germans were to destroy an American vessel and send Americans to the bottom of the ocean, public opinion would get beyond the influence of tradition and natural indifference to European events. Public opinion has been greatly changing in this country since the ruthless treatment of Belgium." The consequences of such a shift, Dodd believed, would be that drift toward militarism and away from American ideals against which he had warned Daniels in the previous month.[16]

Given his fierce dedication to democracy and the possible consequences for America of the European war, it is not surprising that Dodd believed it more important to help guard American ideals than to devote himself to professional concerns. Nowhere was this better illustrated, though, than in his attitude toward the American Historical Association struggle coming to a head in the spring and summer of 1915. Led by Bancroft, John T. Latané of Johns Hopkins, and Dunbar Rowland of Mississippi, a group of "reformers" charged that the Association Council "unfairly dictated succession to high offices..., that [Council] officials used association money for travel to, and entertainment at the annual meetings and that the editors of the [*American Historical*] *Review* erroneously maintained that it belonged to them." While conceding that some changes were in order, Dodd consistently scored the struggle as a tempest in a teapot, and as unworthy of serious concern. "I do not think the stake worth the fight," he said. "If it were the election of a radical for president of the United States," he concluded, "I might feel differently."

The fact, however, that the association struggle became something of a battle royal engaging the attention and energy of the profession's most prominent men only made him feel all the more cut off. "I think I am out of the organization for good and all," he wrote in March, "not that I shall not continue to get the *Review* and pay my dues, but I do not expect to attend meetings and spend time thinking about the ways and means of its best management."

Of course, it was not that simple. Many of the men under attack were Dodd's close friends, like Jameson, Turner, and McLaughlin. Besides, when Bancroft found Dodd unwilling to align himself with advocates of reform, he broke off correspondence in the spring and threatened publicly to "besmirch" him.

Yet none of these considerations did as much to put Dodd off as his belief that Bancroft's fight would contribute nothing to the democratization of American life. "My sympathies are all with the mass of the membership," he wrote William K. Boyd at the end of May, "but I am not willing to start or help start a movement to overthrow the cliques who have governed so long unless I have some guarantee that business shall hereafter be transacted on the open floor of annual meetings. In other words," he concluded, "I would not move an inch to swap cliques. Democracy is the only thing in the world worth fighting for...but democracy is the last thing in the world that the leader of the present fight desires."

But it was not just the leader of the reform group whom Dodd deplored; he also found fault with a majority of the membership and with scholars in general: "The trouble is," he told Boyd in the same letter,

> that men of real learning are none too numerous in this world. In America, the number is spread over such a wide area that they make a very thin covering. Indeed the conversation of such as I meet does not greatly impress me. A farm-house often contains quite as much wisdom as that of a "great German savant." Think of the puerile reasoning of most if not all the so-called great scholars of Germany on this war!...the only remedy for this sort of thing is to get away from the American, German or other worship of Mammon. That is what ruins our scholarship in the great centers; in the small places there is much more real love for the true and the noble than in Chicago, for example.
>
> I wish you could meet some of the so-called leaders of thought in this city.... How dull and stupid to them is the best of books, especially if it breathes an atmosphere of reality, or of democracy.[17]

Given his attitude toward historians and American university men in general, Dodd found it more agreeable to become program committee chairman of the Chicago Literary Club in the spring of 1915 and to take up the cudgels for professors holding "radical views" than to take any part in association affairs. Indeed, a series of academic freedom cases in the spring and summer of 1915 stirred Dodd as much as the AHA battle put him off. "I do not know whether I am a member of the Association of American College Professors..., never having been at one of the meetings or paid any dues," Dodd wrote John Dewey in June, "but I am greatly interested in the [Scott] Nearing case at Pennsylvania. If you think Nearing is really fighting for freedom of teaching..., had we not best seize this opportunity to go on record in vigorous fashion?...If there is anything that I can do, I am ready."

The Nearing case as well as the "wholesale removal of teachers" in Utah and Colorado raised in Dodd's mind the question of the role or position of the college professor in American life. The principle at stake in these cases, Dodd argued in *The Nation,* was the right of teachers "to speak their minds freely on social and religious questions." Indeed, the point at issue was whether "expert opinion in the social sciences" would be permitted to act as a "corrective" on American leaders "whose personal interests run counter to those of the majority of the people." As long as businessmen and religious leaders made up boards of control, Dodd said, the answer would be "no." Only when professors or "representatives of the so-called radical forces of our society" gained a place on such boards would "expert opinion" become a valuable social asset.

While the AAUP was as eager as Dodd to assure free speech or the right of teachers outside the classroom to hold those "political rights vouchsafed to every citizen," the association was less interested in defining the value or goals of free speech than in establishing the means—due process, academic tenure, and standards of professional competence—by which it would be assured.[18] To Dodd, by contrast, a successful fight for academic freedom would assure him not just the right to speak freely but, more important, the privilege to use his knowledge to preserve and extend the democratization of American life. And for Dodd, in the middle of 1915, this meant supporting Wilson's foreign policy and joining in a nation-wide anti-preparedness campaign.

More specifically, in May 1915, it meant defining a position in response to the sinking of the unarmed passenger ship *Lusitania* which had caused the loss of 128 American lives. Though Dodd, like Wilson and the great majority of Americans, still believed that we should stand firmly against involvement in the war, he now began to feel that doing nothing or remaining aloof might also threaten America's democracy. Indeed, like "a small but significant segment of thoughtful American opinion," Dodd was convinced by the *Lusitania* incident that a victory for Germany in the war would directly threaten the United States. It "is deliberate international murder...," he said of the German submarine attack. "It means that the German authorities will balk at no atrocity to carry their point...." "We know you are fighting our battles," he told a French colleague. "We see daily proof that we should be attacked in a very short time if you were beaten...." But "happily," Dodd concluded, "the prospect of victory for the allies is good...."

Given this assumption and the fact that the sinking of the *Lusitania* touched off "a virtual crusade" for preparedness, Dodd made his prime response to the crisis a public appeal against an American arms buildup. Setting forth his case in a Chicago newspaper under the title "Larger Army and Navy? Why?," Dodd warned that embarking "upon a programme of militarism" would mean "imitating the madness of Germany." "Whom shall we arm against?" Dodd asked. England and France with whom we have good relations? Germany whose likely defeat will leave us nothing to fear? South America or Japan whom we would compel to arm against us? No, Dodd concluded, "our mission" must be "to set an example against the militarism which has drenched the treasures of centuries...."

Yet at the same time that Dodd stood foursquare against preparedness, he was mindful of the need for firm opposition to further German violations of American rights. Unlike Bryan, who resigned his post rather than endorse a strong warning from Wilson to the German government, Dodd applauded Wilson's diplomatic note of May 13 as "superb" and his subsequent actions as evidence that Wilson was "doing his utmost to maintain the rights of the country and at the same time not sacrifice those of humanity at large." Furthermore, remembering that "it will be our turn next if the Kaiser overthrows the allies," Dodd was "disposed to rest our case with" the President. Hence when "the exasperatingly futile *Lusitania* negotiations," among other things, made Wilson a convert to "reasonable" preparedness in the summer of 1915, Dodd, despite the vigorous opposition of most progressives, neither endorsed nor opposed Wilson's plans. Indeed, just as Dodd had no inclination to join more "advanced progressives" in demands upon Wilson for "programs of social amelioration" like equal rights for Negroes, woman suffrage, and labor laws, so he now suspended comment rather than fight the administration's preparedness campaign.[19]

But it was not just a reluctance to oppose Wilson which kept Dodd out of the battle. By September when antagonistic feelings began to build, Dodd was again suffering the consequences of his Chicago residence and was about to seek his "nerve restorative" at the farm.[20]

Although six or eight weeks in the fields had previously been enough to "insure" Dodd some "change of thinking," he was still depressed about his Riverside study in November and unable to commit himself to any substantial work. Invitations to contribute a volume to the American Nation series or to undertake a study of Reconstruction were immediately refused with remarks about the unsatisfactory state of current and prospective writing in American history, while agreements for brief essays made in the spring and fall were neither proceeding on schedule nor up to expectation when done. To be sure, letters of praise from Carl Becker, Albert Beveridge, and Frederick Jackson Turner about his *Expansion* study encouraged him "to project extended works" and to undertake some research when he returned to Chicago in January; but his four-month leave nevertheless had been productive of little writing and brought him back to Chicago again in a mood to take up some political work.[21]

The outstanding issue presenting itself to Dodd upon his return was preparedness—now an intense nation-wide battle between various advocates of army and navy expansion and Bryan-led pacifists, who were chiefly from the South and West.

Dodd, like the antipreparedness men, shared a growing fear of an "uncontrolled militarism." "I have always hoped and prayed," he told a colleague in February, "that we might possibly work out a democracy in this country....Now, I begin to think external and to us foreign events will break up our plans....If we ever arm, our social life will rapidly undergo a crystallization not unlike that of the South...in 1861." Such a military establishment would, in the words of one anti-preparedness leader, raise "up a military and naval caste," which, in Dodd's opinion, would serve "capitalists" by shooting down workingmen in the streets. To most southern and western progressives, this was no exaggeration. To them, preparedness, a movement largely supported by men "associated with the great financial and industrial interests," "signified turning America into an armed camp, the glorification of force, and, worst of all, an end to the reform movement at home."[22]

Yet despite the fears Dodd shared with anti-preparationists, he could not bring himself in the winter of 1916 to join in their protests against the administration's plans. In fact, with Germany launching an apparently decisive offensive at Verdun on February 21, and with a new crisis in German-American relations erupting after the torpedoing of the French Channel steamer *Sussex* on March 24, Dodd saw it as his duty to give reasonable preparedness some support. His method was to criticize Bryan and the foremost anti-preparedness Congressman, Claude Kitchin, privately while publicly trying to defend Secretary of the Navy Daniels against Navy League or extreme preparationist attacks.[23]

By May, however, when a German victory no longer seemed imminent and German concessions in the *Sussex* crisis temporarily reduced the threat of war, Dodd again worried chiefly about militarism in the United States or the prospect of an industrial-military oligarchy seizing control. This, however, by no means led him to join the anti-preparedness opposition to Wilson. "Wilson's mistake," he wrote Bryan, "consists in yielding to the militaristic forces of our time." But, Dodd explained, his motives were pure: he "yielded because he thought the people were being led astray by Roosevelt. His idea was to head off" T. R. Let us not therefore, Dodd concluded, punish Wilson by denying him our support; "he is our only hope against men who would hasten the day of our feudalism. If you and he and all the rest of us who want to keep America true to herself can be found fighting for the common cause, there is hope that we may win." This is a "critical" moment in American history, he told Colonel House, "not on account of a possible war, but because of what would surely follow the defeat of Wilson next November." The threat to American democracy, in short, was still greater at home than abroad.[24]

In this spirit, Dodd set out at the end of May to block a move at the University of Chicago to introduce optional military training for undergraduates. Under the terms of the new army bill, officer training could be offered at private institutions of higher learning at federal expense. Although Harvard, Princeton, Yale, and a handful of other schools had already announced their intention to count military training courses toward an undergraduate degree, Dodd opposed the scheme at Chicago on several grounds: first, as he told colleagues at a faculty meeting on June 1, because "it was a political move, supported by a party group—mainly the Roosevelt element and the old guard crowd in the Republican party—and the banks"; secondly, because the university was neither "equipped" to offer such instruction nor inclined to expand its undergraduate offerings; and last, because "we already have officers galore on a waiting list of over 5000, much better trained than we would turn out."[25]

Although the outcome of the faculty "discussion and contest" at Chicago was a victory for the preparedness men, Dodd did not concede defeat. He saw other ways for him to restrain those who "go around the country trying to undermine...what little democracy we have...." One of these was through service in a government post: "If I were a member of the Cabinet or a member of Congress," he wrote Claude Kitchin in June, "I would try to see if a way could not be found to keep these men to their lasts." But since neither was possible, Dodd was more than content to do such work as a member of Wilson's "proposed tariff commission." Indeed, having been recommended to the President as an appointee by Secretary Daniels, Dodd asked Kitchin to second the idea. "...Statisticians and economists will be found indispensable for most of the places...," he told Kitchin, but "I do not believe in turning things over to specialists entirely. Have specialist knowledge at command, but make sure that the specialist serves the public not his specialty."[26]

With the tariff commission bill not yet a law, however, and commission appointees not about to be named, Dodd continued to seek other ways in the interim to secure democracy in the United States. And although a need for money had led him to commit himself in May to a brief volume on the social and economic life of the Old South for Yale's *Chronicles of America* series, Dodd could still not see history-writing as a means to this end. "History," he now said, reflecting the deprecatory tone he had adopted in the previous year, "seldom does justice." And as if to give force to his idea, Charles Beard's *Economic Origins of Jeffersonian Democracy,* a book expressing more "advanced" progressive or New Nationalism ideas in depicting the Jeffersonian ideology as another "outworn" tyranny of the past, came to hand for review. This was a study, Dodd complained, which would chiefly appeal to conservatives for its description of Jefferson as "a rather poor sort of individual, a mere time-server and a consistent representative of certain 'interests,'" Whatever its merits, and there were several Dodd pointed to, the book, in Dodd's thinking, suffered from both an inaccurate assessment of Jefferson as "at heart not democratic" and an excessive emphasis on economic factors to the exclusion of other social forces. The lesson apparently for Dodd was that if even New historians like Beard could not set down the whole truth, then what significant contribution could history possibly make to the "common cause." In sum, he found little incentive to start on the Yale book.[27]

Far more interesting to him was the thought of going to see Wilson at the White House to enter a "mild protest" for himself and faculty friends against all "the military propaganda" and "agitation" for universal military service "led by General [Leonard] Wood." Whereas Dodd in the spring had seen all disagreement with the administration as injurious to democracy, he now believed that Bryan's reconciliation to Wilson at the party's nominating convention in June and Wilson's successful wooing of progressive Republicans with all-out backing for their schemes freed him to voice some mild dissent. Besides, the extraordinary outpouring of peace sentiment at the Democratic convention in June and the general realization that peace would be the single most important issue in the upcoming campaign encouraged Dodd to feel that an anti-militarist protest to the President would be but one more expression of the popular will.

His interview with Wilson on August 23, which was arranged through a Chicago acquaintance, Assistant Secretary of Labor Louis Post, was "frank and sincere." Although Wilson reported himself "in full sympathy with the…anti-militarists," he impatiently explained that since leaving the university world he had come to see that other nations "judge us by our physical power which is…negligible." Our only recourse, he felt, was to develop our strength, which would "give our voice its due influence" and allow us to say to the European nations when the war was done: " 'Let us make a move to maintain the people of the world,' " Expressing his eagerness for American participation in a postwar league of nations, a goal he had already publicly committed himself to in the spring, Wilson envisioned the United States "in concert with others" saying "to the world that he who disturbs the peace of the world is an outlaw" subject to punitive measures. As for General Leonard Wood, a leading preparationist, Wilson explained that his policy was " 'hire a hall for a fool.' " "Wood has tried from the beginning of this administration to make me make a martyr of him," Wilson said, "…but I am not going to play into his hands. Tell your friend[s]…that Wood has no more of our approval than…yours, but we think the best way is to let him hang himself.…"

Dodd came away from the meeting convinced of Wilson's "democracy," "confirmed" in his "former view that Wilson was really the chief of pacifists" and determined to support his re-election in the fall. Other pacifists, however, were not so easily convinced. In fact, it was not until October that Wilson energetically took up the peace cause, and won the pacifists to his camp. But by then, the combination of Republican fumbling and Wilson's strong campaign persuaded Dodd that there was little he need undertake in the President's behalf. "In the last two weeks," he wrote Colonel House on October 12, "there have been frequent changes from [Republican candidate Charles Evans] Hughes to Wilson in our faculty.... The feeling here is that Wilson is almost certain to receive the vote of the city of Chicago and likely to carry the state.... The vote of Republicans for him seems to be controlled by the attitude of the President on foreign affairs, though the Progressive voters depend on the legislation which Wilson has seen through the Congress."[28]

It was more, however, than Wilson's apparent success which restrained Dodd from some participation in the campaign; indeed, a host of obligations that always confronted him after a quarter's leave also played a part. There were rounds of university lectures and seminars to give, the careful preparation and presentation of which drew "heavily" upon his "nervous reserves," while History and Literary Club meetings, faculty discussions, and numerous social calls also consumed many hours of his time.[29]

Not the least of these preoccupations, however, was Dodd's continuing concern with a "militarist" or "reactionary" threat to democracy in the United States. It was a danger which even Wilson's re-election on November 7 could not dispatch.[30] Indeed, even though Democrats and progressives saw Wilson's return to the White House as promising "another four years of peace and an intensification of the drive for social justice," Dodd was less sanguine. For in contrast to those envisioning a "peace without victory" in the European war and a new round of domestic reform, Dodd primarily saw a peace with victory and "reactionary" gains at home. "If the Germans prove to be the conquerors of the world," Dodd wrote on November 25, "then we shall all live during two or three generations under the shadow of a...reactionary power...; if Germany loses distinctly then England will fall under the hands of the reactionary powers there...." In either case, that of German success or English victory, he said, reflecting the current disillusionment with Britain and antagonism toward both nations, "we shall have to keep ready for trouble...." Such a state of affairs, Dodd predicted, would place the country on a constant war footing and deprive the people of real control.[31]

Dodd was so worried about this prospect that in the two months after Wilson's re-election he borrowed time from the Yale book, which he was just getting under way, and shunned the American Historical Association meeting in Cincinnati in order to devote considerable energy to drafting warnings against reactionary trends. Along with letters to Secretary of War Newton Baker and a critique prepared for Congressman Claude Kitchin of General Emory Upton's *The Military Policy of the United States,* a widely quoted defense of preparedness, Dodd reviewed Albert Bushnell Hart's *American Patriots and Statesmen* in *The Dial.* The work, Dodd contended, was preparedness literature masquerading as history, which made the author the unwitting tool of "powerful men...who want nothing quite so much as scholars who will find them justification for deriding democracy and for endeavoring under the guise of patriotism to bring about the overthrow of whatever popular government we have been able to maintain." Their plan, as Dodd warned in "The United States of To-morrow" in *The Nation,* was an entirely different way of life: an America with "standing troops enough to overawe people and make obsolete such things as strikes"; an America seeking overseas monopolies and territorial annexations; an America, in brief, following the German "rule of might" and menacing the world's peace. "Shall we who foresee such consequences," Dodd asked, "tamely submit to what is now being done and urged in every city and from the columns of most of our newspapers?"[32]

The answer Dodd had to give was painfully complicated by the immediate prospect of war. The German announcement on February 1 of an all-out submarine campaign convinced him that we would soon be in a fight and that "every American [including himself] will gladly contribute his share. Still," Dodd predicted, "if we go to war we must lose. A war party in this country is always anti-democratic.... To go into war to maintain democracy or a measure of it in Europe and risk its loss in this country is a hard choice—but there is no other." Woodrow Wilson was of much the same mind. On the day before asking a declaration of war, he told Frank Cobb, editor of the New York *World,* that he couldn't see any alternative, that he had tried every way he knew to avoid war.... He went on to say that so far as he knew he had considered every loophole of escape and as fast as they were discovered Germany deliberately blocked them with some new outrage.

Then he began to talk about the consequences to the United States. He had no illusions about the fashion in which we were likely to fight the war....

"Once lead this people into war," he said, "and they'll forget there ever was such a thing as tolerance. To fight you must be brutal and ruthless, and the spirit of ruthless brutality will enter into the very fibre of our national life, infecting Congress, the courts, the policeman on the beat, the man in the street."...

He thought the Constitution would not survive it; that free speech and the right of assembly would go. He said a nation couldn't put its strength into a war and keep its head level; it had never been done.

"If there is an alternative, for God's sake, let's take it," he exclaimed.

Fighting this war and preserving democracy at home, Dodd told Josephus Daniels the day after the Senate voted to enter the fight, will be "a path strewn with thorns."[33]

VII

Public Service

"TO THOSE OF us who still retain an irreconcilable animus against war," Randolph Bourne complained in June 1917, "it has been a bitter experience to see the unanimity with which the American intellectuals have thrown their support to the use of war-techniques.... Socialists, college professors, publicists, new-republicans and practitioners of literature, have vied with each other in... the riveting of the war-mind on a hundred million more of the world's people."[1]

For all his misgivings, Dodd was no exception to this rule. Like William Jennings Bryan, who contracted "military lockjaw" at the outset of the conflict, Dodd opposed any and all dissent. When protestors against the war invited him to "assign a call for a mass meeting" at the University of Chicago in May, Dodd refused outright and personally boycotted the gathering. "Your duty lies wholly with this country," he told a German-American at the same time, "as I think the cause of mankind is the cause we are fighting.... Let not a false double allegiance mislead you. You are either with us or against us."[2]

It was not enough for Dodd, however, simply to oppose random acts of dissent; he wished to contribute more directly to the war effort. But "being past the age at which the army will take new recruits," he cast about for other ways to serve. Taking his cue from George Creel's Committee on Public Information and the National Board for Historical Services, he thought to "contribute... to the public information on the subject of the war." His chief effort in this direction was an agreement with the Northern Trust Company of Chicago to publish a series of pamphlets on American foreign policy before the war. At the same time, though, he sent along a variety of materials to Creel's Committee and the National Board, including a copy of his carefully drawn letter to a former pupil of German extraction "for use in enlightening similar states of mind."[3]

No act of national service in this first spring and summer of the war, however, appealed so much to Dodd as aiding the national drive for greater food production. With the administration introducing tight controls to satisfy both domestic and allied demands, Dodd looked forward to spending "every day of my [summer] vacation on the farm or in Washington in the hope that I may contribute my share." Whatever hopes he had of influencing administration policy, however, came to nothing when Secretary of Agriculture David Houston brushed aside his suggestion that larger crops would only follow government assurances of "an equitable return" on produce that usually brought only "one fourth what the consumer pays." By contrast, though, four months of work in Round Hill convinced him that he was doing his part: fifteen bushels of potatoes, 300 bushels of wheat, sixty dozen eggs and $800 worth of milk and cream were respectable accomplishments for an amateur farmer.[4]

But farm work was no long-term answer to Dodd's wish to serve; the next eight months, beginning in October, were to be spent in Chicago. Besides, other, more important opportunities soon presented themselves. In September, when Woodrow Wilson charged Colonel House to prepare American proposals for a peace conference at the end of the war, House began recruiting a staff of scholars to aid him in the work.[5] Dodd's name stood high on the Colonel's list as "... one of the rising authorities in American history. A man of accurate scholarship.... A Southerner who had shown a singular open-mindedness." Dodd was recommended to House by Dunning, Shotwell, and others as someone who "might...be of service to the [American Preparatory] Commission [or the Inquiry, as it was more commonly known] in working upon one of its foreign problems." Traveling to New York for a conference on October 20 with House and his chief aide, President Sidney Mezes of the City College of New York, Dodd agreed to undertake "a study and report on the problem of American trade, the open door in the Far East and the Monroe Doctrine of the future." Though German victories on the Italian front at the close of the month made "the work of Mr. House and my journey to New York...look like practical jokes," Dodd determined to go ahead nevertheless and even to agree to serve with Frederick Jackson Turner and William Dunning as a committee of the National Board for Historical Services to advise the commission on all its historical work.

Given these renewed associations with other scholars, it is not surprising that Dodd also saw his way clear to resume the American Historical Association activities he had avoided for over four years. Compelled by his work for the National Board to attend the association meeting in Philadelphia, he found that "the older and more eminent men do not make themselves as imposing as formerly. A lot of water has run over the mill since 1912," Dodd concluded. But whether the change was in him or in the association, Dodd now felt free to accept appointments to the association's program and policy committees for 1918.[6]

The most important result of Dodd's renewed identification as a professional historian, however, was his ability once more to write history. Indeed, resuming work at the beginning of December on the Yale Chronicle volume which he had tried unsuccessfully to begin in 1916, Dodd now wrote the book in less than two months' time.[7]

Though written so quickly and though only a slim volume of some thirty thousand words aimed at the general reader, Dodd's study *The Cotton Kingdom,* about the lower South in the two decades before the Civil War, was anything but superficial. Written out of twenty years of reading in southern sources and after ten years of teaching southern history, Dodd's volume was a composite of southern life which challenged contemporary themes with arguments that hold good to this day.[8]

At the heart of Dodd's book was the argument that the cotton plantation dominated ante-bellum southern life. Most historians already believed this to be true. What was important, though, was Dodd's analysis of that dominance: with ever increasing demands for cotton from European and New England merchants, he explained, cotton became the section's most important basic staple. Hence, a cotton planter "had only to be a kind master and a reasonably good manager, or employ good overseers, and he could not avoid the rapid accumulation of wealth." Indeed, the growth of the cotton crop from two and one half million to five million bales between 1850 and 1860 concentrated the wealth of the section in the hands of three to four thousand planter families, giving one thousand of them a yearly income almost equal to the annual earnings of the South's 666,000 other families.

Though "the great planters were undoubtedly absorbing a disproportionate part of the wealth of the South," this excited little resentment. On the contrary, Dodd showed that the majority of southern men, "the small farmer, the tenant, and the piney-woods squatter... all contributed to the power and prestige of the industrial leaders": "many of these ne'er-do-wells were but the distant cousins of the rich, the cast-offs of the fast-growing cotton aristocracy; many others were prospective planters, hopeful that they or their sons might... set up as planters." But even where such kinship or aspirations did not exist among poor, non-slaveholding whites, Dodd believed the inclination was to support the plantation system nevertheless. Holding Negro slaves in contempt, poor whites saw any movement toward abolition as a threat to their own social standing. All in all, as Dodd put it, "every class of

Southern society...was disposed to lend power and influence to the owner of great plantations...."[9]

Given such support, Dodd argued that it was comparatively easy for cotton planters to fasten their social philosophy upon the entire section. Drawing upon the writings of Thomas Dew, William Harper, John C. Calhoun, Thomas Carlyle, and George Fitzhugh, the planters led "the small farmers and landless groups" to abandon Jeffersonian liberalism for "the contrary ideal of the inequality of men"—the doctrine of social caste and prescriptive rights.[10] The extent to which these ideas dominated southern thinking, Dodd said, was well illustrated by two facts: Walter Scott's novels—romantic depictions of "fine lords and fair ladies" whom southerners might imitate—were shipped South in "carload lots,"[11] and "no newspaper of any importance, no college or university professor, no prominent preacher, and no politician of any party offered effective resistance" to advocacy of inequality. "The society of the Cotton and Tobacco kingdoms," as one later writer put it, "...was not favorable to the preservation of freedom of thought...."[12]

If these planters so thoroughly dominated southern society, they were still, in Dodd's hands, not the stereotyped planters in other books who "sipped mint juleps on spacious verandas" and left their slaves to brutal overseers like Simon Legree. On the contrary, Dodd depicted the average cotton-planter's home as "modest" and his life as marked by "routine, dress and travel" which left little time for wanton dissipation.[13]

But this was not the only stereotype Dodd challenged. "Contrary to a common preoccupation," he wrote, "the people of the lower Southern states were sincerely religious...." He also attacked the idea that the South lagged far behind the rest of the nation in every field of education. Though illiteracy, he conceded, ran higher in the South than in any other section, college training for young southerners was more widespread than among their counterparts in other regions: "twice as many young men per thousand of the population," he wrote, "were in colleges in the lower South or in some of the Eastern institutions as were sent from similar groups in other parts of the country."[14] The most important stereotype, however, with which Dodd contended was the persistent notion of a South with no middle class, a region simply of slaveholders and "poor white trash." "The life of the plain people of the lower South," Dodd said, "is more important than that which displayed itself in the great houses, at the races, or at the resorts. This life was not altogether so crude and raw as...depicted..., nor was it so much out of sympathy with the planter ideal as...represented.... The farmers and the tenants, the piney-woods people and the mountaineers," he concluded, "were like farmers and tenants elsewhere." It was an argument which, like so many others in Dodd's brief book, was to find confirmation in later, more detailed historical works.[15]

If Dodd's writing, then, flourished in this period of renewed identification as a professional historian, he could not say the same for his Inquiry work. Invited to report on "the problem of American trade, the open door in the Far East and the Monroe Doctrine of the future," Dodd hardly knew where to begin. He had no expertise in any of these matters and, worse yet, little idea of what House or Mezes hoped to have. If it were any consolation to him, though, the same was true for other Inquiry scholars. With a paucity of regional experts or students of international affairs, or for that matter any first-rate university personnel not already committed to other war work, House and Mezes resorted to academicians "whose experience in research could be described as generally successful even though it had not focused squarely on the specific problem to be treated by the Inquiry." Furthermore, with "only the haziest conception" in their own minds of what their project would entail, House and Mezes could only give Inquiry workers a general description of what they must do.[16]

Left to his own devices, then, Dodd interpreted his assignment as "a survey of the policies of the United States with reference to the Far East; tariff and 'preferred nation' clauses in general; the relation of big business (especially bankers) to foreign policy; the detection of imperialistic and 'Prussian' elements in America and similar topics." In brief, Dodd aimed to alert the Commission to "certain reactionary tendencies" while gathering "data...which would strengthen the hands of our government in maintaining liberal and forward looking policies."

Such a project, however, was more than Dodd could manage. Beginning with a consideration of American trade in the Far East, he quickly found himself drifting in a sea of documents. "As for documents, such as you mention in your letter of November 4," a Chamber of Commerce official wrote, "I am somewhat at a loss what to send you. The material, of course, is very extensive. If you will indicate the nature of the statistics you desire, and of the consular reports...I shall endeavor to respond." Unable, however, clearly to define his needs, Dodd could neither decide upon specific materials nor, as with other scholars, get beyond a brief preliminary report.

Part of the reason for Dodd's inability to get beyond a preliminary study, however, was the Inquiry's demand that he give priority to other work. No sooner had Dodd launched his study of Far Eastern trade than Shotwell urged that he advise the National Board for Historical Services on how to serve the Inquiry: "There are so many things I should like to have your advice upon," Shotwell wrote at the beginning of December,

the main one being that which [Frederick Jackson] Turner brought up... namely, the need of applying the experience of America in the past in determining to some extent the line of policy which we might…pursue with reference to some of the major questions at issue.

…My interest, as you know, has always been in the field of European history, and I personally feel very much the need of your advice…. [Dunning] is…somewhat at sea as to the way in which he could be of use, since it is his impression that the problems fronting us now would have to be solved without too many entanglements from the past.

The more I think about it the more I hope that you can come here before long, because in these days of preliminary planning tasks are necessarily being assigned in which your judgment will be of great service to us.

Heeding Shotwell's request, Dodd temporarily put aside his Far Eastern study to meet with board members in Philadelphia on December 28, where they accomplished little toward formulating study methods and aims and invited Dodd instead to prepare a written estimate of "the relation of the Monroe Doctrine to the settlement," one of eleven subjects urgently requiring studies by February 1.[17]

Responding again to the shifting needs of the Inquiry, Dodd agreed to prepare such a report in four weeks' time. The result was a twenty-four-page summary history of the doctrine and a thirteen-page essay on its "present status" in which Dodd argued that where the original intent of the Monroe Doctrine had been to guarantee Latin American nations the right of national self-determination, later Americans had transformed the doctrine into an instrument of imperial control, a means of assuring exclusive American domination of the Latin South. Because Dodd's reports emphasized the latter rather than the primary point about the doctrine, Dunning and Shotwell, taking their cue from Wilson's fourteen-point peace program of January 8, criticized Dodd for not making his study a "justification" of the doctrine's original aim. "This is a rather inaccurate, incoherent and unclear development of a point that probably may be made useful," Dunning wrote. "This point is that the Monroe Doctrine is a doctrine of non-intervention in, and protection to, lesser nationalities….A careful reading of the official documents and correspondence touching the Monroe Doctrine ever since its origins might produce a series of quotations from representative Americans that would have much value in debate." "Would it not be well," Shotwell asked Mezes, "to recast; stating the hypothesis and then justifying it historically? Handled in that way, one would know from the first what the real subject is—not a history of the Monroe Doctrine but a justification for the general application of its implications now."[18] Where Dodd saw the justice of the doctrine's "hypothesis" as self-evident and the need to alert peace commissioners to "reactionary tendencies" instead, Inquiry chiefs insisted upon having detailed information which might support the President's peace plans.

Although Dodd never saw these criticisms of his work, at the beginning of March he asked to be excused from his original commitment to a Far Eastern report. His ostensible reason, as he explained it to Mezes, was that the addition of "experts on far eastern affairs...inclined [him] to think that anything I might do would be sort-of fifth wheel to a wagon." Mezes politely agreed. But what may also have decided Dodd to give up his project was the opinion of a colleague that the Inquiry "is [Walter] L[ippmann]'s conception and organization.... S[hotwell]," this scholar explained, "is only an assistant to L[ippmann] who gets all the reports and uses such of them and such parts of them as he pleases. The work of the best scholars may or may not be used...."[19]

Whatever the impact of these considerations, what probably most influenced Dodd to abandon his study for the Inquiry was his eagerness to be free to make some concerted effort to head off a postwar reaction or restoration of conservative control. In January 1918 with the American Protective Tariff League launching a sharp attack on the third of Wilson's Fourteen Points, that endorsing free trade, and with the passage of the Webb bill, an act amending the antitrust laws to allow American manufacturers to combine for the purpose of carrying on an export trade (and one supported by Wilson as necessary to the healthy growth of industry), Dodd became convinced that such an outcome to the war was already under way. In fact, as he explained in an article in February, such a reaction was something of a historical inevitability: "The farmers thought in 1801," he wrote,

> that their day had come and that commerce and finance had been relegated to secondary places among the great forces which then drove this country toward the future. But seven years had not passed before the farmer's president had been definitely checkmated. In 1829 the farmers came back again, but they did not long control affairs. And the case was not very different in 1860; yet three years had not elapsed till finance and industry were in the saddle. Now it would seem that labor has won.
>
> The existence of the great war gives laboring men, especially skilled men, an advantage that no other class has ever had. They will keep this advantage till arms are stacked on the western front. On that day finance and industry and trade will return to their former position.

"What can we do to keep out of the slough of despond at the end of the war?" Dodd rhetorically asked Claude Kitchin in January. "It will not suffice to make the world safe for democracy and then become ourselves the most reactionary of peoples. That is our danger.... Tax laws, tariffs, immigration laws, army and navy, the courts and diplomacy," he warned, "must be watched and guarded." To help in this work, Dodd first "thought of offering for a seat in Congress for Virginia"; but the chance of finding himself "utterly helpless, in the event of success,... discouraged" him. More to his taste, as he told Colonel House in February, would be a place "on the Tariff or Federal Trade Boards.... There are," he explained, "two reasons I would like to be considered: first, that the determination of our trade policy is going to be vitally important at the end of the war; second, I would like to study the men and makers of this administration from a nearer point of vantage than Chicago." Though Colonel House promised to do "what I can" and though Dodd also appealed to Claude Kitchin for aid, neither offered him any real hope of an immediate or even a future appointment.[20]

In the meantime, though, Dodd was prepared to battle reactionaries with the spoken and written word. In February he launched a series of lectures in and around Chicago on "The Chance for Democracy in the Country at the End of the War,"[21] and began toying with the idea of fashioning the theme of his lectures into a paper for the Inquiry and Colonel House. "Quite on my own account," he wrote Mezes at the beginning of March, "I have made a survey of our history with all the emphasis on the critical periods when democracy and our foreign relations were brought into juxtaposition.... From my point of view, this study would offer responsible representatives some angles of consideration not apt to be had otherwise."

Encouraged by Mezes to make his work available to the commission, Dodd prepared a paper entitled "The Evolution of the Present Status of Democracy in the United States" which he submitted to Mezes on April 10. Analyzing "the problem of democracy in this country as influenced by the wars of Europe," Dodd focused on a single theme: "for a democracy to go to war is to take its life in its hands": the Revolutionary War, the Napoleonic struggles with England, the American Civil War, and the Spanish-American conflict of 1898, Dodd said, had aided commercial and financial moguls to take or keep control over national affairs. But, Dodd emphasized, the outcome of the First World War need not be the same: when Wilson led America into war, he "was," Dodd wrote, "in a position to enter... on his own terms. He could wield the two hundred and fifty billions of American wealth on behalf of democracy everywhere. He could make his enemies at home and his rivals abroad hold up his arms while he accomplished their overthrow. That was not possible to Jefferson; nor could Lincoln think of dictating terms to the great capitalists who loaned him money in 1862. Never in the world's history has a leader been so lucky in the circumstances of his position."

But these circumstances, Dodd warned, would change unless Wilson guarded against certain things: "Great corporations, masters of large fortunes and parasitic men" seeking to upset a Wilsonian peace guaranteeing free trade and national self-determination; special interests hoping to saddle "the people" with interest payments on a debt of many billions which only "the very wealthy" should pay; the collapse of "the good understanding among the guarantors of the international treaty" because of American refusal to curtail a greatly expanded overseas trade; the unemployment of "thousands and even millions of American laborers" through the too rapid or radical reduction of that trade; and lastly, the failure of the government to deal more constructively than ever before with laborers and farmers whose war-time incomes might slip from their all-time high. The cost of not coping with these problems, Dodd warned, would be to assure the transformation of the United States into "another vast Roman republic exploiting all who come within our ken,... [or] another Roman empire subjugating all the weaker nations of the earth...."[22]

To assure that Colonel House would also consider these analyses of current trends, Dodd urged him on May 1 to read at least one section of his report and to understand "that liberal-minded people here, and elsewhere, are a little uneasy about... the apparent purpose of the Department of Commerce to take the lion's share of the world's commerce at the end of the war if not before the end. It seems to me," Dodd advised, "...that we ought to go very slowly in the matter of our trade policy until we can sit down with our allies at the peace conference."

Accurate in their analysis of the traditional impact of war on American reform and generally prescient about the dangers which lay ahead, Dodd's arguments did not fall on deaf ears. Mezes, on his own account, passed his "survey" along to House and invited Dodd to submit yet a fuller study of postwar problems. House himself expressed "pleasure" at having seen the report and distress over "the tendency in some directions to push our commerce at the expense of the rest of the world and at the expense of more vital issues...." But anything the President might do, House told Dodd, will have to wait until "the proper time." Indeed, though many liberals across the nation worried about "reactionary tendencies," they, like House, deferred confrontation to "the proper time." In Washington, for example, where Wilson feared "that industrialists would take advantage of the emergency raised by war to seize power," he appointed a majority of Republican businessmen to his Council of National Defense. In New York, furthermore, where *New Republic* writers outwardly supported Wilson and the war with optimistic predictions of a "liberal peace," Walter Weyl confided to his diary that "Wilson does not energetically strive to maintain liberalism. He allows liberalism to go by default... [while] liberals... do nothing to embarrass him."

Only a handful of pacifists like Randolph Bourne, Robert M. LaFollette, and Oswald Garrison Villard or pro-war liberals without demanding government jobs like William Jennings Bryan and Dodd could afford to keep up the fight for domestic liberalism and reform. Without full-time commitments to government work, including particularly the peace-making which would leave so many progressives disillusioned at the end of the war, men like Bryan and Dodd were generally free to keep up their prewar reform activities. In 1917–18, for example, at the same time he acted as a government "propagandist," Bryan devoted considerable energy to crusades for prohibition, woman suffrage, wider and fairer dissemination of public information, government ownership of railroads, and a range of measures which would prevent business from reversing prewar progressive gains.[23] In similar fashion, Dodd divided his time between propaganda, peace research, and familiar prewar warnings against business machinations to end liberal control.

By the spring of 1918, though, Dodd believed it essential to give more than part-time attention to reactionary trends. Viewing the widespread repression of civil liberties and increased power for businessmen—the industrial subordination of American life, Dodd called it—Dodd decided to write a life of Wilson which would "clarify public opinion," or bring "some misinformed people…to a…more historical interest in the development of our country along liberal lines." Actually, the thought of doing a study of Wilson or the evolution of Wilsonian democracy had occurred to Dodd during the previous winter when he explained the "social and economic background" of the President in an article for the *Journal of Political Economy*. It was not until June 1918, however, when he saw "the old Republican party…becoming more and more reactionary" that he decided to carry through on the idea.

To begin such a work, Dodd planned to spend a good part of his summer reading recent newspaper and periodical literature in the Library of Congress and interviewing prominent men on the Washington scene. In the first month of his vacation, therefore, between June 17 and July 15, he traveled from his Virginia farm to Washington once a week to sound out senators and representatives from Illinois, Mississippi, North Carolina, and Virginia on congressional work under Wilson. At the same time, he gathered information on wartime developments from Stuart B. Greene of the "War Service Board," Vernon L. Kellogg, Herbert Hoover's chief assistant in the Food Administration, William L. Chenery of George Creel's staff, and a host of colleagues passing through the Cosmos Club. Moreover, early in August, he met with William Jennings Bryan in Asheville, North Carolina, to hear his version of the campaign of 1896, which confirmed Dodd's picture of that event and provided background for the book.[24]

There was no more important interview, however, than the one arranged for September 13 with Wilson at the White House. In a two-and-one-half-hour conversation on that day, Wilson showed himself as worried as Dodd about reactionary trends. Though, Dodd later wrote, the President discussed war aims, German national traits and problems with the allies, "he came back again and again to our domestic problems": to the fact that he resented bankers and businessmen who distrusted him and made profits from the war, that the Chamber of Commerce held aims with which democratic men can not sympathize and which put it in the same class with German commercial exploiters, that he was required to compel the Congress, at the risk of turning it into a court of registry, to meet the people's demands, that American newspapers were not free, that *The Nation* had become "'a part of that reactionary element in New York which constitutes our greatest danger,'" that the country had never voted for him "'on principle, that is for a definite democratic programme,'" that we were in danger from "'big business men'" who were "'spending immense sums of money'" to get control of Congress and "'set up a reactionary reconstruction regime'" which the people will overturn by revolutionary means, and that he was aiming "to keep the kind of men in office who will support him...." Such opinions left Dodd feeling that Wilson "agreed with most that I said and [that] he saw with the point I made about the evolution of our democracy—namely that we had much of it now and that we had had a hard time keeping it.... I have never heard any high public man talk so frankly and so fearlessly," Dodd concluded. "I doubt if ever visitors to Washington had as clear a view of the President's mind."[25]

Though the conversation was "most inspiring" and a clear inducement to begin writing what Dodd hoped would be a 150-page analysis completed by the following spring, it was also a stimulant to him to find more immediate means of combating reactionary trends, now particularly threatening to engulf the conduct of foreign affairs. Indeed, with the end of the war clearly in sight in early October, and with leading Republicans like Senator Henry Cabot Lodge sounding a call for unconditional surrender, Dodd, like *New Republic* writers, felt compelled to speak out against any diminution or abandonment of initial war aims—a conciliatory peace rather than a vindictive "Prussian" peace. To this end, when he returned to Chicago for the fall quarter, Dodd assumed responsibility for the university's war issues course, exchanged ideas with a group of Chicago "intellectuals," including the British and French vice consuls, working for a "democratic peace," and published a letter in *The Nation* warning against opposition to a Wilsonian treaty from American "Prussians" urging a policy of "brute force"—a policy, Dodd explained, like that of 1865 "which can not but lead to disaster and recurrence to the spirit of war...."[26]

Yet whatever Dodd's interest in assuring a Wilsonian peace, it was his realization that a liberal settlement of the war rested chiefly on continued liberal control at home. And it was just such control which in the autumn of 1918 impressed him as facing a crisis. Informed in mid-October that a plan of economic reconstruction had been worked out and submitted to the President, Dodd warned House on the 22nd that Leon C. Marshall, Dean of Chicago's School of Commerce and Administration, the man expected to take charge of the work, was from the Chamber of Commerce "set." "In other words," Dodd told House, "if great care be not taken ... we shall find after the event that the programme will be mapped out as desired by certain undemocratic leaders, by men now fighting the President night and day."

But with disquieting events like House in Europe for armistice talks and with Republican successes at the polls on November 5, a disturbing conversation with former Senator Albert Beveridge on the 8th, and the presence of Harry Wheeler, President of the United States Chamber of Commerce, in Washington on the 19th, Dodd decided to write the President himself. Summarizing for Wilson what he had already told House, "because House is away and because ... otherwise I should feel that possibly I have not done my duty," Dodd then reported the details of a possible Republican plot:

A week or two ago a man [Albert Beveridge] who is very close to the leaders of the opposition asked me to give him my opinion of some historical work he is doing. After ... the talk turned to yourself and the state of things after the election.

... It is planned to ball up things and bring on serious industrial disturbances, even a financial panic "before Wilson's term is out." That is, he said, "one thing the President can not escape responsibility for if it comes." ... More than once this one great saving disaster of economic distress was mentioned and emphasized.

... The candidate for 1920 he said "is all settled, the issues, in addition to the panic, are to be first and foremost the league of nations and second the need of our taking the lion's share of international trade.["] He said in so many words that England was to be attacked because she is making us take up this league of nations in her own interest. ... I said because the German and Irish votes were at stake?

That was not denied nor acknowledged. But the real reason for the fight on the league of nations is the purpose of having a free hand in Spanish America. He said no man who knows history will deny that we must some day annex Mexico. "Why then tie our hands in any league of nations?"

The same man said a good deal else that convinced me that the programme is pretty much as I have indicated, that we have to be more than careful lest we lose all the war has won and that the most unscrupulous campaign we have had in a long time is to be waged from now till 1920.

While Dodd acknowledged that this "may all be vain imaginings" and that Beveridge's discussion of economic disturbances had been "put hypothetically," Wilson, who already saw "prominent Republicans" as dead set against his peace plans, apparently shared Dodd's fears. But whatever his concern with Republican opposition, Wilson's decision on November 18 to head the American delegation to Paris fixed his thoughts on foreign affairs. Even Joe Tumulty's warning that "domestic affairs would suffer" from his departure "and that the rising Republican tide would swirl into the vacuum in the capitol" could not keep him at home. The President, Arthur Walworth has written, "found it easy to ignore the political reckoning that was being calculated by... [the Congress] as moral impulse drove him toward the New Jerusalem to keep his personal covenant with the millions who had bled and died."[27]

Though Dodd, like other thoughtful progressives, regretted Wilson's preoccupation with foreign affairs to what now seemed like the exclusion of domestic ones, he assumed it was only a temporary condition dictated by events. As he saw it, Republican control of the Senate momentarily precluded "any real reconstruction that [D]emocrats could plan." The President, therefore, was leaving for Europe on December 4 "in large measure to strengthen himself for the bitter fight that he must face here from now till 1920." In other words, as Dodd put it, if Wilson gains his peace program, "he comes back to press his domestic moves...." In the meantime, though, Dodd believed it was the task of American liberals to "strengthen the President's hand"—that is, as league advocates around America saw it, to build support in the country for a league of nations, counteracting anti-league forces and persuading both U.S. senators and French negotiators that a majority of Americans would settle for nothing less than the President's original plan.[28]

To this end, Dodd helped launch Chicago's organized pro-league movement on December 10, while at the same time he asserted his personal influence against "the direction the Chamber of Commerce is taking." The Chamber's annual meeting in Atlantic City, apparently resolving to send "commercial men" to Paris to oversee Wilson's work and encouraging Anglo-American commercial rivalry, struck Dodd as "an affair of war against the President." Urging his old friend Elliott Goodwin, the Chamber's Secretary, to stand against such schemes, Dodd also sought to hasten the publication of a paper he had prepared during the summer, "The Converging Democracies," on the joint responsibility of English-speaking peoples to sustain democracy, heal Europe, and keep the peace.[29]

In the midst of this effort, however, on December 20, Dodd fell ill with influenza, and aside from occasional work on the Wilson book, he did little else for a month.

Moreover, by the time his health was fully restored, it appeared to Dodd that Wilson would carry his program. For with the President's achievement in persuading the peace conference to give priority to drafting a league covenant, it was, Dodd wrote on January 25, "the tendency of men out here, as best I can judge tendencies from papers and the talk of people in clubs like the Union League and the City,...to be ashamed of the attitude of early December. Wilson is immensely stronger than he was four or five weeks ago....I have a long letter from Colonel House this morning giving an intimate account of the state of things in Paris. Confidentially, may I say he says a league of nations is safe...."

Though now confident that Wilson "will secure a peace that will far surpass in wisdom and humane and even democratic arrangements anything the world has ever got," and though predicting that the Senate "will do what he [Wilson] tells it to do," Dodd nevertheless continued in January and February to work for "the cause." On January 30, for example, he became temporary chairman of the Political Equality League's committee for the league of nations, which helped arrange the February 11 Chicago regional congress of the national League to Enforce Peace—one of ten regional congresses marshaling public opinion across the United States. At the same time, Dodd joined Salomon O. Levinson, a progressive Republican businessman in Chicago, in urging Wilson and House to widen support for the league by identifying it with the "outlawing of war": "Tested midwest sentiment by numerous mass meetings and interviews," they wired House on February 6. "Feeling strong for outlawing war. Believe entire country can be quickly won for league with good effect on newspapers and senators. Popular slogan outlaw war timely." It was a conclusion Henry Cabot Lodge himself had reached.

Yet if men as far apart as Dodd and Lodge now saw widespread support for the league, both also recognized that this might change. And if it did change, it would, Dodd believed, in part result from the fact that men did not understand the historical forces at work in their own age. "It has seemed to me," Dodd shortly wrote a colleague, "that the period [of recent American history] has never been analyzed and portrayed in its essential features in any book or paper." "You and your friends," Dodd told Beveridge at the same time, "are now and have been so bound up with historic forces that you have not been able to see...." To help remedy this, or, as he put it to Tumulty on February 18, to "help us all in the struggle for not only the league of nations but for popular control of our own country," Dodd again began to work primarily on the Wilson book.[30]

Having already brought the story up to 1913 in four chapters of some twenty thousand words, Dodd hoped to add a like amount in the spring and publish the work in the fall. But he was less than convinced that his opening chapters were in final form or that his narrative of Wilson's presidential years could be as brief; and before he could reach any firm conclusions, he needed simply to work further on the book. But to do this seemed to require another interview with the President in which he could discuss Wilson's "almost unparalleled unfolding of his powers from 1902 on and his recent ordeal in Paris." Such a meeting, however, was at best difficult to arrange. With the President coming home for only ten days beginning on February 24, he was to be "too rushed [even] to confer with his aides individually." But in an obvious expression of support and high regard for Dodd's work, Wilson agreed to give a half-hour interview on March 1.

Meeting with the President "in one of the middle parlors of the White House," Dodd found Wilson unperturbed by Senate attacks on the league covenant he had brought home to explain and "perfectly sure of himself and apparently of his cause." Launching directly into a discussion of the two topics Dodd had asked information on, Wilson "talked about his gradual change of social philosophy since he wrote the essay on [Edmund] Burke for the *Atlantic* about 1892 or 93. He said my only interest in him was in his growth—and he began to talk of Lincoln.... There is no doubt," Dodd concluded from what he said, "that he now regards the great civil war president as his model...." Turning next to the Paris conference, he described Clemenceau "as a smoothe[*sic*] politician who had tried to double-cross him eight times. He spoke of the French and Italian demands with the utmost disapproval. General Foch he said was a thorn in the flesh demanding the impossible. Lloyd George, he said, was in entire agreement with himself and House. The French treaties of 1915 which were to procure the Rhine boundary for France the English did not regard as suitable to be kept." Coming next to the subject of America and a league of nations, Wilson described "poor stricken Europe" as in "a tangle" and said: "We are their only hope— the hope of the people. We must not withdraw. A league of nations is the only bar against the spread of anarchy and terror. No government in Europe he thought could withstand our withdrawal. Then he indicated his disgust with the Senate opposition. Lodge he said had written Henry White that he favored a league. Yet he talks contrary now." Interspersed through all this was some discussion of "mid-western conditions, the chances of success in Chicago" and the wish that "all his friends...press steadily for a league of nations."[31]

Inspired by his conversation with Wilson and prodded by "the proposed publisher, the Macmillans,...to have the manuscript in hand as soon as possible in order to bring out the book during the coming discussion in the senate and country of the work of the peace conference," Dodd returned to Chicago determined to give exclusive attention to this goal. Indeed, though required to teach his usual two courses in the spring quarter, he departed from his traditional offerings on the South and the West to teach classes on "Recent American History" and "The War with Spain," courses which could be useful in the writing of his book.

To live up to this plan, however, soon proved beyond Dodd's reach. Though working steadily on the book through March with interruptions only to help start "a clean, liberal newspaper" in Chicago and to dissuade Albert Beveridge from anti-league talk, Dodd could not continuously keep from more immediate political work. When a "dark period" of impasse overtook the peace conference at the beginning of April 1919 and Wilson's work seemed to hang "in the balance," he felt compelled to prepare a five-thousand-word essay for publication in England on "Political and Economic Developments in the United States" during the previous six months. While acknowledging a variety of domestic tensions in the United States "that will tend to make the economic and political life of America interesting in the near future," Dodd urged the English above all to understand that the President still held a position of unsurpassed strength. Indeed, his program in the coming summer, Dodd predicted, "will probably be the ratification of the treaty, the adoption of the constitution of the League of Nations, and the acceptance on the part of the country of the mandates for those countries assigned to us. The domestic programme," he forecast with equal optimism, "will probably be Government control of railroads, the settlement...of the relations between employers and workers, and perhaps the public control of the great packers and the coal mines."

Furthermore, though refusing invitations to write history which would distract him from the book, Dodd could not resist a request at the beginning of May for a written appeal to Americans to support the President's work. Believing that an essay for *The World's Work* might "make" United States senators "understand somewhat more the gravity of things" and counteract cynical responses to a published digest of the treaty, Dodd prepared a moralistic brief for a foreign policy of "genuine helpfulness": "We are surely at the parting of the ways in our career," he wrote. "We have more of the riches of the earth than any other three countries in the world. We have less binding traditions to prevent us from embarking upon those inviting ways that lie open before us....If we...set ourselves to the task of genuine helpfulness and not of exploitation in any sense, we should at once win a place in the affections of mankind, an esteem that would far surpass that glory which ancient Rome boasted. Not the beaten paths of history, but the untried ways of international brotherhood, ought to beckon."[32]

Whether they would, however, depended, Dodd believed, on what would now be done for the cause. With the Congress convening for a special session on May 19 and the negotiations in Paris apparently coming to an end, the decision on the President's peace program was now at hand. On the question of whether Wilson succeeds or fails, Dodd told Beveridge on May 26, "the next twelve months will tell."

Since in Dodd's estimate victory for the President turned on the support of "liberal elements...about to be lost" and that of "the great provincial mass...not yet...stirred," Dodd at once began working for these ends. But shortly acknowledging that the "extreme radicals" of the *New Republic* and *The Nation,* liberals who pronounced the treaty and the league vindictive and coercive, could not be held to the cause, he devoted himself exclusively to stirring the mass of men. Like Wilson himself, Dodd believed that once the people appreciated what the President had achieved, they would compel the Senate to approve his work. Beginning on May 19, then, in the realization that he would probably be unable to contribute the completed manuscript of his book to the league debate, Dodd sought to arrange serial publication of several chapters in newspapers across the United States. At the same time he set about to launch a speaking program against "the outrageous misrepresentation of the President that is being pressed daily in this region."[33]

Though unable to arrange for a series of newspaper articles, Dodd quickly found himself committed to a public-speaking program lasting well into July. Agreeing to a number of engagements for himself, he fashioned lectures aimed primarily at the German-Americans who, in his words, were "strong enough here to defeat any candidate they oppose." If these speeches won any converts, it was not obvious to Dodd. In fact, he could not tell whether his appeal to the German-Americans "did good or harm." Furthermore, as he told the President when he returned home in July, "men...wish to see you in person. I think great things would come of a few direct appeals."[34] Given the uncertainty of benefits to be derived from any further speeches he might give and the fact that Lodge's calculated delays in acting on the treaty might permit him to finish the Wilson book before the Senate votes were cast, Dodd decided toward the end of July to leave Chicago for Virginia where he could devote himself chiefly to writing in the seclusion of his farm.

Whatever plans he had for writing, though, quickly gave way to the need for a rest. Having been driven to the edge of his powers by the exertions of the previous six months, Dodd could do nothing more for two months than keep "outdoors" and work "like a farmhand." "This farm is the place to forget that ever men wrought and struggled on a large stage," he wrote Albert Beveridge toward the end of his stay. "I am busy from morn till night with my semi-menial tasks....My hands are hard and my skin tanned...and I eat with a relish and sleep when I go to bed, not trying to think out the construction and form of chapters in some book."

The only thing to mar his two-month holiday was news from the Macmillan Company of New York that they believed his uncompleted "account of Wilson," which he sent them in the summer, too "partisan" for publication. The decision distressed him greatly and reminded him that the "liberal" point of view could not get a hearing in the United States. "I shall be counted partisan, in spite of all that I could possibly do," he complained to the editor. "The reviews, the newspapers that make opinion and the popular magazines are all centered in New York or in the East where...Wilson could not get a fairer historical trial than could Jefferson....I do heartily agree with a remark that Colonel House made to me in 1917, that the press is the greatest single difficulty in maintaining a democracy in our country.... There is not and, of course, never has been a free press in the United States." While other liberals agreed with Dodd's analysis and hoped to raise the issue in the 1920 campaign, Dodd saw "no remedy" for the problem. Even though Arthur Page of Doubleday, Page and Company encouraged him to believe that they would publish his book and urged him to hurry forward the work, Dodd could not trust his word: "the turn of events before I finish the job," he predicted, "may, and likely will, change the attitude of the firm. This in spite of the fact that reasoned and scientific books on present day leaders are of vital importance to this generation."[35]

Had Dodd's study in fact been a "reasoned and scientific" portrait, he would undoubtedly have been confident of publication. But as it stood, his book was really little more than a justification or defense of Wilson and his work. Ending almost every chapter on a melodramatic note—"How would the modern St. George maintain his fight...?" reads one example—Dodd celebrated practically everything Wilson said and did. The President's domestic measures, "the great reforms," were testimony to the fact that "not since the Declaration of Independence had any leader of the country more clearly voiced the ideals which Americans loved to think they believed in."

The fourteen points were "the greatest of all pronouncements ever made by a responsible head of a great government upon the ideal terms of a world federation." Wilson's decision to go to Paris was "natural," while only a "Machiavellian strategy probably would have suggested the appointment of certain bitter opponents as commissioners...." His fight for the treaty and league were of heroic proportions: "without united support in his own party and with the bitterest hatred known to the halls of Congress since the days of Andrew Johnson dominating...the opposition, without powerful economic support in the country, with a cabinet whose members were decidedly deficient in the gift and art of public speaking, and with all the leaders of Europe putting obstacles in his way, Wilson now addressed himself to the greatest task that any American statesman, save Lincoln, ever undertook." The book, in short, in the words of one later Wilson biographer, was "shamelessly partisan and eulogistic."[36]

Yet in spite of his fears that no publisher would be found for so polemical a work, Dodd had no intention of casting it aside. Even during the summer when the rejection from Macmillan was fresh in his mind and he did little writing, he interviewed knowledgeable Wilsonians and sat in the Senate galleries to hear "what passed for debates." If he had any doubts about finishing the book, though, they were entirely overcome at the beginning of October by Wilson's illness and collapse. With the President unable to speak and possibly near death, it was imperative, Dodd believed, that others now speak in his stead. "Wilson's condition makes it...urgent...that I finish my present task and that you publish it as soon as possible," he wrote Arthur Page on October 15. "...[This] is for me the duty of the day."

Through October and part of November, then, while most Wilson supporters fought the last battle in the treaty-league debate, Dodd concentrated on finishing his book and winning his own political fight—the struggle to assure publication of what he wrote. Predicting early in October that Page "will reject it [the completed manuscript] when he reads it in spite of a contract to the contrary," Dodd began prodding him to keep his word by publishing some chapters as articles. "I am anxious to know where you will begin on the book in *The World's Work*," he inquired of Page. "It seems to me that the whole thing might interest readers of all classes. One does not have to be a supporter of the Democratic party to be interested in Wilson." As more of the manuscript went off to the press and "the whole staff" became "perturbed," Dodd made out a more direct case: "Now, pray, do not allow yourself to be swayed from the real purpose we had it in mind to accomplish in this book and the articles by criticism of men who have never made any deep study of American history," he told Page on November 8. "...On the question of my interpretation, I wish you would attend the next meeting of the American Historical Association...and see what scholars say of it....My results as published...have never been seriously attacked. They have been accepted by such men as Turner at Harvard, Dunning of Columbia and West at Minnesota and scores of others of only slightly less importance and scholarship." Whatever the influence of Dodd's appeal to authority and reputation, Page agreed to "stand manfully" by his initial offer and to bring out the book in March.

The promise of publication greatly elated Dodd, but it also left him feeling somewhat distressed. For it was already too late for the book to serve its original goal. On November 19 the Senate voted down the treaty and convinced Dodd that "there is a great reaction going in the country...." Even discussions in the press in December of another possible Senate vote did not arouse him to hope that his book might help work a change. "...My country has proved to be unable to lead the world to a better way," he wrote Erich Marcks at the start of the new year. "...The United States is now the one country definitely set upon the road to imperialism and economic conquest of the world." "Wilson...fought a losing fight...," he advised a friend five days after the Senate agreed to reconsider the treaty. "All that has happened...only shows mankind up in its worst light. Do you ever read Faust second part? That tells the story."

Yet Dodd did not enter the new year without an eye to some bright spot. To be sure, for the time being he saw the treaty and league as lost and Wilson everywhere denounced; "but I should not be surprised," he told a friend, "...to see history reverse all this." For in the light of "true" history, Dodd predicted, "Wilson will not suffer." His league, his treaty, his entire program will be judged sound.[37]

VIII

Unbroken Hope

IF DODD WAS highly optimistic about the ultimate success of Wilson's cause at the beginning of 1920, he was also convinced that it would take "constant pressure in the right direction" to put the movement across. "One only needs to understand and restate a great cause," he wrote Erich Marcks in January, "to win for it sympathetic consideration."

Because his book was not to appear until the spring, Dodd felt compelled in the meantime to carry forward this task by word of mouth. Arranging several lectures for himself in February and March, including talks before the Chicago Woman's Club and university audiences in the East, he stated the conclusions of his book in speeches entitled "The Struggle for a New Foreign Policy," "The Declining Influence of Congress," and "The League of Nations Idea." Once the book reached print, however, he felt constrained to let the volume speak for itself. Besides, there was other, more important work to be done if the Wilson philosophy was to gain the day.

"The election," Dodd told a fellow Wilsonian in April 1920, "is the only thing that men can now take a part in hoping to better the condition of the world." By which Dodd meant that he hoped the Democratic party would make the 1920 election a "solemn referendum" on Wilsonianism and the League of Nations. First, though, as Dodd appreciated, the party itself had to come out of its July convention united behind progressive schemes which, Dodd assured his friends, required no more than a return to the progressive South-West alliance of 1916.[1]

It was at best an unlikely prospect. By April 1920 the Democratic party was already breaking up into rural-prohibitionist and urban-wet factions with but limited interest in economic and political reform. William Jennings Bryan, for example, the party's leading rural-prohibitionist spokesman, was just then declaring his intention to support only a Democratic presidential candidate who was an avowed prohibitionist, while at the same time Irish urban bosses from the Midwest and the East were laying plans to nominate an anti-prohibitionist or a wet. For Dodd, by contrast, the question did not count for much: "On the wet and dry issue," he wrote on April 26, "I am of the opinion that the country is dry to stay.... Personally I have now and then drunk wine or beer. But I never think of it now, except when someone brings it up." Though having been a staunch temperance man in 1903, Dodd could not feel strongly on the issue either way after eleven years in Chicago. Nor could he believe that a southern or western progressive like Bryan would make trouble for the party on such an issue.[2] A forerunner of the Franklin Roosevelt kind of Democrat, a combination of hardy ruralite and urban intellectual, a man at home both in the city and on the farm, Dodd never experienced the rural-urban tensions which were now to tear his party apart. Indeed, unlike other progressive Democrats, Dodd saw it as far more important to get on with the business of continuing Wilson's work.[3]

At the beginning of April then, he began prodding various Democrats toward this end. First, he urged fellow partymen to understand that Wilson's ideas were no unfashionable creed. "...Every audience I have had for a year," he told one Democratic leader, "has, after hearing the facts in the case, shown a certain degree of shame for its hostility to Wilson." "The simple folk of the countryside," he told another, "love Wilson." "May I say," he wrote yet a third, "in speaking at New York University, at Rutgers College and at the Naval Academy and elsewhere... college presidents and trustees frankly said they regretted their recent votes and attitude toward the President." But it was not just Wilson's undying popularity which Dodd put before other Democrats. It was also the fact, as he repeatedly stated it, that failure to unite behind Wilsonianism meant abandoning "our country to a set of bourbons who would bring on something worse than we have heard about in Russia." "...If we are not to try bolshevism," Dodd warned, "you men had better get busy. It won't do any good to denounce Wilson."

Despite the fact that few men seemed to share his views, telling him that he was "the only intellectual in the country who would dare write about the President," Dodd decided at the beginning of May to extend his efforts to preserve liberalism beyond the limits of his acquaintances and friends. In addition to his regularly scheduled classes at the university, he arranged to give five lectures to the Illinois

Democratic Woman's Committee on "The Struggle for Democracy in the United States" as well as several talks in surrounding states. "This struggle of Wilson's for a better world," he told Louis Post toward the end of the month, "has stirred me as nothing else has ever done.... Now I speak two or three times a week in the city or neighboring states."

At the same time, in the expectation that his *Wilson* might disarm critics or win men back to the fold, Dodd worked to assure a wide circulation of the book. Since it was neither well-advertised nor widely reviewed after its publication at the end of April, Dodd understandably assumed that his publishers viewed his study as "bastard children of Southern gentry of the olden time, not exactly hastened upon the market and yet very embarrassing to have about ...," and that newspapers around the country purposely ignored the work. Consequently, Dodd pressed administration leaders and friends to help the book win a hearing. "Could you not get a few of the Southern editors to take notice" of the work, Dodd asked Senator Carter Glass. "... A query or two [to the Boston papers] from such as you," he wrote Charles Haskins of Harvard, "might serve as conscience pricking." Even more important, though, as Dodd told these men, was some effort on their part, to persuade his publisher "to put copies [of the book] on sale at the [Democratic] Convention in San Francisco at the end of June."[4]

Unable, however, with or without pressure, to convince Doubleday of the merits of this scheme and uncertain whether delegates would take the time to read the book should it be sent, Dodd resorted to more direct means of influencing the convention's work. While realistically declaring that "there is little chance that an academic can influence party leadership," Dodd was eager to give it a whirl, especially when the Republican platform and nomination showed that party under conservative control. On June 13, fifteen days before the convention met, he put a detailed program before Assistant Secretary of Labor Louis Post. "All you have to do," Dodd said, "is to be democratic and put up your most progressive candidates and write a platform in line with what the President has done and tried to do these last seven years and you will carry too many states for your own good. Let the platform talk about labor," Dodd urged, "condemn injunctions against strikes, propose constructive legislation about coal mines and packers and railroads and, with the league of nations proposition well to the front, you must really make the party progressive." Conceding nothing to the reaction against Wilsonian progress which was now to dominate the political history of the decade, Dodd put a similar appeal before the party's leading contender for the nomination, William Gibbs McAdoo, a man he had never met.[5]

If Dodd was generally hopeful of a liberal victory at the party convention when he wrote to McAdoo and Post, he quickly found the outcome far from clear. On June

18, when McAdoo "withdrew" from the contest in response to Wilson's apparent eagerness for a third-term nomination, it left the party situation terribly confused. "If you have any wires to pull," Dodd wrote a fellow Democrat on the 20th, "won't you pull them so as to help get a platform and a candidate...which appeal to the liberalism of the country. If reactionaries prevail there, I am undone, as I judge you would be too." Unhappily for Dodd and his friend, most of the wires seemed to be in boss-controlled hands. To be sure, the platform contained enough Wilsonian planks for Dodd to pronounce it "forward-looking," but the decision on a nominee, after a long deadlock between McAdoo and Attorney General A. Mitchell Palmer, fell to the bosses, who selected Governor James M. Cox of Ohio as their man. Actually, despite his machine connections and opposition to prohibition, Cox, who had "an excellent progressive record," did not impress Dodd as all that bad. Unlike Bryan and the prohibitionists, who refused the candidate any backing, Dodd "rather admired Cox." "I could support him now with a will," Dodd wrote shortly after he became the nominee, "if he would only let us know that he does and will not take orders from that gang."

Dodd did not have long to wait. Between July 13 and 15 Cox announced his intention to confer with Wilson at the White House and implied his decision to make the League of Nations the chief issue in the campaign. "The outstanding role of the bosses at San Francisco discouraged all liberals here," Dodd wrote Edward House on the 15th. "But Cox is now making it plain that he is not their man....I believe he will put himself in the way of the best learning and seek to know before he acts."

If Dodd had any doubts about this conclusion, they were dispatched by Cox's public commitment to fight for the League and an invitation to Dodd to support his campaign. "I am...sending you an advance copy of my speech of acceptance," the nominee wrote Dodd on August 5. "...Will you please let me have what you can conveniently spare in the way of text on the League of Nations....I intend to press this question with what force I possess. It is the supreme issue of the century. Won't you please let me have your observations as the campaign progresses?"[6]

While Dodd was, of course, very pleased to co-operate and promptly told Cox so, Cox was probably even more pleased to find a progressive intellectual so eager to render support. Such men in 1920 were rare indeed. Most intellectuals had entertained fervid expectations of triumph and reform as a result of the war and were very disappointed by the compromise peace at the end. "No more dashes into the political jungle" became their credo for the day. Dodd, by contrast, never having seen American participation in the conflict as strictly a force for good or as coming to some utopian end, credited Wilson with a considerable achievement at the peace conference and believed it natural to continue his support. "What was done at Paris," he wrote Carl Becker in July, "represents the wills of all the countries concerned.... Knowing this I can not join such people as edit the *New Republic* and the *Nation* and damn the only important man at Paris who honestly endeavored to compel men to go the wiser way." "There has never been a treaty nor a constitution that was not *compromise* involving cruelty and betrayal of high and noble things," Dodd wrote Alvin Johnson the following month. "... What I lament is the failure of liberal, democratic men in this country... to see what was possible...."

But Dodd had high hopes that somehow this might change, that liberal sentiment might somehow reform and coalesce. After all, to Dodd's thinking, he and other progressives were not that far apart. "You do puzzle me," he told Becker. "The recent political conventions impress me as they do you. The attitudes of the masses of men seem to be what you suggest. The difference between us appears when we undertake to generalize." Even Albert Beveridge, the former progressive who in the previous six years had turned his back on domestic reform to fight Wilson tooth and nail on foreign affairs, could not, in Dodd's estimate, be viewed as totally lost to the cause. At the very least Dodd was convinced that Beveridge would ultimately find it difficult to support Harding. He is controlled by a "senatorial group," he wrote Beveridge in August, "whom you must despise in your heart—as indeed you once wrote me you did despise them and all their ways.... I am your friend," Dodd reassured him. "I see your position. I know what will happen if your party friends succeed. You, for some strange reason, do not recognize the dangers under the togas of your most intimate associates." In touch with reformers and ex-reformers of almost every stripe, including Wilson and House who themselves had recently fallen out, Dodd assumed that progressives could still stand together on common ground.[7]

In this hope, Dodd mapped plans to take a significant part in Cox's campaign. In reply to the Governor's invitation for support, Dodd suggested an early meeting in the East where they could talk over "the situation in the region of Chicago" and discuss means of engaging university men in campaign work. While Cox was more than happy to meet with Dodd after a campaign trip to the West, he was less interested in him as a campaign adviser than as a speaker for the ticket and the League. Instructing Desha Breckinridge, Senator Pat Harrison, and William Jamieson of the Democratic National Committee to arrange a schedule with Dodd, Cox asked that he devote all possible free time to speaking for him in the Middle West.

Dodd, however, was less than pleased at the idea, complaining that "rough and tumble speaking is not my forte." Moreover, Dodd was inclined to let his *Wilson* work speak for him instead. With this in view, he asked Breckinridge to let Cox know that so prominent an opponent as Albert Beveridge believed that circulation of his book would win many to the Democratic camp. At the same time, he pressed his bid for an adviser's role: reiterating his eagerness to talk things over with Cox, he urged Breckinridge to understand that he could give the Governor "the benefit of any information that I, as a student these many years of our history, might possess. I felt all along that I, even with my lack of party experience, could have saved Wilson some of the errors he certainly did make in great matters. But that is only a guess, perhaps a vain one. If you feel differently, I wish you would let him [Cox] know my mind."

Assuming, however, that Breckinridge might well take his suggestion as a vain guess and unwilling to count himself out of what he viewed as a singularly important and, by the end of August, possibly winning campaign, Dodd also expressed an interest in trying his "say" in the West: "It is my opinion," he wrote Breckinridge, "that in Michigan, Indiana, Wisconsin, even Illinois and Minnesota, I could influence people a little." Breckinridge and the National Committee were quick to agree; they scheduled Dodd for several talks in and around Chicago in the fall.

Though kept at his farm by illness until October 9 and though in a "weakened condition" when he returned to the university, Dodd was most eager to tour the area in behalf of "the League of Nations idea." Unaware that party leaders had already privately conceded defeat and "were not even bothering to solicit... would-be contributors," Dodd had before him only the image of Cox and Franklin D. Roosevelt, the vice-presidential nominee, waging a tireless campaign for progressivism and the League. In the months of August and September alone, Cox had traveled almost ten thousand miles in twenty-four states, while Roosevelt had given as many as thirteen speeches a day. Moreover, at the beginning of October, with the Republicans swinging more and more to an anti-league position and losing ground with informed voters as a consequence, the time seemed particularly ripe for Dodd to speak his piece.

Between October 10 and November 1, then, Dodd devoted "every moment I have had to spare" either to speaking or to writing articles for publication "in the newspapers hereabout." Delivering a series of seven talks to women's clubs in Winnetka, Illinois, as well as speeches in Lansing, Michigan, St. Louis, Indianapolis, Frankfort, Indiana, Cleveland, and Chicago, Dodd, like other campaigners, found strong sentiment for the League and even some enthusiasm for Cox.[8] It all came as a painful surprise to him then on November 2 to see Cox suffer an overwhelming defeat.

Worse yet, it was a defeat Dodd found terribly difficult to explain. Resorting to abstractions, he suggested that it was "the law of our social conduct" at work: the fact that "our people will always repudiate its most high-minded leaders at the end of their terms," or that "we can not stand democracy very long at a time." Not content to leave it at this, though, Dodd blamed it on hyphenated Americans who were seeking to punish Wilson for alleged sins against their former homes. While containing elements of truth, Dodd's analysis simply ignored the fact that practically everyone rejected Cox and progressivism at the polls. Given his own circumstances, his sense of continuity with the immediate past, Dodd simply could not accept the fact that the Harding landslide signaled both a profound change in the nation's mood and an end to the prewar South-West, rural-urban alliance for progress. On the contrary, Dodd assumed that political conditions in America were still very much the same and that Wilsonian idealism could still command widespread support. "I have never felt less distressed at the future," he told a fellow Democrat, "for it seems clear to me that a complete reversion is coming in four years."

Dodd found evidence for this everywhere he turned. The fact that university faculties around the country gave Cox substantial backing in response to his campaign for the league convinced him that "nearly every historian" in America had become Wilson's "ardent admirer" and that professors in general, including particularly Republicans, had "quietly turned to Wilson as the great leader of the time." Furthermore, he interpreted an effort at the end of November by the Chicago *Tribune* and the Loyal Legion, "an organization of officers and sons of officers of the Grand Army of the Republic," to have him dismissed from the university as resulting from "the influence that I seemed to have developed during the last year or two in this part of the country. My support of President Wilson in his world policies and the kind of response that came to my efforts," Dodd noted in his diary, "were the causes."[9]

But whatever the causes, the dismissal campaign was a reason for Dodd to keep up the fight for Wilsonian reform. The problem, however, as Dodd saw it, was for the defeated Democrats to find ways and means toward this goal. For himself there was the opportunity to extend his *Wilson* volume to the end of 1920 and once more to put before the public a work of historical "truth." Beyond this, however, Dodd was eager to assure that others would do their share. Beginning with Wilson himself, Dodd urged Newton Baker to persuade the President to make his final message to Congress "a sort of review of his administration and a restatement of his purposes at Paris.... The reasonableness, the democracy and the Americanness of it," Dodd advised Baker, "would set men to wondering once more why they had abandoned all this for the husks of immediate gain." Furthermore, it seemed to Dodd that "many very important matters" could be clarified and the cause aided if Wilson arranged to write an account of his life with the aid of some professional historian.

To suggest such a plan as well as to gather further information for a revised edition of his book, Dodd sought and received an invitation to the White House for December 30. Though reviewing "events that occurred after his [Wilson's] illness in the fall of 1919" and though discussing with the President the disposition of his papers, Dodd found the interview more of an inspiration to himself than a means of either collecting information or pushing the President toward any particular end.

Like Cox and Roosevelt who had been deeply moved by their visit in July, Dodd came away from the meeting primarily determined to extend his efforts for the cause. Arriving at the White House for lunch, Dodd was greeted by the President's wife and daughters who led him

into the large dining room where the President was already seated at the table. He held out his hand and I hastened to him to accept the welcome. He looked broken and worn—one eye, the left, seemed a little drawn and this gave his countenance a slightly deformed appearance. "Poor man, what have you not suffered?" was my momentary thought. But I said nothing being restrained by the fear of excitement which, I had been told, was dreaded by the family. Mrs. Wilson arranged Mr. Wilson's napkin about his neck and prepared his dishes so that he could help himself. He used only his right hand—He ate with some difficulty.

.   .   .   .

After lunch...I...accompanied Mrs. Wilson to the President's bedroom....Wilson lay in bed, propped upon two huge pillows resting from his morning's work....I feared to talk lest I excite him. He explained his illness and talked of his struggle at Paris, of Colonel House, of Lansing and many others. His eyes filled with tears more than once—especially when he described how all men seemed to think he had supernatural power at Paris. "Would to God I had had such power! The great people at home wrote and wired every day that they were against me. But we shall come back, return to those high levels we have abandoned. No good cause is ever lost. Is there anything I can do? I am still ready to serve."
...I remained seated...till 4 p.m. when Mrs. Wilson...came into the room indicating...that the conversation ought to close. I felt profoundly the contrast of Wilson broken as he was in 1920 with the Wilson I had talked with in September 1918.

With this picture of Wilson sharply etched in his memory, Dodd became more eager than ever to take up the President's cause. As a consequence, during the next four years he did almost nothing else. Aside from teaching his classes and satisfying administrative obligations to the university, he relegated scholarly activities to second place in his daily life. Through all of 1921, for example, for the first time since he began his professional career in 1901, he wrote nothing of a scholarly nature, not even a book review, of which he usually did two or three in a year and sometimes as many as fifteen. He did not, however, commit himself to this political work without pangs of conscience. Despite the considerable movement of professors into politics and government during the Wilson years, Dodd still labored under the nineteenth-century notion that academics should be above the political wars. Hence when Albert Beveridge noted his preoccupation with politics in the spring of 1921, Dodd complained that Beveridge was making fun at his expense and emphasized his detachment from public affairs: "Not even the acquaintance I had with Wilson nor the conversations ever led me to try to exert any influence upon his policy or his ideas," Dodd wrote. "It was my job to listen, making such observations as were calculated to keep him talking."[10]

But whatever Dodd's unwillingness to acknowledge openly his devotion to a political cause, it in no way impeded his interest in political work. Devoting the first half of 1921 chiefly to adding one hundred pages to his *Wilson* book, he occupied himself through the summer and fall with lectures in Wilson's behalf. All over the Mid-west and in parts of the South as well, before organizations ranging from college groups to fraternal lodges, Dodd spoke out on "Wilsonism," "Leadership in Recent American History," and "The Meaning of the Wilson Era." That so many people were willing to hear Dodd was less an expression of interest in the former President's ideas than testimony to the fact that Wilson, as Ida Tarbell shortly said, was "the man they cannot forget."

Although such public dedication to Wilsonianism in 1921 was rare among Democrats, it was not entirely unique. Cordell Hull, for one, then a defeated Tennessee congressman, spoke repeatedly for the League, while Franklin Roosevelt urged other Americans to preserve a measure of Wilson's work and to honor the fallen leader with the establishment of a Woodrow Wilson foundation.

Yet whatever might be done in public for Wilsonian principles, Dodd appreciated that there was no more important work than bringing the Democratic party back to these principles. To this end, Dodd arranged his own attendance at the Democratic National Committee meeting in St. Louis, November 1 to 3, to observe for the first time the inner workings of the party structure. Though he came away from the meeting feeling that "some good things were done," he did not think it was enough. Like Bryan, Roosevelt, and a host of what Claude Kitchin called "near-leaders, would-be-leaders and self-appointed advisers," Dodd had his own ideas about party goals. Whether we shall be able to make use of the opportunity just ahead, Dodd advised Cordell Hull, Jouett Shouse, and Henry Morgenthau, depends upon three things: our leadership in the immediate future; the possibility of winning and holding workingmen; and the use we make of the materials at our command. "If I were in your position [as Chairman of the Democratic National Committee]," he told Hull, "I would seek Northern Democrats, far and near, men who can speak well, and enlist them; and I would by all fair means seek to bring into the party the best leaders of the progressive Republicans." In brief, Dodd advised at least partial restoration of the coalition which had worked so well in the past.

Although Morgenthau urged Dodd to believe that a gathering of party leaders, including, among others, Hull and William G. McAdoo, "took up the very proposition" he suggested and wished a fuller statement of his views, Dodd, like Bryan, refused to believe that "the ordinary [or entrenched] organization group" could really lead. While he generally trusted the sincerity and progressiveness of a few party leaders like Hull, Morgenthau, McAdoo, Jouett Shouse, and Bernard Baruch, he considered most of the leadership—the some one hundred members of the National Committee—insincere and intellectually shallow. "The men in charge are not thinkers," he told Morgenthau; "they do not even know the history of the last thirty years; they do not know the country as it now is.... Great victories are not won by such men."[11]

To help remedy this, Dodd urged the party's liberals to help intellectuals like himself gain influence in the party and among the people at large. In January 1922, for example, when he discovered that his name was "being canvassed ... for the presidency of the University of Missouri," he asked Wilson's brother-in-law and secretary, John R. Bolling, to have the former President put in a word. "I have concluded," Dodd told Bolling, "that I might render some better service to the country as a whole if elected—perhaps gain a hearing for ideas and social purposes not now at my command." Although Wilson agreed that such a post "would open up new fields of service" for him and dispatched a letter in Dodd's behalf, he could not influence the trustees who had already committed themselves to another man.

The fact, however, that Wilson was willing to see him take some larger public role encouraged Dodd to raise more directly with Wilson the issue of greater influence for liberal intellectuals in the party. With the Democrats showing no sign of a progressive revival by the end of March and with the Conference for Progressive Political Action, a new coalition of American liberals organized in February, drawing most reformers into its camp, Dodd now urged that Wilson publicly identify himself with "the people who spoke and worked and voted for him in 1918 and 1920" as a means of weakening the organized or boss element in the party. "He [Wilson] has confidence in your judgment," Bolling shortly replied, "and is anxious to know what it is you think he should do." In reply, Dodd suggested that Wilson might like to emphasize his regard for liberal intellectuals by publicly inviting the editors of the *American Historical Review*—namely, J. Franklin Jameson, Carl Becker, Guy S. Ford, Archibald C. Coolidge, and Dodd—to his home.[12]

At the same time, Dodd began a personal campaign to persuade Bernard Baruch to help establish party "lectureships" or "forums." The idea, as Dodd explained it to Baruch in a conversation on April 8, was to enlist the services of university men around the country to give series of lectures on the importance of the Wilson work to audiences recruited by regular party workers. While Baruch declared himself in almost total agreement with such a scheme, he warned Dodd against assuming that he viewed it as a means of scrapping "the old party machinery. If I gave you that impression," he wrote Dodd at the end of May, "I gave you the exact opposite of what I had in mind." Besides, for a party still trying to pay off its debt from the previous campaign, Baruch appreciated that such a project might prove too costly.

Frustrated in this undertaking and by the continuing grip of party regulars over Democratic affairs as illustrated by the primaries of 1922, Dodd began toying with the idea of running for office himself: "More than once," he wrote Wilson in September,

> I have had a vague thought of entering the public service and offering for election and there have been several suggestions looking that way. But such outcomes as…[the renomination of isolationist Senator James A. Reed] in Missouri discourage even where one's physical strength might offer promise of holding out. I am doubtful whether I could make the kind of appeal that would win the complex electorate of a great Northern state. Yet it is clear some men who have a little knowledge of the nation's affairs ought to offer themselves.
>
> Now this letter has taken quite a different turn from what was intended. I leave it as it is, however, in the hope that you will understand. I only wish that you were well enough to be a more active leader of those who try to think straight and that in these days of doubt and distress we might all turn to you.

"Of course I understand…," Wilson replied, "and hasten to say…that I wish with all my heart you would enter public life. I think it is getting to be plain that only by such sacrifices can men who think straight effectively assist in turning the country's face in the right direction." Beyond such private encouragement, however, Wilson was unwilling to go. The fact that Wilson had previously been receptive to Dodd's suggestions for promoting Wilsonian ideas did not mean that he was prepared to help Dodd himself launch a fight for office. Indeed, Wilson's recommendation of Dodd for a university presidency and his willingness to meet with editors of the *Review* were exceptions to a general rule of refusing to give personal endorsements during the last three years of his life.[13]

If Dodd were unable to advance some scheme or suggest an individual or personality around which and whom the party's progressives might unite, he was simply meeting the same problem other party liberals had. Wilson himself, though working with Justice Louis D. Brandeis, Bernard Baruch, Newton Baker, David F. Houston, and ex-Secretary of State Bainbridge Colby to draft a fresh progressive program in 1922, came up with "little or nothing that would have sounded new to a western progressive in 1912." Similarly, though Bryan set forth a twenty-two-point "National

Legislative Program" at the beginning of 1921 and though he repeatedly begged party members to close ranks behind his schemes, he grew less and less certain in his final years that they would. Yet where Wilson was a broken and dying man with little strength to sustain his political work and where Bryan, as with so many other rural Americans, turned increasingly to "extra-political means" like the churches to put across his ideas, Dodd, with undiminished energy for political reform and a distance from rural fundamentalist groups characteristic of urban intellectuals, continued to view the Democratic party as the only logical instrument of reform.

That Dodd might have joined other liberals like Croly, Villard, and Senators LaFollette, Norris, Borah, and Wheeler in the Conference for Progressive Political Action was of course a possibility. But while he generally agreed with the C.P.P.A. in its attitude toward domestic questions, he found himself generally at odds with its approach to foreign affairs and unwilling to support any third-party movement, which, by his historical lights, was doomed to suffer defeat. Despite the fact, then, that these progressives won a considerable endorsement in the congressional elections of 1922 and that the Democratic party impressed Dodd at the time as a "coalition of irreconcilables," he continued to hope that the party's "provincial membership, its Southern and its Western elements" would "admit leadership" or support Wilsonian reform.[14]

In order to encourage such a development Dodd set forth on a four-month speaking tour in November which carried him to every part of the United States. Dodd emphasized the vitality of Wilsonianism when viewed in the context of the American past. Wilson, Dodd urged men to understand, was the political and intellectual heir of Jefferson and Lincoln and would some day hold as lofty a place in our history as they had gained. In fact, Dodd said, "As the great program that was summed up in Wilsonism—the domestic reforms, the changing attitude of the United States toward Spanish-American countries and the proposed new and more democratic organization of modern civilization—recedes and the figure of Wilson becomes historical, men begin to deny that they ever violently opposed his ideals or sought to break his personality." It might not be long, then, Dodd predicted, when people "will come to see that the ideas so widely preached and so nobly sustained in the ordeal of battle offer about the only hope of safety to a civilization which Henry Adams...insisted was in dire straits."[15]

Yet for all this, Dodd also believed that a Wilsonian revival required the efforts of "a more philosophical leader and speaker than any we now have." Indeed, as Dodd saw it, the call was for a new Wilson, a leader who "compelled men by using the historic ideas of the country...a master who knows the history of the country intimately." Moreover, Dodd said, for him to be effective in the Democratic party, he "must connect with the Wilson groups everywhere;...he must rely upon ideas, as Wilson did; and he must have united party support."

At least one man vaguely fulfilling some of these criteria began to emerge at the beginning of 1923: namely, Wilson's son-in-law, William Gibbs McAdoo. With the Democratic nominating convention less than two years off, with the congressional returns of 1922 indicating that a sufficiently progressive Democratic nominee might capitalize on farmer, labor, and independent discontent to return his party to the White House in 1924, McAdoo, with a reputation as a dry and with strong standing among farmers and laborers dating from the Wilson years, began systematically cultivating these groups with progressive pronouncements. Not the least of his concerns, though, was to gain the support of liberal intellectuals like Dodd. Hence after an unsuccessful attempt by Daniel Roper, McAdoo's chief aide, to arrange a meeting in Los Angeles in March, McAdoo made a point of seeing Dodd in Chicago in May.[16]

Although Dodd had described McAdoo in the previous winter as a poor speaker who "does not stir men" and "knows too little of what has happened in times past," he was ready to change his mind. At least their brief meeting in May inclined Dodd to offer McAdoo and Roper advice on their national and local campaigns. While urging McAdoo to avoid "the liquor question" in favor of constructive proposals on farm, tariff, and foreign affairs, and to persuade Bryan to drop his "miserable evolution rot" for more progressive things, Dodd posted Roper on divisions among Indiana Democrats.

Finding McAdoo and Roper sincerely appreciative of his advice and McAdoo eager for another meeting in July, Dodd now wholly committed himself to McAdoo's campaign. Arranging a reception at his home on July 22 for McAdoo to meet "a large number of the faculty of the University of Chicago," Dodd also began working closely with Roper to win McAdoo's endorsement by Illinois Democrats and to mobilize faculty sentiment in his behalf at Harvard, Yale, Smith, Wisconsin, Kansas, and other schools. Furthermore, in the fall when Dodd traveled to Danville, Greensboro, Atlanta, and Tuscaloosa to deliver a series of lectures on "the present situation of the country in the new world and…Wilson's performance for a peaceful international order," he made "a strong statement," as he told McAdoo, "for your ideas and you personally…."[17]

While finding "much strong and unsuspected sentiment in some places in the South and while hearing from McAdoo in mid November that "everything is moving along encouragingly," Dodd appreciated that there was still much work to be done, especially when Bryan shortly announced his intention to put in nomination the name of a Southern Democrat. Believing that Bryan's announcement made this, as he told Roper, "the moment for all of us to do all we can…[against] those who wish to destroy McAdoo," Dodd intensified his watch over Indiana Democrats, extended his efforts to assure faculty and student support in every state with a primary contest and arranged a heavy schedule of talks for himself in Illinois.

All Dodd's efforts and plans, however, like those of other McAdoo supporters, were abruptly cut short by news of McAdoo's business tie to oil millionaire Edward L. Doheny, a leading figure in the Teapot Dome scandal. Appearing before the Senate Public Lands Committee on February 1, 1924, Doheny testified that McAdoo had been in his employ "to represent us in Washington in connection with Mexican matters" during a time when Wilson, his father-in-law, was still in office. While guilty of no wrong-doing, McAdoo could now hardly expect to use government corruption, his party's chief issue, against the Republicans in a presidential campaign. McAdoo, *The* New *York Times* reported on February 2, had apparently "been eliminated as a formidable contender for the Democratic nomination."

Although stung by the "blight" of Doheny's testimony, Dodd believed he saw a way in which McAdoo might stay in the campaign. Along with Colonel House, Bernard Baruch, and a host of other advisers, Dodd suggested that McAdoo publicly declare himself out of the race. Such a tactic, Dodd advised, would then allow the candidate to resume his campaign in response to rank-and-file demand. Men do not "blame a great leader for making a mistake;" Dodd wrote him on the 8th, "they blame him for refusing to acknowledge it." McAdoo, however, on the strength of other advice, decided to confront the issue head on: after both testifying before the Senate Committee on February 11 to prove that he had not helped the oil interests secure leases on government land, and meeting with supporters in Chicago on the 19th to assess his political strength, McAdoo declared himself ready and able to continue the campaign. Though McAdoo asked Dodd, among others, to attend the Chicago conference and to accept his course of action as the only "wise" one, Dodd withdrew his support. "Nothing in recent years has disappointed me more deeply than the debacle in the Democratic leadership," Dodd shortly said. "...The course that has been pursued has ruined McAdoo. I am convinced that he can not get the nomination; I am also convinced that he could not be elected if nominated."[18]

While as a consequence of the Doheny revelations some progressive Democrats abandoned McAdoo's candidacy to support the C.P.P.A. and others moved to support New York Governor Alfred E. Smith, the rest, as Dodd summed it up, found themselves "in a pickle" with "no real candidate from all the group of men who made Wilson." To remedy this, Dodd now urged Daniel Roper to get together with men "who see things a little way in the future" and to "find some man, even if obscure at present, who knows how to fight and then unite all the forces of progress in the party and put him out." While Dodd thought that John W. Davis of West Virginia, Bryan, Governor William E. Sweet of Colorado, and Homer Cummings, the party's keynote speaker at the 1920 convention, "might do," he was much more inclined to favor "Charles A. Beard of New York...an able man, a very able man and a patriotic one."

Whatever Dodd's hope that Roper, who was still working for McAdoo, would take his suggestion seriously, by the beginning of June Dodd himself was moving back into McAdoo's camp. In this, Dodd was like a number of other McAdoo supporters who had abandoned his candidacy in February and then returned to him in June after he won several primaries and piled up enough delegates to enter the Democratic convention as the frontrunner for the nomination. This did not mean, however, that Dodd was ready to forget about Teapot Dome. On the contrary, Dodd joined other Democrats early in June in trying to keep Republican corruption alive as a campaign issue by publishing an article in *The New Republic on* "Political Corruption and the Public: Fifty Years Ago and Today." What drew him to McAdoo, then, was the fact, as he saw it, that McAdoo was likely to win the nomination because he was "rallying all the Wilson men.... It is his relation to Wilson," his progressive qualities, Dodd might have said, "that overcomes his Doheny connection."[19]

But this was wishful thinking on Dodd's part. To be sure, McAdoo, like Wilson, chiefly drew his strength from the South and the West; unlike 1916, however, men were not voting as Wilsonians but as Ku Klux Klansmen and drys. It was a fact which Dodd could not entirely ignore. Indeed, by the middle of the month, with the tensions which were to divide the convention already much in evidence, Dodd began acknowledging McAdoo's dependence on the Klan and predicting that "the party will be ruined if it suffers the religious or the wet factions to come to recognition." To avoid this, Dodd suggested uniting the party behind the candidacy of Brand Whitlock, the writer and former Ohio mayor and minister to Belgium. "He would be our best progressive candidate," Dodd wrote Roper on the 19th. "I have written to several members of the convention about him." When few bothered to answer and when the convention made Senator Thomas Walsh of Montana its permanent chairman on June 25, Dodd sent Roper a plea in his behalf. "Walsh is an unorthodox Catholic. He would carry the states in the east and about everything west of the Mississippi.... He does not make a Romanist issue but a reform issue; yet he is all we want on the farmer and the League." Dodd was quite right. As a Catholic, a dry, and chief investigator of the oil scandals, Walsh could win support in every section of the United States.

But the die was already cast. Through seventeen days of the most intense heat in New York City's Madison Square Garden, urban and rural Democrats gave truth to the saying that "a Democrat would rather fight another Democrat than a Republican any day." Aside from an impassioned but unsuccessful plea by Newton D. Baker for a party pledge to work for American entrance into the League, Dodd found nothing in the convention to his taste. Unwilling to court "boss" George Brennan's approval for a place in the Illinois delegation, he was spared the sight of a thousand New York policemen restraining delegates and spectators from doing each other bodily harm, of bitter debate over specific denunciation of the Klan, of Bryan repeatedly booed, and of McAdoo and Smith deadlocking the convention until John W. Davis emerged on the one hundred and third ballot as the nominee.

Davis was hardly the kind of candidate Dodd would have chosen to support. A Wall Street lawyer backed chiefly by city bosses, he was viewed by most progressives as the candidate of Eastern conservatives and wets. Even the addition of Governor Charles W. Bryan of Nebraska, the brother of William Jennings Bryan, as the vice-presidential candidate could not appease the party's liberals. As a result, a goodly number of them temporarily transferred allegiances to Robert M. LaFollette, the choice of a newly formed Progressive party.[20]

This was a move, however, which Dodd found impossible to make. To be sure, he found "the general progressiveness of LaFollette's programme" highly attractive. But he could not bring himself to support a man who had opposed American entrance into Wilson's League, now the single most important, or even the only remaining, symbol of Wilsonian reform. "I do not know what I shall do," Dodd wrote a fellow Democrat in July. "But the international situation is the great issue for the present. The League is of vital moment. Davis can not be wrong on that. If he takes a forward position on domestic issues, he will be my choice." Besides, Dodd might have added, Davis had some small chance of success against Calvin Coolidge while LaFollette had practically none: a third-party movement, Dodd continued to believe, only worked to make Democrats and Republicans more receptive to reform; an electoral victory was beyond its reach. The best way, then, for progressive men to remain a force for good, Dodd thought, was through continuing work in the Democratic camp. Sharing Dodd's notion that the regular parties were the surest vehicles of reform, other progressive Democrats and Republicans like Bryan and Senator William Borah made a similar choice.

Hence when Davis denounced the Klan for religious intolerance in a speech in the East on August 22, Dodd found reason to begin giving him energetic support. "There is a very distinct change of view among Wilson Republicans and independents since the Seagirt [New Jersey] speech of Davis," he wrote Roper on the 24th. "I have written [Jesse] Jones [Finance Director for the National Committee] about organization problems."[21]

Dodd's scheme was "to organize a committee of mid-west university men as a sort of auxiliary to the Davis campaign." "A very small group of the best informed and the least selfish" on the committee were to "communicate with Davis" after "sift[ing] all the news and propositions and render[ing] decisions." The rest were to arrange for pro-Davis speakers and talks. Though little came of this idea, Dodd took a hand in preparing and circulating a petition among Midwestern university faculty members endorsing Davis as the best friend of the League. Despite the fact that several men who were supporting LaFollette declined to sign, Dodd went ahead with its publication anyway. Finally, in a more practical vein, Dodd helped organize an October 11 conference in Chicago to gather information on state campaigns. "The West Virginia situation," he wrote Roper on the 26th, "was reported to me good.... In Ohio all the evidence that came to me...[shows] the national ticket receives little effective support." With thirty-five other states reacting as Ohio did, Coolidge won almost twice as many popular votes as Davis and almost three times the number of states. LaFollette, despite a surprisingly good showing, finished last.[22]

The party's second dismal showing at the polls in four years, after a convention which revealed more inner tensions and divisions than ties, tried the patience of even the heartiest of Democrats. Yet within six months of the 1924 debacle, several party leaders were back in the field discussing unity plans. Dodd was among the first to advance "a way out of the present impasse." Writing Josephus Daniels in April, he urged first of all that southern men recognize that McAdoo's presidential prospects were at an end and that the party would have to unite behind a Catholic, either Walsh or Smith. Furthermore, it was Dodd's feeling that if Smith showed himself to be "progressive-minded," that is, sympathetic to southern and western men, he would prefer him to Walsh, especially since Smith was more likely to win a national election. For Walsh, Dodd predicted, "would not carry a state east of Pittsburgh (in my judgment not desirable in the long run for the democracy of the nation)." In brief, then, for the sake of party unity and success, Dodd was willing to be convinced of Smith's progressiveness and to overlook those things about him which offended rural Democrats.

Appreciating that many southern and western Democrats might feel like Dodd, Franklin Roosevelt continually prodded Smith through 1925–26 to travel to these areas to court the residents with progressive talk of the kind which had appealed to them before the World War. Smith, however, refused to heed Roosevelt's advice, and his poor standing in the Protestant, dry sections of the country persisted through 1928. The fact, however, that Smith was the one Democrat conceded a chance to defeat the Republicans and that he would probably lose in spite of this concession "prevented the anti-Smith Democrats from combining upon some desperate strategy...to block his nomination...." This did not mean, though, that all southern and western Democrats were ready to support Smith for the presidency. In fact, a number of such Democrats as Dodd, Roper, and Tom Love of Texas deserted the party long before the campaign of 1928.[23]

By the spring of 1926, with Smith giving no indication of a readiness to unite the party behind old-style progressive schemes, Dodd turned for leadership to Frank O. Lowden of Illinois. A former Republican congressman and governor of the state, an unsuccessful contender for his party's presidential nomination in 1920, by 1926 Lowden had become the chief spokesman for economically depressed farmers of the Middle West. Believing that agricultural depression was the country's foremost domestic question, Lowden pictured it as more of a national than a rural problem and one about which city folk should be concerned. "The short-run problem," Lowden's biographer describes him as saying, "ruinous to farmers but advantageous to city dwellers, had crop surpluses at its heart. The long-run problem, rewarding to those farmers who managed to survive the immediate hard times but ruinous to urban folks, was a threatened shortage of food and clothing. To prevent this short-age in the not distant future, [Lowden believed that] the government must at once help make agriculture remunerative again. The welfare of the entire nation, with its fast-growing cities, would soon depend upon adequate sources of food and fiber. Therefore, all citizens should feel a vital concern about helping the farmer during the fleeting period of over production."

Dodd could not have agreed more. Convinced by the beginning of 1926 that the League question would for the time being have to take a backseat to America's agricultural problems, Dodd began talking and writing primarily about "the farmers' dilemma" in much the same terms as Lowden. Hence when Lowden wrote him in the spring for any ideas he might have on the agricultural situation, Dodd praised him for rendering "the country a great service" and told him about an article on the farmer which *Collier's Weekly* had refused as of little interest to their urban audience. "This seems to show a sharper difference of spirit and point of view between the city and the country than I thought existed," Dodd wrote. "…It seems a pity to me that we should have as historians or students to appeal sharply to the farmer readers or to urban readers. It looks to me that we all belong to the same country."[24]

Whatever his complaint about *Collier's,* though, Dodd believed that a majority of Democrats, indeed Americans, would see things his way. As he told Daniel Roper in May, "my opinion is that all patriotic Democrats would help the farmers in this fight [for the McNary-Haugen bill or federal price supports], party or no party; that some understanding be worked out on farm relief, the Muscle Shoals business [that is, assurances of continued federal control over the government-built power plants in Tennessee] and the dry issue. I think there are plenty of men," he predicted, "who think alike in these subjects to unite and set a limit to the kind of exploitation we have had these last years—enough men to take command of the government in 1929…."

If Dodd was ready to bolt his party for the sake of the farmer, he also appreciated that he had nowhere to go. An Illinois senatorial contest in 1926 between Frank L. Smith and George Brennan, both representatives of the Republican and Democratic machines, made Dodd "a looker-on in this house of turmoil," while Coolidge's apparent intention to run for another term seemed to cut the ground from under any Lowden boom. Although thoroughly convinced by the spring of 1927 that Lowden's nomination on the Republican ticket was the only way "some progress might be made," Dodd saw no way it could be done. "Did you ever know a people to be so helpless as ours…?" he wrote Lowden in despair.

Lowden and his advisers, however, were not as pessimistic. Believing that Coolidge's resistance to federal aid to farmers was hurting his popularity and that the President might choose not to run again, Lowden people were busy in the spring of 1927 marshaling support and counting delegates. Lowden himself, though scrupulously avoiding political talk in public, privately encouraged volunteer efforts in his behalf. Moreover, in the spring and early summer, Lowden called on several intellectuals, including Charles A. Beard, Richard T. Ely, John R. Commons, and Dodd, to lend "the weight of their scholarship to his cause."

Though happy to talk over America's past and present agricultural difficulties with Lowden, Dodd could not envision a progressive Republican party until Coolidge on August 2 announced his intention to retire from the presidency. "The withdrawal of Mr. Coolidge," Dodd wrote on the 4th, "has changed the whole political atmosphere, and it is my judgment that Lowden will be the next president of the United States." "All things considered," he wrote Senator Walsh the same day, "he [Lowden] will make an altogether desirable man. The Democratic party has no candidate, and these recent years have consistently refused to have an issue."[25]

Given his initial enthusiasm and optimism, Dodd was now to suffer a series of disappointments. For one, though he and a host of other Lowden men believed it essential that the candidate undertake a vigorous nomination campaign, Lowden, believing the Republican convention unlikely to rebuff Coolidge "by choosing the leading opponent of his farm policy," refused formally to declare himself a candidate. Secondly, Lowden showed himself less than eager to make Dodd a prominent adviser in his camp. Already badly alienated from Old Guard Republicans in the East by his popularity among Mississippi Valley Democrats, Lowden found no more than a limited behind-the-scenes role for Dodd in his campaign.

Yet Dodd was not entirely put off. Though unable to work as closely with or as directly for Lowden as he might have liked, he abandoned the Democrats to vote in the Republican presidential primary in Illinois, while he continued in speeches and articles to agitate the issue on which he believed Lowden or any other good progressive candidate might now rely to win majority support—namely, agricultural depression and economic imbalance threatening a general collapse. "'For whosoever hath,'" Dodd described government economic policy of the day, "'to him shall be given, and he shall have more abundance: but whosoever hath not, from him shall be taken away even that he hath.'"[26]

Contrary to Dodd's belief, however, such an issue was generally limited to the rural South and West and could not give Lowden the nomination in 1928. Indeed, an overwhelming vote at the convention against the inclusion of a McNary-Haugen plank in the Republican platform decided Lowden to withdraw his candidacy even before the balloting began. "The men who have guided the policy of the Republican party...have been these last twenty or thirty years," Dodd said of Lowden's defeat, "utterly ignorant or indifferent to the steady drift of the farmer into ruin....The trouble with [Herbert] Hoover [the party's nominee] is that he can not possibly change this drift...." As for Smith and the Democrats, Dodd could only say the same: dominated by city machines, the Democracy wished to avoid all issues and show itself a Republican twin. "For that reason," Dodd told a fellow Democrat in August, "I have said nothing to hinder or assist either party. There is no place this year for men who knew and believed in Woodrow Wilson."[27]

Since most American intellectuals had reached this conclusion earlier in the decade, it was a tribute to Dodd's endurance and faith that he held out as long as he did. To be sure, one can also picture him as politically unrealistic and naïve for fighting battles which could not then be won. But in light of what happened in the thirties, in the knowledge that American reform was shortly again to be a dominant political force, credit for the fact that a progressive mentality survived at all, indeed that the entire reform movement did not degenerate into repressive and reactionary crusades or into demoralizing clashes between rural fundamentalists and city machines, belongs in part to men like Dodd.

IX

Against the Tide

ALTHOUGH DODD SUFFERED repeated frustrations in his political efforts through the twenties, there was still much in his personal and professional life during this time which afforded him a measure of satisfaction.

In 1920 he lived with his wife and two children in a comfortable greystone house at 5757 Blackstone Avenue just east of the university. Though eleven years in Chicago had transformed Dodd from the shabbily attired, bewhiskered young recluse of Randolph-Macon days into a "neat" if not "nattily" dressed scholar gentleman, he remained as unpretentious as ever. His home was an "informal, casual, friendly" environment in which Dodd moved easily between the quiet of his third-floor study and the animated society of the dining room where "most of the conversations of the family" took place. In this singularly close-knit family, in which each member viewed any separation as an unhappy time, Dodd took particular delight in his charming and brilliant daughter who showed great promise as a writer and poet.

In addition to the pleasures of a happy home, Dodd greatly enjoyed the company of his university friends. With Chester Wright, the economic historian, his neighbor on the north, Quincy Wright, the political scientist, and A. W. Moore, the philosopher, just across the street, and Chauncey S. Boucher, the American historian, close at hand on the south, there was much informal visiting and a sense of community. When added to the usual rounds of more formal entertaining and the conviviality of the university's Quadrangle Club where Dodd often ate and chatted with Robert

Morss Lovett, Merriam, McLaughlin, Schevill, Conyers Read, and many other faculty members, the university provided Dodd with an atmosphere in which he could feel at home.

The pleasure Dodd found in such friendships, however, was not limited to the University of Chicago. Indeed, through the twenties he sustained close ties with historians, writers, journalists, and, needless to say, politicians in every part of the nation. Counting Woodrow Wilson, Carl Becker, Charles Beard, J. Franklin Jameson, Frederick Jackson Turner, Albert Beveridge, Carl Sandburg, Claude Bowers, Ray Stannard Baker, Henry L. Mencken, Josephus Daniels, and Daniel Roper among his acquaintances, Dodd undoubtedly felt himself more or less at the center of American intellectual and political life. That his sense of community with these men was no one-way affair is partly borne out by Charles Beard's suggestion that "about a half a dozen of us...get together for the next ten years and reconstruct the Encyclopedia of Mythology known as American History!" Albert Beveridge had a more elaborate idea: "Now, look here, old boy," he playfully told Dodd, "when on earth are you and I going to get together? It is perfectly plain to both of us that the universe will go all to pieces if we do not meet, discuss and settle questions, problems and everything else."

Equally gratifying to Dodd during these years was his considerable opportunity to provide academic leadership within and outside of the University of Chicago. Having just reached the height of his reputation as a scholar with the publication of his *Cotton Kingdom* in 1919, Dodd shortly found himself a member of the Board of Trustees of Sweet Briar College in Virginia, a member of a select faculty committee to help the University of Chicago raise endowments and find a new president, the chairman of the American Historical Association's program committee for 1925, a member of the Social Science Research Council, a leading light in Chicago's Council on Foreign Relations, the President of the Chicago Forum Council, and the chairman of the University of Chicago's History Department.

Yet whatever the satisfaction derived from such administrative and organizational work, nothing in Dodd's professional life continued to gratify him as much as teaching. In his eleven years at Chicago he had built a reputation as a fascinating lecturer who could attract as many as one hundred graduate students, especially in the summer quarter when southern educators flocked to the Chicago campus in search of masters' degrees. Devoting himself chiefly to courses on the Old South or the South and the Civil War, Dodd developed a distinctive style on the lecture platform which vividly impressed itself on students who years later could still recall the details of his manner.

At first glance Dodd was an unimpressive, rather ordinary-looking figure. Standing only five feet seven inches in height, with sandy-colored hair, high cheekbones, and peaked features, a prominent, rather unattractive mouth and characteristic warts on his face, he spoke quietly in an unmelodic, almost melancholy tone shaded by a soft southern accent, occasionally covering his mouth with his hand or enunciating at an inaudible pitch. Only bright, inquisitive blue eyes shining out from under heavy, triangular brows lent an unusual feature to an otherwise plain face.

But first glances were deceiving. The slender little man who, in the words of one student, occasionally draped himself over the lectern in the manner of one about to succumb to some disease soon impressed himself on his listeners as perhaps the most exciting professor Chicago students would care to hear. Entering the lecture hall with a small loose-leaf notebook or a thin pile of index cards to which he rarely referred, Dodd usually stood in front of the podium, from where he would launch into an informal discussion of his topic. Posing a question "directed at some individual who was not necessarily expected to reply but who, by inference, was given credit for knowing all the answers," Dodd created the mood of a conversation, "of making others think that they were equally responsible for the thoughts which he alone supplied."

The lecture itself was chiefly a series of biographical sketches marked by "the graciousness, the quaintness, and the pathos of the South from which he [Dodd] came"; it was an intimate experience in which Dodd played the cracker-barrel philosopher, the North Carolina farm boy who saw it all, the "inside dopester" who "crept up on his subject, surprised it in undress as it were, commented on it, and passed on...." It was a remarkably effective method, for Dodd, like some conjurer, could make dead men breathe and past years live: an Old South, a distant time paraded itself before the eyes of the listeners with country folk rocking on wood verandahs in a summer's night, or "John Randolph of Roanoke, thin as a sword, slouching in his seat in Congress in his riding habit, and unfolding himself to his full height like a drawn-out accordion as he pointed his bony finger at one of his opponents and launched upon one of his memorable philippics."

The less able student was inclined to complain of a course with no apparent design, no formal reading list, errors in dates and detail, and an instructor who poked his head in the room on examination day to tell his class to write for three hours on why the South fought the Civil War. The more imaginative or intelligent student, however, quickly saw a grand design and filled in the lectures with readings from a variety of books Dodd mentioned parenthetically in class. In the end, students often found themselves doing more work for Dodd than for other professors.

Dodd evoked an equally enthusiastic response in his seminars, which over the years became his greatest joy to teach. Offered under some fifteen different titles in southern and western history and including usually three or four master's and doctoral candidates and rarely more than six, Dodd's seminars between 1909 and 1920 took a significant part in training nine Ph.D.s, still a considerable accomplishment in an era of mass graduate education. Though the students of these years, with the exception of James G. Randall, the great Lincoln scholar, would not achieve the eminence won by several of those Dodd instructed in the twenties, their successes were nevertheless considerable, and the Dodd technique for launching young men and women on productive and scholarly academic careers was already much in evidence.

Around a table on the fourth floor of Harper Tower East, the site of the History Department since the opening of the Harper Library on the Midway Plaisance in 1912, Dodd's seminars, like his lectures, proceeded informally. Requiring only that students write on what interested them in the history of the South or the West, Dodd presented a series of provocative musings on personalities and movements. While adding shrewd or intuitive guesses about what might be rich source collections and profitable fields of investigation, and while helping to open "paths of approach" to his students "with a skill which few American historians have ever shown," Dodd, unlike William A. Dunning, made no effort to build a school of historical thought: for instance, dissertations written under him during these years ranged in subject matter from biography to the treatment of southern Indians. The occasional Sunday evenings at the Dodds, with students gathered in the living room for discussions of historical and current affairs, proved to be extensions of the seminars and proved nearly as fruitful for his students.

Once a student had picked his topic of study, however, Dodd left him to his own devices. Instead of regularly scheduled office hours, Dodd stopped his students in corridors and on library steps for informal friendly chats, and he refused to provide criticism of anything but a final draft. When given, however, his criticism was calculated to make a good study into a publishable work, and nothing about his teaching gave Dodd so much pleasure as to see six of the first nine theses he helped to completion appear in print, including James G. Randall's *Confiscation of Property during the Civil War*.

Yet all the while Dodd was experiencing a growing frustration over his inability to begin writing a projected four-volume study of the Old South. "I have worked for fifteen years on the history of the South," Dodd complained to a colleague at the beginning of 1921, "have done pretty nearly all the research.... But... it sometimes looks as if I would never be able to execute my plan, much as I have done. And if it fails, I should consider my life a failure and really believe a great deal of my research would be lost."[1]

The forces operating against any advancement of this work included both those Dodd could control and those he could not control. In the first category was Dodd's commitment to preserving Wilsonian reform. As he told a former student shortly after his visit to Wilson in 1920, "if I only knew how best to help [save the Wilson goals], it would be the one work of my remaining years to aid in this cause." As an expression of this feeling, at the beginning of 1921 Dodd tried to launch a Wilsonian project which would have taken the better share of his remaining years: a multivolume study of Wilson and his work which, Dodd repeatedly urged Wilson's family to understand, should be in the form of an autobiography written from the personal papers with the aid of a paid professional "helper." The money for such a project, Dodd counseled Mrs. Wilson, could be readily found. Though Wilson vetoed the scheme, Dodd managed to find other Wilsonian work which took countless hours of his time.[2]

Aside from his political commitments, however, there were a number of professional and institutional obligations which Dodd could not ignore. As a member of the American community of scholars, for example, he found himself naturally involved in a series of dialogues with other scholars about their work. Between 1920 and 1925 alone, there was counsel and comment for Albert Beveridge and Carl Sandburg on their Lincoln studies, for J. Franklin Jameson about Andrew Jackson letters, for Carl Becker on the origins of the Declaration of Independence, for Charles Beard on his view of the Puritans, for Claude Bowers on Jefferson and Hamilton, and for Roy F. Nichols, just starting his career, on pre-Civil War politics. Moreover, as a leading member of the American Historical Association, Dodd found himself repeatedly called upon to perform executive duties: first, from 1917 to 1920 as a member of the Executive Council's special committee on policy, next, for a year as a member of the standing committee on nominations of association officers, and then for a three-year term as an editor of the *American Historical Review,* judging articles in United States history since 1800.[3]

Even more distracting to his writing than these scholarly commitments, however, were the growing demands of his Chicago work. Though continuing to teach but six hours a week in the twenties, Dodd found himself directing more doctoral dissertations than any other member of the faculty. With an ever increasing demand for professors of southern history and with Ulrich B. Phillips the only other prominent man in the field to whom students generally turned for training, Dodd bore a major share of the work. Indeed, where Dodd had played a large role in the development of nine scholars before 1920, he was now to oversee the training of an equal number in only four years, not to mention the two or three master's theses he found himself compelled to read each quarter. The pressures on Dodd now became so great that even his best students, like Julius W. Pratt, Frank L. Owsley, and Avery O. Craven, either carried forward dissertations entirely on their own or turned to other department members like Andrew C. McLaughlin to see them through to the end.

But instructional obligations formed only one part of Dodd's university activities in the early twenties. There was also his concern with such institution-wide developments as the growth of the undergraduate colleges at the expense of the graduate school and President Harry Pratt Judson's frugal and lackluster direction of the university, resulting in what one of Dodd's colleagues described as "an atmosphere of resigned stagnation." Particularly disturbed over the fact that the History Department had grown from only ten to twelve members since 1909 while enrollments in graduate courses had almost doubled in the previous five years alone, Dodd and his colleagues devoted considerable energy to urging the administration to preserve the quality of their graduate program: department resolutions to the University's Curriculum Committee repeatedly asked reductions in senior and junior college commitments of between 25 and 50 percent.[4]

This breakneck schedule of activities that left Dodd practically no time for serious writing continually agitated him: "I hardly know how to stop or how to go on," he lamented at the close of 1921, "and my history of the Old South, always pulling at my very heart, lags and is delayed." "If I do not get to writing the chapters of my *Old South* next fall," he wrote fourteen months later, "I despair of ever putting that book into form."

To assure that this would not happen, Dodd determined to spend the fall quarter of 1923 writing the opening chapters of the first volume. Removing himself to "the little stone house in the mountains," he looked forward to "a quiet time and a quiet corner" in both his study and the Library of Congress. But in no time at all he found himself caught up in political discussions with Daniel Roper in Washington and in drafting a study of "The Growing Power of the Presidency." Clearly, free time was no answer to his problem.[5]

The difficulty lay elsewhere: in the need to see himself as a typical progressive or New historian, which he was not. Like the typical professional of the twenties, who found himself called upon to discover the laws of history through the application of the scientific method to past events, or to take inspiration from Charles Beard who described the rise of American civilization, in a book of that title, as the product of economic forces or determinants beyond any one man's control, Dodd saw the New History as generally incomplete. "I do not think there is any new history as yet," he wrote Harry Elmer Barnes in 1925. "Robinson and Shotwell and half a dozen others have made what might be called introductory studies, but not one of these men has ever had the patience or taken the time to master the material to say nothing of putting it into good literary form." Dodd's hope, then, was to have his *magnum opus* fill this need. For he aimed to write a study of vast scope ranging over all aspects of early southern life and illustrate a fact he saw as fundamental to all American history—namely, the progress of the country resulting from the struggle between the many and the few.

But however much he might like to fancy himself the methodical New historian, the truth is that Dodd had little inclination to launch a major scholarly work. Not having written a book informed by weighty documentation since 1907 Dodd was in no mood to begin one in 1923. Indeed, though Dodd might talk about mastering the material and uncovering historical trends, he was in fact the embodiment of what Carl Becker called the relativist perpetuating "useful myths," or what Charles Beard would describe in the thirties as fallible man writing history as an "act of faith." And though he might not care to say it, a fact which kept him talking about a multi-volume study of the Old South, Dodd in the twenties was only willing to commit himself to history which could fulfill some immediate, compelling public need. In itself this was neither anything very new for Dodd nor so far removed from what other New historians saw as their ultimate goal.

What set Dodd off from most other progressive historians in the twenties, then, was the method he used to achieve this end. More like the amateur historians of the decade than the professionals, Dodd abandoned the scientific techniques of his colleagues to cater to what they invidiously called "popular taste." Like Claude Bowers, Albert Beveridge, Carl Sandburg, and even Charles Beard, whose *Civilization* volumes became the most widely read expression of the progressive version of American history, Dodd responded to the avid public demand for "a framework to provide some sense of order and stability behind a world in tumult...." At a time when, as Walter Lippmann said, "the acids of modernity had destroyed the faith that human destiny was in charge of an omnipotent deity," at a time when, in Dodd's words, "clergymen and politicians alike have been dethroned, either by the discoveries of science or by the workings of democracy," Dodd felt called upon to write history and biography which would point a political course and counteract the growing impersonalization of American life.[6]

No category of writings in the twenties catered more to this public demand than biography rich in personal detail—subject matter in which Dodd had already shown himself something of a master. It was only natural, then, that newspapers, magazines, and public groups should repeatedly call upon Dodd through the decade to furnish this need and that he should feel more or less comfortable in the role. Beginning in 1922 with sketches of Jefferson, Lincoln, Wilson, and Grant in *The New York Times Magazine*, Dodd subsequently drew word portraits of Washington, Jefferson, Jackson, Lincoln, Lee, McClellan, and Samuel J. Tilden for Henry L. Mencken's *American Mercury, The Century Magazine,* and the *Times.* Of these, none gained a wider audience than the essays on Lincoln and Lee which the Century Company published as a book in 1928. Extreme examples of the biographical sketches Dodd produced in the twenties, the essays were the least satisfactory writings of Dodd's entire career. Marked by an excessive concern with style or self-conscious efforts at popularization, they read almost like caricatures of other popular works:

When Andrew Jackson, the happy warrior, trim, correct, both feet out of the grave, well dressed and well mounted, bade farewell to Washington that memorable March day, 1837, the next great President of the United States was in the making, far off on the prairies of Illinois: Abraham, son of poor Nancy Hanks and trifling Thomas Lincoln, who had hired the boy to hardfisted farmers on Pigeon Creek, Indiana, for twenty-five cents a day and put the proceeds into his own dirty pockets; Abraham Lincoln, six feet four, awkward, loose-jointed, and uneasy—used to the ills of a life that promised little but ill; meditative, restless, now and then called "the mad Lincoln," a young lawyer, twenty-eight years old, a member of the legislature of Illinois, and engaged, with his hustling, calculating little friend Stephen A. Douglas, twenty-four years old, in a piece of the most foolish legislation that was ever enacted.

This one excerpt is symptomatic of what a later historian meant when he said that "The public's hunger for 'human interest' [in the twenties] fed upon an episodic display of personality rather than an integrated analysis of process, which was history's more fundamental concern."[7]

Dodd's efforts in this direction did not stop with the written word. In the mid-twenties he stumped from one end of the country to the other lecturing on "Little Men of Great Influence: Thomas Paine, Aaron Burr, and Robert J. Walker." The lectures were filled with halfironic pathos, enthralling audiences with what one newspaper called "more of the human touch or more of the things that strike deeper or truer at the emotions" than anything ever heard in their city before. Revealing, in the words of another reporter, "aspects of…character seldom recognized by the non-historian," the lectures played on the listeners' feelings with sad stories of three men who deserved better of their country: "In his death, he [Walker] was not unlike Paine and Burr. He had wrought mightily for the nation; he had done more than a general's part in saving Abraham Lincoln; few men recognized him then; the whole nation has forgotten him since." "Burr came to his end as sadly as Paine," Dodd offered as a variation on his theme, "and was buried quietly at the feet of Jonathan Edwards in the cemetery at Princeton, unwept by a single individual. His reward was like that of Paine, the just and the unjust finding the same public scorn."[8]

But no single American historical figure better fit this pattern than Wilson. And it was Wilson above all about whom Dodd wished to write. Whatever the difficulties in composing the earlier volume, whatever the small financial return, whatever the likelihood of a multi-volume *Old South* standing incomplete, Dodd was prepared at the beginning of 1924 to return to that work. Even before Wilson's death on February 3 raised public discussion of a biography written from private sources, Dodd was sounding out John R. Bolling on the possibility of using the President's private correspondence "to strengthen the narrative" of his earlier study.

Since the President denied his request at the same time he was allowing Ray
Stannard Baker use of such materials for a study of the Versailles Conference, Dodd
might have taken Wilson's response as an expression of the family's final estimate of
his biography. But he did not. On the contrary, Dodd again wanted, at the time of
Wilson's death, to serve Wilson's memory with a full-scale study of his life. His
intention, however, was both temporarily sidetracked and encouraged by an invitation from Mrs. Wilson to collaborate with Ray S. Baker in editing the President's
public papers for Harper and Brothers.

While gladly accepting the assignment which he accurately foresaw taking at least
two years of his time, Dodd shortly began seeking Mrs. Wilson's approval for his
larger goal. Convinced that she would eventually ask him and Baker to extend their
collaboration to an official life and letters, Dodd wished to make clear that he would
be unable to "work that way. My interpretation, method and even style of writing are
apt to be such that a book of that sort," he wrote Claude Bowers in April, "would
have little unity.... My sort of a biography would be a combination of letters and
writing of my own that would have to be done in my own way. That may seem wrong-
headed; but it is my feeling now." Though hoping to suggest this to Mrs. Wilson
through Stockton Axson and her step-daughter, Dodd received no invitation to
undertake the work alone or in conjunction with anyone else. Instead, he received
word from the President's widow of her intention to postpone selecting a biographer
until she had canvassed all previous writings on her husband's life.[9]

With no decision in the offing, Dodd was content in the meantime to pursue
what was proving to be a delightful but exhausting cooperation with Baker on the
Wilson papers. Having agreed to edit six volumes in little more than two years—
hoping to have the entire set in print by 1926—and having been limited by Harper
and Brothers to some 125,000 words a volume, Dodd and Baker found themselves
compelled to work both rapidly and selectively. Indeed, denied the leisure to
undertake a thorough search for Wilson's addresses and writings, the authors
"included only items that were readily available at that time in the Wilson Papers
or which had already been published." Yet in spite of this, Dodd and Baker found
themselves with "an embarrassment of riches," from which they tried to select "all
of the most important and interpretive documents" illustrating Wilson's views on
"politics or government, education, [and] religion." Though Mrs. Wilson was disappointed with the decision to make the work selective rather than exhaustive,
and though Dodd and Baker themselves excused the shortcoming with an unful-
filled promise to do "an exhaustive edition at a later date," the volumes nevertheless "brought together for the first time many fugitive items," and became, in the
words of the present editors of a comprehensive edition of Wilson papers, "an
indispensable tool."[10]

The fact that Dodd was doing this work at the same time he was teaching and preparing essays for the American Historical Association meeting and Mencken's
Mercury convinced him that a Wilson biography must not and probably could not
be done under the same conditions. Determined, then, to avoid a similar division of
his energies in the future, Dodd began to cast about for an alternative to his university post. An ideal opportunity at once presented itself at the Brookings Institute in
Washington. Including duties totaling only five hours a week, the position offered a
chance to escape a variety of complaints Dodd had about Chicago: first, the fact that
he had "four or five times" the number of students he had when he first arrived there
fifteen years before; and secondly, the fact that "the legitimate appeals of the larger
community for time and service are very many...." Besides these two conditions,
though, Dodd saw "another phase of the problem":

> A change has taken place in the University during the last fifteen years [he
> wrote President Ernest D. Burton] that amounts to a revolution: a, the
> community then fairly stable and admirably suited to the growth of a
> community of scholars and scientists has now ceased to be such. Our friends
> are already scattering.... This destroys the social side of our life, takes away the
> compensation that labor amidst smoke and dirt is designed to secure.
>
> b, While this takes place before our eyes, there arises a powerful alumni
> interest that overwhelms us with their demands for grandstand performances,
> after the manner of eastern universities.... You must already have realized that
> it might easily be "millions for such vanities, not one penny" for the silent work
> in the social science workshops.... The way the world is now made up, it seems
> useless to struggle against the tide.

At least this was Dodd's feeling as long as he had some prospect of giving himself
over to a Wilson volume. But when this possibility disappeared with the selection of
Ray S. Baker in January 1925 to do that work, Dodd decided not only to stay on at
Chicago "to struggle against the tide" but also to throw himself into a schedule of
activities which became a substitute of sorts for a Wilson book—namely, an
unyielding effort to return Americans to their democratic faith.[11]

Such work could be done in a variety of ways: through continued publication of
the Wilson speeches which would show the public "some remarkable things";
through arrangement of the American Historical Association program for 1925 in
which Dodd could include good democratic speakers like Claude Bowers and good
New History papers like "The Function of Historical Research in Relation to the
Progress of the Social Sciences" and "Historical Research as a Public Interest";
through setting up a Chicago Forum where "those who see the dangers of the

present drift" could have their say; and through popular essays and speeches suggesting the need for widespread reassessment of "political and social problems as they have been worked out."

There was no better field for this work in Dodd's estimate, though, than the university itself. For the universities, Dodd believed, could restore stability and progress to American society if they devoted themselves less to undergraduate studies and "grandstand athletics" than to "learning and science" or study and research—a university in which researchers discover truths, lay the foundations of "vast social betterment," and teach devotion to public service. If Dodd, then, found himself denied the opportunity to make "at least one of the great American democrats [namely, Wilson] understood before this generation goes off the stage," if he found himself unable to fill in the outlines of the New History with a seminal study of the Old South, and if he found himself more or less stymied in the political arena with Davis' defeat at the close of 1924, he could still hope to advance democracy in America through service in the university world.[12]

At the beginning of 1925, therefore, Dodd returned to Chicago from his Virginia retreat determined to aid President Burton in restoring the university to its former self. Believing Burton eager to revive the dedication to graduate education established in William Rainey Harper's day, Dodd took part in a campaign to raise $17,000,000. When Burton suddenly died in the spring, Dodd feared it might signal an end to "enlightened" administration of the university and a return to the "autocratic" rule of the Judson regime, which, to Dodd's mind, "left the institution in rather perilous condition." As far as he could tell, then, there was "only one situation in the country where," he wrote Daniel Roper, there are prospects for "the sort of ideas in University life which you and I could strongly favor,...[and that] is at Columbus, Ohio. There is a retiring president of the dogmatic type," he replied to Roper's suggestion that he become a candidate for the Chicago job, "...one who, I think, did not run the institution down [and] leaves the way open for forward-looking administration.... A similar situation once appeared in Missouri and Mr. Wilson at once urged me to consider it. It was a rather curious bit of foresight of his; but it was not perhaps wise that I should fall into this scheme, though I did not definitely refuse.... All this is but to lengthen the story. You will probably not take it in any but the true sense: namely that I see nothing that you or any friend could do."

Resigning himself to the fact that a university presidency was probably beyond his immediate reach and that his field of university activities would continue to be in Chicago, Dodd turned his attention to the selection of a six-man faculty committee to assist the trustees in their search for a new president. At the same time, Dodd pressed Gordon J. Laing, Dean of the Graduate School, to urge careful consideration by the trustees of a Graduate Commission report favoring greater emphasis on "productive scholarship and scientific research" and removal, if not total abandonment, of junior college work from the mainstream of university concerns.

The report and Dodd's strong stand were but part of a larger discussion in the university on the role of undergraduate education at Chicago. When a 25 percent increase in total college enrollments took place in the six years after the First World War, it precipitated a debate between advocates of further expansion and limitation. While all agreed that graduate study and research were the prime interests of the university, "one group defended the college because (1) it provided the departments with an opportunity to select promising research students; (2) it brought revenue which helped pay for research and graduate instruction; and (3) it attracted contributions from college alumni—since it was this group, rather than graduate-school alumni, which had greater wealth." In opposition, men like Dodd and Laing argued that the "University can perform its most distinctive service to education through its graduate and professional schools. The limitation of undergraduate instruction appears to be complementary to this...."

Though Burton gave the issue substantial attention during his time as president, including appointment of a commission on the future of the colleges, the question remained undecided at the time of his death. Moreover, whatever pressure Dodd and Laing might bring to bear in the spring of 1925, it was soon clear that future developments would await the selection of Burton's successor.[13]

From Dodd's point of view the delay was welcome. With volumes three and four of the Wilson papers due at the printers in the fall, with the American Historical Association program less than two-thirds complete and with a hundred "main course" papers and ten or twelve master's essays to be read as well as five doctoral candidates to be examined, Dodd had no time that summer for university problems, great or small. By the fall, however, he was generally optimistic that the debate between proponents and opponents of the colleges would be resolved in favor of the opponents. The appointment of Professor Max Mason, a distinguished mathematical physicist in the University of Wisconsin, as president, coupled with the fact that Mason readily granted him an extension of his fall leave from one to two quarters, inclined Dodd to foresee "more and better things at Chicago for the idea and practice of research."

While Dodd was quite right in assuming that Mason would emphasize research in the university, he did not reckon with the fact that the new President envisioned undergraduate participation in such work. Indeed, when Dodd returned to the university in March, he quickly discovered that Mason intended not only to sustain the colleges but also to integrate them more thoroughly than ever into the university. This decision chiefly served to touch off another round in the debate on the role of the colleges, with Dean Laing insisting more forcefully than before that "the teaching

burden caused by the relatively large undergraduate enrollment...cut research pro-
ductivity in two."[14]

In this argument, lasting to the end of Mason's service in 1928, Laing had no more
consistent supporter than the History Department. Believing itself badly hampered
in graduate instruction by junior and senior college demands upon its staff, the
department consistently urged limitations on the colleges. Despite the fact that the
department fared rather well under Burton and Mason, growing from thirteen to
nineteen members between 1924 and 1927, it was still complaining in the latter year
of "overcrowded classes" and the fact that "real graduate work under these conditions simply can't be done." The department, along with other social science departments, actually had good reason to complain. Where the student-faculty ratio in the
biological and physical sciences either stayed the same or decreased in the two
decades after 1908, it showed a marked increase in the social sciences. A good method
of reducing their ratio, the historians believed, was through cutbacks in undergraduate population. It is not surprising to note that the scientists generally took an
opposite tack.[15]

Whatever their wishes, though, the historians appreciated that the successful representation of their interests in the university at large depended upon a prominent
senior member of their department being chairman. Though McLaughlin had served
them ably in this capacity for a number of years, he had been ill a good deal of the
time since 1920 and unable to carry much of the work. Moreover, between 1924 and
1927 he was in residence at the university only in the spring and autumn quarters.

Clearly, by the spring of 1926 there was need for a new chairman who would vigorously work to expand the staff. Moreover, the department needed an executive
who would help close, or at least not exacerbate, an internal breech opened during
the First World War. Dodd qualified on both counts. For one, he had long seen a
larger and more diverse history faculty as synonymous with continued excellence in
graduate training. Secondly, at the outset of the war in 1914, when the department
divided into pro-English and pro-German supporters with McLaughlin, Boucher,
and Read in the first group and Schevill, Carl Huth, and Thompson in the second,
Dodd had managed to hold a middle ground. While highly sympathetic to the
Anglophiles, Dodd had retained an overriding concern with the preservation of
American democracy and fulfillment of Wilson's fourteen points, and this allowed
him to remain on good terms with Schevill, Thompson, and Huth. As a senior
member of the department, then, who keenly appreciated its two greatest needs,
Dodd became the logical choice for the chairmanship.

That he decided to assume the post for three years beginning in 1927 was an
expression above all, though, of his profound desire to make a substantial contribution to the social sciences in America. Having made almost no progress on his *Old*

South and having committed himself to a host of other writing projects, including a two-volume high school history text, which ruled out the likelihood of measurable advancement on the southern history study during the next two or three years, Dodd decided to make the departmental chairmanship his vehicle for aiding scientific research into American life.[16]

Just what all this research was supposed to accomplish, Dodd felt no need to say. In this, however, he was like most other social scientists of the decade, who assumed the value of methodical investigation into social problems without specifically explaining where such research would lead. Whereas men like John Dewey and James Harvey Robinson shunned concrete explanations out of a fear of a rigid commitment to "fixed ends and means," Dodd offered no specific justification for emphasizing social science research chiefly because he assumed everyone doing such work instinctively knew its aims—namely, to undermine privilege and restore America to some earlier Jeffersonian or democratic past. But such an assumption on Dodd's part (as Dewey might have guessed) helped to short-circuit his own work: clear about the results of his *Old South* study before he began to write, Dodd came to see his project as something less than a voyage of discovery or adventurous inquiry—an almost essential condition, it would seem, for a four-volume work. Unable, then, to carry forward his own writing, Dodd hoped to make Chicago the kind of institution where others readily could.

But this was more difficult than he thought. Chauncey S. Boucher, the Dean of the Colleges, stood "in high favor with President Mason," who responded to Boucher's demands for improved undergraduate instruction with directives to departmental officers to make teaching ability one precondition for academic appointments and promotions. Furthermore, Mason encouraged elaborate plans for experimentation and reform in the colleges. Needless to say, all Mason's attention to undergraduate study in the university alienated and angered Dodd, who, by the spring of 1928, described the President as "arbitrary and offensive in relations with the faculty," and, consequently, unfit for his post.

Though Mason announced his resignation on May 7, 1928, to take up the presidency of the Rockefeller Foundation in New York and though Dodd was invited to participate in the selection of his successor, he could no longer feel very sanguine or comfortable about his role in university affairs. Sixteen months as chairman, with no more progress to show for his work than the addition of two tenured colleagues to help cope with heavy student demands, taught Dodd that university administration and policy-making was less satisfying than teaching and writing. For at the same time he suffered the frustrations of his chairmanship, he took great pride in his preparation and publication of the last two volumes of the Wilson *Papers,* of the first volume of his history text, of the *Century* articles, of random essays and book reviews, and of the fact that seven more of his students earned their Ph.D.s and set forth on their own teaching careers. Yet whatever the gratifications of such work, Dodd could not entirely abandon the hope of working some changes in the university at large. Besides, uncertain that renewed efforts on the *Old South* would bring him the kind of satisfaction his other writings had, Dodd was inclined to give university administration another chance. With such divided feelings toward writing and administration, though, Dodd now entered a period in which he vacillated sharply between them.[17]

His ambivalence was most clear in his reactions to the university's efforts to find a new president. As a member of the five-man faculty group aiding the trustees in their search, Dodd was initially elated over the fact that four members of his committee, Deans Laing and Henry G. Gale, also of the Graduate Division, Merriam and himself, agreed to resign rather than allow the trustees to select a man who would advance the colleges at the expense of the graduate school. Moreover, by the middle of June, Dodd was particularly pleased at their success in dissuading the trustees from offering the presidency to Frederic C. Woodward, the Vice President of the University, the fifth member of Dodd's committee, and a leading representative of "the former regime."

By the end of another month and a half, however, Dodd was ready to leave Chicago for a university position which would free him to write. A deadlock in their deliberations, with Dodd and his colleagues urging the appointment of Laing and the trustees countering with suggestions of Harold H. Swift, Chairman of the Board of Trustees, and Dwight Morrow, Ambassador to Mexico, who no one thought would come, convinced Dodd that the trustees "intend to have their way and set about their great undergraduate college." "I do not see how I can afford to be the victim or one of the victims of such a policy," he wrote Laing. "I suspect I never should have accepted the responsibility of sitting on that committee...."

Though Dodd now asked friends at Cornell and Johns Hopkins to sound out opinions at their universities on offering him a suitable job, and though he warned that only a reduced or half-time teaching schedule could keep him in Chicago, he could not see his way clear to leaving the university until he was sure that his side of the battle was lost. Despite "a drift in the board committee [at the beginning of September]...in the direction of a straight businessman without much college background," Dodd continued to exert pressure within and outside of the university for an appointment to his taste. By the middle of September, though, in a state of near exhaustion from both his labors and uncertainty over future plans, Dodd looked forward to his first real vacation in years—a six-week sojourn in Europe with his wife and twenty-year-old daughter—where he might reach some decision about his future.[18]

The opportunity to remove himself from the immediate day-to-day pressures of the university, plus a barrage of letters from colleagues while he was in Europe asking "about details, courses that should go in the announcement" and means of preserving the department's threatened prestige, all but decided Dodd to devote himself primarily to writing on his return. This resolve was put to the test when he returned to the States and found an attractive offer from Cornell promising substantial free time. Demanding that Chicago match the offer, Dodd asked for "an endowed chair for research in the history of the Old South" and an increased departmental budget which "would show appreciation and good faith. Less than that," he told Dean Laing, "will not suffice."[19]

Greeted with strong appeals not to leave and more or less firm promises from within the university to allow him "half-time" whenever he should ask, as well as expressions of interest from prominent Chicagoans like Cyrus McCormick, Julius Rosenwald, and Henry M. Wolf in establishing an endowed chair, Dodd decided to stay at his post. "The strongest reason just now for abandoning this plan," he wrote Laing in January, "is the fact that it became a little clearer than heretofore...that we may be able in our committee to hold the University to its former objective. At any rate there is now a prospect and so long as there is a prospect, I am willing to see an obligation to do all I can." Though Dodd made no mention of his reluctance to confront the fact at Cornell that he had run out of energy to write a multi-volume history of the Old South, he was undoubtedly sincere in his willingness to abandon a certain measure of personal comfort to help keep the university "true to itself." Indeed, twenty years of service in as fine a university as Chicago had built bonds of institutional loyalty which Dodd himself never fully appreciated were there.

Though there were to be three more months of uncertainty with another unsuccessful attempt by one of the trustees to make Woodward president and a refusal from President Ernest M. Hopkins of Dartmouth to take the job, the decision of the board-committee on April 16, 1929, to invite Robert M. Hutchins, Dean of the Yale Law School, to assume the post impressed Dodd as a genuine reward of his patience: "...we shall choose a man who suits and is equal to the position," he wrote his wife. "In so far as my position is concerned, I am free to go on half-time without loss of salary.... It is my *expectation* now that the new administration will suit me and that all round progress will be made."[20]

Dodd, of course, had some reason to expect that the new administration might so accommodate him. And in fact, when he took up the matter with Hutchins and Laing in January 1930, he found them eager to help: the President offered to seek outside funds, while Laing suggested that Marcus Jernegan be made executive secretary of the department as a time-saving device. The fact, however, that Hutchins was primarily occupied with plans for "radical reorganization" in the university and that the Depression was beginning to force economies upon the departments, left Dodd uncertain as to where he stood. Complaining to Laing in the spring that he saw "no way for me to know the honest and uninfluenced opinion of the administration as to my worth and acceptability," he expressed the hope that "by the end of this academic year the responsible officers of the Board [of Trustees] would…give… evidence which could enable me to determine every issue that involves the future of my work."

Unhappily for Dodd, however, such assurances as he might have liked were still unstated by June. Though the Trustees promised him a salary increase to $9,000 beginning October 1 and though the administration agreed to have him teach but one course in the winter quarter after a fall leave, he remained convinced that he had "misinterpreted the University's real position" and that it was now "too late" for him to find some means to get his work done. "If not right," he inscribed a copy of *The Cotton Kingdom* with measured finality on June 2, "the best I could do." The next day he agreed to accept the chairmanship for another three-year term.[21]

Yet whatever his mood of resignation and defeat, Dodd was again ready in the fall to ask for released time to write. Having satisfied standing obligations with the completion of his two-volume cooperative history text in the previous year and having unwittingly relaxed the pressure on himself with the assumption that he would never finish the *Old South,* he suddenly saw his way clear to draft a few chapters of the book. Indeed, he felt so much like his old self during his autumn leave on the farm that he decided once and for all to give up administrative tasks: "Since I have served more than three years as chairman…and had my work delayed," he wrote Hutchins on December 7, "I prefer to decline administrative responsibility when I return about January [1]….I tell you this now so you can be canvassing the situation and make a selection before I return."[22]

While Hutchins was eager to arrange everything to Dodd's convenience, as he told him within five days, he also wished him to stay in his post. Though undoubtedly recognizing what most members of the History Department knew, namely that Dodd was terribly inept at handling administrative detail and relied heavily on colleagues and secretaries for help, Hutchins also appreciated that Dodd had and would continue to contribute greatly to the reform and uplift of the university. Indeed, by 1930, Dodd had not only brought the department to a point where, for all his complaints, he could describe it as practically "equal to our undertakings before the country," he had also helped to infuse it with an *esprit de corps* or mood of attachment and loyalty among students and faculty which even his sharpest critics could not fault. With a faculty in the late twenties consisting of such prominent and promising scholars as Dodd, McLaughlin, Avery O. Craven, William T. Hutchinson, Marcus Jernegan, J. Fred Rippy, James H. Breasted, Ferdinand Schevill, James

Westfall Thompson, Louis R. Gottschalk, Samuel N. Harper, and Bernadotte E. Schmitt, not to mention such summer-quarter visitors as Carl Becker and Arthur Schlesinger, the History Department deservedly stood as one of the foremost centers of graduate training in America. Given the fact that the department was sustaining a tradition of excellence under Dodd's direction, then, it is not surprising that Hutchins wished him to continue as chairman. But no doubt also of considerable weight in Hutchins' thinking was the fact that he could rely upon Dodd to support him in the great reforms.[23]

While Dodd was somewhat disturbed at the way in which Hutchins went about reorganizing the university during the academic year 1930–31, he thoroughly endorsed his goals. A sharper distinction between junior college and upper division, or senior college, graduate work as well as a greater emphasis on student responsibility in the education of undergraduates impressed Dodd as "orienting" the university more toward research and "social responsibility." Of equal importance to Dodd, though, was the fact that he quickly came to see Hutchins as something of an ideal administrator: a president who thought that the "social sciences...may prove as beneficent to mankind as natural science and the technology which rests upon it," and a president who repeatedly gave voice to the most liberal possible interpretation of academic freedom, including the assumption that without "freedom of inquiry, freedom of discussion, and freedom of teaching...a university cannot exist," immediately won Dodd's fullest respect.

Hence, when Hutchins, who thought Dodd America's "greatest historian of the South," informed him in February of his wish that he "be chairman,...have $10,000 a year, [and] such teaching as I think best for [the] department and myself," Dodd announced himself thoroughly pleased. "Hereafter," he wrote Hutchins in March after the Academic Senate gave the President a vote of confidence at a trying moment in his reorganization work, "all of us who are working in your way and seeking your objectives—a big majority—can and will be clearly behind you. The University of Chicago may now become a real university (hardly another in the country) and all of us are proud to help you make it so."[24]

Yet whatever Dodd's satisfaction at the turn of events within the university and whatever Hutchins' eagerness to recognize his standing as a scholar and reward his service to the university, none of this could in fact aid Dodd to return to his "work." Indeed, though placed on a half-schedule through the spring of 1931 and though appointed Andrew MacLeish Distinguished Service Professor in July, Dodd continued to find it almost impossible to write. As in the past, it was not entirely his fault: discussions of the department's relationship to the newly established Social Sciences and Humanities Division, three doctoral dissertations to read between June and August, unusual difficulties arising out of the Depression in locating students in jobs, efforts in behalf of the President's "proposal...to incorporate the last two years of the University High School in the College," and the compulsion to double his work for 1931–32 when one colleague in American history unexpectedly went on leave, all left Dodd under the same pressures he had grappled with for several years.

When on top of all this the department found the Depression and new administrative organization of the university hampering its ability to hire faculty and sustain course offerings equal to the Harvard, Yale, or Illinois departments, Dodd conclusively decided to resign his chairmanship. "Due to the misrepresentations of the proper function of a history department and my growing sense of defeat as a scholar," he wrote Beardsley Ruml of the Social Sciences Division on June 13, 1932, "I herewith attach my resignation...to take effect at the beginning of the summer session."[25] Beyond these reasons, however, was one consideration Dodd left unsaid: the Depression, the bankruptcy of the Hoover administration in the face of the economic crisis, and prospects for a Democratic party revival on a program of reform had renewed Dodd's interest in political work.

X

Ambassador by Default

DODD HAD NEVER entirely lost interest in politics. To be sure, like even the most hopeful advocates of liberalism, he saw the presidential campaign of 1928 as reason for despair. When "the choice is between the greatest and most dangerous oligarchy in the world (the Republican party) and a Democratic party begging the favor of the oligarchy," he wrote Newton Baker in November of that year, there is no inducement to vote. Furthermore, when Hoover's victory margin in the election announced America's undiminished enthusiasm for Republican policies, he lost practically all "hope... that our country may... turn from her fleshpots before our day is done."

Still, unlike so many other liberals and Democrats, Dodd was not ready to concede that anyone can become rich or that big business was about to abolish poverty in the United States. On the contrary, he continued to see the economy as "top-heavy," with deprived farmers and laborers on the bottom and privileged industrialists holding sway. Moreover, while he appreciated that "it is not an easy thing for 'intellectuals,' unofficial statesmen, to render service in an age and in a country where a vast new feudalism is fixing itself upon every department of life... and where scholars and scientists are thought little more than ornaments to the age," he nevertheless shared "a vague hope" with many American social scientists that "books, articles, and lectures may gain hearings, and that the country may be swerved off the wide road and into a safer by-path."

Yet it was all a vague hope, unless, as Dodd acknowledged in the spring of 1929, "the whole economic system of our day...fall[s] upon us with many casualties," which he "anticipate[d] that it must do." Such a prediction, however, was less an expression of any thoughtful conclusions about the economic prospects of the next six months than a statement of belief about the indefinite future.

Hence when the stock market collapsed in October with a loss of almost sixteen billion dollars in less than a month, Dodd, like Franklin Roosevelt and other prophets of economic disaster through the twenties, did not appreciate that that day had come. Indeed, for men like Dodd and Roosevelt, events on Wall Street were "no more than a just punishment which immoral speculators had brought upon themselves." "Everybody has lost his money bag in New York...," Dodd wrote on October 30. "I only wish that Mr. Mellon and Mr. Coolidge might bear their proper share of the losses. I think this reaction," he cautiously predicted, "is going to have a sobering effect upon the whole country."[1]

It was to take some six months of rising unemployment and falling prices before Dodd and most other Americans appreciated the dimensions of the collapse. But such recognition worked no profound change in Dodd's political or economic ideas. Indeed, to Dodd's thinking, the problem in 1930 or 1931 was the same as it had been since the early twenties when Midwestern farmers began agitating about the maldistribution of wealth.

It is not surprising, then, that Dodd viewed the causes and remedy of the Depression strictly in terms of the imbalance between privileged industrialists and poverty-stricken farmers. Like George N. Peek, the father of McNary-Haugenism, and a host of other farm leaders, Dodd identified the origins of the collapse in the wild speculations and unchecked profits of business titans at the farmers' expense: "The Henry Fords," Dodd announced in the pages of *The Atlantic Monthly,* "increased their output and widened the terrain of their operations; the banks increased their loans to amazing volumes and encouraged the building of skyscrapers in place of old buildings hardly worn smooth with usage....It was the heyday of industrial prosperity, all the rest of the country hopelessly in debt. All the rest of the world confronted with collapse."[2]

The way out of this dilemma, men like Dodd and Peek asserted, was through the disintegration of urban industrial centers with a corresponding increase in independent, landowning farmers. Having always felt somewhat ill at ease in "the dirt and foolish rush of Chicago," having always found a need "to spend three or four months each year in the woods...to recover from the effects of eight or nine months of Mr. Babbitt's bright lights and bathrooms," Dodd viewed such a development as entirely to the good: "How to secure to farmers and unorganized laboring folk a fairer share of the returns from our economic life," he wrote in 1932, "is a difficulty...but big business must disintegrate, that is, the Harvester Company must divide its work, set up specialty plants in small cities or towns, lay out small tracts of land around workingmen's homes...the day of the big city is passing." And should business resist, Dodd had an alternate plan: a government-sponsored program of internal improvements—water power, road building, and reforestation projects— which would lead hundreds of thousands to quit the cities, set up small farms and become "non-consumptive [self-sufficient] elements in a changing economic order." "It is not a healthful thing from any angle to have people crowded together in industrial centers where they may become the victim of every 'ism' of any agitator," Peek observed in 1933. "The healthsome atmosphere of the country is far better for all of us." "...Vast urban concentration," Dodd said later in the decade, "...has given us twenty or thirty million proletarians...which all greater American statesmen of 1787–1800 said would defeat democracy." Indeed, the Russian, Italian, and German "dictatorships" were evidence to him of "how completely dependent our unem-ployed masses can be made."[3]

While economists and social scientists in general could agree with Dodd and Peek that agriculture badly needed help and that the fundamental cause of the Depression was a maldistribution of wealth with farmers denied enough purchasing power to help sustain prosperity, they neither saw farmers as the only underprivileged group nor believed that "old-style antimonopoly progressivism" of the kind preached by Dodd and Peek was more than "an obsolescent cliché" or hopeless assault on "inevi-table, unconquerable industrial forces." Though Dodd talked repeatedly in the early thirties of the university community as "the trusted guardian of truth and the disin-terested counsellor of the public in [these] times of disorder and social welfare," and though he continually urged government posts for "specialists" who were to formu-late policies, he had substantially less in common with these experts than he cared to think. Indeed, once the social scientists or instrumentalists of the twenties formu-lated specific New Deal proposals in the thirties, a number of old-style progressives like Dodd quickly found themselves entirely put off. Happily for Dodd, in 1930 such substantive issues were terribly remote. For as both he and Peek understood, the first order of the day was Republican defeat. And this, Dodd believed, could only be accomplished through establishing a good progressive at the head of the Democratic camp.[4]

This was no easy task. With the party still split between city and country Democrats, between northeasterners like John J. Raskob advocating high tariffs, business support, and Prohibition repeal and southerners like Cordell Hull urging an end to "high-tariff greed and privilege" and to Prohibition talk which distracted men from the facts of economic collapse, it was clear in 1930 that the Democrats might be in for another great battle. It was all the more important, then, as Dodd saw it, for the liberals to settle quickly on a candidate for 1932 and to work untiringly to put him across.

Though Dodd began thinking seriously about possible names as early as June 1930, he was still without a firm choice by the end of the year. Robert Hutchins, whom he described as the "second most popular unofficial man in the United States," did not meet the constitutional requirement that a candidate be thirty-five years of age; Franklin Roosevelt, who had compiled a fine progressive record as governor of New York and an unprecedented plurality in his 1930 re-election campaign, could not disarm the westerner's hostility to the East; and Newton Baker, the man most likely to be true to the Wilsonian faith, seemed ruled out by a heart attack he had had earlier. "There is a fair chance a Southerner might be the leader," Dodd speculated. "But the West will want to offer somebody. It is a puzzling situation." It was a puzzle, however, which Democratic gains in the 1930 congressional elections made Dodd more eager than ever to help solve.

And for a short time at the end of 1930, it began to seem as if a solution might be possible. Conferring in November and December with Daniel Roper and Jouett Shouse, Raskob's full-time director of the Democratic National Committee, Dodd came away with the impression that "the Democratic leadership in Washington is pretty well agreed on Newton Baker" as the party's nominee for 1932. Actually, the committee's members, or at least the Raskob men, had not committed themselves. Eager to head off Roosevelt's growing strength, the committee divided its support among a group of possible nominees, including Baker, Governor Albert Ritchie of Maryland, Al Smith, Governor William Murray of Oklahoma, and businessman Owen D. Young. But temporarily oblivious to all this, Dodd fell in with what seemed like National Committee plans and began talking up Baker's case.

Yet at the same time, Dodd was not blind to other possibilities. Indeed, early in March, when Raskob and Al Smith tried to maneuver the committee into committing "the 1932 Democratic convention to Prohibition-repeal and high-tariff planks," a stratagem calculated to identify Roosevelt with the urban wing of the party and lose him ground in the South, Dodd took note of the fact that F.D.R. raised his standing among southern and western progressives by outright opposition to the plan. Roosevelt can become another Wilson, Dodd told a colleague on March 11. "I know him personally as I know Baker. Either of them would suit me. But the political exigencies of the case are such that I rather look for Baker to be nominated...." Within a matter of weeks, though, Dodd had changed his mind. "As the situation now appears," he wrote on April 13, "Roosevelt of New York is about the most promising man we have....I believe...[he] represents so much of the same thing that Wilson, Cleveland and Tilden represented that he will rally the country to him...."[5]

Four considerations had apparently moved Dodd into Roosevelt's camp. First, Baker's reluctance to feed his own campaign: "You think I may have some possibilities as a candidate," Baker wrote him on March 18. "I have never thought so." Secondly, Roosevelt's successful wooing of Colonel House, who entered into an extensive private correspondence on Roosevelt's behalf in the spring of 1931, though Dodd apparently heard of this through Roper, despite Dodd's having been in touch with House as recently as the previous November. Thirdly, a Progressive conference in Washington on March 12 and 13, which included reformers like George Norris, Burton K. Wheeler, and Charles Beard and which announced itself in favor of "another Roosevelt" for President, undoubtedly had some impact on Dodd. And finally, a March public opinion poll which showed Roosevelt ahead in thirty-nine out of forty-four states must have affected Dodd's decision.

Still, fifteen months before convention time when candidates remained unknown quantities in a shifting political spectrum, Dodd could not feel entirely committed to F.D.R. Like other good progressives, he had, for one, lingering doubts about the Governor's attitude toward Tammany Hall and other big-city machines. Caught between demands from reformers across the country for out-right opposition to New York's powerful machine and considerations of delegate support, Roosevelt had managed to steer a conciliatory middle course. In April 1931, however, when he refused to accede to a request from the reform-minded New York City Affairs Committee to oust Mayor Jimmy Walker from city hall, Dodd was temporarily repelled. "I think Roosevelt stands to lose the nomination now," he wrote on May 6. "The opportunity passed when he did not take a vigorous hand...and convince the great independent public...that regardless of Tammany's vote in the next convention he would deal with problems of corruption as they deserve."

Yet despite Dodd's prophecy, Roosevelt continued to attract and hold widespread public support, including Dodd's. Indeed, while Dodd could readily write off F.D.R. in May, he soon found that liberal Democrats had nowhere else to turn. Reviewing the party's prospects at the beginning of June, he saw that Raskob and Smith were "blind...to wise measures"; that Senator J. Hamilton Lewis, while an "able" politician, was unworthy of his presidential vote; that Newton Baker, though the "one man who might start us off right," was still in poor health; that Senator Carter Glass lacked the "temper of a statesman"; and that "Walsh of Montana is only a little less than great. I doubt whether any New Yorker can be elected this year," Dodd concluded. "The country is sick of New York....If only there were a Wilson: character and persuasive voice." When another public opinion poll, however, showed Roosevelt widening his lead over a field of favorite sons, when Colonel House broke a public silence of seven years to endorse F.D.R., and when a progressive speech on national affairs before the annual Governors' Conference set F.D.R. off more sharply than ever from the Republicans and the Raskob wing of the party, Dodd felt compelled to take the Roosevelt candidacy seriously again.[6]

Still, Dodd was not yet ready to declare himself a Roosevelt man. At the very least, he wished some personal assurance that F.D.R.'s progressivism was more than campaign talk. Accordingly, in the summer of 1931, he wrote the Governor directly, urging him to break openly with Tammany Hall and promise an adjustment in the country's economic imbalance which had plagued American farmers for a decade.

Though Dodd was to receive a warm, friendly answer within a few days, Roosevelt never saw his letter. Too much like hundreds of others pouring into Albany to warrant special attention, it was shipped for reply to the "Friends of Roosevelt," "the letter-writing and publicity factory" set up in New York City earlier in the year. There, under the direction of Louis Howe, Roosevelt's chief aide, secretary Gabrielle Forbush ghosted a reply. To convince Dodd that F.D.R. had carefully read, agreed with, and answered his letter, she used the mirror technique of picking up and repeating various Dodd phrases and comments. "There is no doubt but that we have lost the proper balance between the agricultural and industrial elements in this country," she paraphrased Dodd. "What we need," she continued, "is a restoration of that equality which existed before the manufacturer became, very largely through the Republican Party, a master of our nation." The response was very much like Dodd's letter, "lofty in tone and agrarian in leanings."[7]

While this cleverly ghosted reply was not enough to move Dodd firmly into the Roosevelt camp, events of the next few months were. With Baker showing himself willing to be no more than a dark horse candidate or to accept a draft, and with Raskob and Smith becoming more overt in their efforts both to stop Roosevelt and to make Prohibition the prime issue in the 1932 campaign, Dodd found himself more and more inclined to support F.D.R. Moreover, the fact that Roosevelt people like Roper, Cordell Hull, and Henry Rainey were discussing economic plans as opposed to the "liquor question" in the fall and winter of 1931 was yet another incentive for Dodd to declare himself solidly on their side. "The bitter and relentless campaign which Smith and Raskob have been waging upon Roosevelt," he announced to a friend on December 17, "almost convinces me that Roosevelt ought to have the support of all of us. In fact, I think very highly of him and expect to see him nominated."[8]

But Roosevelt was not home yet. Having remained equivocal in his attitude toward Tammany Hall and having said nothing in recent years about foreign affairs, he was bound sooner or later, as Walter Lippmann announced in a syndicated column on January 8, 1932, to disappoint some of his followers to either his left or his right.

Within a month, Roosevelt was proving the accuracy of Lippmann's words. Compelled by attacks upon him as an internationalist in the Hearst press to declare his opposition to American participation in the League of Nations, Roosevelt found himself in serious trouble with his Wilsonian friends. Dodd, among others, immediately lodged a protest: "Your attitudes," he wrote on February 8, have appealed to me on most things: utilities, prohibition, relief for the distressed and the constructive suggestions involved in the forest and agricultural work of your state. On international relations, I think you underestimate the urgency of the case: close and co-operative international relations are as essential now to restored and abiding if moderate prosperity as closer state relations were in 1783–89. This is not the choice of a mere scholar or historian. It is the result of the over-industrialized modern world; and statesmen who do not see it are simply delaying the inevitable. I was sorry you said what you were reported to have said about the league....

It may be possible for your friends to win enough delegates before the convention to defeat the one-third now planned by [Smith]...[though I doubt it].

Of course I may be wrong and I hope I am. If you are nominated I shall be happy to support you, though in one or two matters of importance,... you have weakened your appeal.

Mild in comparison with other messages coming in to F.D.R., Dodd's letter seemed to require no immediate response. Indeed, gobbled up by Roosevelt's campaign machine, it landed at the Friends, where it lay unanswered for over six weeks. Recalling the early and sympathetic answer to his first note, Dodd took the long silence which now greeted his second letter as a sign that Roosevelt had grown unreceptive to his point of view, especially on foreign affairs. Furthermore, aware through Roper that the Wilsonians like Hull, Senator Clarence C. Dill, and Homer Cummings were now thinking of giving Roosevelt token support in the hope that he might aid a candidate "of our liking" in a deadlocked convention, Dodd assumed that Roosevelt himself was probably writing the Wilsonians off.

Through the rest of February and much of March, then, Dodd felt himself as much at sea in his search for a candidate as he had been in the previous year. But with his only other choice for the nomination, Newton Baker, showing himself both reluctant to stand firm on his earlier endorsements of American participation in the League and willing to form closer ties with the Raskob-Smith wing of the party, Dodd shared a feeling with other progressives that he might as well give Roosevelt his backing. Cordell Hull probably best summed up the feeling of this group when he told Josephus Daniels, "I am unable to see what alternative there is [to Roosevelt's candidacy] except chaos and anarchy. It is in the light of this situation," he added, "that I feel justified in driving ahead in an effort to be of some aid in organizing the right-minded and right-thinking forces around Roosevelt."[9]

Dodd was of much the same mind. Though during the next three months he continued to feel at odds with F.D.R. over his failure to act on disclosures against

Tammany Hall, and though he remained distressed with his public stand on foreign affairs, he saw the Governor as having at least "two traits which are rare in public men: 1, the ability to keep to the subject and not enter into personalities; [and] 2, an appreciation of the difficulties of the submerged elements of our society—this last truly democratic." Impressed above all by Roosevelt's willingness, unlike any other candidate, Republican or Democrat, "to think in terms of 'the forgotten man at the bottom of the economic pyramid'" and to urge "bold experimentation and comprehensive planning" in a series of speeches in the spring, Dodd decided to give the Governor his more or less wholehearted support.[10]

Such a decision freed Dodd to talk primarily about issues in the upcoming presidential campaign. Eager to assure that Roosevelt and the party would enter the contest with progressive views on tariffs, agriculture, foreign relations, and political machines, he repeatedly asked Roper, Daniels, House, and Hull to press such attitudes upon the Governor and his staff.[11]

Though all these men warmly endorsed Dodd's ideas and had direct lines to F.D.R., which they continually used to espouse progressive notions, Dodd thought to add to their arguments with direct communications to the Governor himself. Moreover, another Forbush tour de force arriving at the end of March encouraged such a course with phrases like: "I read between the lines of your letter [of February 8] a genuine understanding of the fundamental principles of the Democratic Party.... I yield to no one in my desire to further the cause of international peace.... I know that no nation can live unto itself... [and] if at any time you should be in this part of the country, I should be very happy to have you let me know far enough in advance so that we may make an arrangement to talk over personally our common interests." Though a ghosted reply, the invitation was sincerely meant. Eager for suggestions on how to cope with the Depression, Roosevelt devoted a number of evenings through the spring of 1932 to his favorite means of gathering ideas, namely, conversations with professors who, Raymond Moley relates, usually left such meetings "squeezed dry."

Though he had neither the time nor the money to travel to Albany, Dodd was more than happy to elaborate on his attitudes for F.D.R. Writing again at the end of April, he concentrated his fire on agriculture and foreign affairs. Stating his ideas in the most general terms, including comments on the disintegration of big business, Dodd soon had Roosevelt's ghost repeating the invitation for a talk: "I wish much that I could have a talk with you, for, as you know, I am devoting a good deal of time to studying the tangled economic situation of the country. I know well your contribution to the administration of President Wilson and of your clear understanding and thinking. I am especially interested in what [Alexander] Legge [of the Federal Farm Board] said to you about the disintegration of the huge plants of big business."

Though Roosevelt's chief advisers, Raymond Moley, Rexford G. Tugwell, and Adolph A. Berle, Jr., of Columbia University, all argued that "bigness was inevitable in economic life" and that the Wilson-Brandeis program of breaking up big business was old hat, Roosevelt was still eager to hear all sides. Indeed, as late as June 20, the Governor remained uncertain as to what he would say in an acceptance speech about agriculture, the country's foremost economic problem.

While this letter and invitation to Dodd neither brought forth a visit nor a specific economic proposal, for which he lacked the expertise, it did encourage Dodd to political efforts in the Governor's behalf. Even more decisive in this regard was the behavior of Roosevelt's opponents when they arrived in Chicago for the Democratic convention toward the end of June. "Smith, Raskob and Shouse," Dodd wrote Colonel House, "'blew in' like a storm from the East. They announced to thousands of shouting Chicagoans (our Tammany) 'He [Smith] will stop Roosevelt.'... This disgusted nearly every decent Democrat." When on top of this Dodd found the Raskob people discussing "minor points about whether they will require a two-thirds vote or a majority vote [for the nomination] or whether they will have more or less liquor or whether the country can manage some way or other without ever mentioning the tariff," he decided to reverse an earlier decision to stay away from the convention in order to do what he could for F.D.R.[12]

Dodd quickly found important work. Roosevelt, who would find himself one hundred votes short of the nomination after the first ballot, badly needed the Illinois delegation. Pledged to Senator J. Hamilton Lewis by Mayor Anton J. Cermak as a means of helping Smith deadlock the proceedings, the Roosevelt people were help-less until Lewis publicly announced his withdrawal from the contest two days before the first session. Taking advantage of the news to meet and talk "with a number of responsible people," including Judge Henry Horner, the party's gubernatorial candidate, Dodd urged them to support the will of the majority by voting for F.D.R. When, despite his efforts, more than forty of the state's fifty-eight votes went to Melvin J. Traylor, another favorite son, on the first three ballots, Dodd, as he later told Roosevelt, "circularized the members of the delegation and had a talk with Mr. Traylor who agreed with me: namely, that unless the Illinois delegation turned its attention to the large interests of the middle west which looked more and more to you, the nomination might so turn as to make success in the country more than doubtful." Before Dodd's efforts could show any results, though, California, released from its pledge to House Speaker John Nance Garner, switched its allegiance and all but stampeded the convention into nominating F.D.R.[13]

Though delighted with the outcome and though convinced "that what we need now is a combined effort...in behalf of Roosevelt," Dodd played but a limited role in the campaign. When he met the candidate in his room at the Congress Hotel in

Chicago the night after his acceptance speech, there was some vague talk about working up the historical data for the campaign. But if this was seriously contemplated, it came to naught, and Dodd soon settled into the role of a contact man. In continual correspondence with Roper, House, and several of their aides working out of campaign headquarters in New York, Dodd, usually at their request, kept them posted on progressive Republican attitudes toward Roosevelt's handling of the Walker affair, on when and where President Robert Hutchins and Alexander Legge might find time to see F.D.R., on what Newton Baker was thinking, on the attitude of Judge Robert W. Bingham, publisher of the Louisville *Courier-Journal,* toward organizing independent and Republican publishers for Roosevelt, and on prospects for college and university clubs "headed by some such man as the President of the University of Chicago." Although adding a few speeches to these efforts, this was as large a role as Dodd cared to play.[14]

Convinced early in the fall that Roosevelt was a sure winner, Dodd was more inclined to devote himself to post-election affairs. He was particularly concerned to assure that "liberal-minded" men would become secretaries of treasury and state and that forward-looking policies would mark Roosevelt's handling of foreign affairs. Hence when rumors began reaching him in late September that either Owen Young or Melvin Traylor, men committed to "the high finance of the East," would take the treasury post, Dodd wrote both House and Roper to head off any such step. Furthermore, assuming from Roosevelt's equivocal stand on the tariff in a Sioux City, Iowa, address in September and from his reticence on international relations, "the most important subject before the world," that he was coming under the influence of insufficiently qualified men, Dodd, with Roper's help and House's approval, worked up a "List of persons for consideration in connection with the appointment of a National Advisory Council" to help the future president formulate specific recovery plans. Encouraged by strong expressions of interest in such a council from Chicago colleagues and by a promise from Colonel House personally to take up the matter with Roosevelt, Dodd sent the president-elect the details of his proposal on November 9.[15]

By the middle of the month, however, with no answer to his "memorandum," Dodd began to bridle under the suspicion that other, less able advisers had the inside track. "I notice the Governor is to have a conference with Hoover next Tuesday," he wrote Roper on the 18th, "and that he is taking Raymond Moley with him. When we canvassed all these personalities in our conference about two weeks ago the estimates of…Moley…were not quite as favorable as I had hoped.… The titles of his publications do not suggest any period in his life in which he made a prolonged study of some great subject. I think every man who is going to be a safe authority in any one great social field must sometime in his life have made a prolonged and careful study of human beings…over a critical period of history—preferably American history if he is going to play a role in American public life." "Some of the men who are apparently very much trusted in the new executive circle," he told Richard Crane, another Roosevelt aide, "seem to me not to be sufficiently qualified.…I hope you may be able to bring your influence to bear at the proper time." By December, it was becoming increasingly clear to Dodd that the Old Wilsonians were not to be at the heart of the new regime. "Perhaps you and I," he told Roper on the 23rd, "have no influence whatsoever, and I have the feeling that Colonel House's influence is beginning to wane."

In light of all this, Dodd believed it essential that men like himself put themselves forward for government work. But when he inquired of Roper about serving the new administration, the latter could only promise to "keep in mind the personal matters to which you referred in your letter, against the possibility and opportunity of my being able to assist." Despite his central role in the Roosevelt campaign, Roper could promise no more; increasingly fearful that the influence of Wilsonians like himself was evaporating, Roper joined Cordell Hull at that moment in asking Josephus Daniels to press the President-elect to be more progressive.

It was not until the end of February, then, when both Roper and Hull found themselves in Roosevelt's cabinet as secretaries of commerce and state, that Dodd could realistically think of government service. In the meantime, though, any thoughts Dodd held of personally influencing F.D.R. had been all but snuffed out by a reply from Louis Howe to his "memorandum" of November 9. "Mr. Roosevelt has been holding your good letter and the interesting list of consultants…," Howe wrote on January 16. "He has asked me to act for him…in expressing his appreciation of your thoughtfulness in presenting this material to him and to tell you that he will refer to it often and is glad to have it." The note left Dodd pretty well convinced that "it may be utterly useless for us in university circles to attempt to do anything…," and that he would do just as well to accept reappointment to his departmental chairmanship for another term.[16]

When Hull and Roper won their appointments, however, Dodd again found reason to believe that he might serve the new regime. On February 23, therefore, he sent Hull a hortatory letter about foreign affairs, while writing Colonel House, the man most widely assumed to have arranged the Hull and Roper selections, of his "wish [that] some university man might tie in somewhere…." When Hull announced his intention "to see something of you from time to time, [to] have the benefit of your wise counsel," and when House and Roper, too, expressed their desire to have him "closely connected with the administration" or serving "in some capacity," Dodd explained just what he thought he might do: "You do not know how delighted I am to receive your letter," he told House, indicating you wish to have me appointed to some position in the complex down in Washington. This is to say that I know of no position I would be justified in accepting. I have been engaged for twenty years in the writing of a book called *The Rise and Fall of the Old South*. . . . It is my duty and obligation to finish this work.

The only sort of thing that I could do would be on occasion to talk over with you or the Secretary of State, possibly even Roosevelt, some critical situation at a critical moment, and for that sort of work I would not think of taking any compensation or asking any official status. I am inclined to think that you have set an example which thoughtful people ought to note very carefully. . . .

The only other point . . . is this: that the administration does need some representative of the university world who can speak to hostile audiences without offense, somebody who, with the authority of the government behind him, can talk about foreign relations in a frank and honest manner to people who do not understand. . . . That is what I had in mind when I wrote you. Professors Moley and Tugwell may be able to perform the latter function. I do not know them personally. I do not think their expert advice very valuable.

"As to House's and your suggestion," he likewise told Roper, "there is no position that would justify my abandoning my work on the Old South—unless the University goes bankrupt. A position without portfolio, such as the English have now and then might have appealed. The need is for some such man as Merriam, or perhaps Beard. If a Democrat of long standing, possibly myself, to stand for progressive and frank ideas before dinner and university groups. . . ." Arranging to see Cordell Hull at the State Department later in the month, Dodd was prepared to tell him much the same thing.[17]

If House, Roper, and Hull, however, were inclined to see Dodd serve in some capacity, they were unprepared to encourage him in this plan. For all three apparently recognized that someone as remote from Roosevelt and as internationalist in outlook as Dodd was not about to be made a minister without portfolio or an administration spokesman on foreign affairs. Even Moley, Tugwell, and Berle would not receive assignments of such scope. House, therefore, ignored Dodd's suggestions with the comment that "I understand now why you cannot take part in the new administration," while Roper turned them aside with the explanation that "there will be many ways and many times in which you can render service. . . ." Roper, with genuine respect for Dodd, shortly accepted his suggestion for an assistant director in his Commerce Department. Hull, however, gave Dodd more immediate and specific recognition, offering him a choice of apparently minor diplomatic posts.

But with no interest in such assignments, Dodd refused the jobs. "I told Hull I would not take any diplomatic appointment," he wrote his wife. "He said all of them were expensive; but my objection is to the fuss and feathers and the daily absorption with petit detail. Hull and Roper want me to be handy about Washington but I see no point in that—and cannot afford it. The radio business [apparently an invitation to make regular broadcasts for the party] would wear me out besides being partisan which is belittling. It is one thing to be a democrat, quite another to be a Democrat. So I shall not be asked to take any place and of course shall not ask for anything. I do not know what you might say except nothing."[18]

If Dodd was greatly disappointed by the end of March that his discussions with administration leaders had yielded no opportunity to help advance what he thought would be a new round of Wilsonian reform, he was soon to find himself with an ideal chance to serve. For on March 9, five days after Roosevelt assumed office, he began his search for an ambassador to Berlin.

Apparently eager at first to use the post to help satisfy claims from the conservative side of the party, Roosevelt initially invited James M. Cox, his running mate in the 1920 campaign, to take the job.

As you know [he wrote Cox], the problem of world relations is going to be of at least equal importance [to domestic issues] during the next four years, and the key localities will be Berlin, Paris and London.

I regard Berlin as of special importance at this time, for many reasons which you will understand [only one of which the President cared to elaborate]. The future of the League of Nations and our cooperation with the League are also very definitely linked to German action.

It is not only because of my affection for you but also because I think you are singularly fitted to this key place, that I want much to send your name to the Senate as American Ambassador to Germany. I hope much that you will accept after talking it over with your delightful wife.... Do send me a telegram saying yes.

Despite the President's flattering letter, "the operation of several...business enterprises" caused Cox to decline. Overwhelmed by domestic concerns, Roosevelt dropped the matter until April 20, when he sounded out Cordell Hull on appointing another conservative Democrat, former Secretary of War Newton Baker. Though Hull thought it best first to sound out the Germans on their attitude toward a high-ranking member of Wilson's war government, he considered the idea "fine." Baker, however, according to Roper's record of a conversation he had with Roosevelt in June, refused the assignment, as did a third choice, millionaire businessman Owen D. Young.[19]

At this point—probably late May—the President turned the German ambassadorship into a complex patronage scheme to satisfy two staunch supporters, New York's Senator Royal Copeland and Democratic "Boss" Ed Flynn. Informed that the Senator "was...fed up with the life in Washington and eager to have a major diplomatic appointment," Roosevelt averred cautiously that he was willing to send Copeland to Berlin; but only on the condition that Flynn be named heir to the Copeland Senate seat. The choice of Copeland's heir rested totally with New York's Governor Herbert Lehman, and Flynn, following possibilities through on his own, telephoned Lehman directly. Governor Lehman informed Flynn that he would feel compelled to offer the post first to Al Smith. And Smith, queried by Flynn about his intentions, was in no mood to favor Roosevelt with a promise to stand aside. Hence, Roosevelt scrapped the plan and asked Flynn to go to Germany instead. But the New York politico, explaining that his children were too young for travel, also declined the post.[20]

During these three months Roosevelt could have ended his search for an ambassador at any time with the appointment of a career man. But the fact is, he never asked or considered one for the job. Holding a "deep-rooted prejudice against members of the American foreign service" which dated from his earliest years in Washington and which told him that career people had been "appointed for social rather than for more practical considerations," Roosevelt instinctively viewed such men as likely to be unfriendly to his liberal domestic and foreign policies and as possible sources of confidential information for "opposition circles."[21]

For what sort of man, then, was he looking? Judging from the five asked, he sought a well-known Democrat with no ties to the State Department. Judging from four others considered but apparently never asked, namely, Harry Emerson Fosdick of New York's Riverside Church; Glenn Frank, President of the University of Wisconsin; William Mather Lewis, President of Lafayette College; and Ernest Hopkins, President of Dartmouth, he was willing to settle for a nationally known minister or academician with democratic leanings. Indeed, by the end of May, after almost four months of repressive Nazi measures against opposition parties, newspapers, churches, universities, and minorities, such an appointment apparently had great appeal for Roosevelt as a means of expressing America's standing hostility to all such deeds.

Yet despite these seemingly simple qualifications for an envoy, Roosevelt, by the first week of June, was further from establishing a man in Berlin than he had been in March; now he had even run out of candidates. The simple fact was, then, that F.D.R. could not find an ambassador for the most dynamic and dangerous power on the Continent—dramatic testimony to both the unattractiveness of the Berlin post and America's insulation from world affairs. What made it so bad, though, was the fact that circumstances required a quick appointment: with no ambassador in Germany since Frederic M. Sackett's retirement at the end of March, with attacks upon United States citizens, discriminatory actions against American business firms in violation of the German-American treaty of 1923, threats of suspended payments on a debt of almost two billion dollars owed to private investors in the United States, and prospects, from the American side, of congressional adjournment without provision for ambassadorial funds, the President found himself under heavy pressure to select a man.[22]

All this led Roosevelt to complain on June 7 to a group of intimates, including Daniel Roper, that he "could not decide upon a suitable man" for Germany. "How about William E. Dodd?" Roper records himself as saying. "Not a bad idea," responded the President. "I'll consider it." Within twenty-four hours Roosevelt was on the phone to Dodd. "'This is Franklin Roosevelt,'" the President shouted into the receiver. "'I want to know if you will render the government a distinct service. I want you to go to Germany as ambassador.' ...I hope you will ascertain whether the German Government takes exception to my *Woodrow Wilson*," Dodd in part replied. "... 'I am sure they will not,' the President said. 'That book, your work as a liberal and as a scholar and your study at a German university are the main reasons for my wishing to appoint you. It is a difficult post and you have cultural approaches that would help. I want an American liberal in Germany as a standing example.'"[23]

The offer to Dodd was not simply a case of Roosevelt succumbing to the need for an immediate decision; Dodd more than met his minimum requirements. Indeed, Dodd's strong ties to the Wilsonian wing of the party, his active part in the 1932 campaign, his Ph.D. from Leipzig, his knowledge of German, and his considerable reputation as a progressive historian—all moved Roosevelt to herald his selection as the end of a careful search for just the right man.[24]

Dodd had little difficulty making up his mind. Though he was not prepared to agree at once, he did, under Roosevelt's prodding, say yes within two hours' time. The appointment no doubt appealed to him as a welcome relief from the recent frustrations of his professional life, and one colleague who saw him that week recalls him as "elated" by events. Yet Dodd did not view the ambassadorship as a means of escape. On the contrary, he primarily saw the position as an opportunity to help reverse the isolationist policy of the United States—an achievement which Dodd considered both possible and vital to economic well-being in America and the world. Indeed, for more than a year Dodd had been urging leading Democrats to understand that "there can be no recovery without closer and friendlier international relations, including in the end American co-operation with the League of Nations." Such co-operation, he also believed, "would meet with ready approval, if presented properly": "an active, driving policy toward co-operation with the League, immediate recognition of Russia…and a real entente with England and France," he counseled Cordell Hull, "would be immediately supported by large masses of people who have hitherto been opposed."[25] While Hull and other internationalists might not have been quite so optimistic, they substantially agreed that such economic and political cooperation was the surest road to economic recovery and world peace.

If United States senators had any objections to these views held by Dodd, they did not make them known. When Roosevelt presented them with Dodd's nomination on June 10, after clearing it with Berlin, they gave swift approval, confirming the appointment on the same day without public hearings or debate.

When Dodd arrived in Washington on June 15 for conversations with Roosevelt and the State Department, he was first apprised of the revolutionary character of the new German regime. Although he undoubtedly followed German developments in the newspapers after Hitler's takeover on January 30, it was not until he read Embassy dispatches that he fully appreciated just how revolutionary, confused, and uncertain was the course of German events. Indeed, while at once seeing that this new anti-democratic, nationalistic regime had ruthlessly dispensed with traditional democratic methods to gain control over almost every meaningful institution in Germany, from the central and state governments to the newspapers, trade unions, and schools, Dodd also appreciated that it was next to impossible to predict with confidence in which direction the Nazi government would now turn, an attitude his predecessor Sackett had expressed previously on March 5 when the Nazis had scored an election victory. Other observers, such as George S. Messersmith, the Consul General at Berlin, and Norman Davis, Roosevelt's representative to the Geneva Disarmament Conference, who visited Berlin in April, agreed.[26]

Though the Hitler government continued its relentless drive in the spring toward *Gleichschaltung*—co-ordination of all institutions under Nazi control—and though continued mistreatment of Jews as well as a threatened moratorium on payment of certain foreign loans gave Americans specific cause for complaint, there were some signs that Hitler's new Reich might yet show itself reasonable in dealings with the rest of the world. Eager to avoid foreign difficulties which might distract him from consolidation of power at home, Hitler was more than willing to hide temporarily all aggressive designs. In his now famous *Friedensrede* or peace speech of May 17, which produced "euphoria" in capitals around the world, the Führer announced his wholehearted support of continued disarmament negotiations in Geneva, along with his willingness to disband Germany's entire military machine in return for sim-ilar actions by other powers. Moreover, this reasonable attitude on Hitler's part seemed to show itself in efforts to restrain more radical or Socialist-minded mem-bers of his party, like Gottfried Feder, from revolutionary experiments with the economy—measures which might impede or destroy cooperation with business and industry to end the depression and reduce unemployment. This attitude was brought home to American representatives especially by the fact that Hitler's so-called moderate faction responded to informal appeals to prevent Dr. Adrian von Renteln's Combat League of Middle-Class Tradespeople, "the intermediary leaders and the masses of the party," as Messersmith described them, from taking discriminatory actions against American-owned business firms. In sum, then, by the middle of June, Dodd had some reason to put a positive face on his assignment and to hope that reasonable representations in Berlin would encourage the Nazis toward restraint in domestic and foreign affairs.[27]

In this, Dodd had substantial encouragement from the White House. At lunch on June 16, Roosevelt urged him to work for three things: continued repayment on all private American loans; moderation of Jewish persecutions by use of "unofficial and personal influence"; and trade arrangements on certain items which could increase German exports and aid them in their debt payments. For the first, Roosevelt explained that a failure to prevent a moratorium "would tend to retard recovery," though he also acknowledged a personal antipathy toward American bankers who "made exorbitant profits" on their loans. As to Jewish mistreatment, Roosevelt thought it shameful, and this was reason enough why something should be done. On his last point, however, trade concessions, Roosevelt himself was skeptical that anything could be worked out. Reflecting the attitude which had already led him to abandon any attempt to press Congress for a reciprocal trade agreements bill and the feeling that the London Economic Conference—then in its fourth day—could do little to reverse America's economic collapse, Roosevelt told Dodd that the drift in the world "is all toward economic nationalism. What do you think of that tendency with us?" Like Cordell Hull who believed that economic recovery was simply "beyond the powers of individual states," Dodd thought economic nationalism patently wrong. "Pyramiding of the economic structure in the United States," he told F.D.R., "would soon lead us into a new feudalism which would tend to make peasants and day laborers of farmers, and proletarians of all unorganized city workers." While Roosevelt was willing to give his general assent, he also sounded the nationalistic note which he felt compelled to follow in these hard times: "If European states refuse to make tariff concessions," he told Dodd, "we shall make special arrangements with Canada and Latin America and develop a mutual trade policy which will give us markets for our surplus products."

Though generally preoccupied with the international Economic Conference in London at that moment, Roosevelt actually saw all such squabbles over trade and tariffs as distinctly secondary to European disarmament. Believing, as he also told Dodd, that "limitation of armaments is necessary if the world is to avoid war" and fearing that "events in Germany" might touch off "an insane rush to further armaments in Continental Europe," the President closed his conversation with his new ambassador by asking him to consult with Norman Davis about the Geneva talks. Particularly pleased at Roosevelt's interest in disarmament, Dodd came away from their meeting convinced that they saw eye to eye on most things and that the President trusted him to find sensible means to contribute to their common goals.[28]

His first exchanges with the State Department were considerably less cordial. Meeting to arrange the practical details of his assignment with Jay Pierrepont Moffat, a career diplomat in charge of the Division of Western European Affairs, Dodd was undoubtedly put off. Moffat, who believed Dodd naïve for thinking that he could run his Embassy with a family of four persons on his $17,500 salary, something which Roosevelt specifically approved, at once described Dodd as "extremely sure of his opinions." Moreover, a first meeting with Raymond Moley, now an Assistant Secretary of State, greatly bothered Dodd. Astonished at Moley's ignorance of the workings of earlier American tariffs and at his apparent differences of opinion with Roosevelt over "the American attitude towards the Jews in Germany" and the virtues of economic nationalism, Dodd predicted an early end to his confidential relationship with the President. On top of all this, a formal dinner at the German Embassy attended by both Embassy and State Department personnel left Dodd unimpressed and bored at the want of "good talk." Missing the fact that other members of the State Department also disliked Moley's views and that such diplomatic dinners could serve a useful purpose, Dodd came away from these first encounters convinced that professional diplomats were frivolous in the extreme. It was the beginning of unhappy relations which would make for unfair attitudes on both sides.

If these first meetings bothered Dodd, though, he was even more annoyed later in the month when "State Department people" pressured him into meeting with bankers and Jewish leaders in New York before leaving for Berlin on July 5. Fearful that such meetings might lead to adverse publicity or might be exploited in the press by the bankers and the Jews for their private aims, Dodd reluctantly agreed, leaving Moffat with the strong and generally accurate impression that he did not have "any interest in the financial end."

These unhappy crosscurrents tended to exacerbate certain natural reservations Dodd held about his assignment. Uncertain whether at the age of sixty-three he would be able to recall the German he had spoken some thirty-five years before and fearful, despite the hopeful tone of Embassy dispatches, that he might find himself totally stymied by an intractable Nazi regime, Dodd repeatedly urged his family to count on a Berlin residence of no more than a year.

Yet despite both the comforting thought that he could resign his post after a year and the kind words of Wilsonian friends, who on the eve of his departure urged him to believe that he had a better approach to the problem of the Germans than almost any other man, Dodd, accompanied by his wife, daughter, and son, set sail on July 5 on the *Washington* with "a disproportionate amount of sadness and foreboding."[29]

XI

Peaceful Negotiations

HAVING SET OUT for Germany believing most strongly that hopes for constructive work would probably prove false, Dodd was pleasantly surprised with what he
initially met: rather than a revolutionary regime systematically destroying the past
and closing itself off from any voice of reason from abroad, Dodd found, somewhat
as earlier reports out of Berlin had indicated, a country still steeped in history and a
government outwardly eager to satisfy American demands.

From almost the first moment he set foot in the country, Dodd saw reason to
strike a positive note. Arriving in Berlin on the afternoon of July 13, after eight days
crossing to Hamburg and four hours in "an old-fashioned German train," he found
the station platform crowded with friendly reporters, Embassy officials, Foreign
Office representatives, and fellow Americans. Handshakes and greetings all around
opened the way to a reassuring automobile tour of the capital on the way to the
hotel.

Berlin was still a historian's dream; monuments and landmarks announced the
unrelenting grip of the past: the Kaiser-Wilhelm Memorial Church, the Tiergarten,
the Brandenburg Gate, Unter den Linden, the Staats Bibliothek, the University, the
Opera House, government buildings along the Wilhelmstrasse, even the Reichstag,
despite the recent fire, appeared untouched.

And the Germans themselves were enthusiastic and kind. Turning aside the
Ambassador's request for modest accommodations, the centrally located Hotel

Esplanade insisted on the royal suite—six "embarrassingly elegant rooms" bedecked with flowers at a cost of only ten dollars a day. An excellent dinner served by almost obsequiously courteous waiters pronouncing endless *Dankeschöns* and *Bitteschöns* encouraged Dodd, now "in magnificent humor," to pour out jests and questions in German.

An after-dinner walk closed out a nearly perfect day. Heading up the Bellevuestrasse for a stroll along the Sieges Allee in the Tiergarten, Dodd delighted in the statues of former Prussian kings lining both sides of the Allee and the serenity of dully lit streets reminiscent of small American towns. It was one of the happiest evenings he was to have in Berlin.

The next morning Dodd was ready to begin his work. But a host of preliminaries came first: How should he describe his mission to the press? Who were the people on his staff? When could he present his credentials to the German government? Where would his family find a suitable house? And what were the most pressing needs of his job?

However challenging it all at first seemed, things quickly fell into place. The American and German correspondents who gathered at the Embassy on the morning of the 14th were more or less content with general statements of greeting and purpose, including vague expressions of interest in "older cultural elements." The Embassy staff was too large for Dodd to get to know all at once: a twenty-two-man mission, it included eight military, naval, agricultural, and commercial attachés, three secretaries of Embassy, and nine consuls and vice consuls serving in the Consulate at the north end of the Wilhelmstrasse. Besides, it was only George A. Gordon and George S. Messersmith, the Counselor of Embassy and the Consul General, with whom Dodd needed to work closely at first.

An Alabaman, trained at Harvard and Columbia universities, the forty-eight-year-old Gordon was a career officer of substantial experience and three years' residence in Berlin. Though Dodd initially thought him "generally accurate as to facts" and a man rendering "great service" to his country, he soon came to feel that the Counselor set too much store by diplomatic protocol. Dodd was more favorably impressed with Messersmith. Though also a career man of long standing and equal service in Germany, he seemed less concerned about form and a bit more devoted to his work, which he had performed "to the limit of his physical strength" when Dodd joined him in Berlin. The difference Dodd saw between the two men emerged more clearly for him in a few weeks when Gordon upbraided him for attending a conference in Messersmith's office. By Gordon's diplomatic lights, it was degrading to Dodd's status.

The other questions Dodd confronted in his first day were more difficult to arrange. With President Paul von Hindenburg away in East Prussia until the end of

August, Dodd had to accept temporary status as an "appointed Ambassador," a matter arranged through a brief official meeting with Foreign Minister Freiherr Konstantin von Neurath on the 15th. Actually, it was an arrangement much to Dodd's taste: not compelled to participate in the demanding social life of the Berlin diplomatic corps until he had full ambassadorial status, Dodd relished the thought of devoting himself exclusively to study and work. The following Monday morning at nine o'clock, while his wife and daughter went off to look for a house, he began just such a routine.

His first task, as Dodd conceived his assignment, was to inform Washington about the pace and direction the Nazi revolution might now take. With the help of Gordon and Messersmith, who had done the lion's share of the reporting in the absence of a mission chief, Dodd constructed a first dispatch which summarized what astute diplomats and journalists saw that summer in Berlin: Hitler was slowing down or halting his revolution. Fearful, Dodd told the State Department, "that any further attempts at Nazification of business and industry might throw [the] German economy completely out of joint and thus imperil the existence of his regime," Hitler and other leading members of his government, including Vice Chancellor von Papen, Interior Minister Wilhelm Frick, and Economics Minister Kurt Schmitt, had been warning against radical economic experiments or unauthorized interference with business which might "sabotage" the Nazi state. Moreover, to reassure the entire business community, Hitler, Dodd pointed out, had organized a council of conservative business leaders who were to advise him on economic affairs.[1]

These steps soon impressed Dodd as a single expression of a larger trend. Indeed, as he settled into a regular schedule of reading German papers, studying staff reports, listening to journalists and chatting with a variety of visitors passing through the Embassy, Dodd became convinced that the new regime might well take a more moderate turn. By the end of his first month, in fact, he had found abundant evidence to that effect. For one, though on June 9 the Germans had declared a moratorium on the transfer abroad of payments on foreign debts, they had not ceased payments on American loans or, in other words, actually defaulted on this debt. Furthermore, both Bernhard von Bülow, the second ranking member of the Foreign Office, and Hjalmar Schacht, Reichsbank President, had expressly assured American representatives in mid-June that they had no intention of discriminating against American creditors or of using debt payments to extract trade advantages from the United States. Lastly, by early August, Dodd found that American and German bankers had "worked out a compromise fairly satisfactory to both parties": Americans were to receive 75 percent of what was owed them on their interest coupons—50 percent in cash and 50 percent in scrip, which the *Golddiskontbank* offered to purchase at half its face value.[2]

In addition to these debt matters, Dodd could point to other indications of growing reasonableness and restraint. On July 22, for example, he noted that "strenuous Jewish persecutions" were "on the decline," with "general and specific instructions to the police everywhere to put a stop to maltreatment of all American Jews or others resident here or in German business." Secondly, between the last week in July and the middle of August, Dodd saw Hitler's government issuing new laws and regulations aimed against "rebellious" Nazis, including one dissolving the militant *Kampfbund* or Combat League of Middle-class Tradespeople. Finally, conversations with von Neurath, Hans Luther, the Ambassador to the United States, and other "unofficial Germans," who all showed themselves "most agreeable," more or less convinced Dodd that the government wished further "to ease down off" its "dangerous position" and to improve relations with the United States.

Yet Dodd could not be sure. For however moderate the new regime might now seem inclined to become, Hitler, Göring and Goebbels still impressed him as "adolescents in the great game of international leadership and even national guidance. They affect to believe in sheer regimentation and force," Dodd wrote on August 12. "With a free hand they would...soon be at war with France, Austrian annexation being the pretext." "The Nazis," Dodd said a few days before, "do not seem to me to know what are the natural consequences of ruthless procedure."

On the other hand, von Neurath, Schmitt, and Schacht—"cultural Germany," as Dodd called them—wished, from what he could tell, "to stop all Jewish persecutions, to co-operate with remnants of German Liberalism and continue effort[s] to bring [the] outside world to more conciliatory attitudes." It was the aim of this group, as Dodd understood it, to eliminate privately sponsored British-American trade boycotts lest they aggravate unemployment and bring on a Communist coup. What made the strongest impression on Dodd was the fact that von Neurath and Luther seemed to believe that Hitler was inclined to share their point of view. And in this they were entirely sincere: after six months in which Hitler had shown himself willing to follow a conservative lead in foreign affairs, old regime diplomats were confident that the Chancellor would prove to be "a reasonable, and a manageable, man." Whatever Dodd's reservations, then, it was his "hope" that "Hitler will fall into line with these wiser men and ease up a tense situation."

And because he believed this was possible, Dodd wished to give the conservatives a chance to exercise their influence. He hoped, therefore, that pressures from abroad would not become too great: for "if the boycott goes [as] far as [the] British are now driving," he told Newton Baker, "unemployment will greatly increase and [a] Communist revolution will upset Hitler, the Jews here and elsewhere and not a few of the rest of us. I feel this is fairly certain," Dodd added, "if German industry is stalled by America joining British boycott! So; two results that way, if adolescents here and the unwise elsewhere drive too far.... You can see, therefore, how I must react to the urge for immediate action on the Jewish issue—much as I abhor much that is being done." Striking a similar note with Roosevelt, Dodd urged the President to "restrain [the] English and [the] French" who were "ready...to apply the utmost force against Germany...." With Germany politically isolated, economically depressed, and militarily weak in 1933, rumors abounded that other European states would respond to Germany's new nationalist regime with a preventive war. Opposition to such an undertaking, Dodd told F.D.R., was not a "defense of German armament and anti-semitic attitudes (both contrary to liberal philosophy)," but rather a statement of his belief that things might soon improve and that "a people has a right to govern itself and that other peoples must exercise patience even when cruelties and injustices are done. Give men a chance to try their schemes," he concluded.[3]

All this, however, did not mean that Dodd wished to see an end to external pressure. On the contrary, he firmly believed that Hitler's increasingly moderate approach to domestic affairs had in part resulted from "growing opposition in the United States and England." Continued, measured pressure from abroad, then, was to Dodd's thinking very much the order of the day. But fearing that extreme reactions to Nazism might undermine the position of the reasonable German officials who remained, he wished only to encourage a restrained opposition which would serve a delicate diplomatic game. Hence, when Edgar A. Mowrer, the *Chicago Daily News* correspondent in Berlin, who was about to be tossed out of Germany for critical descriptions of the regime, asked Dodd to make a test case of his order to leave, Dodd refused, urging his early departure as much more to the "interest of all concerned." Similarly, in mid-August, Dodd advised the State Department to delay a formal protest against Nazi mistreatment of traveling and resident Americans.

Instead, Dodd wished to see American, British, and French opposition take the form of united absence from the Nuremberg Nazi party congress of September 2–3. A joint decision to refuse formal invitations, Dodd advised, "would strengthen the hand of the liberal and peace forces in Germany." By contrast, attendance at the congress, Dodd said, would establish "a vicious precedent," allowing the Nazis to trumpet it around the world "as an endorsement of [both] the present regime and...the theory that the Nazi Party is synonymous with the German Government and nation."

Despite Dodd's contention that the matter was "a vitally important one" and that the Department should arrange a common policy or stand with Britain and France, Under-Secretary of State William Phillips "refused to take any initiative or act directly...." "This Government should not take the lead in this matter," Phillips said. "The British and the French have as much if not more at stake than we, and I should not wish to give them an opportunity to later justify a decision by claiming that it was made at the instance of this government...." Moreover, Phillips urged Dodd to assess "the implications of the local situation" and to pursue the course which promised "the minimum of embarrassment" to himself and his government in deciding whether to attend. Beyond this, Phillips would not advise.[4]

Though somewhat shaken at the Department's apparent failure to understand the "vital" need for American participation or initiative in restraining the German regime, Dodd nevertheless decided to refuse the invitation and to pursue the line of action he had already begun to take. Indeed, if he were to take Phillips at his word and assume that he were in the best position to evaluate local developments, he could hardly ignore the inducements and opportunities to continue such a course. On August 23, for example, he found Undersecretary of State von Bülow "deeply concerned about Germany's American relations...hopeful that the demonstration in Nuremberg will not take a belligerent tone..." and eager to assure that "not a single aggressive move will be made...." Furthermore, on August 29, Karl von Wiegand, the experienced and well-informed Hearst newspaperman, reported that Mussolini's intervention on the side of Chancellor Engelbert Dollfuss had compelled Hitler to call off an Austrian putsch scheduled for September 6. Dodd was also pleased to note that English, French, American, and Spanish decisions to stay away from Nuremberg might have played a part. Even more heartening, though, was the news from von Wiegand that the eighty-six-year-old President von Hindenburg had written a will which contained an appeal to the German people for the return of a Hohenzollern king, a limitation on Hitler's powers, and a restoration of some popular control.

Still other indications that he might realistically press for German moderation came to Dodd in the next two weeks. Scholars and Nazi officials at a luncheon indirectly acknowledged "that Hitler has undertaken too much and for too long a period"; Henry Mann of the National City Bank reported Hitler in conversation as "a fanatic on the Jewish problem," and wanting in any conception of international relations, but probably open to reason nevertheless; Friedrich von Prittwitz, former Ambassador to the United States, representative of the old regime, and a man "in some danger of imprisonment," announced the Chancellor in "a conciliatory spirit"; Schacht, Hans Dieckhoff of the Foreign Office, Mayor Heinrich Sahm of Berlin, and "other members of the government circle" expressed understanding at Dodd's unwillingness to go to a "purely Party gathering" in Nuremberg; while André François-Poncet, the French Ambassador, repeated the story about von Hindenburg's will and predicted that improved economic conditions and strict control over party chiefs would forestall an "outbreak for some time, perhaps a year."[5]

Given all this, Dodd had good reason to believe that some straight talk to Germany's "wiser men" would now serve the cause of international harmony and peace. Hence on September 14, when he conferred with von Neurath at the Foreign Office, he went directly to the point: economic blunders, street violence, and Jewish persecutions were ruining Germany's chance to improve relations abroad. Reminding von Neurath of a government order of early August against travel on other than German ships, Dodd warned that such measures "would greatly injure our exchange." Secondly, "the violent and disgraceful attacks upon Americans," Dodd said, were evidence "that the attitude of responsible police and law enforcement officials was almost childish." Indeed, "speeches about terrorizing opponents of the Hitler regime," Dodd added, " ... seem to me to be the boasts and shouts of adolescents just raised to power. On the Jewish issue the talk was much the same," with characterizations of official conduct "as utterly unstatesmanlike" and likely to intensify Anglo-American boycotts. As a parting shot, Dodd "observed that Germany could never recover except through a long period of international peace."

Since von Neurath seemed "embarrassed" by Dodd's complaints and personally eager to satisfy all demands, repeating a Göring promise to stop "Nazi idiots" from further street attacks and offering assurances that Germany's Geneva delegates "would make no move that could furnish any pretext for foreign intervention," Dodd was inclined to keep some pressure on the regime. And invitations to lecture at the University of Munich in October and to write a preface for a German biography of F.D.R. impressed him as offering more than one good chance. "I think I can serve the cause I am here for," he wrote Secretary Hull on the 14th, "by accepting and carefully preparing what I shall say in German. They asked me to speak on the 'American Revolution of 1776'—a good subject for this era in Europe. I can say all I want, press home the lesson and violate no conventions of my station." As to a preface, Dodd envisioned a brief statement stressing the President's "objectivity of purpose, independence of group or party control and interest in European problems"—a statement which he thought "of value at this time."

While Hull reluctantly agreed to let him lecture if he refused an honorarium which might provoke criticism, the Secretary advised against a preface as inconsistent with his official position.

The two decisions nettled Dodd, principally because he thought them at odds with the whole purpose of his mission as outlined by F.D.R. "My understanding of the President's conversation before I accepted," he told Hull, " ... was that my best service was apt to be in the form of occasional lectures in German before university groups. My conviction is now stronger than when I talked with him. They asked for the very kind of lectures which German intellectuals need these days of stern ordeal." And "the same," Dodd believed, held for "the excellent, friendly, unpartisan book for which I had written a brief German preface without a sentence that could have been quoted to our disadvantage or to anger Germans."[6]

What also bothered Dodd about Hull's response was the fact that it appeared to have been drawn by "some protocol man" or professional desk diplomat. That Dodd was probably not far off the mark may be deduced from Moffat's statement at the time that Dodd "has not yet got an idea of the functions or the best technique for an Ambassador, particularly to Germany, to apply." No doubt Moffat's harsh appraisal was partly a response to criticisms Dodd had already passed along to the President and Colonel House about the inefficiency and waste in the American diplomatic establishment in Berlin.

As a Jeffersonian democrat, a man rooted in the idea of personal and government frugality, Dodd was antagonistic to lavish diplomatic practice long before he took up his assignment. Moreover, at a time when America faced grave economic hardship and the President had ordered reduced government spending, including salary cuts, he thought it particularly outrageous that his staff saw fit to emulate traditional protocol. Irregular office hours, sumptuous cocktail parties, and formal receptions impressed him as a shameful waste of money and time. Yet, as he quickly learned, even antagonists of the system were compelled to toe the line: "the modest and intelligent" Ambassador from Spain, Luis Zulueta, lived in an elaborate "palace built and furnished during the heyday of German imperialism," while Dodd himself, against his better judgment, paid out one thousand dollars for living costs in just one month. "Not being a rich man," he told Hull, "it is a little difficult to get on here on the salary—that is and meet reasonable expectations." Now, however, when he found an opportunity to earn additional income to help satisfy just the reasonable social demands of his station, the diplomatic code said no. The whole system was almost too much for him to bear: "a practice," he wrote Hull, "as far from public service as Louis XIV...."[7] In response to Dodd's complaint, the Department later added an entertainment allowance to his salary.

But there were other more substantive arguments against such lectures—in fact, against Dodd's whole conception of what he might achieve in Berlin. Consul General Messersmith summed them up in a remarkable dispatch of September 29: Hitler, Göring, and Goebbels, he wrote the Department, were uninformed and little concerned about foreign attitudes. "Schacht who could talk with him [Hitler] about it and has tried has about given it up. Schmitt has little influence except so far as the internal situation is concerned....von Neurath, the Chancellor distrusts, but respects, and I think that any illusions which we may have had as to the influence which von Neurath may have on the Chancellor, should no longer be nourished. He wants to retain von Neurath," Messersmith suggested almost five years before others saw this fact, "as a decorative and protective front because of the confidence that the diplomats here and chanceries outside have in him, but I am beginning to wonder whether we are not playing the party's game by placing too much confidence in Mr. von Neurath."

If Messersmith saw through the role Hitler assigned his Foreign Minister to play, he yet underestimated the Führer's concern that foreign opinion and power not mobilize to bring down his regime. On further thought Messersmith was willing to acknowledge the "possibility...that the pressure of public opinion from the outside will eventually bring about a more moderate system here." But of this, he quickly added, "I am somewhat doubtful. I believe that if our newspapers and our public men are kept adequately informed as to what is really happening here, there is some hope that through economic pressure and practical isolation a change will be brought about, for Germany cannot exist except as a secondary country without her foreign markets. This, however, is a somewhat slender reed on which to lean, for it is difficult for other peoples to maintain their interest in the German situation....And it would seem that already the rest of the world is less shocked and horrified and concerned by what is happening in Germany...."

Messersmith nevertheless hoped that such outside pressure would continue to be applied, for he was "more convinced...than ever...that in some way or other a more moderate Germany must be restored or else political and economic peace will be definitely disturbed." Indeed, "in the long run," he predicted, "what is happening here may be more disturbing to our peace and comfort than the other problems which concern us [today]."

Whereas Dodd, of course, readily agreed with Messersmith's prognosis should foreign opposition collapse, he differed with the Consul General's estimate of both the strength and likely impact of external pressure on the regime. But after only ten weeks in Germany, compared with Messersmith's three and a half years in which he had seen the rise and ruthless consolidation of Nazi power, it was only natural that Dodd should be more optimistic about what foreign influence could achieve. In this, moreover, Dodd had encouragement from F.D.R., who wrote him on September 13 to urge that "you do everything possible to pave the way for the possibility that France and England, and indeed most of the rest of Europe, will try to put it up to Germany at the Disarmament Conference [in October]. The crux of the matter," the President explained, "will be some form of continuous international inspection. This is a sine qua non on the part of France, and I think, a reasonable one. Perhaps the German Government," he proposed, "could use as a face saver the claim that they would have equal rights to full knowledge of what the French were doing." Despite Messersmith's pessimism, then, and the State Department's inclination to have Dodd play a passive role, the President, like his Ambassador, thought something could and should be done, at least about disarmament.[8]

And at no time, in fact, did Dodd see a more urgent need for foreign pressure than in the days after September 15. For in the three and a half weeks, from September 18 to October 14, the Germans undertook a series of nationalist actions that set back hopes for international co-operation and peace. Beginning on the 18th, the German Ministries of Finance and Agriculture announced an agreement to import eight thousand tons of prunes from Yugoslavia during the next ten months. In and of itself the grant of a prune quota to Yugoslavia, though threatening to reduce American exports by one-third, did not count for very much. What worried Americans in general and Cordell Hull in particular was the possibility that the Germans would now see fit to "embark upon a general policy of customs quotas"—a policy which could sharply cut back most German-American trade. For if the Germans, as was the case in the Yugoslavia exchange, should refuse to grant the United States future quotas equal to earlier ones in the German trade, the United States would find itself denied access to German markets. This, of course, is exactly what the Germans had in mind, as von Bülow made clear to Dodd in an interview on September 29. Eager to reduce their unfavorable balance of trade with America, the Germans were now willing openly to violate the most-favored-nation clause of their German-American Treaty of 1923.

Similarly, an announcement on October 3 of German intent to pay Swiss holders of scrip at face value was viewed as "blatant discrimination" against American creditors who refused to take German exports in place of "blocked marks." The whole policy, Hull complained, was in total disagreement with Schacht's promise of June 13 not to "sanction any policy of discrimination as between creditors of different nations" or to tie debts to trade. Schacht, however, refused to concede "that discrimination had taken place in the advantages…accorded Swiss holders of scrip…and appeared to give no consideration to the impression which Germany's action would create in the United States."[9]

As if all this were not enough, Hitler added to American and international uneasiness with the first of his Saturday surprises on October 14. Announcing Germany's withdrawal from both the Geneva Disarmament Conference and the League of Nations, he complained of humiliations and unequal rights. Promised only a four-year freeze on existing forces before France would even begin to reduce her armaments to Germany's level of strength, Hitler declared himself unwilling further to compromise Germany's self-respect.

However harsh or arbitrary such actions appeared to some at the time, Dodd and other American and European liberals considered them almost just. Believing Germany's trade and financial discriminations against the United States primarily a just response to America's "foolish loans" and "high tariffs," men like Dodd could not describe German economic nationalism as strictly the work of a Nazi mind.

Moreover, though Dodd believed German withdrawal from the Conference and the League a "huge blunder," he (again like so many others) could not but acknowledge the injustice in a system which kept Germany disarmed without reducing military might in other heavily armed states.[10]

Since all these actions, then, were generally what a more moderate German government might have seen fit to undertake, Dodd held undiminished faith in the ultimate reasonableness of some influential men in the new regime. And nothing served to bolster this trust more than interviews with von Neurath and Hitler during the week of October 10. Meeting first with the Foreign Minister on the 13th, he found von Neurath friendly and agreeable as usual and extremely eager to assure an end to street attacks on Americans by the S.A., the paramilitary wing of the Nazi party. To Dodd's objection that despite past promises nothing had in fact been done to halt such assaults, Neurath replied that "he had been engaged the whole day in arguing (impliedly with Hitler, Goering and Goebbels)...on the question of adequate deterrent measures." Moreover, within forty-eight hours the Foreign Minister reported specific actions against assailants of Americans, stating both their names and places of internment. Hence, by the time Dodd came to see Hitler on the 17th, the Führer's promise that "he would personally see to it that any offender of this kind would be punished to the limit of the law" seemed to have the ring of truth. Moreover, "the total effect of the interview was more favorable from the point of view of the maintenance of world peace than...[Dodd] had expected." Presenting himself in much the same spirit of his withdrawal announcement of the 14th, that is, as devoted to international peace and justice, Hitler told Dodd "that he would not allow any incident along the Polish, Austrian, or French frontiers to develop into a war and affirmed his recognition of the efficacy of convoking a further conference should matters take such a turn as to make armed activity seem imminent."

In spite of, or because of, his assumption that Hitler and other German leaders were still open to reason, Dodd believed it imperative that America counter German actions with increased pressure. Indeed, whatever the justifications Dodd saw for German behavior, he nevertheless thought it essential to discourage them from believing that "a country can be economically independent and [can] discard international codes of behavior...." It was Dodd's feeling, therefore, as he told Hull, "that desired results from the German Government," that is, an end to trade and debt discriminations, could "only be attained through fear of retaliatory measures...." And should "no effective means of pressure in the commercial field appear to be available," Dodd suggested the use of such pressure "in totally unrelated fields." Moreover, were street attacks on Americans to resume, Dodd thought it a good idea to threaten the Germans with a warning to American citizens to stay out of Germany unless they had specific business there.[11]

Whatever the State Department might see its way clear to do, Dodd was resolved to apply pressure on his own. Turning to the technique he had hoped to use in Munich, Dodd prepared an eleven-page speech for delivery before the Berlin American Chamber of Commerce on Columbus Day. "Informed beforehand that members of the Foreign and Economic ministries [including Schacht and Wilhelm Keppler from the latter and Doctors Fuehr and Davidson from the former] would be present," Dodd aimed "to point out the hazards of arbitrary and minority government under the subject of *Economic Nationalism*." The speech in fact was a pointed moral in historical dress: departures from democracy, whether in ancient or modern times, have never had much success. "In times of great stress," Dodd said, "men are too apt to abandon too much of their past social devices and venture too far upon uncharted courses. And the consequence has always been reaction, sometimes disaster.... It would be no sin," Dodd urged, "if statesmen learned enough of history to realize that no system which implies control of society by privilege seekers has ever ended in any other way than collapse." It was Jefferson's belief, Dodd concluded, "that the way to develop the ideal social order was to leave every man the utmost freedom of initiative and action and always to forbid any man or group of men to profiteer at the expense of others."

If Dodd had any qualms about personally applying pressure in a public speech, he was immediately reassured by the German response. The reaction, he told Roosevelt, Hull, and House, was one of "extraordinary approval." "When the thing was over, about every German present showed and expressed," in Dodd's words, "a kind of approval which revealed the thought: 'You have said what all of us have been denied the right to say.' One of the higher Foreign Office men said: 'You have become another Philip Melanchton [*sic*]; keep on, we need you.' Yesterday...Dr. Georg Solmssen, Director of the Deutsche Bank-Disconto, called to say that he was present, agreed with everything I had said and then added: 'Silent, but anxious Germany, above all the business and University Germany, is entirely with you and most thankful that you are here....' Scores of eminent Germans have said to me what Dr. Solmssen said, begged that I keep their names confidential and not telephone their houses or offices." What with a good number of German newspapers also carrying "fair digests" of the speech, Dodd was wont to conclude "that all liberal Germany is with us—and more than half of Germany is at heart liberal." "Germany," Dodd was also willing to say, "is now very impatient of the arbitrary behavior of eminent official[s], the belittling propaganda and above all the domination of the schools and universities." In fact, it was all evidence to Dodd that a "liberal and intellectual group" had won the right to remain in office and promised in the event of Hindenburg's death to "exercise much steadying influence."[12]

That the reaction to Dodd's speech implied all that Dodd said is at best doubtful. To be sure, a number of those praising his words were entirely sincere. "An intelligent and highly placed German," for example, told Messersmith "that the Ambassador's speeches had been exceedingly helpful to thinking Germans and had reached a much wider audience than we might think." A *New York Times* reporter, moreover, shortly described Dodd as "a lodestone to German scholars of distinction and his home...[as] a favorite place for their foregatherings." Thomas Wolfe saw much the same thing: his "home in Berlin," he wrote Maxwell Perkins in 1935, "has been a free and fearless harbor for people of all opinions, and people who live and walk in terror have been able to draw their breath without fear, and to speak their minds." Yet for all this, it was probably also the case that men like Schacht and Fuehr, men with an almost natural aversion for democracy, were cultivating Dodd with an eye to the help he might ultimately give them in a drive to win trade concessions from the United States. To assume, then, as Dodd did, that more than half of Germany was at heart liberal was a miscalculation on his part; indeed, even if every expression of praise had been sincerely meant, it would still have signified less than Dodd seemed to think. Why then did Dodd exaggerate the significance of the German response?[13]

The answer has more to do with his assumption about German reasonableness and his relationship to the State Department than with realities in Berlin. In the first instance, his conviction that moderate and intellectual elements in German society, like those in America, were responsive to the truth encouraged him to see more in the reaction to his speech than was actually there. Secondly, his fear that criticism of what he said would be voiced by members of the Department, who had apparently opposed his earlier request to state a case, also encouraged him to overemphasize the value or impact of his address. Hence, the day after he spoke, Dodd sent Roosevelt a long defense of his action, describing the German response, its great significance, and the prospects for "embarrassing interpretations" and State Department complaints which he hoped the President would ignore. Likewise, he urged Cordell Hull to understand "that I am not meddling in German affairs, only speaking (on important occasions) just what educated people must know is the truth. If an American can do otherwise, I do not know what it would be." Messersmith added his voice to Dodd's defense: "...every effort," he wrote Phillips, "...is made to force him [Dodd] into positions to say things favorable about Germany, which can be used here and abroad. He has absolutely refused to allow himself to be used in this way and has turned every one of these occasions into one of drawing historical parallels, which cannot be offensive, but which is very effective. He has shown a cleverness and a resource which are highly admirable and extremely useful....The Ambassador," Messersmith concluded, "has in an extraordinarily short time reached a comprehensive and objective viewpoint of the situation here, and his appointment I consider one of the wisest that could have been made."

But the State Department did not quite see it that way. No sooner in fact did Dodd deliver his speech than the Hearst press, in Moffat's words, "tried to make trouble." Though neither Moffat nor anyone else in the Department would offer even unofficial comments, except to say that they had not seen the speech before it was delivered, it clearly annoyed them, moving Moffat to remark that it was a case of "the schoolmaster lecturing his pupils." Moreover, the speech served to remind the professional staff that Dodd was "continuing to bombard the Secretary with letter after letter extremely critical not only of his staff in Berlin but [also] of the reaction of the Department to his suggestions." When Colonel House visited the State Department the following week, he found its members, unlike Roosevelt who reported himself "pleased beyond measure" with Dodd's work, less than enthusiastic about their Berlin representative who "did not keep them well informed."[14]

Aside from some indication that Dodd had been slow in reporting the introduction of German discriminations against American debtors at the end of September and the fact that he had failed to foresee or warn of Germany's withdrawal from the Geneva talks, it is difficult to know just what the Department had in mind. Furthermore, in his surprise at Hitler's announcement on the 14th, Dodd was no more caught short than the British, the French, or his own Embassy staff. If the Department, then, viewed Dodd with less enthusiasm than Roosevelt did, it probably had less to do with the richness or promptness of his reports than with his challenge to their whole scheme and style of life. Complaining repeatedly that "wealthy staff people want to have cocktail parties in the afternoon, card parties in the evening and get up next day at 10 o'clock," he was inclined to describe his professional staff as inefficient and "indifferent to [the] costs of their reports." Given both the fact that he was relying heavily on his experienced staff for much of the information he sent back and that reports and telegrams were bound to be long and numerous in a country undergoing dynamic change, Dodd was taking issue with something other than the quality of their work.[15]

Happily for all concerned, though, Dodd's strained relations with the Department did little to impair his judgment of German events. For whatever his inclination to perceive a substantial opposition working some ultimate check on the regime, he did not blink the immediate realities of German life. And so his reports after the speech of October 12 remained as competent and balanced as before. If the Chancellor "stressed peace to the limit" in their talk, he was also at one with Goebbels and Göring in "arousing common men's ire against the outside world." If "liberal and intellectual Germany" were made "uneasy" as a result, it was also clear that they "dare not speak out." If Göring and Rudolph Hess issued orders "for the protection of foreign citizens from attack," they would no doubt still find "over-enthusiastic Nazis" taking the law into their own hands. If Hitler and his government declared the pleb- iscite election of November 12 an expression of the people's will, an honest endorse- ment of German withdrawal from the League, which Dodd and others could not help but describe as fact, it was nevertheless a one-sided affair, a rigged campaign in which the slightest opposition was "rigorously suppressed." If Nazis campaigners billed themselves "as apostles of peace," victory at the polls assured at least "defensive" preparations for war. If Dr. Schacht declared himself a free trader in the privacy of his home and Germans denied discriminations in their debt agreement with the Swiss, they nevertheless practiced economic nationalism of the most blatant kind— economic nationalism which only "concrete actions…rather than representations" or formal protests could reverse.

Yet despite all this, there were still some bright spots to which Dodd could point. For one, the Economics Minister, Kurt Schmitt, was waging an almost tireless campaign against the systematic elimination of Jews "from active and gainful partic- ipation in any phase of German life." And though Schmitt had hardly brought about "any change of importance," it was Dodd's and Messersmith's feeling that the Minister had already "had an influence in laying a groundwork towards more moderate action.…" Secondly, it was of considerable pleasure to Dodd that "in spite of the success achieved by the National Socialist Party in the political field, its attempts to obtain complete control over the religious life of the country" were "encountering great difficulties." "For the first time," Dodd could add in a dispatch of November 23, "the Nazi *Gleichschaltung* steamroller…has struck a formidable obstacle." In particular, Dodd had in mind the fact that some "four thousand Protestant preachers" were then refusing to accept the centralization of religious authority under a Reich Bishop, Ludwig Müller, while at the same time relations between Nazi officials and the Roman Catholics, despite a four-month-old concordat, left "much to be desired." Thirdly, two more speeches in Berlin and Munich along the lines of Dodd's earlier address evoked "extraordinary applause" and reaffirmed Dodd's belief that "Germans wished me to say in public what they are not allowed to say in private, especially about religious and personal freedom." Finally, and most important to Dodd's mind, there were renewed indications that Hitler was inclined to undertake "peaceful moves."[16]

In this regard, Dodd saw two encouraging developments. On the one hand, he received confidential information from Secretary of State von Bülow on November 20 that German talks with the Polish government were likely to result in a ten-year nonaggression pact, which, in the eyes of men like Dodd, meant that Nazi leaders were trying to settle "one of the most dangerous and intractable problems of Europe," namely Polish-German antagonism over Danzig and the

Corridor. It was exactly the reaction Hitler wished and foresaw. Secondly, Dodd was also pleased to learn that armament talks were not completely dead, that, in fact, Hitler used the occasion of a conversation on October 24 with the new British Ambassador, Sir Eric Phipps, to propose a new arms limitation plan and the British were considering a reply. Moreover, though the French were reluctant, first, to admit Germany's right to rearm and, second, to substitute arms-limitation talks for disarmament discussions, François-Poncet nevertheless felt compelled to raise arms questions with Hitler in an interview on November 24. The best summary Dodd could make at the end of November was that Hitler had been and remained "wholly belligerent." But considering his "many, many announcements of peaceful purpose" during the previous eight months, Dodd was inclined for the moment to give him the benefit of the doubt. "At the time being," he told F.D.R., the Chancellor "is perfectly sincere" in his wish for peace "and is consequently willing to negotiate with France. However, in the back of his mind," Dodd urged the President to understand, "is the old German idea of dominating Europe through warfare."

Messersmith, who was then also trying to chart the German diplomatic course, was of much the same mind. "Hitler and his associates," he wrote William Phillips, "really and sincerely want peace for the moment, but only to have a chance to get ready to use force if it is found finally essential." This would soon be illustrated, Messersmith said, by German disarmament moves, or by the fact that Germany would "make all sorts of protestations with regard to the reduction of armaments by other countries, but what she is interested in is not so much the other countries cutting down their armaments, as having a free hand to go ahead and rearm herself."[17]

Still in a more optimistic mood than Messersmith after only four and a half months in Berlin, Dodd was inclined to take German arms proposals more seriously, as were the British. Hence when Sir Eric Phipps approached Dodd on December 8 to inform him that his government had replied to Hitler's October 24 proposal with suggestions that Germany be allowed one-fourth the armament strength of her neighbors, and that she agree both to ten-year nonaggression pacts with these states and a supervisory commission for periodic and automatic inspection, Dodd urged Washington to take "advantage" of "an improving attitude" or "real move toward disarmament." Moreover, two days later in another meeting with Phipps in which the Englishman added a request for American moral support of a British-German pact, Dodd took the initiative to suggest that in return for such backing England consider joining Russia and the United States to head off further Japanese aggressions in the Far East or, more specifically, a Japanese attack on Vladivostok rumored for the next April or May.[18]

Whatever British thoughts about such a scheme, the response in Washington bordered on rage. Though Roosevelt had clearly encouraged Dodd to contribute what he might to the earlier disarmament talks, he had no interest in supporting as bold a scheme as Dodd's. And so while he sent Dodd no personal rebuff, he agreed to the one Phillips immediately dispatched. In a nine-point reply on December 11, the Under-Secretary cautioned Dodd primarily about three things:

> The problem under discussion is in its final essence a Franco-German one, with England playing both ends against the middle. We cannot offer to participate or play the role of honest broker between them outside the Disarmament Conference, as this would inevitably draw us into the general European political picture....
>
> The President and I are somewhat concerned over your references to the Far East. We assume, of course, that you did not convey the impression that our disarmament policy was dependent on the development of British policy in the Orient. In our view the two problems should be as far as possible disassociated.
>
> More specifically, we are particularly anxious to avoid any step which might give the appearance of endeavoring to isolate Japan. During the recent visit of Litvinoff and the discussions surrounding the recognition of the Soviet Government great care was exercised not to give the impression that recognition carried with it any thought of cooperation with Russia against Japan. We spoke only in general terms of mutual effort to maintain peace throughout the world.

Clearly, in suggesting Anglo-American co-operation in both Europe and the Far East, Dodd had challenged the central policies by which the new administration hoped to live: non-entanglement and passivity in practically everything connected with foreign affairs. Where the State Department had already given Dodd indications in the Nuremberg exchange that it had no intention of playing a leading role in the European give-and-take, it was then, under the influence of its Far Eastern Division, moving with increasing determination to do all in its power to avoid provoking Japan. Hence, a few months later, in April 1934, when the British thought close Anglo-American cooperation necessary in the face of Japan's Amau declaration against foreign technical or financial aid of any kind to China, Washington declared itself unwilling "to assume or be placed in a position of leadership in initiating proposals for joint or concurrent action." All this, of course, had the blessings and specific approval of F.D.R.[19]

But it was something which Dodd simply could not accept, and he felt compelled to let Washington know. While sending off immediate assurances to Phillips that he had not intended "to convey any impression of inter-dependence of policies" and that he had done no more than "put forward a personal and informal suggestion," he refused to give ground on his idea. Isolationism, he wished the President and his Under-Secretary to understand, was a short-sighted policy or "a false self-interest" which more likely than not would ultimately lead to war. More specifically, with British-German negotiations apparently continuing along "reasonable" lines, Dodd urged Roosevelt and Phillips to appreciate that it was time for an American move: "My analysis," he wrote F.D.R. on December 28, "is that if you could get [the] English and [the] French together and put through present ten year pact tied on to similar pact for Far East, you might do what our great friend, Wilson, failed to do: actually start [the] world on [the] road to peaceful negotiations in place of [the] old road to war.... [But] if you can not get actual agreements from England and France," Dodd warned, "Italy, Germany, Poland and Russia, [the] autocratic powers, will unite on French-Balkan problems and leave [the] Far East to us alone. [A] change of German attitude as to Poland and Russia is obvious here. If this sort of pact is agreed to, it won't be peaceful very long. Perhaps I am wrong," Dodd conceded, "but such is my mature judgment—nor am I either German or British!"

If Dodd had grave doubts as to where Roosevelt stood on all this (after all, he had not heard directly from the President about his ideas), he was greatly reassured by F.D.R.'s address before the Woodrow Wilson Foundation on December 28. Transmitted to America's leading European embassies as an expression of the President's current attitude toward disarmament and the League, the speech praised the League as "a prop in the world peace structure" and reiterated the President's suggestion of the previous May for disarmament and a non-aggression pact. Though the President specifically denied the idea of American participation in the League and though he showed himself as reluctant as France to acknowledge the collapse of disarmament talks, Dodd took the speech as "a good and a timely thing" and an inducement to repeat some "adventurous" ideas.[20]

Before this second appeal could even reach the President, though, Dodd himself began to see a downturn in the prospects for any immediate improvement or change. The gulf between the French and German arguments remained as great as ever after another exchange of views on January 1, while the English themselves, according to Sir Eric Phipp's report, were about to fall into a "wavering" course. On top of all this, Dodd began to reflect on the fact that the American public was "not going to allow wise international action unless somebody with a national hearing will state the truth and the whole truth...." And though Dodd believed that it would take a "statesman" rather than a "politician" to effect such a goal, he could not help but appreciate that Roosevelt needed a decisive victory in the November congressional elections before he could undertake even the smallest step. Hence, Dodd now thought it reasonable to put aside political matters for more pressing trade and debt affairs.[21]

Having added a special arrangement with Holland at the end of October to the one already concluded with the Swiss for full reimbursement of interest payments on its debt, having indicated its intention to renew these agreements in January for another half year, and having unilaterally announced on December 18 that the debt service on American bonds would now "be curtailed" from 75 to 65 percent, the German government shocked the State Department and even the President into a sharp response. Reacting, first of all, to a British request that the United States join them in protesting the German announcement of the 18th, Phillips wired Dodd to back up a British note of the 23rd with both an identical written statement and an oral explanation of growing American impatience with "successive curtailments" followed by the repurchase of German bonds "at prices depreciated mainly because of the action of the German Government in halting or reducing service...." Secondly, Phillips asked Dodd to arrange to work closely with British officials on all matters relating to these developments, while also keeping in touch with Laird Bell, a vice president of the Foreign Bondholders Protective Council, and the council's representative to a foreign creditors conference scheduled for Berlin in late January. Finally, Phillips arranged with the President to call in the German Ambassador for the presentation of an aide-mémoire, to which Roosevelt himself saw fit to add a final paragraph warning that continued discrimination against American creditors might lead to direct "practical" steps.

While these latest acts of German economic nationalism aroused Washington to challenge the Nazis more forcefully than ever before, they did not provoke Dodd to the same extent. To be sure, Dodd shared and represented to the Germans his government's distress with "known buying of large blocks of German bonds on American markets" once their value had been driven down and with discriminatory debt and trade agreements which ran counter to all hopes for freer trade; but at the same time he could not comfortably accept Washington's decision to give forceful support to American demands for interest payments at a higher rate. Like his Wilsonian counterpart in Mexico, Josephus Daniels, Dodd opposed sacrificing international co-operation for special interests of an American kind.

Had the Germans themselves all taken a hard nationalistic line, Dodd would undoubtedly have felt himself at an impasse in his post, caught between two tough-minded and unyielding governments. But as things stood, Dodd found his formal protests to the Foreign Office and to Hjalmar Schacht greeted with understanding and restraint. Moreover, though Schacht refused to concede that Germany could satisfy her obligations in full, he readily acknowledged his opposition to the "Dutch-Swiss agreements," even going so far as to tell Dodd "in great confidence that he had used his influence against discrimination involved." And in this, Schacht was entirely sincere. For, as German documents show, Schacht believed that the special arrangements with the Swiss and the Dutch were then doing more harm than good to Germany's overall balance of trade.

What Schacht did not say, of course, was that he favored other nationalistic measures which could better do the job. And one such measure, in Schacht's view, was the temporary agreement reached with the foreign bondholders on January 31. Including a promise to meet again with these creditors in April "to prepare [a] permanent settlement on the basis of [a] cessation [of] special agreements involving discrimination" as well as a commitment to increase interest payments on British- and American-held bonds from 75 to 81 percent, the agreement met with favorable comment in "the London press." Yet this, Schacht told Hitler on February 1, "does not mean that the agreement is unfavorable for us." On the contrary, Schacht considered it highly beneficial to the Germans: for, as he explained it to Hitler, "the Anglo-Saxon creditors" were now recognizing the scrip system, "which they had so far opposed in principle," and this, Schacht assured him, would soon lead to larger German exports.[22]

Whatever the complicated economics by which Schacht foresaw this end, the agreement appeared to most foreigners, including Dodd, as a reasonable concession to their demands or as a willingness to be more co-operative in international affairs. As Dodd reported it to Roosevelt the following week, "the German Finance and Economics authorities here are now and have been quite aware of the wrong involved in their rulings. I have had 'set to's' with all responsible parties. Schacht finally declared to me that he had never favored the discriminations. There are really two groups functioning here: one is composed of Foreign Office, Reichsbank and Wirtsschaftsministerium; the other of the curious combination of Hitler, Göring and Goebbels who hardly know there is an international opinion to reckon with.... In view of the above facts, I feel that the bond matter was decided as well as we could have hoped for." More important, though, it was evidence to Dodd that a reasonable group of men continued to hold enough influence in Germany to block their government from destructive international acts.

In light of Washington's willingness to do battle for higher returns on private debts, Dodd could not be entirely sure his own government would not be destructive. For, as he told Roosevelt in the same letter, "the 6 percent and 7 percent interest rates which our New York bankers fixed are regarded here as far too high; and our tariff rates of 1922 and 1930 are regarded as largely responsible for [the] existing state of things.... We forgot Jefferson's *dictum,*" he reminded F.D.R., "that no man or group must be allowed to profiteer and now the profiteers, as well as the rest of us, are paying the penalty." To remedy, then, what in Dodd's view had become the worst problem an American president ever had to face, he urged Roosevelt to work "to redistribute population, open world markets, put all banks under control and then show Europe how to stop [the] barbarism of war...." It would, Dodd acknowledged, take uninterrupted peace and electoral victories in both 1934 and 1936 to carry this scheme, but such a program, Dodd sincerely believed, was very much within reach. Since the President was reared on Wilsonian internationalism and was about to put the reciprocal trade agreements act before the Congress, he must have been sympathetic to these ideas.[23]

Whatever Roosevelt might think, Dodd was determined to continue using his post to promote international co-operation of every kind. Hence, at the end of February 1934, when the Germans approached him about improving trade relations between the two states, he was inclined to encourage such talks, especially since the Germans appeared to be ready for some real give-and-take. Arguing that they faced "a foreign trade situation which threatens to become [a] catastrophe," warning that they might have to devalue the mark, and citing "recent general statements of American officials recognizing the desirability of better balanced trade" between the two countries, the Germans specifically pressed Dodd and the State Department to give them a wine and spirits quota equal to the most favored nation, to consider a two-year scheme for increasing German cotton purchases in America, and to receive a trade mission in March which would seek "a broad reciprocity agreement" with the United States.

Behind these expressions of economic internationalism and pleas for help were Schacht's earliest efforts to increase raw materials for use in German rearmament as well as an attempt "to find out definitely, by using a conspicuous example [namely, the United States], whether" expressions of willingness to take greater exports from debtor countries could "be converted into [a] practical reality. Our aim in the April negotiations with foreign creditors," von Neurath wrote Hans Luther, the Ambassador to the United States, "is to institute a comprehensive conversion of the German external debts in agreement with the creditors." A plan, in brief, to pay creditors in goods rather than cash.

While Dodd and Hull, who was the chief architect of the administration's reciprocal trade agreements act, were eager for better trade relations with the Germans, both appreciated that they had to proceed with extreme caution. When, for example, Hull asked Dodd's opinion on the advisability of "linking up action on wines and spirits with both the broad question of Germany's commercial policy" and the possibility of suggesting "an agreement mutually defining most favored nation rights under quota and monopoly purchasing agreements," Dodd advised that "the Department make no definite proposals" until his Embassy completed a full survey of current discriminations against American goods. Moreover, once this report was completed in the following week, it led Dodd to argue that one should not expect too much from simply a contractual agreement with the Germans: "Experience shows," he said, "that unless commercial agreements are made worthwhile to the German Government, the latter will devote considerable ingenuity to finding some technical reason for circumventing them." The way, therefore, to extract meaningful concessions from the Germans, Dodd and his staff believed, was: first, to agree to take more German exports; second, to intimate to the Germans that we might place easily marketable goods in America like toys and pharmaceuticals on a quota system; third, to enlist the services of American bankers in threatening to reduce or cut off short-term credits on which Germany relied to import "indispensable raw materials" from the United States; and fourth, to tell the Germans of our willingness to respond to increased duties with higher tariffs of our own.

With such an arsenal of weapons, Dodd believed it reasonable for Washington to begin trade talks at any time. Hull, however, wished to be more cautious than that: under political pressure to delay all talks until Congress made clear its wishes on the trade agreements act, the Secretary told Dodd and the Germans at the beginning of March that discussions simply could not be opened now and that, furthermore, as he indicated to Dodd alone, he would be unreceptive to any talks if it were Germany's aim to put trade relations with the United States "on a strictly bilateral basis."

Hoping and believing that this was not the case, Dodd encouraged the Germans to prepare to send a commission of their "best economists" who would be ready to offer "real concessions if they expected results.... I saw hope in the [German] plan," Dodd confided to his diary on March 6, "and promised to advance it all I could."[24]

At the same time and in much the same spirit, Dodd also tried to reconcile German-American differences over propaganda in the United States. In February, after more than a year in which America had been subjected to strenuous Nazi propaganda urging, by State Department estimates, the establishment "of a form of government inimical to our constitution and civil liberties," Hull asked Dodd to broach this problem informally and unofficially with Hitler. Before Dodd could see the Chancellor, however, the Germans themselves objected to American counter propaganda which was about to take the form of a mock trial of Hitler. Handed an informal memorandum about the matter on March 5, Dodd "held his ground" and offered a strong defense: "...many things still occur here shocking to foreign public opinion," he reminded von Neurath, and explained "that nobody in the United States could suppress a private or public meeting...without violating the constitutions of the nation and of the several states." At the same time, however, Dodd did not think it a bad idea, as he told Hull, "to soothe injured susceptibilities [with] a press interview deprecating irresponsible expressions of opinion in regard to problems outside our frontiers as tending to stimulate international ill will...."[25]

Clearly, it was still very much Dodd's hope that America would show herself both firm and reasonable in her dealings with the Germans and that the Hitler government would eventually respond in kind. Scheduled to see the Chancellor on March 7 before leaving on the 14th for two months of work and rest in the United States, Dodd thought to make this the governing theme of his talk. Meeting privately with Hitler in his office for an informal discussion, Dodd directed the conversation to those problems—debts and trade, Jewish persecutions and disarmament—which Roosevelt had asked him to put at the center of his work.

Beginning their conversation with a query about Hitler's interest in sending the President a personal message and the need for improved trade relations between the two states, Dodd found the Führer taken aback by the former and without "very definite opinions" about the latter. When he turned the discussion to Nazi propaganda in the United States, however, he found the Führer prepared to speak. Denouncing "everything of that sort" as "almost certainly put out by Jews," Hitler declared himself convinced that the Jews above all were responsible for anti-German feelings in the United States. Taking advantage of Hitler's diatribe against the Jews to describe James McDonald's Commission for Refugees Coming from Germany and to emphasize the need to solve the "Jewish problem" "in a humane way," Dodd again found the Chancellor uninformed and unreasonable, asserting in reply that "nothing could come of such a movement" and that in fact the Jews would only use such an organization "to make endless trouble." Unwilling, however, to let the matter rest there, Dodd began to argue "a bit with him about the effects of violent treatment in the United States," hoping as a result "to suggest a different procedure from that which has been followed here...."

But seeing "that there was little chance to do more than emphasize the embarrassments" which Nazi policy "creates at home" and growing somewhat impatient with his inability to make headway on this point, Dodd bluntly turned the conversation to the fact that American public opinion was beginning to see Germany as "aiming one day to go to war." Evoking an emphatic denial qualified by the prediction that "Germany will have equality of rights in the matter of armaments," Dodd now pressed him for an opinion about the value of another disarmament conference. But unable to get more from Hitler than a restatement of his recent arms proposals to the British and the French, Dodd closed out the talk by explaining that improved German-American relations greatly depended on continuing close ties between their respective universities, which, in turn, required that academic freedom be restored in full. Though Hitler said that he agreed with this view "and that the universities here would not be improperly treated," it was "plain" to Dodd "that he did not care to talk about the subject." In fact, Dodd's whole impression of the conversation was that Hitler "talked as if he would never yield an inch. . . . " That Dodd accurately measured Hitler's response is testified to by Ernst Hanfstaengl, the Nazi party's foreign press officer, who arranged the interview. "Dodd made no impression," Hanfstaengl recalled. "Hitler was almost pitying: *'Der gute* Dodd,' he said, 'he can hardly speak German and made no sense at all.'"

Hitler's response to Dodd is not surprising. Indeed, it is doubtful that Dodd—whatever approach he might have thought to take—could have influenced Hitler one whit, for the Führer's mind was already made up about America and Americans. In his view, the United States was a "mongrel society" which "could not possibly construct a sound economy, create an indigenous culture, or operate a successful political system." But even more to the point, as far as Hitler was concerned, America "was hopelessly weak and could not interfere in any way with the realization of. . . [his] plans." Limited in his knowledge of America almost exclusively to facts about the Depression, "gangsters in Chicago and the scandals surrounding Jimmy Walker. . . of New York," Hitler stood convinced that "'any country which cannot even master its own internal police problems cannot hope to play a role in foreign affairs.'"[26]

Although Dodd more or less detected this attitude behind Hitler's expressions of interest and restraint, he was still not ready to believe that better relations were beyond reach or that the Führer could be in fact as unreasonable as he seemed. High government officials, after all, were almost passionate in their desire for better trade relations with the United States, and it seemed incomprehensible to Dodd that the Germans would not sooner or later feel compelled to moderate their economic nationalism or ease up on their persecutions for the sake of this trade. Like others who would be even more seriously fooled later in the decade, Dodd assumed that Hitler and his ministers would have to act like reasonable men.

And, in fact, within five days after their conversation Dodd began to see solid evidence to that effect. At a German Press Club luncheon on March 12, two days before Dodd left for the United States, Hans Dieckhoff of the Foreign Office announced "the re-establishment of a warrant system in making arrests" and the closing of Columbia House near Templehof airport, a private S.A. prison where Jews and political opponents of the regime were maltreated. Moreover, when he docked in the United States on the 23rd, Dodd found a German consulate official waiting for him with a ceremonial letter from Hitler to the President and words to the effect that Hitler had called a halt to propaganda in the United States. It all inclined Dodd to believe that his efforts to improve German-American relations were beginning to show results. "It is my hope," he told *The New York Times* on the day of his arrival, "that in the next few years commercial and national barriers shall be so modified that world-wide recovery and general peace may become fixtures."

Given what he now saw as conscious decisions in Germany "to ease up on the Jews" and to eliminate Nazi propaganda in America, it was Dodd's conviction that Americans should respond in kind. Hence, as soon as he landed in New York, he began something of a personal campaign to prevent a mock trial of Hitler in Chicago which he thought "would tend to undo the work I have done in Berlin." Enlisting the aid of Colonel House and Chicago Jewish leaders like Max Epstein, Leo Wolf, and Leo Wormser to "quiet things" down, Dodd also thought to arrange more positive steps like a moderation of the Jewish boycott of German goods and "a conciliation mass meeting in which both German and Jewish organizations might" take part.[27]

If Dodd hoped such measures would facilitate trade talks and improve relations between the two states, neither Messersmith in Berlin nor State Department officials in Washington were of the same mind. Believing credits and increased exports to Germany out of the question for the time being because of her callousness "with respect to existing obligations," Messersmith asked Dodd not to consider him "too pessimistic." "You know that like you," he wrote the Ambassador on April 3, "I never fail to remember that there are 65 million people here with whom we want to live in peace and to have very close relations. But it is increasingly obvious that if this government remains in power…, there is no room in Germany for any foreign interest." It was Messersmith's conviction that Germany aimed to make herself "self-supporting in every possible way…" and that the only thing the Germans planned to have come out of negotiations with the United States was a "one-sided" agreement which would aid her rearmament program. Hull and practically everyone else in the Department shared this view, announcing themselves convinced that Germany was "deliberately trying to get the American creditors to finance her rearmament" and that a German trade delegation would come over "demanding a great deal but offering nothing in return…."

Dodd was greatly troubled by this attitude. Not because he wished in any way to help sustain the Nazi regime, but because it seemed to cut the ground from under everything he hoped for. Indeed, if the American government showed itself tough and uncompromising in its dealings with Germany, it would, Dodd believed, only add to existing antagonisms and encourage an even more militant attitude in Berlin. Moreover, at a personal level, Dodd was pained to think that his mission had nowhere to go, that he might, in fact, serve only as an observer or reporter of events. And this role as yet he was unprepared to accept. On the contrary, he still had hopes of pushing the United States toward some meaningful negotiations with the Germans and, even more important, toward some substantial role in world affairs. As he stated it in a "Memorandum as to Existing World Complex," which he prepared for presentation to the President before returning to Berlin in May, "There has not been so terrible a social and economic situation for Western civilization since the collapse of the Roman empire.... From Rome to Tokyo governments of the dictatorial type are in power...[and] with all newspapers, radio, armies, churches and universities at their command, they are apt to remain in power and finally subordinate modern civilization, returning the next generation...to the medievalism of Frederic II,...1200–1250. Personally," Dodd argued, "I think England and the United States...are the two peoples who can solve the situation." But, Dodd explained, it would take a revolution in foreign policy: America would not only have to join with Britain and Holland to guarantee the "existing status of the Far East," she would also have to join the League of Nations which would "hasten better commercial relations with Europe" and save us from economic nationalism or national socialism of an American kind. Indeed, such a shift in policy, Dodd concluded, would preserve the peace and save democracy from medievalism's on-rushing tide.[28]

It is not surprising that Dodd prepared such a memorandum for the President without thinking to send a copy to the State Department. For by the time he returned to the United States in March, Dodd was more or less convinced that the Department stood firmly against an internationalist approach to German, European, or world affairs. Its reprimand for having suggested political co-operation with Britain against Japan, its apparent inclination to help American bankers collect on their German bonds at the highest possible rate, its unwillingness to encourage any immediate commercial negotiations with the Germans, and its reluctance to accord the Germans even some small measure of satisfaction in the mock trial affair, all convinced Dodd that the Department could not be relied upon to take a more co-operative or internationalist approach to foreign affairs. It is something of a tribute to Roosevelt's political resourcefulness at this time that he left Dodd feeling that he would favor co-operation. For in matters of international economics, Hull was far more committed to co-operation than F.D.R., who waited a year before presenting the Congress with Hull's reciprocal trade agreements act and then, as a counterweight, appointed George N. Peek, a staunch economic nationalist, as his Foreign Trade Adviser. Yet in matters of international politics, Dodd correctly sensed that Roosevelt would ultimately prove more flexible and less passive than Hull and the State Department. In the next five years the President inched his way toward cooperation with the democracies, while Hull repeatedly urged caution and restraint, and "permanent career men" worked to assure that a reactionary and isolationist successor to F.D.R. would find "their records clean of New Deal or one world taints."[29]

It was this attitude of the career diplomats which particularly bothered Dodd. "The further I go in my study of State Department policies," he wrote in March, "the more evidence there is that a clique of kinspeople connected with certain rich families are bent upon exploiting the Foreign Service for their set, many of them Harvard graduates who are not even well informed. Snobbery and personal gratification are the main objects with them."

One of the main reasons, in fact, why Dodd had arranged to come home for two months was in order to talk with the President and others about reforming the Foreign Service. "The condition of the Foreign Service," he wrote Roosevelt at the beginning of the year, "requires some attention—some points best not to commit to paper.... Pardon me if I add, in all confidence, the appropriate officials in Washington can not be induced to see the situation aright without some very positive pressure from above."

Yet despite this conclusion, Dodd was ready to put his case before these "officials" when he returned to the United States in March. On the afternoon of the 28th, in fact, he appeared before the State Department's Personnel Board, where he urged Assistant Secretaries R. Walton Moore, Wilbur J. Carr, Sumner Welles, and Hugh Wilson to understand "that American diplomacy had a new role to play" and "that the time had come for a new kind of service": specifically, one in which merit rather than social class would form the chief prerequisite for "new recruits." To illustrate his point, Dodd described his own staff, and particularly his Counselor and Second Secretary of Embassy, as undisciplined in their work habits and inclined to spend too much time and money in social display. Men of this kind, Dodd asserted, "think more of wearing good clothes than doing good work...."

Needless to say, the Department did not take kindly to his remarks, particularly because Dodd offered little or no evidence to show that such social preoccupations actually undermined the quality of Embassy work. As a consequence, Moffat and Phillips dismissed his criticisms as springing from envy of other men with greater financial means. "It is, of course," Phillips believed, "a small town attitude" toward diplomatic life.

Even though Dodd relied more heavily on his convictions than on the facts in presenting his case, it was nonetheless unfair of Moffat and Phillips to assume that envy motivated him and that they could dismiss his ideas out of hand. Dodd, after all, was not the only ambassador complaining of inefficiency and waste, as testified by what Josephus Daniels had to report from Mexico. Moreover, whatever the State Department might think, Roosevelt was inclined to accept Dodd's picture of the Foreign Service, deciding in the spring of 1934 to recast State Department groupings a little by insisting on more and faster transfers between the diplomatic and consular services in general and on the shift of Dodd's Counselor and Second Secretary of Embassy in particular.[30]

Despite Dodd's being at odds with Department leaders over practically everything he wished to achieve, he was nevertheless able to conclude his stay in the United States on a positive note. With the President showing himself generally sympathetic to most of his ideas, with Jewish leaders in Chicago and New York agreeing to call off a mock trial and possibly ease up on boycotts, and with twenty of the country's "foremost editors and newspaper executives" expressing themselves in an off-the-record luncheon as more than friendly to F.D.R., "open and frank" in their "support" of Dodd's approach to "leading problems," and convinced that Germany was "profoundly important," Dodd took ship for Europe on May 9 hopeful that better relations and international peace might yet be assured.[31]

XII

War and Not Peace

THROUGH ALMOST ELEVEN months as Ambassador to Germany Dodd had sustained the hope that Hitler's Nazi regime would sooner or later moderate and change, that under the weight of economic and political pressure from abroad Germany would soon once more speak the language of reasonable men. As later events revealed, this was no more than a variation of the baseless faith held by British and French leaders down to the outbreak of the Second World War.

For Dodd, however, it was a hope which could not outlive 1934. For even before he got back to Germany on May 17, Dodd was beginning to feel he had been naïve to assume that Hitler's regime was about to change. Reading a Goebbels speech aboard ship which declared "Jews...the syphilis of all European peoples" and finding extensive evidence of fresh anti-Semitism on his return, Dodd could only conclude that German leaders never meant what they said, or that conservative officials had no power to moderate the destructive actions of the regime. "I was put in the position of having been humbugged," he told F.D.R., "as indeed I was."

As a result, Dodd was now determined to take a wait-and-see attitude toward practically everything the Germans proposed. Hence, when one of Hitler's adherents approached Colonel House about going to Berlin for a talk with Hitler about "the Jewish situation" and when House suggested that Dodd open the way, the Ambassador adopted a highly cautious line. Reading Colonel House's letter to von Neurath in the privacy of the Foreign Minister's home, Dodd suggested that von

Neurath have "some Nazi chief make a speech calling for moderation" before he encouraged Colonel House to come across. Needless to say, nothing came of this exchange.

Similarly, in matters of debts and trade, Dodd was no longer ready to encourage the dispatch of a trade commission to Washington from Berlin. With Germany adding lard to the list of American products closed out of German markets by quota agreements and with Schacht announcing a moratorium on medium- and long-term American loans for July, Dodd countered renewed suggestions for trade negotiations with a long list of complaints: Jewish persecutions; unanswered treaty violations, such as a failure to give most-favored-nation treatment to American lard; and moratoria on American loans at the same time other creditors were paid and foreign exchange went for raw materials and aircraft for use in building a German war machine. These things, Dodd said, impressed Americans as an unwillingness to appreciate "the effect of failure to meet existing obligations" and as sufficient reason to refuse talks.

In the face of these reprimands from Dodd, Schmitt, von Neurath and other Foreign Office "conservatives" showed themselves more sympathetic to his point of view than ever before. Indeed, in response to Dodd's complaints that he had been taken in and could no longer accord German leaders a substantial measure of trust, von Neurath assured him that anti-Semitic outbursts were entirely against his wishes and that "he, Schacht and Schmitt had gone to Goebbels and protested." Dieckhoff, likewise, "revealed his whole attitude of opposition to Goebbels and his expectation that Hitler would be overthrown soon." "I felt the deep concern of a high official," Dodd wrote at the time, "who could thus risk his life in criticism of the existing regime." Conversations with Schmitt and Karl Ritter of the economics section of the Foreign Office yielded much the same response.[1]

While such expressions of distress and good faith may have somewhat disarmed Dodd, they no longer left him feeling that conservative opposition or dissatisfaction with Hitler guaranteed an imminent or even an eventual turnabout. Moreover, Dodd now believed that protests to government officials would bring no results, that Hitler and the Nazis were almost indifferent to economic and political pressure from abroad, especially from the United States, and that, even more important, the Hitler government was here to stay.

Other observers on the Berlin scene at the time, however, were less certain than Dodd. François-Poncet, for example, saw "Nazism…weathering a crisis. There was the open clash against the churches; there were the enormous Nazi expenditures which raised the ghost of inflation; the increase of arrests and deportations to concentration camps about which terrifying rumors ran rife; and a general distrust and hostility throughout Europe." The French Ambassador later recalled that it all "created a deep-seated uneasiness" and an opposition coming "especially from the high military command and from the Prussian nobility, from former Steel Helmet supporters and even from the tiny circle of Hindenburg's familiars." And though "an iron curtain had been drawn down over reality…the atmosphere was heavy, stifling, as before an imminent storm." Even the cautious and generally pessimistic Messersmith, who departed for the American Ministry in Vienna at the end of May, was ready to conclude that continued loss of prestige and dissensions within the party might shortly join with economic and financial difficulties to "bring about a change of regime" to one "along more reasonable and cooperative lines."

Though Dodd, like François-Poncet and Messersmith, also saw "evidences of dissatisfaction" or "decided discontent…prevalent in various portions of the German population," he did not believe it portended some important change. Although the conservative opposition to the regime had reached a point where Vice Chancellor von Papen openly spoke against "a second revolutionary wave" in a "remarkable" address to university students on June 17, Dodd was mindful of the fact that Nazi radicals continued to hold enormous strength, including the backing of their two-and-one-half-million-man S.A. Moreover, Dodd assumed, with apparently a good bit of accuracy, that Hitler wished to avoid a confrontation with either the Left or the Right, preferring, as before, to govern "with divided counsels." Given all this, Dodd was wont "for the present" to see Hitler "holding the situation in check." "I do not anticipate," he wrote Roosevelt and Hull on June 27, "any immediate radical change in the German Government."

Dodd, of course, was only partly right. Three days after he wrote F.D.R. and Hull, an upheaval took place. Pushed by "an uncompromising message" from President Hindenburg and Defense Minister Blomberg that he bring about a relaxation of the state of tension generated from the Left or face martial law and rule by army decree, Hitler purged the opposition to his regime. Though moving primarily against radicals like S.A. leader Ernst Röhm, the Führer spared few opponents on the right, simultaneously striking down Generals Schleicher and Bredow as well as two of von Papen's aides. "For anyone less blind than the [German] generals," Alan Bullock has written, "the way in which Hitler dealt with the threat of a second revolution must have brought consternation rather than satisfaction. Never had Hitler made so patent his total indifference to any respect for law or humanity, and his determination to preserve power at any cost. Never had he illustrated so clearly the revolutionary character of his regime as in disowning the revolution." "…It was Hitler, not Papen and the *Reaktion,* the peddlars of Christian Conservatism," Bullock concludes, "who emerged triumphant from the test of June 1934."[2]

If Dodd was surprised by the swiftness with which the threatened outbreak took place and if he was never entirely clear about the immediate origins of the clash, he at once appreciated its significance. While Röhm's elimination seemed to mean "increased strength to the conservative elements" at the expense of the radicals, the killing of Schleicher, the alleged deaths of one or two of von Papen's followers, and "rumors that he [Papen] and other conservative Ministers are under a cloud if not under arrest" seemed to him to "prescribe that this [first] deduction should be made with all reserve." Dodd was soon ready with an even more precise report: the elimination of radicals and conservatives as well as the continuation in the government of men of the Left and the Right indicated to him that the so-called revolt increased the power of neither side. The real victors in the affair, Dodd concluded, were Hitler and the established regime.[3]

The situation from Dodd's viewpoint could not have been much worse, for a government which operated along such ruthless lines could hardly be expected to contribute anything to better foreign relations and peace. Indeed, it was now Dodd's conviction that nothing positive would ever result from a Nazi presence in Berlin and that negotiation, a dialogue, or some real give-and-take with Hitler and the regime was no more than a contradiction in terms. In short, Dodd no longer saw any point in meeting with Hitler on other than ceremonial or "official grounds." "I certainly would not ask to see any man who has committed a score of murders the last few days," Dodd told his diary on July 4. "He [Hitler] is such a horror to me," he told Eric Phipps on July 13, "I cannot endure his presence." Though Dodd decided on intuitive and moralistic grounds never to seek another interview with Hitler, he was doing no more than reflecting the realities of his position in Berlin. Representing a country that wished no part in determining the course of European events—especially once dreams of disarmament ended—and confronting a government which held the United States in contempt, Dodd really had very little to discuss with the highest officials of the regime.

Yet in acknowledging this fact, Dodd initially felt as if he were repudiating the very reason for which he had come to Berlin. By July 8, in fact, he was asking himself: "Ought I to resign?" But his answer was at once "no," for he by no means felt entirely bankrupt in his post.[4]

For one, he continued to see important work for himself in the field of Foreign Service reform. Having found an enthusiastic supporter for his ideas in Assistant Secretary of State R. Walton Moore, a fellow Wilsonian who joined the Department in 1933 after a long congressional career, Dodd continued to press for change through him. And Moore, who gingerly repeated his arguments to F.D.R., assured him that "the views you expressed to the Personnel Board and your communications have been exceedingly helpful, and…if we find a better basis on which our Foreign Service should rest, the credit will be largely due to your clear conception of what conditions now are and what…they can be made." Much to Dodd's delight, this was more than mere rhetoric. For by the end of June, Moore was telling him about the President's "coordinating plan" and how his suggestions were now "bearing fruit." On top of this, Dodd took considerable pleasure in a *New York Times* article of July 1 describing him as an almost model diplomat who saved the government's money and lived within his means.

Secondly, and no doubt equally gratifying to Dodd, his Berlin Embassy now became something of a catalyst for renewed efforts on his *Old South*. Stirred by Nazi excesses to a defense of democracy such as he had not felt compelled to undertake in several years, he turned once more to the origins and growth of democratic habits in the United States. "I walked home...and had a quiet afternoon and evening, writing two hours on my *Old South*," he recorded on July 14.[5]

Yet if Dodd were now repelled by the Nazi government, considered resigning, and showed considerable interest in Foreign Service reform and in writing his book, he was not about to withdraw from diplomatic life or become a recluse far removed from the daily consideration of events. On the contrary, Dodd's inclination to abandon his work was no more than a passing mood which, to be sure, would recur, but by no means dominate all he did. Indeed, in the first two weeks of July, while he was ruminating over the ruthlessness and undiminished power of the Hitler regime, he was also busily engaged in a variety of diplomatic tasks, including a discussion with the State Department over how to answer a German decision to meet its Dawes-Young loan obligations to the British without offering equal treatment to the United States.

On hearing of the British-German arrangement of July 4, the State Department instructed Dodd "to spare no efforts either with von Neurath or with any other high German official to impress upon them the growing feeling of exasperation in this country at the discriminatory attitude being practised...." Dodd, however, had little interest in pressing a case. Convinced that a four-to-one advantage in America's balance of trade with the Germans ruled out the possibility of collecting on the loans and that America's tariff policy of 1923–30 had gone a long way toward pushing Hitler as well as the Italians, British, and French toward "economic autarchies," Dodd saw neither practical nor moral reasons for carrying empty protests to the Foreign Office and Schacht. While correctly assuming, as Under-Secretary Phillips was ready to admit, that America, unlike Britain, with whom the Germans had a greater export than an import trade, had "no weapon with which to force Germany to give American holders of...securities equal treatment," Dodd erroneously believed that Hull shared his view and would be receptive to arguments against asking the Germans repeatedly for what they could not give. The Secretary, however, rejected Dodd's opinion: recognizing that "transfer difficulties" were less the result of America's past trade policies and current German inability to pay than of Nazi determination to use German money for other things, Hull was morally outraged and wished Dodd "not only to take but also to create every possible occasion to bring about a change of attitude toward the just demands of this Government."

At the same time Dodd sparred with Washington about American loans and reluctantly carried messages of protest to the Germans, he kept in close touch with the diplomatic corps, gathering what information he could on internal affairs. In the two weeks between Hitler's public explanation of the purge and the abortive Nazi coup in Austria on July 25, Dodd held both formal and informal talks with a variety of officials, including Schacht, Finance Minister von Schwerin-Krosigk, von Papen, von Neurath, von Ribbentrop, Lev Khinchuk, Russia's Ambassador to Berlin, Phipps, and François-Poncet. Moreover, whatever the extent of Dodd's antagonism to the Nazis by this point, he was eager to appear outwardly neutral or to avoid being accused of some undiplomatic act. Appreciating that Nazi hostility to Berlin diplomats had just been driven to a new high by rumors of foreign involvement in the alleged June 30 plot, Dodd went out of his way to assure that the Germans would not think him urging a diplomats' boycott of Hitler's purge speech or inclined to involve himself in a diplomatic "intrigue" over the Austrian affair.[6]

Though terribly concerned about being watched and constantly worried lest he appear indiscreet, Dodd nevertheless managed with the help of his staff to gather sufficient information to conclude that the country stood in jeopardy of another revolt. "The people show great concern," he wired Hull on July 21, "and consular reports indicate increasing hostility to the regime.... Collapse of financial structure or death of the President," he suggested, "might produce another revolution." The belief existed, François-Poncet recalls, that Hindenburg's death would provide "a ready-made occasion to submit Hitler to a higher authority more apt to keep him in hand than Hindenburg had been or to get rid of him altogether." Yet none of this then appeared certain or even likely: for while the "economic crisis" and "rumors... that more bloodshed would take place in about two months" were not improving "public confidence," it also seemed to Dodd that traditional submissiveness and widespread intimidation made a new revolt unlikely. Indeed, stories like the one about the young man who was shot for making derogatory remarks about the regime while buying a newspaper undoubtedly made people hesitate to express their views.

Yet the conviction Dodd held earlier in the month that the regime was more or less permanently ensconced was now further challenged by external events. The failure of the Austrian Nazis, who were generally viewed as controlled by Berlin, to succeed in their July 25 coup both embarrassed Hitler and added to the forces ranged against him from the outside. Indeed, the efforts in the summer of 1934 of Louis Barthou, the French Foreign Minister, to surround Germany with defensive alliances and Mussolini's addition to this group of Western and Eastern European states after the events of July 25 seemed to foretell "the completest encirclement Germany has ever known" as well as a renewed effort among Germans to drive Hitler from power. If Dodd, in short, was convinced at the beginning of July that the Nazi government was unshakable, his conviction had weakened by the end of the month. "It is not my purpose to resign," he now told Cordell Hull, "until I am sure this system has come to stay."[7]

Events following Hindenburg's death on August 2, however, at once struck Dodd's reviving hopes a sharp blow. Instead of the "possible putsch in Berlin which so many people expected and many thousands had, doubtless, prayed for," the President's passing proved to be but another example of Hitler's ability to turn a possibly dangerous situation to his advantage. Declaring the incorporation of the President's and Chancellor's powers into one office under his control and winning an immediate oath of allegiance from the German army, Hitler at once destroyed the last meaningful possibility of opposition to his rule.

Dodd could not blink these results. "My hope had been that when Hindenburg passed away there would be a change in the direction of more rational international relations," he wrote Daniel Roper on August 14. But now "on the contrary, everything tends the other way." Above all, Dodd complained, there was no longer an opposing conservative force likely to moderate or possibly frustrate Hitler's plans. Von Neurath, for example, might tell Eric Phipps of his trepidation over Hitler's assumption of presidential powers, but, Dodd concluded, he was ready to "*heil* Hitler" with the rest. "I have never seen evidence," Dodd wrote in his diary, "that the Secretary ever resists the arbitrary conduct of the Führer." Dieckhoff, moreover, might inform him that the Foreign Office had worked a change in Hitler's attitude toward the Jews, but Dodd appreciated that Hitler "allowed his most intimate and trusted counselor [Rudolph Hess] to do the opposite of what he promised," if he had, in fact, ever promised. The Foreign Office, in sum, now appeared to Dodd as an organization "unquestionably" molding "its general policies to the dictate of the Nazis." Likewise, the Protestant churches, which Dodd had previously viewed as a major source of discontent, emerged from a National Synod in Berlin on August 9 as a force Dodd now wrote off as more than ever under government control. The final act in the drama recording Hitler's unassailable grip on power was the plebiscite vote of August 19 endorsing the Führer's assumption of presidential duties. While all dangers to the regime had not been removed, the Embassy told Washington on the 21st, "it would be rash to predict that any of them will cause the Dictator's downfall."[8]

What chiefly troubled Dodd in all this was the fact that Nazi dominance at home portended Nazi adventures abroad. At the very least, Dodd could point to considerable evidence of widespread preparations for war. "More men are trained, uniformed and armed (perhaps not heavy guns)," he told F.D.R., "than in 1914, at least a million and a half; and the funeral all the Ambassadors and Ministers attended at Tannenburg August 7 was one grand military display.... Every diplomat with whom I spoke," Dodd added, "regarded the whole thing as a challenge under cover.... It seems to me that war and not peace is the objective, and the Hitler enthusiasts think they can beat Italy and France in a month—nor is high-power aircraft wanting, the Wrights having sold them machines last April."

Given these developments, Dodd once more felt terribly distressed with an assignment which promised so little result. What, he asked, could he accomplish in a country where "we cannot depend on the promises of the highest authorities" or where Americans could not look forward to any fruitful exchange, even in commercial relations in which the Germans clearly wanted something from the United States? Dodd's answer was a more or less concerted effort to have his government directly confront the German threat. If conciliation and generous actions, in other words, were futile in calling forth a reasonable response, then Dodd believed it the business of his government to encourage collective security through the League. "Much as our people dislike the idea," he told Roper on the 14th, "it seems to me that we must come into closer relations with Geneva, urge more positively than ever abandonment of war methods and gradual acceptance of the League of Nations as a means of closer political and economic relations." "I am inclined again to look at the League of Nations when Russia is admitted" in September, he urged F.D.R. Indeed, the only answer Dodd could see to Germany's "everlasting military enlargement" was "closest cooperation of all greater powers." And "as a means of carrying the same idea in the Far East, where there is another military-naval urge," Dodd revived his proposal for a British-American entente. Resistance to such a policy now, he warned Roper, would result in Japanese domination of "the whole East...in a few years—[and] then such a war!" A war, Dodd concluded, which "will delay, if not destroy, a progressive civilization which we have done so much to advance since 1776."

Since it was obvious to Dodd that official Washington would be in no position to take up or implement such notions at once, he toyed with two or three means of giving them substance on his own. For one, he raised with François-Poncet the possibility of a "concerted withdrawal" by the British, French, and American ambassadors in answer to some future Nazi attack or threat of war. François-Poncet, who had already decided to block or combat Hitler with a "policy of accommodation" rather than one of "frontal resistance," was cool to the idea. Similarly, the British Ambassador was unprepared to provide Dodd with "useful answers" to questions about the Far East.[9]

Yet despite the unenthusiastic response of François-Poncet and Phipps, Dodd was not disposed to abandon his call for collective action against militarist regimes. An invitation to speak at the centenary celebration of the Bremen YMCA on September 9, therefore, became an occasion to give voice to his remedy for "A Troubled World." The Christian principles of "self-sacrifice, love of one's neighbor and co-operation among rivals," he announced as the key. For if men were ready "to abandon minor differences of creed and denominational particularism for the greater purposes of Christianity," Dodd said, "…both Catholics and Protestants may for once work together and save themselves and their fellows—[that is, they may] get the twenty million unemployed back to self-respecting self-help and stop the suicidal spirit of hatred and militarism which marks the attitude of every great people of our time." Though his Counselor of Embassy warned that such a speech might "make a sensation" and possibly bring "a rebuke from the State Department," Dodd was ready to risk it, hoping, along with one American correspondent who read an advance copy, that it might do "great good…at Geneva."[10]

Yet such vague hopes were a poor substitute for a sense of marked accomplishment or meaningful work in his Berlin post. To be sure, Dodd found considerable comfort in an enthusiastic response from the five thousand Europeans listening to his speech and in a reply from Roosevelt of August 25 telling him that "I watch for any ray of hope or opening to give me an opportunity to lend a helping hand"; but Dodd nevertheless found it difficult to sustain a positive attitude toward an assignment which in truth was an almost impossible one from the start. If it was difficult to accept the fact that improved German-American relations were out of reach, it was even more painful to acknowledge that prospects for a meaningful response to Nazism from the United States were almost as bleak.

Attendance on September 12 at a formal diplomatic reception for the new President of the Reich forcefully reminded Dodd of these facts. Presented with a chance for a direct exchange with the Führer as he moved along a reception line greeting representatives of foreign states, Dodd struck an ironical note: "As the happy Führer extended his hand to me," Dodd later wrote, "I reminded him quickly of the peace note in his speech to us and said that it would be approved in the United States, especially by our President, who had asked me to say to him that these peace speeches always interested him. Hitler bowed pointedly and talked for a moment as though he were a pacifist, a type he always damns in his public statements. As he passed on to the Spanish and British Ambassadors, I felt a little badly because he seemed not to have understood my ironical meaning. He assumed that I actually believed what he said!" Feeling intensely his inability to have an impact, or do any "good" in a country moving inexorably toward a European, or even world, war, Dodd wondered again whether he would not be better off quitting Berlin. "What can one, of my way of thinking, do in a country where the atmosphere is so disagreeable?" he asked Schacht.

Dodd needed no reply. In almost the same breath with his complaint, he pressed the economist to oppose Hitler's war plans. "Why do you not, when you speak before the public, tell the German people they must abandon a war attitude?... 'I dare not say that,'" Schacht replied. "'I can only speak on my special subjects.' How, then," Dodd came back, "can German people ever learn the real dangers of war if nobody ever presents that side of the question?" Immediately carrying news of his conversation with Schacht to the British Ambassador, Dodd also hoped to use his talk with Phipps to prepare the ground for later discussions "with him if President Roosevelt tries again to bring American arms manufacturers under government control." Believing, along with millions of other Americans at this time, that Senator Gerald Nye's investigation of the United States' arms industry offered irrefutable proof that munitions manufacturers favored wars and that "the arms manufacturers over the world are the cause of this trouble in Europe," Dodd hoped "to enlist" Phipps in a move to persuade his government to undertake a similar exposé.[11]

At the same time Dodd pressed his personal campaign to prevent war, he fashioned yet another answer to his own question of what he could do in the disagreeable atmosphere of Berlin. Continuing to gather and read masses of documents and reports on conditions in Germany, Dodd and the Embassy maintained a steady flow of information to the Department on a wide range of subjects: labor decrees, Jewish persecutions, and conflict with the churches received their regular attention or review, while rearmament in the Reich came in for a special report. Aided by the American consuls around the country—and especially in Stuttgart and Munich—Dodd gave the State Department an eight-page account on September 24 of "Germany's Will for Peace." Contrasting official protestations of peace with actual preparations for war, Dodd could only conclude that the first was but a smoke screen for the latter: "material preparations" and "indications that the Government is prepared to effect a material increase in the size of the Reichswehr," Dodd told the Department, were both evidence of Germany's will for war.[12]

As if all this were not enough to test Dodd's endurance in his post, a new series of developments at the beginning of October made a bleak picture seem worse. A conversation with Quincy Wright, a former colleague and international relations specialist at the University of Chicago, plus fresh evidence from the Nye committee in Washington, revealed the League of Nations as helpless before the intrigue of arms dealers in Britain, France, and the United States. On top of this, Dodd had to confront reports "of forcible measures applied to recalcitrant clergy" in Germany and of the emergence of a fascist regime in Spain. "I shall almost weep for my Spanish friend if it turns out that way," Dodd wrote in his diary on the 6th. "I must write somebody frankly and in confidence," he announced in a sorrowful letter to Moore. "Hitler I think...is here to stay....All intellectual Germany, with rare exceptions, is miserable. But where correspondence, telephone, telegraph, radio, sermons and all public speaking is absolutely controlled by a single person and he is a curious fanatic, I can not see how resistance and reform can begin." What makes things so very terrible, though, he also told Moore, is that "the German people are thoroughly indoctrinated with war idea and drilled to the limit. They intend to destroy France, break English power and annex territory where it seems to be needed: Austria, Hungary, part of Poland and all Holland. Pan-Germanism of 1910–12 is fully alive. If this succeeds," Dodd concluded, "Europe will give our people something to think about. They refuse to think now: Borah and Johnson examples. The only nation that can stop this course is the U.S.A., but the U.S.A. will not do it. Note the Nye investigation," which, as Dodd understood, had now been turned into an additional argument for American isolation from world affairs.

This head-long rush toward collapse seemed to speed up in the following weeks. Informed by Zulueta that he would resign his post and return to Madrid rather than serve an autocratic Spanish regime, Dodd felt as if he were losing his "one personal friend…in the diplomatic corps." Worse yet, King Alexander of Yugoslavia and Louis Barthou were assassinated by an Italian-trained Croat terrorist in Marseilles on the same day. "It was a shock," Dodd wrote, "especially because the visit to France was for the purpose of binding France, Italy and Yugoslavia into closer relations against Germany and Poland." At the same time, Washington demanded another protest to the Germans over renewed discriminations against bondholders in the United States; Schacht declared "the whole modern world crazy" and Germany on the verge of economic collapse; William Hillman, a Hearst journalist, brought news of increasing hostility to America in Britain over debt payments with little prospect for a pact; reports reached the Embassy of current and promised British-American arms sales to Hitler's Reich; while Armand Bérard, François-Poncet's confidential secretary, warned of a German attack upon France around the first of the year.

In the midst of all this gloom, Dodd could still pick out a few bright spots. For one, Hitler was not yet strong enough to risk war and would probably hold back for some time. Secondly, England and Holland were apparently giving some consideration to a mutual defense pact against Germany and Japan, in which the English were promised military passage through the Netherlands in return for common defense of Dutch possessions in the Far East. Thirdly, and most heartening to Dodd at this point, the German resistance to Hitler seemed to be finding new life in the Protestant Church. On October 22, at least, the Embassy was ready to report that "the controversy which is disturbing German Protestantism has suddenly assumed new and unexpected aspects." These included a controversy among the "German Christians," the official church-group under the Reich, over a plan to combine Protestants and Catholics into a national church and, "of greater importance," the attempt of the dissenting "Confessional Synod of Barmen to secede openly from the [state supported] Unified Evangelical Church."[13]

Further evidence of increasing tension over the church-state conflict came to Dodd in the next few days from Schacht. In a conversation on the 26th in which he expressed the belief that Hitler's church policy "hurts us more in America than our Jewish persecutions," Schacht asked Dodd to let him arrange a meeting with the Führer on just this point. Doing all he now could to reduce economic pressure on Germany from the United States or to remove opposition to trade negotiations between the two states, including the publication in the October issue of *Foreign Affairs* of an appeal for greater understanding of the new Germany in America, Schacht also thought to reduce provocations from the German side. "He [Hitler] is so completely surrounded by *Partei* people," Schacht told Dodd, "that I think you ought to tell him very frankly what outside opinion is. It might have a good effect."

Though Dodd declined, refusing to "intermeddle in German domestic affairs," or to attempt something which he apparently believed would do no good, he nevertheless kept a close watch on this latest trend. "To judge from the most recent reports," he wrote the State Department on November 2, "the Confessional Synod's position has become steadily stronger, at the expense of Reichsbischof Müller and his legal adviser, Dr. Jäger." As proof of this, Dodd pointed to the fact that Jäger had lost his post and that Hitler told a "deputation from the opposition ... that the Government would have nothing more to do with the Church dispute. This statement, which is probably correct," Dodd said, "is of considerable importance," for it seemed to show that Hitler was fearful of weakening the party in southern Germany and that the National Socialist principle of the total state had not yet been successfully applied.

Yet even if this were in fact the case, Dodd was unprepared to herald it as some major turning point in the history of the Reich. Additional reports from the consuls about military preparations, reinforced by personal observations on a four-day motor trip through Wittenberg, Leipzig, Nuremberg, Stuttgart, and Erfurt, were stern reminders of the extent of Nazi control. "In almost every city or town there was marching, either of Hitler Jugend or of SS and SA men in uniform.... In some places they ... [were] making poison gas and explosives in great quantities. The Consul in Dresden reported ... 1,000 airplanes in that district." Despite the fact, then, as Dodd told Moore, that "a great minority in Germany" showed "considerable uneasiness," it was clear that the majority stood "entirely committed to the philosophy of complete German unity in every direction and of war as soon as that unity is attained.... I am not saying that this is certain," Dodd concluded, "only all the contemporary evidence points that way."[14]

Since nothing was certain and since "discontent" among an "indeterminate part of the population" seemed to have "ebbed and flowed at different periods" during the previous year, Dodd thought it well that he keep a specially careful watch on this latest round of antigovernment discontent. Drawing on what he heard from his intellectual and conservative acquaintances in Berlin, he was able to report on November 14 that "criticism is again becoming more outspoken." Fed by the "severity of the Government's economic policy" and the resistance of the Protestants to government efforts "to dragoon their Church," leading university men were beginning to break their "cowardly silence," while farmers or peasants in general and Saxon industrial workers in particular were showing greater restlessness than before. "…Notwithstanding the more or less confidential mutterings of countless pessimists," Dodd told Washington, "it is impossible to predict any change." Indeed, despite the recent ostensible gains of the churchmen in October, it was clear to Dodd that Reichsbischof Müller and the German Christians had not been put to flight and that Hitler might yet openly espouse their cause after the Saar plebiscite in January 1935. Yet there were enough "eminent clergymen" and non-church leaders privately promising resistance to the death against government control for Dodd accurately to foresee a "real struggle" over the religious issue resuming after February 1.[15]

At the same time Dodd kept close watch on these domestic developments, he continued to assess and report on the international scene. And here he was beginning to find support for his assumption that there would be no immediate war. The fact that the Germans were negotiating a commercial and possibly military-political pact with the Russians at the same time they were accepting an ad hoc international force to supervise the Saar plebiscite on whether the territory would again come under German control, all seemed to indicate that Hitler now wished to fight the encircle-ment with diplomacy rather than force. Moreover, the fact that the British government was publicly expressing its disquiet over rapid German rearmament impressed Dodd as likely to compel even greater German restraint. Yet none of this, Dodd urged Moore and Phillips to understand, in any way changed his long-term estimate of events. In due course, Germany's expansive plans would precipitate a European war, unless, of course, America was prepared to act.

And since she was not, Dodd felt more intensely than ever the need to press this point. "If the United States and Great Britain fail to restrain Japan and continue to quarrel about war debts…," he wrote Phillips on December 5, "the policy here for alliance with Japan (I believe it already exists) will be pressed." Or, as he stated it for the British Ambassador on November 30, an Anglo-American guarantee of "the existing status in the Far East, will bring a halt to Japan's naval arms race, which she was beginning to run, and, coincidentally, open the way to British-American co-operation against the German war plan." Even though the usually noncommittal Englishman—he had "a perfect poker face," William Shirer recalls—was ready to announce that "our two countries could agree," Dodd could not promise such a response from the United States. Indeed, the chief obstacle to any such co-operation, Dodd appreciated, continued to come from the American side.[16]

Consequently, he believed it high time that American leaders undertake to change some minds. Moreover, scheduled to return home for a presidential address to the American Historical Association at the end of December, Dodd was determined to do his share. Hence, in the five weeks after he arrived in New York on December 23, he wrote and spoke privately to individuals and groups, including the President, Colonel House, John D. Rockefeller, Jr., the National Committee on the Cause and Cure of War, Princeton's Institute for Advanced Studies, and the Foreign Policy Association of Washington, D.C., about the urgent need for a change in America's conduct of foreign affairs.

Dodd pressed the President particularly hard. Urging him to set forth at once on a policy of co-operation with Britain and Holland in the Far East, Dodd also suggested "a joint resolution" to the Congress approving admission to the League. By Dodd's account, Roosevelt shared his desire to do "something" about Japan, or to arrange a settlement in the region before the Japanese controlled "all of Asia" and the United States spent a billion dollars on warships which would be "antiquated in ten years." Although he showed himself alive to the dangers from both Germany and Japan, Roosevelt was unprepared to undertake more than symbolic gestures toward involvement in world affairs. Waving aside the idea of a joint resolution as likely to meet overwhelming defeat, he explained his intention to begin with an effort to join the World Court. If that carried, he told Dodd, he would ask "authority to send an ambassador to Geneva." But remembering that "no President has ever been able to accomplish anything worthwhile during his second term," Dodd urged Roosevelt to understand that "delay might defeat the final purpose."

Roosevelt, however, could not see it that way. And the defeat of his World Court proposal in the Senate on January 29 confirmed him in his estimate of what he could try. Touching off a wave of isolationist sentiment which led initially sympathetic senators to vote no, the resolution suffered a clear-cut defeat and temporarily destroyed all the President's hopes for a larger American role in world affairs. "We shall go through a period of non-co-operation in everything, I fear, for the next year or two," he frankly told Dodd.[17]

But this was a fact Dodd stubbornly refused to accept—primarily because he could not believe that such a decision represented the majority mood. Indeed, as far as Dodd was concerned, the Senate's veto was no more than "minority control of foreign policy." Hence, his first response to the defeat of the Court resolution was to find a scheme whereby the President and the people could exercise their legitimate will. His first idea for effecting this goal was for him to create a sensation by resigning in protest against the Senate vote. Such a move would then allow him "to say to the country how foolish it seemed…for our people to denounce minority dictatorships in Europe and then allow a minority of men, largely under Hearst and Coughlin influence, to rule the United States in such an important matter." When Assistant Secretary Moore advised against the idea, however, Dodd thought he saw a way for the President himself to assure majority control: let Roosevelt, he told Moore, wait for a strategic moment when he could appeal to the country for entrance into the League and press a joint resolution through both houses of Congress.

Behind all this was an assumption on Dodd's part that the American people had not lost their Wilsonian faith. That, indeed, despite fourteen years of propaganda "against any connection or cooperation anywhere," the American public, like Dodd himself, was still eager to have its country defend democracy and lead the world away from war.[18]

This, of course, was not a widely held view. Charles Beard, for example, Dodd's fellow historian and old friend, was closer to the public mood when he abandoned Wilsonian internationalism at the end of 1934 for the view that America should do all in her power to stand aloof from events abroad. To Beard's thinking, it was far more important that the United States give the world the example of "a national garden well tended" than for her to become involved in international disturbances which, as in Wilson's day, would sidetrack domestic reform. In short, it was more important for Roosevelt to devote American energies to building a "collectivist democracy" or a Planned National Economy than for him to divert progressive energies into the folly of another war.

Stated yet another way, Beard's attraction to isolationism, or what he preferred to call "continentalism," was an expression of his belief "that the United States, either alone or in any coalition, did not possess the power to force peace on Europe and Asia, to assure the establishment of democratic and pacific governments there, or to provide the social and economic underwriting necessary to the perdurance of such governments." Set against the backdrop of his whole career, Beard's words illustrate the fact that his "pragmatic relativism" left him hard pressed in the thirties to meet the ideological challenge of fascism and communism. Indeed, no longer convinced that "science, facts, and the scientific method" could "provide inescapable and irrefutable policies," or no longer sure that history could be objective or lay bare some ultimate truth, Beard underwent what he himself called a "crisis in thought," a philosophical turnabout in which he used his 1933 presidential address to the American Historical Association to summon other historians to see "Written History as an Act of Faith."

Never having been a relativist like Beard and other progressives, Dodd suffered no "crisis in thought." And so his presidential address to the association in December

1934 entirely ignored philosophical and methodological questions for a discussion of America's democratic origins in "The First Social Order in the United States." "Previous presidential addresses," Dodd said, "have generally dealt with 'how history should be written' or 'what is the proper realm of history.' I think this has been over-done, and feel I should make a definite historical contribution instead." If others were puzzling over the validity of their beliefs, Dodd had few, if any, questions about his democratic faith. "...In a world where interference with freedom of expression is so common," he told his colleagues, "the American historians now have opportuni-ties of leadership and should feel a new sense of responsibility." American democ-racy, Jefferson, and Wilson continued to be firm guides in a dark age.[19]

Yet this is not to say that Dodd was entirely sanguine. He was, in fact, deeply trou-bled by attitudes in the United States. Like other "intelligent observers" around the country, he "could almost believe that the traditional structure of American politics was on the verge of dissolution," that the Coughlins, Hearsts, and Huey Longs were aiming to dispense with the democratic past. A dinner at the home of Assistant Secretary of Agriculture Rexford G. Tugwell on the evening of February 1 aggravated his fears: in the presence of congressional and administration leaders, Senator Burton K. Wheeler repeatedly attacked F.D.R. as too conservative, defended Huey Long, and in general upset Dodd with what sounded to him like National Socialist talk. "We shall soon be shooting up people here, like Hitler does," Dodd remembered him saying in answer to a comment on Long. As bad, Wheeler impressed Dodd as favoring "German domination of all Europe, our domination of the Americas, and Japanese domination of the Far East." Worse yet, Dodd thought most people at the dinner agreed.[20]

If Dodd had hopes that Hull and Roosevelt were ready to counter such beliefs, he was greatly disappointed. A meeting with the Secretary of State on the following day relieved him of any such notion. Hull agreed that Americans were being misled, confessed his helplessness, and despaired for domestic recovery "so long as interna-tional relations remain so chaotic." Roosevelt was no more encouraging. In reply to Dodd's description of Wheeler's remarks, the President outlined "an ominous situation" in which Long would challenge him for the nomination in 1936 and strive for a Hitler-style dictatorship in the following four years. Adding to this the impres-sion that Roosevelt "did not seem too regretful about the Senate vote," Dodd came away from their talk convinced that he was "in a position in Germany in which nothing can be done. No amount of optimism," he said, "relieves my doubts. Since the January 30 vote of the Senate, a minority of old-timers in the Senate will insist on guiding American foreign policy."[21]

Dodd, it would seem, now had every reason to resign, for not only had his assign-ment reached something of a dead end, it was also beginning to take a personal toll.

Having suffered progressively poor health since 1921, including some "obscure" digestive disturbances, he was increasingly bothered by medical problems in Berlin: headaches, backaches, neuritis, and colitis. Though his doctor prescribed a regimen of exercise and holidays which would reduce the "fatigue, tension and worry" of his work, both Dodd and his physician appreciated that real improvement could only come with permanent residence at the farm. For it was only there in his "remote mountain home" with "the little old room…, the hot stove in the corner [and] the ghosts of departed farmers knocking about the attics" that he could find peace "from a crazy world."

Yet Dodd gave no indication that he would in fact resign, mostly because he continued to think that things might change, that America might shed her isolationism and contribute to world peace. After all, isolationism, to his thinking, was chiefly a product of misinformation which might still be argued away. As he explained to one acquaintance in a letter of February 4,

Senators with whom I have spoken for brief moments, even the broader-minded ones, show such a lack of understanding of the effects of European attitudes upon our own recovery programme. They seem to think in terms of the old extremest [sic] protectionist policy.

…There is no permanent recovery save by planned international co-operation, not sacrificing of independence, as some seem to think; but friendly planning of trade and armament matters so that we may not all swing backwards towards the medievalism in which serfdom was the rule for the masses and absence of culture for nearly all populations. I could give expert judgments on these matters from some of the most far-seeing and best trained men in Europe, if it were necessary.

Though Americans in general and senators in particular were so misinformed, it was nevertheless Dodd's feeling that they could still be taught. A luncheon meeting with the Senate Committee on Foreign Relations on February 8 confirmed him in this belief. "I had the feeling as the luncheon broke up," he recorded in his diary, "…that a real discussion of the merits of foreign relations would have changed the Senate's attitude, i.e., if there had been a real presentation of the facts and their probable consequences to the Foreign Relations Committee."[22]

In addition to such hopes for an American turnabout in international affairs, however, there was at least one other consideration tying Dodd to his post— namely, his continuing contribution to Foreign Service reform. For by the end of 1934, no one, aside from Moore, was more deeply involved in such work. Having completed a careful survey of the consulates in Germany and having repeatedly recommended changes looking toward greater Service efficiency at lower cost, Dodd impressed Phillips, Moffat, and Carr as the man, next to Moore, most responsible for the President's inclination to cut the Foreign Service budget and speed integration of the diplomatic and consular branches. While this association with Roosevelt's Foreign Service reforms continued to put Dodd at odds with the State Department, it also left him with a certain sense of achievement in his work. Nothing, in fact, pleased him quite so much at the beginning of 1935 as the conviction that his Embassy, "except for certain individuals, is pretty close to a model so far as actual costs go." Still, whatever his accomplishments and hopes for future Service reform, it is doubtful that Dodd would have been content to stay in Berlin for this alone. Undoubtedly more central to his thoughts was the belief that America might yet be steered onto an internationalist course. There was also a matter of "ideals," of continuing to fight, as in the twenties, for what he deemed correct. "I can not see how our country is willing to allow minority control of foreign policy," he told the President the day after the World Court vote. "However, one has to fight for one's ideals and I admire you for this in every direction. All success attend your heroic efforts."[23]

XIII

Roosevelt's Ambassador

IDEALS ASIDE, DODD was profoundly unhappy going back to Berlin. To his "instinctive distaste" for Nazi chiefs and general boredom with diplomatic highjinks, he had now to add one more unpleasant fact: America's increasing isolation from world affairs deprived him of the opportunity to operate on the premises of Woodrow Wilson and consigned him unhappily to what he called "the delicate work of watching and carefully doing nothing."

His distress at having to represent a country stripping itself of moral and political influence did not much undermine the performance of his work. For, like most historians with a fascination for political affairs, Dodd remained enthralled by developments in Berlin—Europe's most dynamic center of current events. Indeed, even before he got back to his Embassy desk, Dodd was writing Moore about the Anglo-French proposal of February 3 inviting Hitler to join in new discussions of European affairs. Hoping that Germany's great success in the Saar plebiscite of January 13 had put Hitler in a more conciliatory mood, Britain and France proposed an extension of the Locarno Pact of 1925 to cover unprovoked attacks from the air, while also suggesting the negotiation of mutual security treaties for Eastern and Central Europe. Believing that these proposals "will compel Germany to show her hand or hasten her entente with Japan," Dodd promised to cable more facts as soon as he arrived at his post.

But once there, Dodd initially found himself caught up in the assessment of other information or trends. A conversation with von Neurath on the 26th in which "so much was said that…[he] returned at once to the Embassy to wire Washington a full report," a review of the continuing church struggle against "National Socialist extremists," and a warning from the Uruguayan Minister of Japanese plans to buy oil lands in Latin America gave Dodd more than enough to think about in his first week back.[1]

All these matters, however, were quickly eclipsed by the response and counter-response to the suggestions of February 3. The announcement that Britain's Foreign Minister Sir John Simon would visit Berlin on March 7, the publication of a white paper stating Britain's intention to increase her armaments in answer to Germany's growing preparations for war, followed by Hitler's postponement of the Simon visit and a German admission of the existence of an air force, pressed Dodd into new efforts to chart and explain the course of German and European affairs.

As before, he showed himself very much up to the task: unwilling to believe that Göring's announcement of an "air program" was in direct response to the British white paper of the 4th, Dodd accurately set it down as the "completion of the first portion of a military program on the part of the Nazi Government." He was of the same mind about the bolder unilateral denunciation of the disarmament clauses of the Versailles Treaty on the 16th. Though Hitler represented this action as a defensive answer to France's decision of March 15 to lengthen the service period for conscripts and to lower the age limit for enlistees, Dodd considered it another fulfillment of long-term plans: "…the decision to announce military service in violation of treaty provisions does not appear to have been predicated upon or precipitated by the recent French and British action," he wrote the State Department. "The creation of a military air force was a trial balloon and was undoubtedly decided upon prior to the release of the British white paper.… Furthermore, it has been reported that the Chancellor had written the general military service law prior to the decision of the French Chamber to increase military service on March 15th." Before the Germans were willing to proceed with further peace talks, Dodd concluded, they were determined to establish themselves on an equal footing with the other powers, or, put another way, to free themselves from having to pay for their rearmament with multilateral agreements which would tie their hands. For as far as Dodd could see, despite renewed professions of peaceful designs, Hitler's appetite for territorial expansion was as great as before.

If these disturbing events, then, reinforced Dodd's impression of a Nazi Germany bent upon war, they also taught him that America's isolationism was beginning to deprive her of even the smallest voice in foreign affairs. Not only did Hitler ignore him when he personally notified the French, English, Italian, and Polish ambassadors of his rearmament plans, he also directed his press "to make it appear that America, at most, was indifferent" to his actions. If this were not enough, though, to indicate the growing attitude of disregard for American opinions about European concerns, it was further brought home to Dodd by the actions of his colleagues. Deciding to stay away from the annual Heroes Memorial Day service on the 17th as a sort of protest against German rearmament, Phipps and François-Poncet saw no need to include Dodd in their scheme. Failing on his side to inquire after British and French intentions, Dodd found himself the only Ambassador attending the ceremonial rebirth of German arms. On top of this, Armand Bérard informed him on the following day that François-Poncet was thinking of asking his government to arrange "a united protest against German military preparations" through the simultaneous withdrawal of the English, French, and Italian representatives from Berlin. "I believe I would ask to be recalled too, if those three powers withdraw," Dodd told Bérard "half-jokingly."

Whatever personal embarrassment or slight Dodd suffered in all this, he discounted it as nothing beside the consequences for America if she continued on her isolationist course. It was a view shared by Messersmith, who agreed with Dodd that the continued existence of a Nazi regime would eventually give the United States "something to reckon with...." America's "innocent isolation" or failure to recognize what the Nazis were "really after," they both told Washington, would sooner or later bring their countrymen considerable grief.[2]

But Dodd had been telling this to Washington for better than a year, and now with events moving so fast, he found little time to dwell upon this larger fact. For, first of all, there was the important business of sorting out what the reintroduction of military service would mean for the future of the Nazi state. Or more specifically, as Dodd put it in a dispatch of March 26, the question now arose as to what impact the increased strength of the Reichswehr would have on the National Socialist regime. Dodd had no definite answer, suggesting that either Reichswehr conservatism would be transformed "into a more universal influence" or the army would become more National Socialist than before. But then neither did Hitler, who also had this question uppermost in his mind.

Equally important for the moment, though, was the question of what relevance Hitler's rearmament announcement would have for the latest round of European peace talks. And here, Dodd again went to the heart of the matter: where the British now had "little hope of material results from the conversations, [believing] that Germany has taken all she can by unilateral action," the Germans, regardless of future plans, were now compelled to be conciliatory "if for no other reason than self-preservation." Within that context, though, Dodd thought it well to keep in mind that Hitler "is more powerful than ever in Germany" and consequently "he is more than ever a potential menace to the peace of Europe."[3]

If the State Department had any doubts about Hitler's improved or strengthened position, Dodd relieved them with detailed information to the effect that "the period of internal calm" and "the declaration of military conscription" had encouraged the regime to undertake both a new anti-Jewish drive, which included above all a further restriction of legal rights, and central government control of the "various administrations" of the German judicial system which had remained under provincial control. When Secretary Hull, as indicated by a circular telegram to America's leading European diplomats, asked for up-to-date estimates of "the political situation in Europe" and for predictions of what might now be in store, Dodd obliged him with further warnings as to Germany's ultimate aim—namely, the seizure of the Polish Corridor or Austria, which in turn would "release the dogs of war."

If Hull, however, was after more immediate information, like what might be expected in the Danzig Volkstag elections of April 9, or what were the likely results of the British, French, Italian discussions scheduled for Stresa on April 11 and the League Council meeting called for April 15, Dodd began helping him on the 10th. When the Nazis failed to win anything like a substantial victory in the Free City elections, Dodd sent the Secretary some predictions about events in the upcoming weeks: "My guess now is," he wired Hull, "that war spirit declines considerably and that Hitler will listen more favorably to English proposals. Information from Paris is that France and Russia are about to sign a defensive alliance. [Maxim] Litvinov [Soviet Commissar for Foreign Affairs] is here and we look for heavy pressure on Germany. Poland likely to yield to Eastern demands. If these evidences are real the proposed League conference is apt to become very important."[4]

Coming hard on the heels of the Danzig election, the Stresa conference, the League meeting, the Franco-Soviet Pact of May 2, and another anti-German treaty, the Czech-Russian agreement of May 14, challenged Dodd more than ever to keep up with what seemed like important changes in Europe's affairs. Indeed, the tough British, French, Italian stand at Stresa, including condemnation of German rearmament, rededication to the existing treaty system, and reaffirmation of Austrian independence, seemed to compel the Germans toward a more conciliatory line, which Dodd thought might include their return to the League. Though Hitler's sharp reply on April 20 to the League's censure of his Versailles Treaty violations caused Dodd momentarily to back away from this interpretation, he soon came back to his initial point: the "complete encirclement" of Germany was provoking a widespread reassessment of the country's internal and external affairs. For in contrast with the "spirit of solidarity" which prevailed immediately after the Chancellor's announcement of rearmament in the middle of March, the country now seemed beset by "a tug-of-war between moderate and extreme elements in the Cabinet, a bitter struggle between government authorities and branches of the Christian

Church, misgivings and uncertainty among the middle classes..., active discontent among large classes of workers due to a declining standard of living,...a feeling amounting almost to despair among the unemployed," and an eagerness to restrain Hitler from any precipitous action in foreign affairs.

Yet if Hitler were in fact weathering another crisis of sorts and if he successfully "lulled the suspicions and raised the hopes of the gullible" with a Reichstag address on May 21 in which he "redoubled" his "assurances of peace" and appealed to "reason, justice and conscience," Dodd was not fooled in the least. From all Dodd could see, there were few signs that the Chancellor was about to act like a reasonable man. On the contrary, Dodd was inclined to take at face value a story from one Foreign Office official who reported that Hitler "believes 'he is Joan of Arc and simply awaits the Command of Heaven, commands which no other human being hears.'" For say what he might about peace, Hitler, Dodd warned, had not changed his plans in the least: his "urge for eastern expansion" remained, with hopes of taking "part of the Corridor, part of Czechoslovakia and all Austria." And though the current encirclement would act to force a delay until 1937 or 1938, Dodd accurately foresaw that the Stresa front would soon fall apart. Indeed, in an extraordinary letter to William Phillips on May 29, 1935, Dodd described Europe's immediate diplomatic course:

> The Hitler speech was designed, very cleverly for him, to divide his opponents and give the necessary time for preparedness. The English Administration, sorely pressed by differing groups, is practically compelled to accept Hitler's speech as aimed at permanent peace. As you know from the press accounts, the London *Times* and other influential papers argue strongly for negotiations on aircraft and naval agreements. Sir Eric Phipps...shows considerable concern; but he said the Germans have agreed to an international Air inspection commission which is to limit activities. He also thought naval limitation would be similar.
>
> The French are for the present yielding, their population being pacifist, like the English, and Mussolini, denounced here for a year, is making friendly gestures toward Berlin; and the German press has ceased all criticism of the Italian dictator.
>
> The representatives of the whole Balkan region show less belligerency than at any time since I have been here. Perhaps your reports contradict this. But the Ministers from Czechoslovakia, Yugoslavia, Hungary, Bulgaria and Roumania all indicate more disposition to patch up their quarrels and make economic agreements than heretofore....You see then that the solid front of Stresa and Geneva is weakening and the former sharp rivalries of the Danube zone declining. As to [the] German-Polish-Russian front, one can hardly venture a prediction.

The effect of Hitler's quoting Wilson's Fourteen Points and ridiculing the use of tanks, bombs and submarines is evident outside Germany; but inside Germany arms manufacture of every possible kind goes on night and day.[5]

The vindication of Dodd's views came with almost lightning rapidity. Without so much as informing the French or the Italians, the British, as Dodd more or less predicted, jumped at Hitler's suggestion that they head off a naval race between the two countries by allowing him to build a naval force equal to 35 percent of British strength. It was an act, in the words of one historian, "hardly compatible with that respect for treaties which the Stresa powers had just proclaimed." Moreover, as Dodd analyzed it, the British were giving Hitler a free hand in the Baltic where he might provoke a fight with Russia. And this, Dodd began warning repeatedly at the end of June, was producing a German-Japanese entente whereby the two powers would encircle the U.S.S.R. Though Dodd exaggerated the identity of interests between the two totalitarian states at this time, he was very much on top of the German attitude toward Italy's inclination to expand her East African empire through the annexation of Abyssinia. Indeed, the prospect of an Italian attack upon Ethiopia, Dodd explained, delighted the Hitler government in two ways: on the one hand, an adventure against the African state would weaken or further test the Stresa front, and on the other, it would also undermine Mussolini's ability to assure Austrian freedom from German control.[6]

Because all these matters, with the exception of the Anglo-German naval pact, were open to question in the summer of 1935, they continued to keep Dodd vitally involved in Europe's diplomatic give-and-take. At the same time, however, he was compelled to keep up with German domestic affairs, which also continued to shift and change in response to both internal and external concerns. A third Synod of the dissenting Confessional Church in June, for example, was apparently freed from substantial government pressure by Nazi reluctance to provoke anger in England while the naval discussions were still going on. Stated more generally at the beginning of July, Dodd asserted that "the active reentry of Germany into foreign politics, marked by the evident aim of concluding direct agreements with European countries, ... may lead to the realization that the understanding achieved with England and that apparently sought with France, are likely to be profoundly affected by the state of public opinion in these countries concerning what happens in Germany itself."

When a new wave of anti-Semitic and anti-Catholic actions erupted in mid-July, however, Dodd found himself compelled to revise his most recent estimates of domestic events. Conferring with members of his Embassy staff and drawing on what information he could gather from his usual sources in the correspondents' and diplomatic corps, Dodd could only conclude that this was a general reaction against recent conservative successes by dissatisfied or radical party groups. And though it was clear that conservative government leaders like Schacht, von Neurath, and von Schwerin-Krosigk had suffered a setback or been temporarily eclipsed by radicals like Goebbels and Agriculture Minister Walther Darre, Dodd, like everyone else, was unable to predict where this latest round of internal rivalries would lead. One thing was clear, though, the renewal of intra-party squabbling required that he now give as much attention to domestic affairs as that recently given to foreign ones. In sum, the requirements of a demanding and exhausting job promised to grow rather than decrease.[7]

It was a particularly disturbing prospect for Dodd. And chiefly because he was beginning to feel more and more the strain of his task. Indeed, by the middle of the summer he was beginning to have days when he was "too unwell for office work." "...During the last thirty days," he wrote Moore in mid-July, "there have been signs that I may have to ask a leave in September. I hope not but the Doctor's definite advice will have to be followed. The atmosphere here is to a person of my social attitudes and political prejudices so tense that relaxation is almost impossible. The remedy would be six weeks on my little farm." His doctor, however, believed that a more permanent move was in order, urging him to "seriously take stock and see whether it is not possible for you to return to the farm...."

Given his condition and his physician's advice, it seemed logical for Dodd to return gracefully to the United States and to leave his almost thankless job to a younger man. Although he had returned to his post in February with the hope of helping steer America off her isolationist course, he could now leave Berlin with the feeling that for the moment this was an impossible task. For while continuing to press Roosevelt and the State Department to understand the need for American cooperation in halting the slide toward war, he could not help but observe the growing drive in America for presidential and national neutrality in response to any conflict. Finally, had he been the only American diplomat arguing against America's retreat from international affairs, it might have made more sense for him to accept the personal sacrifice involved in staying at his post. But as things stood and as he appreciated, at least one other man in the field, namely Messersmith, was arguing the same point. Everything, therefore, seemed to argue an early retirement from Berlin.[8]

But Dodd would not go. Doing "nothing in a world in such a dangerous position" was an intolerable idea. In the best progressive tradition, Dodd believed it his personal responsibility to continue wrestling with public problems, especially since his country's policies had done so much to create them in the first place. "Since our country is so deeply involved and has made such terrible blunders," he wrote F.D.R. in May, "I would endeavor in some way to retrace our steps. If we had entered the

League in 1919, Mussolini and Hitler would not be in existence today." And now in the face of yet further damages to world peace through American deeds, Dodd felt more compelled than ever to struggle with past, present, and future wrongs.

The most he would concede himself, therefore, was a three-week holiday in a Lake Constance health resort some three hundred miles from Berlin. And though the vacation "did considerable good," relieving him of tension and aches, it was no more than a temporary release. For as soon as he got back to the work, he came under the same pressures as before. First, he had to marshal the facts about recent developments on the domestic scene in order to apprise Washington of what they could expect from the Nazi party's annual Nuremberg congress scheduled for the week of September 10. And to do this required that he sound out a number of "usually exceedingly well informed" sources. Once this careful research effort was completed, though, he was able to give the Department an accurate picture of continuing right- and left-wing pressures on the government producing another uneasy compromise: in return for a temporary halt to violence and "individual action," Dodd wrote the State Department, the radicals were promised "a status of complete subordination for the Jew." Through the pronouncement of Reichstag laws at Nuremberg, the Jews of Germany were now to find themselves restricted by statutes which for all practical purposes had long been in force. To protect German dealings abroad, however, particularly of a financial character, the conservatives, Dodd added, were seeing to it that such measures would be "offset by certain appearances of moderation": to wit, the Jews were to be described as a "national minority" whose treatment was compared with that given to German minorities living abroad. Such a deception, though, as Dodd explained after the Nuremberg meeting, would lead "very few people" to think "that new discriminatory measures will not eventually follow within the limit of what is possible without bringing about too great a disturbance in business."[9]

At the same time as he caught up on internal affairs, Dodd felt compelled to sound out the Italian, British, French, and Egyptian representatives about the increasingly tense Italo-Ethiopian situation, springing from Mussolini's unwillingness to settle his differences with the African state. Though Rome, Geneva, London, and Paris were much more at the center of this conflict than Berlin, Dodd appreciated that the prime beneficiary of a war would in fact be Berlin. "All opinion agrees," he wired Washington in late August, "the League is about dead. If England does nothing her decline begins and dictatorial Europe will hardly be limited. The only chance of more democracy in the world," he concluded, "depends upon a blockade of warring Italy."[10]

When his discussions with his colleagues in September added little to what he already knew and, above all, did nothing to change his fundamental view, Dodd again fixed his primary attention on domestic events. And here, by contrast with the

Nazi "attitude of 'splendid isolation'" toward the Abyssinian clash, a great deal was
going on. To be sure, what happened in the highest government circles remained
"complicated and very much obscured," but despite this, Dodd was able to draw a
picture of unrelenting party gains at the expense of traditional habits of mind. The
army, the churches, the Foreign Office, and the conservative student societies were
all succumbing to the Nazi wave. Though the Reichswehr greatly resented the establishment of heavily armed S.S. divisions under party control, for example, they were
the first to admit that it was a matter over which they had no control. Secondly,
though opposition continued to emanate from the Protestant churchmen, it was
now being cleverly split by the new Minister of Church Affairs, Hans Kerrl. Adopting
a more conciliatory approach than Reichsbischof Müller, including the organization
of a governing committee for the Protestant churches made up chiefly of pastors
close to the Confessional front, the opposition church group was being weakened
and split into militant Calvinists and moderate or co-operative Lutherans. Thirdly,
the Foreign Office "professional group in the Reich League of German officials" was
being "incorporated in [to] the Foreign Organization of the Party," while rumors
were rife that a full-fledged Nazi would sooner or later replace von Neurath as
Ministry head. Finally, the dissolution in October of both the graduate and undergraduate units of the student corporations marked the demise of "an institution...in
which apathy, if not actual hostility, to the Party has been fostered...." It all added
up to a situation in which, Dodd told Messersmith, "no sacrifice of Nazi principles
is even thought of...." Hence, whatever Germany's shortage of raw materials and
food stuffs, whatever the need for foreign exchange, Dodd felt justified in predicting
no change in any of the radical platforms to which the party was committed.

But with a considerable body of business and academic opinion in Germany convinced that Hitler's armament program portended "eventual economic disaster,"
Dodd looked for any and all reversals of increasing Nazi control. And though he
found some evidence in the next two months of deepening resentment and opposition to the regime among academicians, church leaders, and old regime officials, he
appreciated that it sprang chiefly from a desire to make some last stand. For as far as
Dodd could see, everything continued to point to unrelenting Nazi party efforts to
"carry through its program against [what Hitler called] 'pigmy remnants of' resisting
organizations...." Moreover, that Hitler was likely to succeed in this undertaking
with ever greater power accruing to radical Nazis was pointed up in Dodd's mind by
the fact that Heinrich Himmler, Reichsführer for the S.S., had taken advantage of the
radical swing in internal policy during the previous six months to appropriate to himself both "armed might" and "a considerable degree of influence in forming German
social policy...." In short, by the end of 1935, Dodd was no longer hopeful that any
sort of effective German resistance could be mounted against Nazi plans.[11]

This fact alone was enough to remind Dodd just how important it was to resist Hitler abroad. And the issue was made even more poignant now by the outbreak of the Italo-Ethiopian war. With Mussolini's armies breaking into Abyssinia on October 3, Dodd believed that the response to Italian aggression would have a profound impact on German schemes: "One thing is certain here:" he wrote F.D.R. at the end of October, "the early defeat or forced withdrawal of Italy from Ethiopia would be considered a serious set-back for German autocratic-military procedure. If [on the other hand] Italy succeeds, it is the common feeling that the two dictatorships would unite upon a policy of aggression."

The fact, however, that Britain and the League at once put up a stiff show of resistance to Italy by voting sanctions did not impress Dodd as assuring Italian defeat. Indeed, to his thinking, the success or failure of Italian arms depended primarily on the United States. "…The United States," he wired Colonel House on October 27, "will save or destroy the League by its attitude on war materials.…" "…Our country may still bring the 'civilized' world to pursue peace policies," he told Roosevelt at the same time, "if it can stop all shipments of arms material.… One of the Ministers here said to me today: '…your country alone can save civilization.'"

Though Roosevelt was not sure that the United States could save civilization, he was inclined to offer at least passive resistance to Italian aggression by invoking the Neutrality Law of 1935. Halting the flow of arms and recommending an embargo on trade, the President was hoping to cut off the shipment of strategic supplies which only the Italians had been buying from the United States. It was a means, in Dodd's words, of giving "the League actual power to stop Italy." Moreover, believing that Washington had at last come alive to the dangers abroad, Dodd began pressing the administration to do more—namely, to join an oil boycott, which most people at the time believed would seriously undermine Italy's ability to make war. More than this, though, Dodd hoped that such a move would have a profound impact on the German regime: "…Certain people here would be tremendously concerned about an oil and gas boycott," he told Moore. "The Germans produce some oil from coal, and they have certain crude gasses which they are able to use for very ordinary purposes. But when it comes to airplanes, war vessels and tanks in the midst of conflict, they would be almost helpless without the importation of what the Standard and Shell Oil companies give them."[12]

If Dodd believed that such an argument, or for that matter any of his arguments for collective security, could have some influence on Moore and the State Department at large, he was sadly mistaken. With Moore, for example, the fact that they had an entirely friendly relationship and that he had been putting his point of view before the Assistant Secretary since the beginning of 1934 seemed to make no difference at all. When it came to a debate in the Department over endorsing a mandatory arms embargo favored by the isolationists or a discriminatory one allowing Roosevelt to join other nations in penalizing an aggressor, Moore gave his full support to those in the first camp. Moreover, when Roosevelt prepared to pursue a bold neutrality policy in answer to Italy's war, the Assistant Secretary urged a more cautious line. Apparently more concerned with appeasing isolationist congressmen than with responding to developments abroad, Moore gave Dodd's reports and recommendations less than careful thought.

Dodd had even less impact on the thought of career officers like Moffat and Phillips. Seeing Dodd as out of step with traditional diplomatic style or technique, both men set him down as inadequate to his task. Despite the fact that Dodd's reports were generally of a high quality, with both short- and long-range predictions usually proving correct, Moffat believed Dodd unable to keep the Department "fully informed." The trouble, as he saw it, was a lack of "power to describe" the situation in Berlin. As he stated it in his diary in March 1934, "[I] lunched with Jules Henry who read to me the French résumé of the recent German disarmament note. We had recently had a summary from our Embassy in Berlin, and while in substance the two summaries did not differ, the art with which the French telegram was drafted was a pleasure to note." Offended by Dodd's "small town" attitude toward diplomatic affairs, Moffat found stylistic reasons to ignore the substance of what Dodd said.

It was much the same with Phillips. After visiting Berlin in December 1935, he complained of the fact that Dodd's living arrangements were "scarcely ambassadorial" and that unlike Ambassador Jesse Straus in Paris, who took "infinite pains with regard to every detail," Dodd seemed unable to give his Embassy the kind of influence or standing it should have. More important, though, Dodd seemed to be out of touch with Nazi officials, and, as Phillips confided to his diary and later told F.D.R., "what in the world is the use of having an ambassador who refuses to speak to the government to which he is accredited?"

Under normal circumstances, Phillips was, of course, perfectly right. But normal diplomatic conditions did not prevail in Berlin. The representative of an isolationist state in a country contemptuous of American ways, Dodd had almost nothing to discuss with the regime, from the German point of view as well as his. Moreover, greater intimacy with Nazi officials was little calculated to assure more accurate information about affairs in the Reich. Had Phillips been able to compare Dodd's work with that of François-Poncet, a master of the diplomatic art and "the Führer's favorite ambassador," he would have seen that personal relationships were no guarantee of astute reporting. Or, more to the point, had Phillips been inclined systematically to compare Dodd's dispatches with those sent by Messersmith, he would have found less difference than he probably thought existed. But as things stood, Phillips apparently never had the time to make a careful study of even Dodd's dispatches. For, according to Dodd, when he and the staff gave the Under-Secretary "up-to-date information about all phases of German activity" during his visit to Berlin, Phillips "was amazed and distressed, although," in Dodd's words, "all this information had been going to the Department for two whole years." While Phillips himself observed that "…as a result of these morning talks…I had learned a good deal about the German situation," he believed that it was the kind of information he "could not have learned from documents in Washington."

Yet probably more to the point was the fact that as Under-Secretary of State and occasionally acting Secretary of State, Phillips held a variety of obligations which simply would not allow him the leisure to peruse the thousands of pages of telegrams and reports coming into the State Department from the American diplomatic missions abroad. Indeed, during Dodd's ambassadorial service, the Berlin Embassy alone sent Washington about one thousand dispatches a year, of which some were as long as one hundred and fifty or two hundred pages. It is probably fair to conclude, then, as Dodd himself did after this meeting with Phillips, that "no high official can master all the reports as they pile up there" in Washington.

It is regrettable that Phillips and Dodd did not openly discuss Dodd's intelligence-gathering technique. For not only might it have set Phillips' mind at rest about the need for personal contacts with Nazi chiefs, it might also have led the two men into a constructive discussion of a legitimate failing in Dodd's reportorial work. Having committed himself to Embassy economies which might become a model for other American missions and help the government bring its overall spending under control, Dodd reduced the flow of telegrams to Washington to a point that occasionally deprived the Department of immediate details about developments in Berlin. Since he compelled the State Department to wait ten days sometimes for diplomatic dispatches containing information it should no doubt have had at once, Dodd perhaps should have been persuaded to be freer with his telegraphic reports. To judge from a long letter of explanation Dodd sent Moore in the fall of 1935, it is likely that Phillips could have had a more than worthwhile discussion with him about all sides of his reporting. "As to the telegram deficiency here," Dodd wrote,

I must say that it is my fault. When I came here I found three and four page telegrams going back to Washington the contents of which could easily have been put into one or two hundred words. My first effort was to get men to write briefly and succinctly. In that I have not succeeded. My second was to send only real information, not rumors. Since a dictator never confides to his officials items of real policy, information can not be had, in spite of the seven-page telegrams I have seen from other representatives of our people in Europe. Neither von Neurath nor Schacht here can [or will] give information; others are even less able to do so. The press pick up all that can be had and a lot more. They are most friendly and loyal, in spite of the fact I am a mere school teacher, and they bring all to me. When it seems that they have real facts, I always have a telegram sent. When I see an official, German or British, Italian or French, I try to put his talk together briefly and send it. I also ask Mr. [John C.] White [Counselor of Embassy] to see people every day and night, also [Frank] Lee [First Secretary of Embassy], and get what seems worth telegraphing. But I do not send what I think I should have to contradict in a week. This is my explanation. It may not be what the Department likes.[13]

Yet if it were not, this still did not leave Dodd feeling that the Department would give little thought to what he said. In December, for example, when the President wrote him that an effective foreign policy required a discriminatory rather than a mandatory neutrality bill and when the British and the French cut the ground from under their own position and that of the League with the conciliatory Hoare-Laval offer to Italy to end the war, Dodd pressed the State Department to support the President's view and to follow a "strategy" assuring "American pressure for peace." More specifically, Dodd used a conversation with Phillips, two telegrams to Hull, and a letter to Moore to continue to stress the need for some kind of American effort to head off war.[14]

Yet whatever response he might evoke from the Department, Dodd saw it as secondary to any influence he might exert on F.D.R. It was the President after all who would have to lead the way. Between October 1935 and January 1936, therefore, he did all he could to encourage Roosevelt in his peace drive. After the President's initiation of his anti-Italian neutrality stand, Dodd praised him for his efforts and reminded him that "while the domestic situation must be your fundamental problem, world peace is not less important." Moreover, when the President answered with assurances of his own awareness of German designs and his eagerness for a discriminatory embargo law which he could apply against aggressors, Dodd apprised him of the shortcomings in the Hoare-Laval idea and expressed the hope that "you may be able to rouse our people to the dangers that lie ahead—next year perhaps a decisive year in many parts of the world." Finally, when the President found confirmation for his "previous feeling of extreme disquiet in regard to European and Asiatic affairs" in Dodd's letter and when he voiced his disquiet in his annual State of the Union message, telling Americans that "a point has been reached where the people of the Americas must take cognizance of…a situation which has in it many of the elements that lead to the tragedy of general war," Dodd wired him his "congratulations." "I am sure the people of the country are with you," Dodd advised him. "The McReynolds proposal to Congress [for a discriminatory neutrality bill] is given front page publicity all over Germany. If your address receives similar publicity tomorrow the effect is going to be great in spite of all limitations of free speech and I believe the whole of Europe is going to be deeply moved in the direction of peace."

If Roosevelt were not as optimistic as Dodd, explaining that "I do not anticipate much of a response within the autocratic nations," he nevertheless appreciated Dodd's enthusiastic response and in general accepted the validity of what his ambassador had to say. At the very least he held a rapport with Dodd and a positive estimate of his worth which the State Department lacked. Indeed, in September 1935 when Moore raised the question with him of a leave for Dodd in 1936, the President expressed the hope that Dodd would not "consider resigning," saying "I need him in Berlin." To be sure, Roosevelt may have been reluctant to change ambassadors in the face of the approaching Italo-Ethiopian war, or he may have recalled how difficult it had been in the first place to find a good man for the post; but whatever part these considerations played in his thinking, it is clear that he did not accept Moffat's contention that Dodd "would be hopeless if war should break out." Moreover, despite the fact that Phillips asked him in January 1936 to replace Dodd with a more understanding representative, Roosevelt made no effort to make a change. In short, though the President may have found Dodd a bit too idealistic, he appears to have considered him a more than adequate representative who fully understood the drift of German and European affairs.[15]

The fact that Roosevelt managed to communicate this attitude to Dodd undoubtedly served to boost his Ambassador's spirits. For by the beginning of 1936 there was almost nothing else either within or outside of Germany to give Dodd cheer. The Hitler regime was solidly ensconced; Nazi ideas everywhere held sway. A survey of political conditions in the first month of the new year showed him that church opposition was weakening under the stress of internal divisions, that Jewish persecutions were going forward with less and less "external evidences" of which foreigners could complain, and that compulsory service in the *Deutsches Jungvolk* for children between the ages of 10 and 14 meant "conscription of the entire German youth" into Nazi ranks. Moreover, attendance at the Nazi propaganda film *Unsere Wehrmacht* revealed a huge audience enthusiastically applauding scenes of "vast army fields with tanks and machine guns operating and soldiers falling to the ground…; great parades of heavy trucks and big cannon; air attacks with hundreds of flying machines dropping bombs on a city. I could hardly endure the scene," Dodd noted in his diary, "and what seemed to me the brutal performances."

Only in international affairs could Dodd see any chance for a reproach to Hitler's designs. And in January with both Foreign Ministers Hoare and Laval forced from office by the outcry against their plan and with new moves underfoot to punish

Italian aggression, Dodd momentarily envisioned an effective alignment against German schemes. But when the likelihood of meaningful action disappeared by the end of the month, Dodd could only report that German fear of League power was practically dead and that the entire Abyssinian episode had "rather stimulated" Germany's "adventurous spirit" than dampened it down.[16]

By the beginning of February, then, in light of all that had happened, Dodd could no longer put any faith in collective action to restrain Berlin. Indeed, despite the fact that the Franco-Russian agreement was just coming before the French Chamber for ratification and that Britain and France were supposedly coordinating plans in case Hitler responded to the Chamber's ratification with a reoccupation of the demilitarized Rhineland zone—his just response, he said, to France's violation of the Locarno Pact—Dodd accurately foresaw that the "Encirclement Powers" were offering no more than "an idle threat [which] would only be to the advantage of the extremist element in Germany and…would only further 'inflate Germany towards a more adventurous attitude and a contemptuous feeling towards the other European states.'"

"The only policy toward Germany," therefore, which Dodd could now "view with any hope," was one of "deflation," or channeling "German energy and the German dynamic spirit…into as constructive a direction as can be devised. This, however," Dodd explained, "would be at a price" paid by the "Possession Powers," Britain and France, in the form of colonies and a revised Treaty of Versailles. And though "only extreme and forceful measures" might ultimately serve Britain and France, Dodd believed conciliatory proposals temporarily worth a try. For, after all, Germany, by contrast with Italy, was momentarily quiet or passive toward foreign affairs, with von Neurath and the Foreign Office saying concessions might bring Hitler back to the League.

Yet if Dodd thought it worthwhile for Britain and France to respond to what "appears to be an opportunity to take Hitler's May 21st [1935, peace] speech at its face value and explore that other [conciliatory] policy which was not tried in 1918…," he was also aware of how little could actually be expected from this idea. For with Germany threatening to use France's Russian treaty or so-called breach of Locarno as "an excuse for military occupation of the demilitarized zone," with Britain "absolutely committed to great armament" after repeated unsuccessful invitations to Hitler to join them in disarmament talks, with rumors circulating that Hitler was in failing health and that Göring, the "most warlike of all the leaders," was about to take his place, and with the American Congress approving neutrality legislation which left Roosevelt even less control over foreign policy than before, Dodd was hard pressed to convince anyone that Europe was ready for reasonable talks.[17]

Still, having lost all faith in the ability of the democracies to take a collective stand, Dodd hoped Britain and France would gamble on Hitler's willingness to negotiate differences and keep the peace. Hence, when the Führer marched his troops into the Rhineland on March 7 and simultaneously announced "new and far-reaching peace proposals," Dodd was inclined to take Hitler's pacifist language more seriously than before. In contrast with his reaction to Hitler's major peace address of the previous May, Dodd was ready to describe this latest speech as "impressive" and as "a sort of compromise" between the desire of the Foreign Office to "bring Germany back into the European diplomatic arena" and the demands of the radicals for the restoration to Germany of her "equality." Moreover, during the first week of the crisis, Dodd was ready to believe that the Foreign Office might persuade the Führer to send representatives to a League Council session, "confirm[ing] by action the constructive proposals in Hitler's speech," that the Germans had "a practical plan for bilateral demilitarization of the Franco-German frontier," and that Hitler might be provoked into military action by French failure "to consider the constructive aspects of the Hitler proposals...." Like a large section of the British public which "was inclined to pay more attention to...[Hitler's] specious projects for the future than to the manner in which he had torn up the pledges of the past," Dodd hoped that this crisis, in the language of the London *Times,* would provide "A Chance to Rebuild."

Probably of equal weight in Dodd's attitude, though, was a growing bias against France, which consisted of the belief that a nation which was so quick to give in to Mussolini's aggression should not expect the world, and especially the English who tried to hold the line against Italy, to rush to its aid when Germany took what was more rightfully hers. "Frenchmen here and in Paris," Dodd wrote the President, "seemed to have no real understanding of their blunders.... If she [France] approved the Italian seizure of territory, how could she complain if Germany re-seized her historic Rhine country?"[18]

Even after the middle of March, therefore, when Dodd acknowledged that German reoccupation of the Rhineland meant an inability of French arms to march quickly to the aid of her Central and Eastern European allies and that Hitler was likely to follow one or two years of peaceful appearances with the application of Germany's "medieval claims to the Danube zone all the way to the Black Sea," Dodd continued to hope that something might result from multilateral talks. And even after von Neurath and Schacht revealed their extreme satisfaction with the events of March 7, leading Dodd to complain that "it is impossible to trust even the most conservative members of the government," and the German Foreign Office rejected proposals for negotiations from the Locarno Powers as "entirely unacceptable," Dodd was still willing to counsel talks. The response to the German counter-proposals of March 31, he advised the State Department, "should rest on a different ground than that of sincerity. We feel," Dodd explained, "that the best present chance is to call Hitler's bluff for peace, since the powers concerned do not seem willing or capable of calling his bluff for war.... If, after negotiations, it appears that Hitler is not bluffing for peace and is working for a harmonious settlement of European problems, then well and good; Europe would be on its way out of its present major difficulties. If, on the other hand, after a few months' consideration and negotiation in a real spirit of equality, it is found that Hitler's proposals are a sham and only a façade for conquest then European opinion and indeed world opinion will have a sounder basis for common agreement and doubtless common action and meanwhile little will be lost."[19]

Dodd himself, however, could hardly take this analysis seriously; he knew all too well that Europe was on a different course. And so when Roosevelt asked him in a letter on March 16 to send "immediate word" if "events should by chance get to the point where a gesture, an offer or a formal statement by me would, in your judgment, make for peace," Dodd could only prophesy a continuing downward trend.

France, he told the President, "is now on a definite decline," with her Russian peace pact and her Eastern European alliances unlikely to preserve her from domination by German might. Likewise, having failed to co-operate with the United States against Japan in 1931 and having failed more recently to halt Mussolini's drive, England was "beginning a similar decline." Finally, with Hitler further strengthened by a nearly unanimous plebiscite vote in favor of his Rhineland move and Germany likely to grow from sixty-seven to eighty million people "when Austria (including part of Czechoslovakia) is annexed," all Europe would soon find itself under German control. "If Woodrow Wilson's bones do not turn in the Cathedral grave," Dodd lamented, "then bones never turn in graves. Possibly you can do something, but from reports of Congressional attitudes, I have grave doubts. So many men, including my friend Beard, think absolute isolation a coming paradise."

If Dodd needed any confirmation of this attitude, it came to him from George Messersmith, who visited Berlin on April 6. Unfettered by an anti-French bias or an inclination to blink the facts of European affairs for even a moment, Messersmith caught the precise drift of events. "The most important single basic factor disturbing Europe today," he told the State Department on March 9, "is that facts are not being generally faced and given the interpretation which common sense dictates and met with the action which elementary prudence obviously requires." As evidence of this, Messersmith pointed to the fact that the Locarno Powers were seriously entertaining Hitler's offer to follow his march into the Rhineland with "the establishment of a demilitarized zone on both sides of the western boundary.... The height of cynicism," Messersmith said, "is reached by this offer of Hitler Germany, which must be appraised at what it really is—a step by which the defense of the western powers toward German aggression in all directions is to be weakened. It is known," Messersmith added, "that National Socialist Germany holds as one of its primary doctrines that agreements are only entered into as means to an end, and that they must be denounced ruthlessly when they have served their purpose." Moreover, it was Messersmith's conviction that Hitler's latest peace speech was another fraud, "that the words of the peace offer mean nothing and that it [the speech] was full of veiled threats in every direction." In the face of all this, Messersmith could see "only one way to deal with the German regime of today, and this is to meet its brutal ruthless action by an equally determined stand. It is the only language which that regime understands," Messersmith concluded, "as it is the only language which it can talk."

Though Dodd could not agree with Messersmith on every point in their conversation on April 6, disagreeing in particular about what Mussolini's response to a German move against Austria might be, he did come away from their talk feeling that he and Messersmith were "not of a really different view." To judge from his diary notes of the next several days, this was very much the case. For instead of entries about negotiations and possible sincerity from the German side, Dodd could only recall his earlier estimates of German methods and plans, repeating the fears he had expressed in his most recent letter to F.D.R.[20]

Although things were as bleak as they seemed and Roosevelt, as Dodd believed, stood more or less hopeless before it all, there were still symbolic gestures and indirect criticisms which Dodd wished to encourage and voice at every turn. Having added an occasional address in praise of democracy to those offered during his first months in Berlin, Dodd believed it more important than ever for an American representative to speak his mind. In a speech before an American Chamber of Commerce gathering on April 17, therefore, Dodd pointedly lauded Thomas Jefferson as a great American who opposed wars, favored low tariffs, and fought America's slave system. The fact that a selfish minority defeated Jefferson's objectives, Dodd said, led to widespread suffering in the United States. And so, Dodd urged upon his audience, "these facts illustrate the dangerous performances of minority leaders who think more of personal and group interests than people's interests."[21]

In the same spirit and at the same time, Dodd helped arrange a "hearty reception" in the United States for Dr. Hugo Eckner, "the one outstanding authority for Zeppelin aircraft," and a man at odds with the regime. Having refused to meet Goebbels' demands for election work in the March plebiscite campaign, Eckner was privately vilified and publicly denied attention in the press. To celebrate Eckner's "ability and genius" and to counter the tactics of an authoritarian regime, Dodd urged official attention for Eckner when he flew his Zeppelin to the United States. Taking Dodd's proposal to heart, Roosevelt invited Eckner to the White House and, according to *The New York Times,* helped restore him to favor in Berlin: apparently unwilling to forego associating Eckner's achievements and prestige with the "new" Germany, the Nazis once more permitted accounts of him in the German press.[22]

Yet gestures were not enough to satisfy Dodd; he badly wished some more direct involvement in democracy's defense. And since the only prospect for this involved another trip to the United States, Dodd arranged to leave Berlin for three months beginning on April 18. The attraction at home, of course, was the election of 1936; in Dodd's words, "one of the great decisive campaigns of our history." Indeed, as he reflected on what he had seen in America on his last visit and as he watched further developments from Berlin, he became increasingly convinced that the very survival of democracy depended on Roosevelt's return to the White House for another four years. Roosevelt, he remarked in July 1935, was "the only man who can hold liberal groups together and thwart the extremists of left and right." It was the extremists on the right Dodd most feared. With the Supreme Court applying the conservative principles of John Marshall, "no state or Congress has the right to limit or regulate the claims of property holders," and with "big business leaders" aiming "to rule the nation against majorities," Dodd became increasingly worried that selfish businessmen might push the country into a class war by the defeat of F.D.R.

Dodd was not alone in his fears. Since the decisions of the highest court were making it appear that "regulated capitalism was impossible, then," New Dealers were asking themselves, "what could ensue but the anarchy of reaction, leading in the end to the violence of revolution? The impasse," Arthur Schlesinger, Jr., has written, "threatened the future of democracy in America." And Roosevelt himself, eager to assure his liberal friends that he was mindful of the problem, announced in his January State of the Union message that "the struggle to return the government to the people had 'earned the hatred of entrenched greed.' Now the nation's former masters," the President warned, "were conspiring to recapture their power [and]…'serve discredited special interests.'" Even without his opening remarks about the dangers from abroad, these words were enough to have Dodd wire his approval of a "masterly and unanswerable address."[23]

Besides lending what aid he could to Roosevelt's campaign, Dodd was also determined to take time out at home for a rest. "I am going direct to Virginia," he wrote his family on April 19, "in the hope of adding to and prolonging my days." Sixty-six years old in the previous October, he was increasingly feeling the strain of the Berlin post. His headaches, backaches, neuritis, colitis, loss of appetite, and sleeplessness caused almost constant complaints. "My food does not digest properly," he wrote on board ship, "headaches spread over the nerve connections between the stomach, shoulders and brain until sleep is almost impossible." The rest, exercise, and freedom from strain which he could only find at his farm were reason enough to make him come home. Within four days after his arrival at Round Hill, "there was not a touch of aches of any kind."[24]

In addition to his rest in Virginia, Dodd found time in his three-month stay in America to discuss private and public affairs with the President and to lecture in the University of Chicago summer quarter. Aside from the fact that Roosevelt asked him to continue at his post "for some time to come" and expressed the desire to apply "a definite reform scheme for the Service...[as] soon as he is reelected," Dodd apparently found their meeting uneventful, making no reference to it in his diary and drawing no specific memorandum of what was said. By contrast, his return to Chicago revived strong feelings: first, of affection for the university he had served for twenty-five years, and secondly, of distress with Hutchins' "scheme of limiting departments and avoiding departmental selection of professors...." Three years in a country systematically destroying the freedom of its universities, or turning them into "mere technical academies," left Dodd feeling that the University of Chicago with its "many real, truth-seeking professors and many promising young scholars" was "the most appealing" to him of any in the world. And because this was so, he "sometimes" wished that he "might again bring pressure to bear" against those qualities of the Chicago system which he now deemed incorrect.[25]

Whatever his inclination to pick up where he had left off at the university in 1933, Dodd did not lose sight of the fact that he had primarily returned to America in order to voice his support of F.D.R. By the end of June when he arrived in Chicago, he felt more than ever the need to give Roosevelt what aid he could. With the earliest polls showing surprising Republican strength and with a great majority of the country's newspapers ranged against F.D.R., Dodd, like other Roosevelt supporters, continued to feel that the "present struggle in this country...[is] most serious," and that unless the President could win re-election by a wide margin, he would not be able to reduce the number of unemployed, which remained close to eight million, or "to do what his many experiments show must be done," which would likely mean the collapse of democracy in the United States. And "the failure of democracy in our country," he told Josephus Daniels, "would almost certainly mean a reversion to semi-medievalism all over the western world." With all this in mind, therefore, Dodd did not hesitate to arrange several speaking engagements for himself, which while ostensibly non-partisan were calculated to help the President's election campaign.[26]

Dodd thought he saw at least one other way to support the President's case. Distressed by the opposition to Roosevelt from some former progressives, Dodd tried to persuade at least two of them, Newton Baker and William Allen White, to vote for F.D.R. But they were not easily moved: put off by the experimentalism or intellectual inconsistency of the New Deal, horrified at the way in which Roosevelt intervened in the economy through the machinery of the state and catered to special interests of every kind, men like Baker and White saw the President encouraging class warfare, centralized power, and an end to constitutional restraints. As Baker put it in a reply to Dodd, "the bread and circus appeal which is at present being made to the American voter to reelect the President, the class warfare which the present administration has declared, and the fundamental lack of morality of the adminis- tration's policies…are just a few of the things which make me sad, but they are all much too serious and complicated to be more than adverted to in a letter, and I do not point them out to ask any comment from you because I realize that in Berlin you are a long way from the sort of evidence which is daily thrust upon me.…"[27]

To be sure, Dodd had no great understanding of what the New Deal was about. Occasionally urging the administration to cure the depression with free trade and back-to-the-land policies, he obviously had little feel for the complicated monetary and economic theories applied by Roosevelt to restore the nation's economic health. Moreover, had Dodd been in the United States, he would no doubt also have been troubled by the New Deal's "disturbing adventures in federal power." Though it is possible that Dodd, on the order of other old Wilsonians like Albert Burleson and Edgar Lee Masters, might have turned against F.D.R. after unsuccessfully urging him toward a briefer, clearer program such as free trade, it is more likely that he would have followed old loyalties and voted for the Democratic party's man.

But as things stood, of course, Dodd was not in the United States and so he had other, more forceful reasons to support F.D.R. The fact that he was part of the administration cannot be overlooked, for this allowed him a much different view of the President than the one held by Baker and White. Where the latter, for example, saw Roosevelt as profligate, spending government monies at an unheard-of rate, Dodd knew him as a responsible executive eager to economize. Having consistently shown himself sympathetic to Dodd's appeals for greater efficiency and economy in the Foreign Service, Roosevelt made a fresh expression of interest in early 1936: under heavy pressure from Morgenthau in the spring to reduce government spending, the President invited Moore and Hull to discuss a number of Dodd's proposals for reducing Foreign Service costs. More important than this, though, Dodd could not share the progressive fear of a Rooseveltian drive for dictatorial power. Listening to the President privately declare his distress with Nazi rule, hearing Roosevelt publicly attack economic autocracy and "economic royalists," and recalling his three years in Berlin where he saw totalitarian government as a fact of life, Dodd could find no ground for comparison between Hitler and F.D.R.[28]

But it was hardly necessary for a progressive to have lived in Germany to appre- ciate this. And so in the final analysis, the difference between the Bakers and the Dodds, as Otis Graham, Jr., suggests, was probably more a matter of instinct and experience than anything else. Schooled in law and keenly attracted to "a sort of mental tidiness, a desire to think carefully and have the theory straight before act- ing," Baker was profoundly offended by the New Deal's intellectual chaos. Dodd, by contrast, though strongly committed to Jeffersonian principles and a systematic approach to government and life, was a more intuitive and flexible man who valued insight and style as much as theory and logic. Moreover, his long residence in Chicago, during which he gained a firsthand acquaintance with problems of urban life and developed a healthy respect for New Nationalists like Charles Merriam and social welfare advocates like Jane Addams and Graham Taylor, no doubt made him more sympathetic to government involvement in urban problems than the average Wilsonian. At the very least, Dodd's career as an academic in Chicago made it more difficult for him to ignore the harsh realities of twentieth-century America than it was for a Baker who pursued a successful corporate law practice in the twenties with the feeling that progressivism had completed its work when it reorganized municipal and state governments. In the final analysis, then, it was instinct and experience which allowed Dodd to give and prevented Baker from giving enthusiastic support to a president who subordinated abstract principle to human need.

XIV

Four Years' Service Is Enough

THREE MONTHS IN the United States, including six weeks in the Blue Ridge Mountains of Virginia, refreshed Dodd for his return to Berlin. But no amount of rest and quiet could have fully prepared him for the unpleasant events which now lay ahead. Nazi victories and promises of yet greater Nazi strength soon had Dodd complaining that "nothing is more oppressive to a democrat...than the situation in Europe." And like his friend Limburg-Stirum, the Dutch Minister, he was soon ready to believe "we shall probably never have another happy day in our lives."

Nothing contributed so much to this mood as the outbreak of the Spanish Civil War with its likely consequences. Beginning on July 17, it quickly developed into a symbolic fight between fascists and antifascists around the world. Dodd saw little hope of success for his side. With Britain so pacific and France so divided that neither seemed likely to undertake effective aid to republican Spain, Dodd at once envisioned Mussolini and Hitler intervening to establish a third totalitarian state. And this, Dodd wrote Moore, would be the fulfillment of "my sad prophecies these last eighteen months about Europe's steady move toward a solid dictatorship," which in due time would threaten the United States. "The idea of a European dictatorship against the last great democracy in the world!" It was a fear millions of other Americans would come to share.[1]

But the Spanish Civil War was only one of several unhappy facts greeting Dodd on his return. Asked by Roosevelt to let him know "what would happen if Hitler were personally and secretly asked by me to outline the limit of German foreign objectives during…a ten year period, and to state whether or not he would have any sympathy with a general limitation of armaments' proposal," Dodd began by approaching Hjalmar Schacht, who "spoke for the first time almost with bitterness" and violence about the United States. Locked in a losing argument with Hitler and Göring over the speed of German rearmament and its threat to the economy, Schacht was apparently convinced by the summer of 1936 that Germany could not last out the year without outside help, or, more specifically, greater supplies of raw material and foreign exchange. The fact, therefore, that Washington had applied countervailing or increased duties to subsidized German exports, forcing Schacht to abandon the procedures which had provoked this retaliation in the first place, and the fact that German trade plans with Brazil had been undermined by Brazilian-American trade talks helped Dodd understand Schacht's anti-American outburst. But it was of little comfort next to the fact that he could neither get "a quiet answer" to Roosevelt's inquiry or shake the feeling that Schacht was now willing to see Germany "resist to the limit, perhaps even fight the United States."

Moreover, to complete this picture of so-called reasonable or conservative men in the government falling completely under Hitler's sway, Dodd had only to visit the Foreign Office, where he found for the first time "a large portrait of Hitler" in the waiting room and another one on Dieckhoff's desk. Since Dieckhoff also spoke as if he wished a fascist government in Spain, Dodd could only conclude that Foreign Office officials who formerly showed themselves "friendly to democratic institutions and resentful that innocent Jews were being so roughly treated" had now entirely gone over to the Führer's side.[2]

If all this were not enough to make Dodd more than uncomfortable in Berlin, he now also had before him the picture of incredible Nazi dynamism and strength put on display during the Olympic Games. "In the history of the Nazi regime," François-Poncet recalls, "the celebration of the Olympic games in Berlin in August 1936 illustrated a great moment, a climax of sorts, if not the apotheosis of Hitler and his Third Reich. Hitler had impressed himself upon the consciousness of Europe as an extraordinary personage.…Crowned heads, princes, and illustrious guests thronged to Berlin, eager to meet this prophetic being who apparently held the fate of Europe in his hand and to observe the Germany which he had transformed and galvanized in his irresistible grip." And though Dodd might come away from a magnificent Goebbels reception remembering that the host was a man "who had helped in June 30, 1934, to murder Germans," he was compelled to admit that most foreigners were more forgetful and readily taken in.

In the face of all this, it is not surprising that Dodd now tended to see some things as worse than they were. Ferdinand Mayer, his Counselor of Embassy, had taken it upon himself to cultivate Göring in the hope of negotiating a new commercial treaty with Berlin; Messersmith and Ambassador John Cudahy to Poland had taken Dodd's long residence in America as an invitation to put themselves forward for his post; and former Ambassador Jacob Gould Schurman had apparently been "captivated" by Nazi chiefs and persuaded "to stimulate Republican opposition [to the President] among Germans" in the United States—these events impressed Dodd as a signal that Foreign Service people were generally favorable toward "German-Italian domination of Spain" and a victory of "privileged capitalists" over F.D.R. Moreover, the fact that the French were so politically divided and that Schacht went to Paris for talks was enough to convince Dodd that Léon Blum's Popular Front government would shortly give way to a fascist regime.

Still, these exaggerated reactions to events were the exception rather than the rule. With a tenacity developed during years of fighting reform battles against impossible odds, with an "excellent group of [Embassy] workers" and newspaper people like Norman Ebbutt, Louis Lochner, Sigrid Schultz, William Shirer, and Otto Tolischus to feed him news, and with a native ability to cull the central theme from almost any mass of fact, Dodd was able to stay at his post and send the State Department accurate estimates of German affairs.[3]

Jewish persecutions and church-state controversies showed no signs of abating or taking a fundamentally different course. The introduction in August of a policy denying passports to Jews had Dodd immediately writing the Department that it was an attempt, first, "to prevent Jews from following their capital abroad and enjoying its use"; secondly, "to limit the emigration of elements who would certainly be hostile to Germany once they left the country"; and finally, to lay the groundwork for the introduction of new travel documents which would recognize the division of the population into the two classes of citizens created by the Nuremberg laws. As for the immediate future, Dodd reported that "the Jewish population awaits with fear and trembling the termination of the Olympic period which has vouchsafed them a certain respite against molestation, although," he was quick to add, "it may be doubted whether the National Socialists will be quite so foolish as to spoil the good impression upon foreign opinion made by the management of the games by an immediate resumption of the more spectacular anti-Jewish activities." With regard to church affairs, Dodd reported a temporary lull brought on by both the Olympics and the illness of Church Minister Hans Kerrl. Both conditions, Dodd explained, accounted for recent inactivity on the part of the secret police as well as the leniency of the government in its response to a manifesto read in Confessional Front churches denouncing Nazi interference in religious concerns. As with the government's anti-Jewish policy, though, the post-Olympic period was to bring a renewed offensive against ecclesiastical opposition to the regime.

Similarly, though Dodd confidentially predicted the ultimate, disturbing Italo-German impact on the Spanish Civil War, he still felt compelled to trace the tortuous course by which it would proceed. Dodd cabled the State Department on August 17 "that the real danger lies in Italy rather than in Germany and that from the former will come any lead towards intervention...." Moreover, in the face of the German announcement on the 24th that she would join other European states in embargoing arms to Spain, Dodd advised Washington to look beyond this declaration to the fact that "the German Government would look with apprehension on a Communist Spain, which after all is a western power and influential with respect to the uncertain conditions in France."[4]

More important, though, Dodd began telling the State Department that the Civil War, with its threat of communism in Spain, was driving Hitler and Mussolini into each other's arms. Indeed, appreciating just what Hitler himself saw at the beginning of September 1936, Dodd was able to write Washington that "if it is true, as many believe, that Italy has definitely limited her imperial aspirations, for the time being at least, to the Mediterranean and is willing to see the other Fascist imperialism, Germany, control Central Europe, there would be no reason why these powers, under the pressure of the Soviet menace...should not join to press for unity in Central and Southeastern Europe and the creation of a solid defensive position in the middle of the Continent."

To Dodd's vocational, if not political, satisfaction, he soon began to find a good bit of evidence to bear out what he said. Preoccupation at the Nuremberg Congress with the Bolshevik menace, or Nazism's "defense of Europe against Bolshevism," he wired Hull on September 11, "consorts readily with the consolidation of Eastern Europe under German leadership...." The anti-Bolshevik drive, in other words, was providing the basis for a German-led fascist bloc. And though there was no proof of a "definite German-Italian tie-up," it was clear that such an arrangement was fundamental to such a bloc and was already in the works. An identical Italian-German response to a forthcoming five-power Locarno conference, evidence of military discussions in Rome between high-ranking German and Italian officers, and a visit to Mussolini by Minister of Justice Hans Frank and Nazi Youth Leader Baldur von Schirach, during which friendly speeches were exchanged, gave indications of at least a mutual desire to co-operate in a joint enterprise.

But if this were not enough to show that Hitler was beginning a new diplomatic offensive, Dodd was able to point to parallel economic and military measures calculated to strengthen Germany's position in international affairs. The proclamation of a Four-Year Plan by which "German skill, German chemistry and German mining" were to render the Reich "as independent as possible from foreign raw materials and food stuffs" and the unpublicized decision to expand the army from 24 to 36 divisions

impressed Dodd as attempts to give Germany the strongest possible hand in dealings with the Locarno states. Further, since Hitler's future diplomatic course in part
depended upon the extent of his power at home, Dodd thought it of interest to the
State Department to assess "the [current] state of feeling among the German people
toward a possible armed conflict." And here it seemed safe to assume, as Hitler himself well knew, that "an overwhelming majority of the German people" stood ready
to follow the Führer "in any venture he might undertake, whether it be one of outright conquest or one cloaked in the guise of repelling an invader."

But because the Italo-German alliance was still vague and because the Four-Year
Plan was no more than an improvisation devoid of substantive schemes, Dodd saw
no immediate threat of war. Moreover, with news of polls showing that Roosevelt
would gain reelection by a wide margin, Dodd began to feel less pessimistic about
the ultimate course of events, or at least optimistic enough to believe that Roosevelt
could use his second term to organize democratic states into an effective bulwark
against fascist plans. To aid the President in this work Dodd asked Moore at the
beginning of October whether he could discuss foreign problems with the Senate
Committee on Foreign Affairs. "I suppose not," Dodd himself at once said, "yet
I feel that a confidential discussion of the situation might help."

Settling instead for a long letter of explanation to F.D.R., Dodd urged the President
to use the next four years to strike out on a new path. Explaining first of all that
Europe might avoid a war if Hitler and Mussolini were given all they wanted, namely
continental control, Dodd asked the President to consider what kind of a peace that
would be. Answering his own question, Dodd explained that "anyone who knows
the sophomoric and egotistic mentalities of these men and their chief supporters can
hardly fail to forecast the coming state of European civilization," which was another
way of saying that German-Italian domination of Europe equaled "the breakdown of
democracy in all Europe" and "a disaster for the people" of the United States. "One
thing," then, Dodd saw as certain: "…modern civilization is in grave danger,
and…the cooperation of the United States with European democracies is the only
hope we have." Though Dodd had no answer to the question of how Roosevelt could
"lead our people to a correct understanding of things," he believed it incumbent
upon him to try. For only then could he "get the great nations to see things as they
are and apply their coercive power to any leader who wishes to go back to the
fifteenth-century morals! That would be what Henry IV of France tried to do, what
Jefferson hoped for in 1807 and what Wilson almost accomplished in 1918–19."[5]

In the meantime, though, Dodd recognized that events would not wait on F.D.R.
Though Franco's armies had not yet vanquished the Republic, they seemed on the
verge of capturing Madrid and gaining Italian recognition of their existence as the
legitimately constituted government of Spain. Secondly, though between Rome

and Berlin there was "a fundamental mutual distrust if not indeed an active rivalry in jockeying for position among the Danubian and Balkan states," it was clear by the end of October that Italy and Germany had reached a definite rapprochement, or formed an "axis," in Mussolini's words, around which other nations might strive for peace. Thirdly, the fact that Hitler was now spending most of his time at Berchtesgaden was "portentous" of some new surprise move by this "eccentric and instinctively clever and audacious lawmaker." Indeed, Hitler, Dodd warned, might use his freshly won alliance with Mussolini to move against Czechoslovakia, the "one situation in Central Europe where Italy and Germany could happily combine" and strike a blow against the U.S.S.R. Fourthly, the fact that Hitler saw fit to join Mussolini on November 18 in recognizing the Franco government before it captured Madrid impressed Dodd as signifying that the Führer meant to go all out in assuring a fascist government in Spain, a decision which increased the likelihood of a wider war. Finally, the fact that Germany and Japan were about to announce an anti-Comintern Pact convinced Dodd that "if the time ever should come when Japanese assistance would be desirable against Russia, that situation would work out so automatically for the best interest of both Germany and Japan that there is no necessity meanwhile to have an alliance or [public] understanding to this effect...."

Yet despite all this, Dodd continued to hope that Roosevelt could and would do something about the fascist threat. To be sure, the President's call for an embargo on arms and munitions to Spain was hardly evidence that he planned to support the Republic against Franco's revolt. Nor did Roosevelt's answer to his appeal of October 19 give Dodd much reason to think that the President planned any bold strokes. "I am off in a week to, I hope, Buenos Aires," he wrote on November 9. "That visit will have little practical or immediate effect in Europe but at least the forces of example will help if the knowledge of it can be spread down to the masses of the people in Germany and Italy. Incidentally," the President concluded, "I think the results [of the national elections] last Tuesday may have made the German and Italian populace a little envious of democratic methods."[6]

Still, Dodd found reason to believe that Roosevelt might be willing to go beyond such limited means to save the peace. His advocacy of an embargo, after all, was primarily an effort to co-operate with England and France in heading off a general or world war. His idea of an inquiry to Hitler, newspaper reports that he was thinking of an international peace conference after his re-election, as well as the possibility that he would use his attendance at the Buenos Aires meeting to "organize all American peoples against Fascist Europe" led Dodd to think that Roosevelt might be persuaded to announce for "an economic boycott of any nation that precipitates war," or to turn the inter-American conference into a world peace conclave.

That either measure would in fact prove effective was something Dodd felt no one could assure. But he certainly believed the measures worth trying, especially the suggestion of a conference, which he saw the Germans as almost ready to accept. With the Foreign Office and the high command fearful that Hitler's growing involvement in Spain might plunge Germany into a disastrous war, and with Dieckhoff talking as if the Foreign Office would welcome a proposal to settle the conflict by peaceful international means, Dodd thought the time ripe for general peace talks arranged by F.D.R. "From what information I can get," he wrote the President on December 7, "there is a rising doubt here as to Hitler's success in his Italian, Japanese, Spanish procedure. High army generals were positively opposed to the recognition of Franco, and rumors circulate that Hitler fears now that he will not succeed this time as on former occasions.... There is no doubt that democratic countries in Europe would welcome a call for a world conference.... What Hitler will say no one can say, certainly not Foreign Office Officials. But if the Fascists don't conquer Spain, I am convinced that there will be a silent popular demand here for international cooperation.... And Germany," Dodd concluded, *"might* assent to representation if the Führer listens to the officials indicated above and actually fears, as the intelligent people do, that he might not win a war before 1938."

Though Hitler shortly showed his contempt for any international settlement of the Spanish war by sending more troops, airmen, and engineers to Spain than ever before, Dodd continued to find some hope for his idea in the opposition of Schacht, the Foreign Office, and the generals. Indeed, on the same day he received conclusive evidence of the Führer's increased support of Franco, Schacht urged him to believe that Hitler would accept the French-English "neutrality demands" and with prior concessions, like the return of Germany's former colonial empire, would no doubt also join in a peace conference of the great states.[7]

That the Germans would ever show themselves receptive to productive talks or his own country to meaningful steps toward peace, Dodd was now unprepared to say. By the end of the year, though, he was all but convinced that he could no longer hope to do vital work in Berlin and would thus do well to retire. Having entertained such thoughts during earlier moments of frustration, he could no longer contain them after reading a Washington newspaper report about himself on December 12. Described by Drew Pearson as a complete failure in the eyes of both the State Department and the President, who, Pearson reported, would replace him with Ambassador William Bullitt in Paris, a man bound to be more sympathetic to the German regime, Dodd considered resigning immediately. But when reflecting on the fact that his immediate retirement "would at once be recognized as a confession of failure," he decided to wait until July. Still, the episode galvanized him into a consideration of what seemed like unanswerable arguments against a longer residence in his post. "No man who represents the people of the United States," he told Moore, "can do anything very positive with a Foreign Office absolutely ignored on all vital matters. Yet anyone who is recognized as a democratic American in my position will be popular with most of the people he is apt to meet. He can not accept half the invitations that issue from all groups and individuals, except the dictators. These facts with the tense situations from month to month make one's work most trying; and I have concluded that four years' service is enough."

And yet Dodd was not saying that Berlin had become an inconsequential assignment. As from the first, and as illustrated by his comments to Moore, he continued to believe that an American ambassador could perform a valuable service as a standing example of American liberalism in Berlin. More than that, though, Dodd feared that the wrong man in Germany could do America some small harm. A Bullitt, for example, who had shifted from enthusiasm for the Soviets to an advocacy of a Franco-German alignment against Moscow, was hardly Dodd's idea of a satisfactory ambassador in that post. Professor James T. Shotwell of Columbia University was much more to his taste. "He knows Europe as few men do," Dodd told Moore. "He speaks German admirably. He is not a man who would fall for fascism or communism and he would actually work in the office…Another thing, he represents our university life most of which was enthusiastic for the President and democracy.…For this reason and others I take the liberty of naming him." If Dodd, then, was ready to give up his post in six months, it was not because he believed it a meaningless task. Though he saw nothing "Very positive" as likely to occur in German-American relations in the near future, he nevertheless considered it essential for the United States to have a talented, democratic man in Berlin.

But neither Roosevelt nor Moore was ready to give Dodd any answers about who his successor would be, apparently because they themselves had not given the matter much thought. To judge from their response to Dodd, they had no intention of finding someone else for perhaps another year. Urging Dodd to understand that Pearson's comments were "regarded as both truthless and ruthless," Moore explained that the President wanted him to put aside all thoughts of tendering his resignation now and to "feel free to postpone your retirement until after next summer." Though Roosevelt, of course, appreciated that Pearson had accurately reflected feelings in the State Department toward his ambassador, he was unprepared to accept the idea that "anything could have been gained by more intimate contacts with Hitler and some other officials. We both believe," Moore told Dodd, "that you have had a most desirable influence on relations you have maintained with some of the intellectual people whose views are more nearly in accord with your own." The President would shortly repeat this estimate of Dodd's performance in an off-the-record conversation with a Washington reporter.

What Roosevelt left unsaid in urging Dodd to remain in Berlin was that, in addition to Dodd's satisfactory handling of the Embassy, a change of ambassadors might entail a hard search for another able man. After Joseph Grew, the Ambassador to Japan and one of the most thoroughly professional diplomats in the Service, told him in the fall of 1936 that his prejudice against the Germans would not let him comfortably serve in Berlin, Roosevelt no doubt concluded that Nazi Germany was the last place an American ambassador wished to be.[8]

Though Dodd was undoubtedly pleased to be assured of the President's eagerness to have him remain at his post, the events at the start of 1937 reaffirmed his decision to leave Berlin later in the year. The vague hopes he held at the beginning of January that an effective world peace conference might yet be convened, or that Congress and the President would find some economic formula in conjunction with other states for punishing aggressors, he all but lost by the end of the month. First to go was his assumption that Congress and the President might see their way clear to commit themselves to an internationalist act or scheme. For the introduction in Congress of a joint resolution on January 6 specifically embargoing all arms ship-ments to Spain brought a warning from Dodd that "the Neutrality Act…is expected here to expand the Fascist-Nazi dictatorships.…Our members of Congress," he complained, "may think this only emphasizes American isolation but our business people have billions of dollars invested in these countries and innocent American investors would be the real losers." Though he anticipated what many liberals and businessmen in the United States would say, neither they nor Dodd could influence the congressional vote.

As frustrating to Dodd, both Roosevelt and the Germans killed his world conference idea. By contrast with Dodd, who primarily saw such a meeting as an expression of America's renewed determination to work for peace, Roosevelt wished assurances of some practical gain. He agreed, for example, with his Ambassador to Poland, John Cudahy, who asserted that an attempt to assemble the European heads of state "would result in nothing but propaganda and recriminations" unless some meaningful program were agreed upon before the conference met. As Roosevelt himself stated it to Dodd: "The trouble about any world conference…is that it would bring fifty-five or sixty nations around a table, each nation with from five to ten delegates and each nation, in addition, with no authority to agree to anything without referring the matter home. From a practical point of view, that type of conference is an impossibility unless, as in the case of B[uenos] A[ires], there are one or two simple principles on which all will agree beforehand." More to Roosevelt's taste was a secret, personal consultation of the kind he had mentioned in the previous year: "If five or six heads of the important governments," he also told Dodd, "could meet together for a week with complete inaccessibility to press or cables or radio, a definite, useful agreement might result or else one or two of them would be murdered by the other! In any case it would be worthwhile from the point of view of civilization!"

But Hitler gave Dodd no reason to tell the President that the Führer was ready for talks, private or otherwise. With evidence that "additional German Volunteers'" were being sent "continuously" to Franco and that Hitler had "rebuked" his generals for opposing his policy, Dodd could hardly be less than skeptical of a renewed Schacht proposal for world peace talks and Foreign Office promises of Hitler's inclination to withdraw his "volunteers" from Spain.[9]

If Dodd needed any other reason to see his prospective retirement as coming at a good time, he found it in what he saw as a resurgent threat to democracy in the United States. With the President's proposed reform of the Supreme Court and the sit-down strikes driving America into angry debate, Dodd feared that the very fabric of the society might soon fly apart. He wrote Moore in February: "The economic situation in our country is certainly none too safe: big business and nearly all newspapers tending toward dictatorship; labor men urged to form one solid front; and farmers likely to vote simply for their own interests." Reflecting no doubt on the Senate opposition to the Court packing plan, Dodd added that "five times in our history Senate minorities of the successful party have refused to cooperate with the most popular Presidents we have ever had and defeated overwhelming votes of the people.... I fear the Senate may do this thing again in spite of Roosevelt's majority. If they do I am afraid the Democratic party will go to pieces and under existing world conditions, we would be in grave danger of losing our democratic system. What seems to me to be the facts is the major cause why I wish to be at home after this year."[10]

For the time being, though, Dodd could only "wait and watch until my time to retire." But it was an active vigil. In addition to office work running from the early morning hours to seven in the evening of almost every day, there were unceasing dinner parties and receptions lasting until ten, eleven, or even midnight. And though he usually found these entertainments dull and tiring, they occasionally helped him keep up with the latest turn of events. Even though the ground seemed to be "swept clear of organizations which might serve as centers of opposition" and the general outlines of Nazi foreign policy were unlikely to change, there was still the radical-conservative, or Göring-Schacht struggle for control of the economy as well as Hitler's immediate foreign efforts to be watched.

And as in the past, Dodd managed to keep Washington well informed. Though Schacht was under heavy fire and clearly losing ground to Göring, whom the Führer celebrated as a man who did not know the word "impossible," Dodd was close enough to things to see that Schacht was not about to resign his place and power.

This, however, was the only indication of conservative influence holding its own. Almost everything else seemed to point the other way: with "recent changes in the character of the German moderate press," with the seizure of three Spanish merchant ships, or what Dodd called "drastic naval steps" to punish the Loyalists for actions against the German ship *Palos,* with the elevation of an "adventurous officer" to the head of the German fleet, with the resignation from the Leipzig Mayor's office of Dr. Carl Goerdeler, a leading conservative, and with the integration of the Party's foreign organization, the A.O., into the Foreign Office as a "first step toward a breaking down...of that last remaining citadel of conservatism," Dodd pronounced the party and country solidly in radical hands.[11]

Moreover, from all Dodd could gather in the first ten weeks of the new year, Hitler was working as hard as ever to assure German domination of the Balkan zone. Sending Göring to Rome in January and von Neurath to Vienna the following month, the Führer was still trying to arrange Mussolini's acquiescence in his plans, especially for Austria, where von Neurath went to head off any restoration of the Hapsburg throne. And so while Hitler might sound a conciliatory note in his speech of January 30 celebrating the fourth anniversary of his regime, his demand for the return of Germany's colonies, coupled with an outright refusal to hear any talk of limitations on German arms, impressed Dodd as fresh evidence of Hitler's fundamental lack of interest in an agreement with the West. Moreover, despite Dieckhoff's assertion that von Neurath's visit was no more than "a return formality" for the Austrian Foreign Secretary's visit to Berlin, Schacht's reassertion of his eagerness for a world peace conference, to which he announced he would persuade Hitler to agree, and von Neurath's contention that there would be no war and that Germany was a proponent of gradual disarmament, Dodd found enough contradictions in all they said to show him "more clearly than formerly that the German government is now determined to control, and actually annex neighboring countries."

Further confirmation came in the next four weeks. Rumors that Hitler rejected a proposed rapprochement with Czechoslovakia reminded Dodd that "Germany will have her own way as to the boundaries and status of the Balkan states...the *Mein Kampf* doctrine," and moved him to advise Messersmith to talk over with Chancellor Schuschnigg of Austria the establishment of a cooperative confederation among the Balkan peoples. "That would be a union of 80,000,000 people," Dodd observed, and "Germany would have to think twice before she moved against such a union." The fact, moreover, that Schacht was "reported to have challenged Hitler's Four Year Plan in some of its items" was made even more ominous in Dodd's eyes when Schacht himself reported, "My position is critical; I do not know what is to happen."

As if to highlight this general downturn, Dodd simultaneously found himself at the center of a minor crisis in German-American relations which aroused his ire and reminded him of how little could be expected from relations between Washington and Berlin. Apparently eager to divert attention "from the evil impression made abroad" by a recent Ribbentrop speech, the German press made headlines of a public attack upon Hitler by New York's Mayor Fiorello La Guardia. What amazed Dodd and provoked an answer from the State Department was the viciousness of the German reply.

"When one considers that this is the official language of a 'new-born Germany,'" Dodd wrote Hull, "and reads in it a revolting contrast between the noble and cultured civilization of Goethe, Kant, Beethoven, and Dürer, with which, according to history at least, National Socialism has had but little to do, and the 'gangster civilization' of the United States couched in billingsgate terminology, one may pause to think. It may be said that at least one branch of science, still, presumably, endowed with the characteristics of culture, is being furthered by the Ministry of Propaganda and Public Enlightenment. That science is philology—even though it may be limited to philology of the invective and the obscene. There would also appear to be reason to believe that in transplanting the word 'gentleman' from the original English into other languages, the connotations thereof become varied indeed." Though the Department won an easing of the press attacks through informal protests, the episode convinced Dodd that "nothing can be done in the United States or in Nazi Germany to better relations."[12]

With this conviction, Dodd now laid final plans to quit Berlin. Taking up Moore's suggestion that he postpone his retirement until the end of the summer, he now asked the Assistant Secretary to arrange for his resignation on September 1. Actually such a plan was calculated to coincide with his earlier scheme to leave his post in July. Entitled to several weeks' vacation, Dodd correctly assumed that he could depart Berlin roughly a month before his separation from the Foreign Service. Winning approval from the President and the State Department for his plan, Dodd had only to submit his official resignation, which all agreed to keep confidential until later in the year.[13]

Though now something of a lame-duck ambassador representing a country trying to declare its independence from European affairs, Dodd continued to act as if German domestic and foreign events both were in direct relation to or of direct importance to the United States. In this, of course, he was much closer to the truth than most Americans cared to believe. He told Hull in April, for example, that "the suppression of the B'nai B'rith [the Jewish benevolent society] appears to have been activated by the desire to retaliate against foreign [and particularly American] anti-Nazi agitation, to deliver another blow at the freedom of association of Jews and finally to carry out a profitable raid upon independent Jewish funds." What impressed Dodd as most significant about this action, though, was that it seemed to foretell that the future tempo of the "permanent" policy of Nazi anti-Semitism would "be influenced by outside circumstances."

Nothing, however, was more important to America in Dodd's eyes than the course and fate of Hitler's diplomatic offensive. And in April, it seemed almost likely to stall. With the war in Spain apparently shifting in favor of the Republic, with the London Non-Intervention Committee arranging naval and frontier patrols to halt the flow of equipment and "volunteers," with the Führer seemingly delayed in his moves against Austria and Czechoslovakia by economic difficulties in the Reich, and with "frequent and repeated interchange of visits, discussions, and negotiations among so many of the European powers" opening new possibilities for "political and economic stabilization," Dodd could strike a fairly optimistic note. He qualified the optimism for Washington with evidence that Mussolini was reducing his commitment to Austrian independence in proportion to his increasing reliance on the Italo-German rapprochement and a warning that the deepening isolation of Czechoslovakia was a growing temptation to "radical German designs."

Convinced that none of this diplomatic maneuvering would result in anything definite before the fall, Dodd felt free to use up some of his accumulated vacation time in a five-day motor trip through Hanover, Marburg, Luxemburg, Verdun, Geneva, Basle, and Heidelberg and Frankfurt on his return. Though Dodd was right about international affairs, he could not foresee that another sort of crisis would greet him shortly after he got back.[14]

Having written Senators Robert Bulkley and Carter Glass at the beginning of March to urge support for the President's Court plan and having won no converts, Dodd thought to give public expression to his views by asking Moore to have Virginius Dabney of the Richmond *Times-Dispatch* release his letter to newspapers in the South. Though Moore asked Dabney to withhold publication of Dodd's letter until the Ambassador had a chance to reconsider his desire to project himself into "so heated" a public debate, a Greensboro newspaper printed a summary of the letter on the 10th of May. When Dabney followed with a complete copy on the 11th, other newspapers around the country picked up the story, which now created something of a national debate. Entitled "Should not the Majority Govern?" and arguing at great length that earlier democratic presidents like Cleveland, Roosevelt, and Wilson had been foiled in their efforts for the people by court decisions, Senate filibusters, and party splits, the letter urged that F.D.R. be preserved from a similar fate, especially since American democracy faced its gravest threat since Lincoln's day. To emphasize the last, Dodd concluded on a sensational note: "There are individuals of great wealth," he warned, "who wish a dictatorship and are ready to help a Huey Long. There are politicians who think they can gain powers like those exercised in Europe. One man, I have been told by personal friends, who owns nearly a billion dollars, is ready to support such a program and, of course, control it."

The warning at once became the focus of all the newspaper stories and the basis for a demand by Senators Borah and William King that Dodd resign his post and return to the United States where he could testify before a Senate committee as to the facts behind his charge. Borah, however, had already made up his mind about the substance of Dodd's report, describing it for the press as "the figment of a disturbed mind." Other critics were equally harsh. A Cincinnati newspaper quipped in verse:

> There's a billionaire,
> Can't you see his hand?
> He is out to make
> This a Fascist land!
>
> …
>
> I see him here
> And I see him there;
> He has big green eyes
> And long purple hair.
>
> He has uncut claws,
> And wears iron spats,
> And his favorite dish
> Is boiled Democrats.
>
> Help! Assistance! Quick!
> Save me from that wad.
> What? the cops can't come?
> Well, send William Dodd![15]

Having heard similar warnings about the threat to democracy for over three years, few people in the United States were ready to take Dodd's contention seriously, and so in a matter of days the whole episode disappeared from public view. Roosevelt himself, for example, simply dismissed Dodd's billionaire story as regrettable and set the general outcry down to partisan politics. Taking a Borah statement warning against fascism and comparing it to the Senator's answer to Dodd, the President told the writer Raymond Clapper on May 16 that he found the "two statements directly opposite of each other." Moreover, the President said "that outside of that crack in Dodd's letter it was a pretty good letter on the Court question." To Dodd himself, Roosevelt wrote that "frankly, I was delighted with your letter to Bulkley. But because you are too honest and sincere to be a publicity expert, you did not realize that that one sentence about the billionaire would be the one thing in the whole letter seized on by the Press and a certain type of false liberal like Borah." Finally, in the face of renewed talk about State Department dissatisfaction with Dodd's work, the President "said that Dodd did a good job of getting undercurrents and reporting on them and that this was about all an ambassador could do....Dodd was in with professors and intellectuals," Roosevelt added, "and was thus able to keep tab on undercurrents....Hitler and Göring wouldn't tell any of the diplomats anything anyway and that therefore Dodds [*sic*] couldn't get anything else...and he did have the advantage of being in with the intellectual group....He," Roosevelt concluded, "finds out more that way than other diplomats there do."[16]

Yet the fact that Roosevelt took a certain satisfaction in Dodd's letter and thought his overall performance worthy of praise is hardly proof that Dodd used good judgment in releasing such a statement to the press. On the contrary, the letter suggests that Dodd was beginning to let his anger toward the Nazis and his fears of fascism in the United States get out of control. For having included the "billionaire" warning, as he later told a friend, "rather casually and without thinking much about it," and, as he wrote Moore, on the strength of what he learned from "three influential and well-informed Americans" and "an influential European," all of whom insisted on remaining anonymous, Dodd was publishing a charge he could neither effectively prove nor defend.[17]

Although Dodd showed a lack of sound judgment in this affair, in his conduct of the Embassy and his assessment of European events his judgment was still good. In one particularly trying case of an American citizen condemned to death for conspiring to kill Julius Streicher, editor of Germany's leading anti-Semitic paper, *Die Stürmer*, Dodd acted with energy and restraint in seeking a commutation of sentence for the accused. Appreciating that the Nazis would resent any attempt to turn the matter into a cause célèbre, Dodd, like the State Department, confined himself to brief, factual statements to the press at the same time he worked through the Foreign Office, the Ministry of Justice, and the Chancellery to gain his end. In a direct appeal to Hitler as well as conversations with von Neurath, Hans von Mackensen, the new State Secretary in the Foreign Office, and Otto Meissner, the Führer's *Staatssekretaer*, Dodd first emphasized that Helmut Hirsch was only twenty years old and "may well have been misled by older and more experienced minds whose influence may have been primarily responsible." But when these humanitarian arguments gained nothing, Dodd began emphasizing that Hirsch, after all, had not in fact committed the crime, nor been caught doing it, and that American public opinion would be outraged and German-American relations further undermined by the execution of an American whose crime was in no way proved with a display of evidence to his government. Only after commutation had been denied in a manner which, in Dodd's words, revealed Hitler's "failure to understand and act in accordance with the procedure and usage to be expected in normal relations between governments" did Dodd confidentially give the press the full story of the Embassy's unsuccessful effort to save Hirsch's life. Moreover, in a review of the case for the State Department, Dodd reasonably urged that Washington vigorously protest German disregard of American wishes by refusing either to postpone the execution or to make available the evidence on which the conviction stood. But as in the whole range of international affairs, the American government refused to challenge the Hitler regime.[18]

More important to Washington than his handling of this case, Dodd's conclusions about European political developments remained as shrewd as before. In the middle of May, for example, he accurately depicted von Neurath's recent visit to Mussolini and the Foreign Minister's statement to him "that Germany was getting into closer relations with England" as evidence of a double game: "It was plain from the talk," he wired Hull, "that Germany is at present cultivating England but not abandoning its relations with Italy as to control of the coveted Balkan areas." If there were any question, though, as to which alliance Hitler valued most, it was made clearer for Dodd at the end of the month. With Germany and Italy simultaneously responding to republican Spain's attack on the German patrol ship *Deutschland* by withdrawing from Non-Intervention Committee discussions and patrols, Dodd warned that the Germans and the Italians were "once more leagued for the domination of Spain," which in turn would assure Hitler's plan of Balkan control. Never, in fact, "since my acquaintance with Balkan ministers became fairly close," Dodd reported, "have they revealed such anxiety as now." Their anxiety was well founded, for Dodd reported that the new British Ambassador to Berlin, Sir Neville Henderson, was "representing his country as willing for Hitler to annex Austria and other countries in that zone," the Belgian Minister was declaring himself in favor of "German expansion to the East," and von Neurath was planning a trip to Belgrade, Budapest, and Sofia in the hope of defeating the Czech-Austro-Rumanian effort "to enlarge the Little Entente for mutual protection." That the British and the Belgians should think to assure themselves from war and domination by such a policy impressed Dodd as foolish in the extreme. German domination of the Balkans, he said, would mean Belgian annexation, British decline, and Hitler's unlimited European control.

If an Italo-German return to the Non-Intervention Committee in mid-June and an announced visit by von Neurath to London momentarily shook Dodd's conviction of a fascist commitment to Italian domination of the Mediterranean and German hegemony to the East, he was shortly reassured by a second withdrawal and the cancellation of von Neurath's trip. Though ostensibly outraged by a torpedo attack on the cruiser *Leipzig* and Anglo-French unwillingness to join a naval demonstration against republican Spain, Hitler, Dodd believed, was actually withdrawing from the international patrol in order to advance Franco's fortunes at a time when Russia and France stood weakened by Stalin's purges and Blum's ouster. Yet if these were Hitler's aims and tactics, it was Dodd's conviction that he could still be stopped. For Germany, he advised Washington, was in no position "to wage a major war and…she knows it.…Germany has an inconsiderable trained reserve; an inadequate matériel reserve; a highly inadequate reserve of raw materials, gold and foodstuffs and is facing at best a less than average crop. Her air force both as to matériel and personnel is nowhere near satisfactorily organized and completed and will not be ready for another 2 years. Likewise the German navy is in process of organization and her army generally requires at least the same period to bring it up to a satisfactory level to fight a major war on two fronts which she must envisage as possible, if not probable, should she cooperate with Italy in endangering any vital Franco-British interests."

What troubled Dodd so much in the face of all this was the extent to which the democracies refused to head off Hitler with a show of unity and force. At the very least, it was time, Dodd said, "for the British to adopt a firmer attitude and be their more normal Elizabethan selves...." For such a posture, Dodd correctly understood, would either push the dictators into some "immediate action" or "a more temperate frame of mind." With German arms still less than well prepared, either result would be to Britain's good. But as Dodd appreciated, exactly the reverse was taking place; earlier Anglo-French equivocation was giving way to all-out acquiescence in Nazi demands. "The pressure here for English approval of German control...of the Danube-Balkan zone," he wrote Sir Eric Phipps on July 1, "is greater now than at any time since my residence here began. I can see how English public opinion might even favor that rather than a risk of war. Your Ambassador here has said more than once to me that English agreement for such 'Bismarckian' expansion is the proper thing, and even asked if the United States would not approve such a move and join a moral triple alliance." As for France, Dodd judged her "so overwhelmingly against war" that Hitler could annex Czechoslovakia without a fight. The French Ambassador, moreover, was doing nothing to alter that course, and, in fact, like Henderson, was now entirely playing into Hitler's hands. Yet even if men like François-Poncet and Henderson were symptoms of the Franco-British attitude rather than the cause, or even if "you and I may not be able to do anything," he told Phipps, "...we may at least let our convictions be known to our government."[19]

And in that spirit, Dodd now thought to extend his stay in Berlin. Actually, he had been considering such a move since the beginning of May. When he heard that Ambassador Joseph Davies in Moscow, a man Dodd unfairly believed close to Bullitt in ideas as well as background, was slated to replace him, and when the controversy over his letter seemed to invite future suggestions that he had resigned under fire, Dodd asked Moore to take up with the President the question of how long he could remain at his post. But when Moore strongly opposed the idea, Dodd temporarily abandoned it for a direct appeal to Roosevelt to make either Shotwell, Stephen Duggan of the Council on Foreign Relations, or Charles Merriam his successor.

But uncertain that the President would follow his advice, he continued to worry over who his replacement would be. "My predecessors here since 1921 spent from $50,000 to $100,000 a year," he wrote Colonel House in June. "And there are now in troubled

Europe three or four who do the same thing. How can an Ambassador who knows no language but his own, no real history of Europe, and spends $50,000 a year really master the situation?" If such a man comes here, he also told House, "that means that England, France, Germany and even Italy would have the kind of [American] Ambassadors who have injured our Service [for] forty years. Under present circumstances we need the best informed and most industrious representative we can possibly get."

Though as unfairly prejudiced against wealthy career officers as some of them were against him, Dodd was understandably eager to torpedo the appointment of anyone who might fall in with Henderson, François-Poncet, or Bullitt in seeking to appease Berlin. Hence, by the first week in July, with news that Sumner Welles, another wealthy career man, had been appointed Under-Secretary of State and nothing to indicate that the President would appoint a Shotwell to his place, Dodd decided to discuss the situation with Roosevelt and Moore when he got back to the United States. Before he could do that, his own time as ambassador was extended to October 1. Compelled by the absence of the Embassy's First Secretary to delay his departure from Berlin from July 10 to the 24th, he asked and received permission to put off his resignation for a month, or, as originally agreed upon, until he could use up his accumulated leave.[20]

The one-month extension in no way settled in Dodd's mind the problem of arranging for a democratic successor, and if he needed any added incentive to press for this, it came in the form of renewed warfare in the Far East between China and Japan. Convinced that the Japanese were the aggressors in the conflict and that this was but one expression of what he described for the press on his arrival in the United States as "a basic objective of some powers to frighten, even destroy democracies everywhere," he more than ever saw a need for an informed representative in Berlin who would "help his Government know what to do."

Consequently, when he met with Roosevelt on August 11, Dodd apparently asked him for assurances on this point. But with the President still indicating an intention to send Davies to Germany, the best Dodd could arrange was a two- to three-month extension for himself beyond October 1. More important to him for the moment, though, Roosevelt showed himself "greatly troubled about the danger of war" and eager for Dodd "to accept all the lecture invitations I could" and to "'speak the truth about things.'"

And so, though withdrawing to his "lonely mountainside farm for a real vacation" from the strenuous work and headaches which had plagued him ever since the end of winter, he determined to devote a part of his time to counseling Americans on their best interests in foreign affairs. In a letter to the President on August 26, for example, he urged Roosevelt to understand that it was time for America to make a bold move abroad:

The situation in Europe is such that American action as to Far East tyranny in conjunction with England would not start Germany into her war scheme, even if Mussolini were ready.... Therefore, I would, in your position, press conservative England (the Government) to join us in pressure upon Japan, even to send American-British navies across the Pacific. Later Germany and Italy would act together if this were done—now they would not move.... Russia is in such a critical position at home that she can't act to save China alone. If Russia acted alone...Germany and Italy would be far more apt to act in the Black Sea region. So, it seems to me that just now our Government, England and France with the Holland Navy in the Far East, can ask co-operation of Russia and save the situation. Certainly if this dictatorial system goes on two more years unchecked, as in Ethiopia, Spain and now China, a combination of democratic...states may not save themselves. I am taking the liberty to write you because I know we have the same ideals and because I have watched and studied things in Berlin four sad years. All representatives of democratic countries in Berlin have again and again said: the United States is the only nation that can save our civilization.

Though Dodd's appeal came at a time of mounting indignation in the United States against the Japanese and of considerable discussion in both diplomatic circles and the press of some concerted action by the Western powers to halt the hostilities in the Far East, it was almost totally at odds with what the State Department and the American ambassadors in China and Japan, Nelson Johnson and Joseph Grew, had seen fit to advise. Moreover, though Dodd's suggestion was in line with what others were telling Roosevelt about his part in preserving the world from another war, the President was in no mood to take the kind of steps outlined in Dodd's letter. Indeed, though eager to find some formula for the future which would allow non-belligerents to defeat an aggressor without provoking reprisals or involving themselves in hostilities, an attitude he would express in his Quarantine speech of October 5, Roosevelt had no intention of applying such a plan to either China or Spain, for, as he told Harold Ickes, what had been done could not be undone. And so, the President at once answered Dodd that "I agree with you—but the rearmament complex in England seems to hinder any positive action." Since the English had put forward more than one proposal for Anglo-American co-operation in the Far East in July and August, it was hardly a fair representation of the facts.[21]

At the same time he wrote the President, Dodd tried other methods of alerting the administration and the country to the dangers lying ahead. At the beginning of September, he successfully helped arrange an interview between Hull and Dr. Carl Goerdeler, the man destined to become the leader of civilian resistance in the 1944 plot against Hitler's life. Such a meeting, Dodd told the Secretary of State, "would be a good thing—[because] many questions might be asked." Secondly, taking the President at his word, Dodd delivered speeches in the North and the South in September which reflected just what he had been telling the administration for almost three years: American democracy is threatened both at home and abroad, and unless people moved from cities to small farms and unless Washington co-operated with other democratic states, or applied the Wilsonian principles to our foreign affairs, self-government was doomed.

Though apparently finding a positive reception for his speeches and though detained in the United States by this work until the end of October, Dodd still felt it important for him to return to Berlin. Moreover, compelled to make living arrangements which could not be conveniently terminated before the end of winter and feeling "pressure" from people in the United States, his "whole staff, but one," "the consular chief about Germany," and "the ministers of European democracies...to stay another year," Dodd was inclined to remain until March.[22]

But this was now becoming very difficult to arrange. For both the Germans and the State Department were applying pressure to Roosevelt to remove Dodd from his post. At the beginning of August, first of all, Dieckhoff, who had been Ambassador to the United States since May, was instructed to register an informal protest with Hull against Dodd's statement to the press of August 4 in which, Dieckhoff said, "the German Government is reported to have been singled out and seriously criticized by the Ambassador." Though Hull assured him that Dodd knew better "than to make a personal attack on the government to which he is accredited," he conceded to Dieckhoff that the Ambassador "has almost an obsession on the question of peace and democracy," or, as Dieckhoff recorded it, that Dodd is a "little insane" on the subject of Jeffersonian democracy. But whatever Hull's precise words, he apparently left Dieckhoff with the impression that he was eager to have Dodd retire from Berlin.

The situation was further aggravated at the beginning of September by a public controversy between Dodd and the State Department over a decision to allow Prentiss Gilbert, the Chargé d'Affaires in Berlin, to follow the British and French Ambassadors in breaking a four-year policy of absenting themselves from the annual Nuremberg Party Congress. Dodd took strong exception to this decision in a letter to Hull, and his views, without his approval, were soon known to the press and provoked a protest from Dr. Hans Thomsen, the German Chargé d'Affaires in Washington, who expressed the personal opinion that "it was hard to see how he [Dodd] could usefully go on with his mission...." In response, on September 18, Assistant Secretaries of State Moffat and Hugh Wilson conveyed Thomsen's opinion to the President, who agreed to have Wilson notify the German that Dodd "would be relinquishing his mission around the end of the year." But even if Roosevelt had not agreed to such a proposal then, he would have been compelled shortly to issue such a directive. For Dieckhoff, who had been on leave in Germany for a month, carried instructions with him on his return at the end of September to tell Hull that "his Government did not request the recall of Mr. Dodd but desired to make it plain that the German Government did not feel that he was *persona grata*."[23]

Though believing that Sumner Welles had in "some way slipped" his letter to the New York papers in the hope of forcing him from his post, and though appreciating that the Germans had protested to the State Department, Dodd was unaware that the President had in fact promised the Germans to recall him by the end of the year. And so he continued to feel that Roosevelt's invitation to him to stay for two or three more months could be extended beyond that, or at least until he could persuade him to appoint a successor who, like him, would fearlessly represent democracy in Germany. Hence, in conversations with the President "about the middle of September" and on October 19, the day before he left for Berlin, he pressed Roosevelt to extend his appointment into 1938 and to have Shotwell take up his assignment when he left.

Though Roosevelt had already committed himself to a terminal date for Dodd's services and though he apparently had no serious intentions of appointing Shotwell his successor, he gave Dodd no indication of either fact. On the contrary, he made no objection to Dodd's request for an extension to March and said: "I will appoint Shotwell or [Hugh] Wilson." This bit of indirection on the President's part was, under the circumstances, characteristic. When pressed too hard, Roosevelt, as Arthur Schlesinger, Jr., has explained, "resorted—almost, it would seem, as if he considered himself entitled to do so—to deviousness and to deceit. Those who did not press," Schlesinger adds, "rarely complained of being cheated."

Yet Roosevelt's small deception of his ambassador was done casually and without malice, and their last official meeting at F.D.R.'s Hyde Park home on October 19 was marked by a cordiality of spirit which represented the President's largest feeling about Dodd. Apparently seeing in his ambassador a man who cared too much to hold back on a demand and who radiated that idealism and simplicity of faith which made up his own "heart of hearts," Roosevelt was friendly and accepting: talking candidly about foreign affairs, he revealed his anxiety over the Far East war, the possibility for meaningful gains at the upcoming Nine Power Brussels conference and the question of whether the United States, England, France, and Russia could actually co-operate for peace. Moreover, asking Dodd and his son to stay to lunch, he made it "a delightful occasion" which he ended with an invitation to write him personally about things in Europe. "I can read your handwriting very well," he said.[24]

Although Dodd came away from his meeting with the President believing that he was to retain his post until March 1, he was also aware that the Germans were pressing for his removal and that more than one man in the State Department thought it a good idea that he leave Berlin about December 15. Despite this, when Hull cabled him within three weeks of his return that he arrange his departure for that date or by no later than the 25th, he felt deceived and cheated. To be sure, he was understandably annoyed to have to bear the inconvenience involved in leaving earlier than he planned and to think that the Nazis would take satisfaction in assuming that they speeded his retirement from his post; but, nevertheless, the quality of his reaction seems to indicate that something more was at stake.

But what? Certainly not the news that Roosevelt wished to make Ambassador Hugh Gibson in Belgium his successor. Dodd viewed Gibson as a career officer of liberal persuasions whom the Nazis would probably not wish to have in Berlin. Nor was he subsequently distressed by Roosevelt's selection of Hugh Wilson when Gibson turned him down. Viewed by the Department as "a colorless, smooth career man" who could "get contacts [with the German government] worked up again," Wilson also seemed unobjectionable to Dodd.[25]

Nor could Dodd's frustration be attributed to any feeling that he was being removed at a moment when some improvement in relations or success in negotiations was about to be achieved. On the contrary, everything Dodd found on his return to Europe seemed to point toward further fascist gains at democracy's expense. The reaffirmation of Polish-German friendship symbolized by a minorities treaty signed on November 5, the addition of Mussolini to Germany's Anti-Comintern Pact with Japan on the 6th, and a German inquiry in Paris as to France's attitude toward a possible move against Austria or Czechoslovakia seemed to promise increased German pressure in the Danube zone. Further, an almost total lack of progress at the Brussels conference coupled with fascist pressure on China to concede its northern territories to Japan seemed to foretell the success of a "cruel and amazing imperialism" which would bring another "vast region into close cooperation with the European dictatorships." Lastly, the accession to power of a new dictator in Brazil followed by reports from Chilean and Colombian officials of expanding Nazi influence in their countries and across the continent seemed to threaten a general Latin alliance with Rome and Berlin. In short, after two and a half weeks back at his post, Dodd was more convinced than ever that a solid fascist front from Rome to Tokyo threatened to take the world in its grip.

This was just the point. The thought of giving up public work at a time when democracy stood in such jeopardy seemed to him equal to abandoning his own defense. Indeed, the Nazi threat to democratic men was in Dodd's eyes no abstraction. It was a terribly personal affair, with the fascists putting his life, his liberties, his rights under direct personal attack. And the best way to combat such a threat, he felt, was to meet it head-on in Berlin. Though you and I may have little immediate impact on events, he had recently told Sir Eric Phipps, we may at least let our convictions be known and our apprehensions be expressed. "All that we can do in every nation to raise the question of what would happen if Fascism were to spread greatly throughout the world and dominate it," Roosevelt was then telling his ambassador in Poland, "ought to be said and ought to be done. We cannot stop the spread of Fascism unless world opinion realizes its ultimate danger." And it was chiefly to help sound the alert that Dodd wished to stay at his post. But as he also knew, an end to his assignment did not necessarily mean a halt to his anti-fascist work. His recent speeches in the United States were enough to tell him that.[26]

And so something other than an assumption that he could only fight Nazism from America's Berlin Embassy was tying him to his post. And this something was a sense of failure, of nagging doubt that he had exhausted all the possibilities of his office to help halt the slide toward war or to alert Roosevelt and the nation to growing threats. This concern weighed heavily on him as he returned to the United States, leading him repeatedly to ask: "Could one be successful?" Should an American ambassador have acted differently in Berlin? Was there anything more which could have been done? Though the answer seemed to be "no," he was not perfectly sure, recording in his diary that after four and a half years in Europe in the service of his country, "how much one could do is an open question."[27]

It is sad that Dodd came away from Germany questioning his own success. For it is hard to see how an ambassador could have been much more astute than Dodd in his judgment of events. At the very least, compared with the erroneous conclusions drawn by Henderson and François-Poncet about Nazi leaders and plans, Dodd made an excellent record of assessing German and international trends. Moreover, if any one thing contributed measurably to this success, it was probably that very quality of unorthodoxy which so bothered the State Department, or that unwillingness to operate strictly within the limits of the European diplomatic tradition, which allowed him sharper vision than either his British or French counterparts. For though Dodd, like his two colleagues, started out to see, in Henderson's words, the "good side" of Nazi Germany, he soon concluded that there was no such thing and that he was up against ruthless, unreasonable men who would prove unresponsive to traditional diplomatic means. By contrast, the British and French representatives could not break with their original idea: Hitler and the Nazis were traditional German nationalists with traditional goals ready to be satisfied by acquiescence in their limited demands. Moreover, as traditional diplomats, Henderson and François-Poncet believed negotiation their chief task in Berlin. And so for Henderson to assume that there was no basis for co-operation with Germany was for him to consider "the reasons for his appointment futile." It was much the same with François-Poncet: seeing Hitler on business at least once a month, he never gave up hope of reaching some accord, especially on economic affairs. "You should stop while it tastes best," he commented after closing out his Berlin Embassy with the Franco-German nonaggression pact of December 1938.

Though it was occasionally difficult for him, Dodd never succumbed to the feeling that his limited assignment or the want of something important to negotiate made his work inconsequential. And the same applied to Robert Coulondre, François-Poncet's successor. Having "the rare political virtue of asking the right question, which he permitted no sentimental consideration to obscure," Coulondre was quick to acknowledge that his mission was devoid of "positive aspects" and that he would have to "remain in Berlin as a scout in an advance observation post." Though a professional like Henderson and François-Poncet, Coulondre had a humanity in outlook and purpose which transcended the dictates of his profession, permitting him, like Dodd at an earlier, less certain time, to find no room for agreement with a man he described as "the monstrous specimen of a debased humanity."[28] And so in the face of the evil generated by the Hitler regime, the simple manliness and humane generosity of Dodd and Coulondre proved itself superior to the sophistication of the traditionalists—not merely as a moral posture but even as an instrument of human understanding.

XV

Reaping the Whirlwind

WHEN DODD LANDED in the United States on January 6, 1938, he faced a difficult choice: should he retire to the quiet of his Blue Ridge home to preserve what remained of his failing health and to work on his *Old South*, or should he give himself over to lecturing and writing about the fascist threat?

Everything seemed to argue in favor of the former and against the latter. Careworn and enervated by his Berlin labors, he badly needed a period of rest; secondly, at sixty-eight years of age he could little afford to squander precious time if he meant to complete a four-volume study of the Old South. Moreover, having found the time in the midst of his exhausting labors in Berlin to complete the first volume of that work, *Struggles for Democracy,* a study of the seventeenth-century southern colonies, Dodd now had good reason to assume that he could make rapid progress on the remaining volumes. As much to the point in January 1938, there was not a ghost of a chance that Dodd could move a substantial number of people to abandon isolationism for involvement in world affairs. With the country in the grip of a five-month-old recession which had added two million people to the unemployment rolls and brought some Americans to the brink of starvation, and with the President unable to formulate a meaningful response and looking more and more like a repudiated leader, it was out of the question that Americans in general and Roosevelt in particular could be persuaded to shift their attention primarily to foreign affairs. Finally, if Dodd needed any additional evidence of isolationist strength, he had only to consider that the sinking of the U.S.S. *Panay* by Japanese planes in the previous month had produced a demand that American ships be recalled from Chinese waters and that the constitution be amended to place the war-making power more directly in the hands of the people.

Yet if questions of personal convenience and success primarily moved Dodd, he would not have gone to Germany in the first place. Further, since his *Struggles for Democracy* received unenthusiastic reviews, Dodd probably had second thoughts about immediately plunging into the next volume. And so during his first two weeks back in the states when he received more than thirty letters and telegrams a day inviting him to make lectures "all the way to Minnesota, Texas and California," he did not hesitate to arrange a three-month speaking tour of twenty cities in the eastern, mid-western, and southern United States. Beginning at a testimonial dinner given him by two hundred friends in New York City on January 13, Dodd set forth the theme which stood at the center of all his later talks: the world's democracies are threatened with annihilation, and the responsibility for this rests in good measure with the United States. Rejection of the League of Nations followed by indiscriminate economic nationalism helped establish fascism in Italy, Germany, and Japan, and now only a policy of co-operation among the democracies could save the world another war and preserve the civilization which began with the Renaissance.

"Mankind is in grave danger," Dodd told the New York gathering, "but democratic governments seem not to know what to do. If they do nothing western civilization, religious, personal, and economic freedom is in grave danger. The United States are as much to blame...as any other country...in that it failed to join the League of Nations...and that it later erected trade barriers and made enormous loans to improvident foreign interests." "The world would be enjoying calm, with no threat of war today," he said in a Washington Town Hall lecture on January 23, "...if its nations had agreed at the close of the World War to...effect a real union. The collapse of such a union in the guise of the League of Nations [may be] blamed in large part [on] our Congress's refusal to join the League. The United States [has also made] war debt settlement impossible by our high tariffs. To our high tariffs [may be] attributed world-wide tariff barriers, to world-wide tariff barriers [may be] attributed the modern intensity of nationalistic feelings, and to such [may be] attributed the current bellicose spirit noticeable in some countries."

What conclusion was to be drawn from these facts? What lesson to be learned? The very one Dodd had been urging upon Roosevelt and Hull for almost five years: that ideals and self-interest, that morality and self-preservation dictated a policy for Americans of international co-operation among democratic nations. "The one chance of keeping peace," Dodd assured a Carnegie Hall rally on January 30, "is for all nations to co-operate in economic matters, applying pressure to bear on peoples who are forced into undeclared wars and stringently applying boycotts against governments which violate solemn treaties."

When Hitler and the Nazis moved successfully in February and March to bring Austria under their control, it gave Dodd fresh evidence for his case: "The German appetite for expansion of territory and power," he warned a Rochester audience on February 21, "will not be satisfied with the Nazification of Austria. This will be succeeded by more bold steps.... Poland is scared and Czechoslovakia, the only democracy remaining in Central Europe, threatened.... The program of the dictators will be carried on without arms and the democracies will probably make concessions rather than fight. Democracy's one hope in Europe," Dodd concluded, "depends on the ability of the great powers to co-operate, a fact they have thus far been unable to accomplish."[1]

If Dodd had any doubts about undertaking such a speaking tour, they were partly alleviated by the reception given him everywhere he went. His audiences were large—reaching seven thousand people in one instance—and highly enthusiastic; local newspapers were generous with front-page coverage; and his mail was almost uniformly favorable. Moreover, it was of considerable satisfaction to him that both the Germans and the Italians felt compelled to take note of his anti-fascist campaign. Ambassador Dieckhoff carried a formal protest to Secretary Hull against Dodd's anti-Hitler talk, while the Führer himself was "considering the idea of not receiving the new American Ambassador until…the American Government should…straighten out the matter in a manner satisfactory to the Reich." Though Hitler did in fact receive Hugh Wilson without delay, German and Italian propagandists struck back at Dodd on the radio and in the press as a man undermining opportunities to improve relations between their countries and the U.S.A.[2]

Despite all this, Dodd could not help but appreciate that he was having little impact on the course of American foreign policy. The groups he spoke to, after all—like the Federation of Jewish Women's Organizations, the Massachusetts League of Women's Voters, Women Shoppers for the Japanese Boycott, the Church League for Industrial Democracy, the Chicago Council on Foreign Relations, the Zionist Organization of America, and the Medical Bureau to Aid Spanish Democracy—were generally committed to his point of view before they heard him, while those who were less receptive to his ideas remained out of reach. Roosevelt, Hull, and members of the Senate Foreign Relations Committee, for example, were unwilling either to take his advice or even to give him a hearing. Indeed, though he tried three times between February and April to arrange "to talk over European affairs and the reactions to my addresses with the President," he could not win his way into Roosevelt's crowded schedule. Similarly, though he sent hortatory notes to Hull and a request to Senator Key Pittman, Chairman of the Foreign Relations Committee, for a meeting, he received no more than ceremonious replies in the first instance and nothing at all in the second. After only one month back in the States, Dodd was ready to announce that he saw "no leadership anywhere willing to try to save Modern Civilization."[3]

It is not difficult to find reasons why these men were reluctant to confer with Dodd. With the suspicion growing that the administration might seek to cover up its domestic difficulties through foreign involvements, and with Dodd a member of what isolationists called the "messianic" group eager for a larger American role in heading off fascist plans, it is understandable that Roosevelt, Hull, and Pittman, all of whom viewed themselves as treading a middle ground between the isolationists and internationalists, would not want to associate themselves publicly with a man so clearly in one camp. In Roosevelt's case, however, there may have been at least one other reason for him to put off Dodd. With Dodd's son, William E. Dodd, Jr., laying plans to challenge conservative Congressman Howard W. Smith for his seat in Virginia's Eighth District, Roosevelt may have wished to avoid a personal appeal from Dodd for a public endorsement of his son. To be sure, the President was then giving his unofficial blessings to a council of liberals, including Harry Hopkins, Tom Corcoran, Harold Ickes, and his son James Roosevelt, working to assure the elimination of conservatives from their party. Moreover, there were probably few congressmen Roosevelt wished to replace more than Smith, who held a seat on the House Rules Committee and generally opposed his liberal measures, including most recently the controversial wages and hours bill. But, nevertheless, in the first months of 1938, Roosevelt was still not willing to inject himself personally into the party's liberal-conservative struggle, or to put his prestige on the line with liberal candidates in local primaries.

Though Dodd was greatly discouraged by all this and would shortly express the opinion that the President and the Secretary of State were under the influence of semi-fascists or "half-Nazis" in the diplomatic corps and State Department who pressed them to do nothing about foreign affairs, he was not ready to abandon his fight for a more enlightened policy. To be sure, by the beginning of April he was too exhausted to keep on with the kind of schedule he had sustained for almost three months, and so he limited himself to a handful of talks during April and May while he rested at his farm. But he was not about to call off his campaign.[4]

And nothing testified to his commitment more than his willingness to continue his public efforts in the face of great personal sufferings. On the 28th of May his wife died suddenly at the age of sixty-two from heart failure. Deeply devoted to her through thirty-seven years of marriage, Dodd "could hardly believe what had happened.... A terrible shock and surprise," he wrote a friend, "... a calamity to me and our children." Though he continued to live at the farm where he "hoped to have rest and quiet," he now fell into a mood of melancholy which plagued him through the last eighteen months of his life. "I am still not quite well from the troubles we have had," he told Walton Moore in July. "...The death of my wife," he wrote Josephus Daniels the following month, "has been such a calamity that my health has not been good...: nervous and some kind of heart trouble."[5]

Dodd nevertheless determined to keep on with the schedule of talks he had arranged to give in the summer months. Slated to speak primarily at colleges and universities in the North, South, and West, Dodd felt compelled to write a lecture which included his plea for collective security and something of special interest to the educator. He achieved this balance in a lecture he called both "The University and the Totalitarian State" and "Democracy and Education." But this was not a device for setting American academicians against the German educational system. The idea was still to win converts to an internationalist approach to foreign affairs. And to do this Dodd first sought to establish that the Nazi system of education was anathema to Americans: "...education must be purely partisan," he told his audiences, "...so that in the school where a six- or seven-year-old child is studying, every teacher must be sympathetic with the Nazis. If they are not absolutely sympathetic...they will be immediately dismissed. Sixteen hundred and thirty teachers were dismissed before the end of 1936...." Responsibility for such a state of affairs, Dodd next suggested, rested heavily upon the United States: "I don't know whether I need to recommend to you the educational system which Hitler has applied," Dodd said ironically, "but if I remind you that we are more the cause of Hitler's rise to power than any other nation in the world, you may be a little bit sad—and I think we are." Having appealed to the conscience of his audience, Dodd was ready to invoke his earlier warnings and recommendations: "When China and Japan, Germany, Italy, and...the Danube zone, all come into co-operation, I cannot help thinking democracy everywhere will be in grave danger....I hope the teachers of the rising generation, in co-operation with various other institutions, will be able to bring the coming legislators to a fuller realization of the dangers of democratic countries always being rivals to one another....I hope that something like that will come before it is too late. I don't think it can wait very long."[6]

At the same time Dodd appealed to American educators for a new approach to world problems, he contributed what he could to the general effort then under way to alert Americans to an internal Nazi menace. With anti-fascist congressmen calling for a congressional investigation of Nazi activities in the United States, Dodd was moved to tell a radio audience on June 25 that Hitler's propaganda organization had five hundred workers, was the second most important office in the Department of Foreign Affairs, and had a current budget of thirty million dollars for propaganda in the Americas. "...The United States is only one country which the Nazis wish to control," Dodd added. "All over Latin America great activity of the propaganda office in Berlin goes on day and night. All over the world the Nazi chiefs are doing all they can to weaken the trade of our country and to prevent democracies from co-operating in any way." To Dodd's satisfaction, his charges were incorporated into an American Civil Liberties Union pamphlet calling upon the newly created House Committee on Un-American Activities, chaired by congressman Martin Dies, to investigate Nazi espionage and propaganda in the United States. But when placed alongside the fact that neither his words nor any number of pamphlets could move the Dies Committee to consider anything besides communist subversion, Dodd, as in the spring, could feel little satisfaction with his efforts.[7]

The same frustration dogged his attempts to rescue German and Austrian scholars. Having helped find positions in America for some of the 2,800 professors and instructors dismissed from German universities during the first five years of Nazi rule, Dodd thought to continue this work when he returned from Berlin. He at once tried to enlist the aid of leading Americans: House and Senate Foreign Relations Committee members were asked to hear Gerhart Seger of the *Neue Volks Zeitung* on the German refugee problem; Berkeley's President Robert G. Sproul was urged to find a place on the faculty for historian Ernst Kantorowitz; Frank B. Hanson of the Rockefeller Foundation was asked to provide financial assistance for a Dr. Walter Lascar; while Walton Moore and Messersmith, now also a member of the State Department staff, were repeatedly urged to solve the specific emigration problems of Old World scholars.

But National Origins Act quotas and continuing massive unemployment now permitted no aid for these people: "I have your note...regarding Dr. Emmy Sachs in Vienna," Messersmith wrote. "But the Department can't intervene directly—she must apply for a Visa in Vienna." "Reference is made to the letter to you from Dr. Hans Seiffert stating that he desires to emigrate to the United States," the Leipzig Consul answered Dodd. "...I regret to tell you that our present quota is entirely filled and will not be open for some time." Louis P. Lochner's "suggestion that Dr. [Max] Immanuel might be employed by this government is not one I believe which would be considered," Messersmith told Dodd. "I think you will agree...that it would not be advisable for this government to take on...a person who is not an American citizen. It would lead to a great deal of unfavorable comment in this country...." Besides, Messersmith added in a few days, "some of these refugees...seem to think that it is not hospitality which we are offering them and an opportunity to make a new life but rather that there is a debt which we owe to them. They are not willing to come here in the spirit of the pioneers who helped to build up the country." With but one or two exceptions, Dodd could not overcome the prejudices and regulations which abandoned the Max Immanuels to their fate.[8]

On yet another score, Dodd felt himself stymied in his efforts during the summer to counter fascism at home and abroad. His inability to help assure a primary victory for his son over Howard Smith impressed him as yet another defeat for democracy. "There is now in Virginia," Dodd warned in a speech at the state university shortly before the election,

> a general movement against democracy because certain leaders think the President is wrong.... Are they not afraid of Nazi and Fascist propaganda for a dictatorship? Think of what has happened in Europe since 1933 and in Spain and China the last two years. These circumstances have caused my son, William, to yield to pressure to enter the congressional primary of the 8th district, whose representative has voted many times in the House of Representatives against democracy, majority rule. He is now canvassing our public and representing democracy—the old Virginia ideal and the philosophy of Thomas Jefferson.... I can't help thinking that if Virginia once more accepted the principle of majority government she might do a great deal to avoid the dangers ahead, especially efforts to defeat democracy.

Particularly galling to Dodd was the fact that despite Roosevelt's decision publicly to endorse his son and other liberal House and Senate candidates opposing party conservatives, almost all of them, including William Dodd, Jr., lost.

To make matters worse, after the election Dodd could not even arrange an interview with the President to discuss Virginia's "curious situation" which he hoped the President "might change...so its people may vote freely for democracy." Roosevelt, who now had no desire to put Dodd off, was away on a campaign trip until September, when, his secretary advised Dodd on the first, he would be happy to see him. In the more than three weeks, though, during which he had no reply, Dodd became so doubtful of the President's commitment to his point of view that a letter of criticism from an Alabama businessman suggesting that most Americans, including the President, were relieved to have him out of Germany moved Dodd to ask Moore whether in fact "the President felt as this man said." Moreover, when scheduling difficulties again intervened to deny him an interview in September and when Hitler's demands upon Czechoslovakia and English and French moves to satisfy them again vindicated Dodd's forecast of events, he gave direct expression to his anger with both the President and the Secretary of State in a letter to Hull. Reminding him that the democratic peoples of England, France, and the United States must co-operate if Europe were to avoid falling entirely under Hitler's control, he added: "I have reported this necessity to you and the President for fully two years; but I have been told my reports, even hand-written letters, were not delivered to you and the President. I may doubt these reports to me, but no real replies were ever written."[9]

Though Dodd was shortly reassured by another expression of the President's intention to meet with him soon, he felt more compelled than ever to carry his case to the people. And though this could only be done at considerable personal sacrifice because of an unrelenting condition of "nervous strain," Dodd set out at the beginning of October for a two-week speaking tour of Kansas, Texas, and New Mexico followed by engagements at the end of the month in Boston, Milwaukee, Chicago, Springfield, Baltimore, and Cincinnati. Despite some new titles like "Our Democratic Hopes and Disappointments" and "The Nazi Philosophy of Life," the familiar themes were all there. We are responsible: "...the work done at Geneva by the secret spokesmen of the American munitions makers in the early days of the League of Nations had been responsible for the rise of Hitler and the conditions in Germany today." We are threatened: "In the event a general war is precipitated, the United States will inevitably be involved. The Neutrality Act is not a sufficient guarantee that the nation can keep aloof." We must co-operate: "Hitler would not have risked war if the democracies had united against him over the Czech question." "There is only one hope for peace. That is for the peoples of England, France and the United States, and all other countries ready to co-operate in peace efforts, to join in action against fascism, an action more aggressive and constructive than has been done up to the present....An uncompromising boycott, or even an embargo, should be applied to nations that violate their solemn treaty obligations or go to war to seize other nations' territory....Every lover of liberty and democracy should work in all ways to fight fascism—this unparalleled encroachment on world civilization."[10]

When he completed his tour and returned to Virginia at the beginning of November, Dodd could no longer slight his medical problems or subordinate them to his lecture schedule. Plagued by headaches growing out of his nervous tension and beginning to complain of a "laryngitis" or "nervous throat trouble," which was in fact bulbar palsy, a progressive paralysis that made it difficult for him to speak and swallow, Dodd was to find it increasingly troublesome to fulfill lecture assignments. The most immediate result of his organic and functional problems, however, was a nightmarish hit-and-run car accident on December 5, 1938.

On that date Dodd was driving alone to a speaking engagement near Petersburg, Virginia. On Route 2 some three or four miles from Hanover Courthouse, he struck a four-year-old girl who had wandered unattended onto the highway. Considering his highly nervous and weakened condition, it is understandable that what followed were less than the actions of a rational man. Though he had swerved his vehicle abruptly to the side, thereby believing he had missed the child, he stopped his car and asked a woman who had been driving behind him "to look into things." Then, without actually looking to see if the child had escaped injury, he returned to his car and drove on to Petersburg. The next day he "explained the incident—or accident—to the chief

of auto police in Richmond....As I had not seen evidence that my car hit the young-
ster...I left the woman to look into things....Besides, I did not wish to give my name
because of publicity...." Two days later two policemen, "two large pistols on their
sides," took him from his home to Hanover and "insisted my giving a bond for
$2,000...." On January 9, Dodd waived a preliminary hearing on the charge of
hit-and-run driving because "the state of his health [was] such that he could not stand
the strain of a trial." Indicted a week later by a grand jury, he pleaded innocent and a
trial was set for March 2.[11]

Through all this Dodd managed to give another dozen talks in the South and the
East. But by January 24, too ill to continue any sort of work, he entered Georgetown
University hospital for observation of his throat condition and rest. Despite his con-
finement, he could not give up his preoccupation with public affairs. With the
President asking for increases in America's defense spending and for revisions of the
existing neutrality law which would implicitly free him to act more energetically
against aggressor nations, Dodd felt compelled to remind him how badly the democracies needed such support. "Hitler is bent on dominating Europe," he wrote
Roosevelt four days after entering the hospital,

with an army of ten million men and perhaps ten thousand bombing planes.
He has violated all treaties his country had agreed to; he has formed an alliance (secretly) with Mussolini, Franco and Japan. He hopes to force Russia
into the world combination by the overthrow of Communism. Then he pro-
poses to ally himself with Latin America and Canada and rule the world.
Every move he has made since 1935 has been successful. He knows all people
are opposed to war; so he threatens. What a world we shall have when he
dominates Christianity. You are the greatest leader in the world and I hope
you may be able to block things before too late: a master's job unequaled in
history.[12]

Though Roosevelt was too busy to send him more than an expression of thanks and
wishes for his rapid recovery, Dodd at least had the satisfaction of hearing from
Josephus Daniels that "events in Germany have more than justified your vision of
what was to take place. I am not at all surprised at what you say about the views of
some of the officials [in the State Department]," Daniels added. "They were dealing
with conditions as they saw them and in the old way. You had the vision and
background of history, and could see further than those who lack that training and
experience."

Yet whatever personal satisfaction Dodd and Daniels himself could take in having
seen more clearly into the future than most of their contemporaries, it was dwarfed

by the feeling, as Daniels expressed it, that "the world has gone mad. If those who have gone before can know what is happening in this sphere," Daniels speculated, "our good friend Woodrow Wilson can not be happy in Heaven, when he sees that the people who shattered his dream are reaping the whirlwind."

Though as distressed as Daniels about the world situation and though more convinced than ever that there was "no way to prevent the dictators going to war," Dodd stood more or less helpless before it all. When he was released from the hospital on February 28, his condition was too delicate for him either to resume his speaking schedule or to stand the strain of a trial. When at the advice of his lawyers he reluctantly changed his plea to guilty, the judge, taking account of his poor health and medical payments to the child of eleven hundred dollars, limited his sentence to a $250 fine.[13]

Still, despite his condition, Dodd could not entirely remove himself from the public arena. Traveling to California at the advice of his physician in March, he could not resist all of the many invitations to speak before a variety of groups in and around Los Angeles. In spite of a speech handicap and the exhaustion which followed even the smallest exertion, Dodd managed to give five speeches during two weeks on the West Coast.[14]

But when he returned to Round Hill at the end of the month, even this was too much for him. Too unwell to undertake any further work or even to attend more than an occasional social function, Dodd pretty much kept to his farm, where he wrote an occasional letter on world affairs and suffered a further deterioration in his condition. "I have been…ill four months and no doctor knows what to do," he wrote Josephus Daniels at the beginning of May. "It is a nervous throat trouble which gets worse every month. Today it took 1–1/2 hours for me to eat luncheon." Ending his letter abruptly, Dodd added at the top of the page, "This is all I could write at this time. I am to see a nerve specialist in Washington tomorrow."

The loss of his wife, the growing realization that he was suffering from an incurable disease, and a profound sense of distress over the injuries to the child (from which she eventually recovered) left Dodd somewhat irrational and incoherent. Convinced that his arrest and conviction were the work of Virginia "politicians who are trying to get all they can out of me," he wrote to ask Moore what he thought of "their forcing me to say I was guilty. You know the girl was the sole cause of the accident…," Dodd insisted. When a former student of Dodd's saw him at this time at a social gathering in Washington during one of his rare outings, he encountered "a strange man sitting by himself. 'Father,' Bill [Jr.] said, 'I want you to meet an old student of yours.…' Dodd, his face ravaged, blinked at me, murmured: 'What did you say your name was?' Surprised, I repeated it. 'How do you spell it?' My surprise growing to consternation, I started to tell him that we had known each other for many years, when I noticed that his eyes did not quite focus and that his attention wandered....I was sick with shock."

Though Dodd's family knew the exact nature of his illness, they tried to keep it from him and his friends, who they feared might accidentally tell him. "Father's health remains about the same," his son wrote Walton Moore on May 25, "but the doctors have considerable hope that through a new method of feeding, they may be able to preserve his life for many years." Though Dodd himself sensed the gravity of his condition, he never described it as more than a "nervous throat trouble," and he always held out more or less fanciful hopes for its cure. "I hope to recover my nervous strength," he wrote on June 7. "If I do not recover, I am afraid my life will not reach 70 years."[15]

Unfortunately, Dodd was all too right. With the paralysis spreading along his pharynx, larynx, and tongue muscles, Dodd was admitted to Mount Sinai hospital in New York on July 1 for an abdominal operation to facilitate feeding. He developed bronchial pneumonia and was placed on the critical list, and a persistent melancholia put his recovery in doubt. A State Department official notified Roosevelt that this melancholia was due largely to Dodd's feeling that Roosevelt thought he had failed in Germany. The official urged Roosevelt to send Dodd a telegram. To this, Roosevelt's informant might have added the fact that Dodd had been terribly distressed over the loss of his voting and driving privileges in Virginia as a result of his hit-and-run driving conviction. Hence, when F.D.R. and Hull wired him messages of concern and Governor James Price restored his citizenship, Dodd was cheered immensely. He recovered temporarily and departed the hospital for Virginia on July 27.[16]

Though showing some alleviation during his first month at home, he took a turn for the worse in September and was compelled to live out his last five months under the most trying conditions: confined to bed, fed through a tube, and entirely deprived of speech. Yet through these months he never lost interest in public affairs, nor hope for recovery and accomplishment. When the outbreak of the Second World War came, against which he had warned, Dodd ventured to write Roosevelt about Hitler. "Hitler intends to conquer the whole world. If we do not join England and France, we shall have a hard time. All democracies must co-operate, else they: the Swiss, the Hollanders, the Swedes and others will be annexed....The democracies in Europe have neglected their statesmanship. If they had co-operated on several occasions, they would have succeeded. Now it is too late. Hitler ridiculed Communism and democracy almost every time the party met [at] Nürmberg." "Our world did not learn anything from the last war," he wrote Josephus Daniels on New Year's Day 1940. "I am sorry for that method of keeping the peace would have been effective. But your life and mine can't last much longer. Ten years would be good for me. I wish to write my other two or three volumes."[17]

But they could only remain a wish. On February 8 he contracted pneumonia and had to be placed in an oxygen tent. Too ill to be moved, he remained at the Round Hill farm with his son and daughter keeping vigil. The following day, February 9, his strength gave out: he succumbed at ten minutes after three in the afternoon. Twenty-four hours later he was laid to rest in his beloved Virginia.

The obituaries, the summing up, justly celebrated Dodd's accomplishments as a historian, educator, and public servant: one of the outstanding scholars of American history, the author of several notable books and popular essays, the architect of Chicago's southern history center, one of the truly great teachers of his generation, a statesman without portfolio, but a statesman in the true sense of the word. Beyond these accomplishments stood the man himself: "a curious blending of frailness and strength, gentleness and daring, whimsicalness and crusading spirit...a genial, help-ful man who approached greatness and merited our sincere affection." A democrat of unyielding persuasion, an uncompromising defender of human rights: "He never forgot Virginia. He never forgot Jefferson. He never forgot America. He never apol-ogized for liberty, equality, democracy....He never despised the lowly lowers; he never made social capital by hating or boycotting the Jews; or bowed the knee to the idolatry of so-called Supermen. His voice was the voice of liberty, of reason, of justice."

"When all was black around him," Charles Merriam recalled,

> Dr. Dodd lifted up his eyes to the hills, took courage and went forward—away from Doubting Castle and the counsellors of timidity and cynicism, pessimism and fear. And this is the grandeur of the human spirit which Dr. Dodd embodied and represented in his sharpest hours of life. Over against the "Imponiren" war lords he placed a figure—perhaps a relatively small and relatively quiet figure—a Pauline figure—but a figure representing a great idea and a great ideal. The greatest force in the world is not steel and explosives but the ideas which made them. Ambassador Dodd held aloft the standard of the greatest idea of our time.

And so for the many students and colleagues who cherished their association with him, for the thousands of professionals and interested laymen who read and learned from his books and essays, for the hundreds of thousands in Europe and America who took satisfaction in his unflinching defense of democracy in a time of uncertain faith, Franklin Roosevelt summed up their feeling when he said: "Knowing his pas-sion for historical truth and his rare ability to illuminate the meanings of history, his passing is a real loss to the nation. He served his country devotedly and well as edu-cator and public servant."[18]

But the story does not end here. For after the obituaries always come the hard questions posed by the passage of time: a century after his birth and a quarter of a century after his death, what can we say of his life?

As a nineteenth-century man, a rural southerner dedicated to a Jeffersonian America of yeoman farmers, Dodd, I suggested at the outset, tests the assumption that men like him found themselves out of place in or even unable to cope, as they wished, with a radically altered twentieth-century world.

It cannot be disputed that Dodd's Jeffersonianism handicapped him and limited his impact on historical studies and public policy. Never able, in spite of what even he himself thought, to accept the relativism and scientific assumptions of the progressive writers of his age, Dodd produced works of scholarship which now appear to be more derivative and less salient examples of progressive history than those constructed by a Turner or a Beard. Hence, where the partisanship and ideas of Beard, Turner, and Vernon L. Parrington, the chief figures in this school, have recently come under sharp attack, Dodd's more extreme and less convincing statements of the same ideas have been all but ignored.

Further, it is also clear that Dodd's staunch Jeffersonianism somewhat isolated him from the mainstream of both Democratic and American politics. Viewing twentieth-century problems primarily in terms of nineteenth-century solutions— the substitution at home of smaller economic and social units for the trusts, machines, and unions of the new era coupled with co-operation abroad, especially in the form of free trade—Dodd, whatever his association over the years with Wilson, Franklin Roosevelt, and other Democratic leaders, could never gain a central place in the counsels of the nation or the party such as that won, if even for a short time, by Charles Seymour, James Shotwell, Raymond Moley, and Rexford G. Tugwell.

Lastly, Dodd's Jeffersonianism generally accounts for the pointed lectures, the bursts of well-meaning political credulity, the preoccupation with Foreign Service economies, and the rejection of traditional procedures which mark his Berlin Embassy as partly another chapter in the long and familiar story of American innocence and European experience—a chapter that no doubt would have bemused and perhaps vindicated the most distinguished teller of this tale, Henry James.

Yet whatever the naïveté and failings flowing from this attraction to somewhat outworn ideas, Dodd's traditionalism was at bottom an excellent guide. For one, his commitment to an earlier, less complicated America provided him with an intuitive understanding of the Old South which makes his writings on that region a lasting contribution to our knowledge. Indeed, even if his *Macon* and *Davis* volumes will sooner or later be surpassed, even if his portraits of the statesmen are already out of date, and even if his last work, *Struggles for Democracy,* was a generally unsuccessful discussion of the seventeenth-century southern colonies, the interpretive schemes in both his *Statesmen* and *The Cotton Kingdom* still have much to recommend them. Secondly, the inspirational quality of his teaching, which was unusually effective with students, setting a number of them on the path to distinguished careers, can no doubt be partly attributed to his steady faith in the virtues of an earlier West and South. Further, his prominent role in building a first-rate history department and a great University of Chicago can readily be seen as an expression of his Jeffersonian commitment to excellence.

It was much the same in the public sphere; Dodd's Jeffersonianism helped him to see to the heart of almost every great political issue of his day. Committed above all to the dignity of the individual and the supremacy of human rights, Dodd stood with the progressives against concentrated wealth and power, assailed the First World War as undermining progressive change, foresaw reaction at home and conflict abroad following liberal disaffection with the Treaty of Versailles, opposed Democrats' urban-rural squabbles as choking off continued advance, shared Roosevelt's inclination to put human need above familiar means, and struggled tirelessly against Nazism much before others were ready to announce it the scourge of the age.

And so, as Charles Beard wrote, "Of William E. Dodd, scholar, teacher, writer, and servant of the Republic we may say, therefore, to paraphrase a maxim of Chateaubriand, 'He will live in the memory of the world by what he has done for the world.' And I can vouch for the statement that Mr. Dodd, indomitable foe of the meretricious, would not have it otherwise. Here the argument may rest, for beyond it none can rise."[19] This epitaph any man would do well to earn.

FRONT MATTER

1. Allen Weinstein and Alexander Vassiliev, *The Haunted Wood* (New York: Modern Library, 1999), p. 62.

CHAPTER I A RACE OF SETTLERS AND FARMERS

1. "Autobiographical Notes," 1933, William E. Dodd MSS, Library of Congress, Washington, D.C. (Unless otherwise indicated all manuscripts in the footnotes are from the Dodd collection.)

2. What information I have been able to gather about family origins comes chiefly from Dodd's own researches and records: "Autobiographical MSS," August 31, 1933; ? Dodd to W.E.D., July 26, 1904; W.E.D. to Edna Harris, November 24, 1926; W.E.D. to Ruby Yvonne, May 3, 1927; W.E.D. to Mrs. William E. Dodd, January 24, 1928; W.E.D. to Abner F. Dodd, February 7, 1928; W.E.D. MS Diary, January 20, 1928. A search of the genealogy records in the Library of Congress adds nothing to Dodd's own accounts.

3. See Ian C. C. Graham, *Colonists from Scotland: Emigration to North America,* 1707–1783 (Ithaca, N.Y., 1956), pp. 106–108, 154–161. W.E.D. MS Diary, January 20, 1928.

4. Clement Eaton has shown that "in North Carolina on the eve of the Civil War nearly three-fourths of the people owned no slaves, and of the small minority who were slaveholders, 70.8 percent owned less than ten slaves"—A *History of the South* (New York, 1949), p. 458. Neither John nor John Daniel Dodd have records of military service in the war. Walter Clark (ed.), *North Carolina Regiments,* 1861–1865 (5 vols.; Raleigh, 1901). Untitled newspaper clipping, January (?), 1938. Calculated from the *United States Census Office: Ninth Census: A Compendium* (Washington, 1872), the average Johnston County farmer in 1870 owned 202 acres of land and total property

valued at $803. Stanford Creech, by contrast, held 450 acres and total property of $1500. Eighth United States Census, Agriculture Schedule, Johnston County, Clayton Township, State Department of Archives and History, Raleigh, North Carolina.

5. See W.E.D. to John Daniel Dodd, April 23, 1924; "Autobiographical Notes," 1933; and W.E.D. to J. Franklin Jameson, February 7, 1913.

6. For a description of the southern farmer in these years, see C. Vann Woodward, *Origins of the New South, 1877–1913* (Baton Rouge, 1951), chap. vii. The plight of the North Carolina farmer is described in Hugh T. Lefler and Albert R. Newsome, *North Carolina* (Chapel Hill, 1963), chap. 36.

7. "Autobiographical Notes," 1933; "Professor William E. Dodd's Diary, 1916–1920," *The John P. Branch Historical Papers of Randolph-Macon College,* ed. W. Alexander Mabry, New Series, II (March 1953), 67. Calculated from the *United States Bureau of the Census: Tenth Census: Statistics of Agriculture,* Vol. III (Washington, 1883), the average Johnston County farmer in 1880 owned 131 acres and total property valued at $1454. John Daniel Dodd in that year held 109 acres and total property of $1300. Ninth United States Census, Agriculture Schedule, Johnston County, Clayton Township, State Department of Archives and History, Raleigh, North Carolina.

8. In all, William had four brothers and two sisters. Walter, two years his junior, became a Baptist minister; Alonzo, four years younger than William, became a judge; John, seven years younger, was the only brother to become a full-time farmer; and David, twelve years William's junior, became a Methodist minister. David Dodd to Lowry Price Ware, February 2, 1955, in Lowry P. Ware, "The Academic Career of William E. Dodd" (unpubl. Ph.D. diss., Department of History, University of South Carolina, 1956), p. 3. "Autobiographical Notes," 1933.

9. Jack L. Whitaker to L. P. Ware, June 10, 1954, in Ware, p. 5. "Autobiographical Notes," 1933; Wendell H. Stephenson, *The South Lives in History* (Baton Rouge, 1955), pp. 29–30; W.E.D. to John M. McBryde, Jr., June 23, 1933.

10. In describing Dodd's arrival at Blacksburg in January 1891, I have relied on his "Autobiographical Notes," 1933. His memory, however, may have been faulty since McBryde apparently did not take office as president until September 1891. *Dictionary of American Biography,* Vol. II (New York, 1933), pp. 554–555. "VPI: Historical Data Book," *Bulletin of the Virginia Polytechnic Institute,* LVII, No. 3 (January 1964), 8, 49–52, 56, 64, 67; "Virginia Colleges," *State Board of Education,* XXIV (January 1942), 17–18.

11. "Autobiographical Notes," 1933; "VPI: Historical Data Book," *loc. cit.,* pp. 55, 61; *Annual Catalogue of the Virginia Polytechnic Institute,* 1900–1901; Ware, p. 8; Stephenson, p. 30; *The Gray Jacket,* I, No. 6 (February 1893), 175. Cf. I, Nos. 2–5 (October 1892–January 1893), Carol M. Newman Library, Virginia Polytechnic Institute, Blacksburg, Va.

12. *The Gray Jacket,* II, Nos. 3, 4, and 8 (December 1893, January and May 1894); III, Nos. 1, 3, 4, and 8 (October and December 1894, January and May 1895).

13. Ware, pp. 6–7; W.E.D., "Josephus Daniels," *The Public,* XXI (1918), 791–794, 822–825; Josephus Daniels, *Tar Heel Editor* (Chapel Hill, 1939), p. 496; for an account of Daniels' public activities, see chaps. XLII–XLVIII; untitled newspaper clipping, January (?), 1938.

14. F. W. Simpson to W.E.D., n.d.; "Autobiographical Notes," 1933; "VPI: Historical Data Book," *loc. cit.,* pp. 10–12, 49; F. W. Simpson to W.E.D., May 10, 1898, and January 7, 1899; Ware, p. 9.

15. For a brief sketch of Sheib, see W.E.D., "Freedom of Speech in the South," *The Nation,* LXXXIV (April 24, 1907), 383. For Sheib's influence on him, see Sheib to W.E.D., August 14, 1899; Ware, pp. 9–10. See Laurence Veysey's comment: "Germany connoted not so much a nation or an

educational system as the promise of a great 'master' under whom one might study"—*The Emergence of the American University* (Chicago, 1965), p. 157.

16. Joseph J. Mathews, "The Study of History in the South," *Journal of Southern History,* XXXI (February 1965), 7–8; see C. H. Fahr to W.E.D., April 9, 1897; "Autobiographical Notes," 1933.

CHAPTER II THE LEIPZIG ADVENTURE

1. "Autobiographical Notes," 1933. In general, Dodd's recollections of his two years abroad are supported by J. N. Bowman, a fellow Leipzig student. J. N. Bowman to L. P. Ware, March 31, 1955, in Ware, pp. 12–18.

2. Herman Horne to W.E.D., August 6, 1897, February 27, 1898, July 10, 1898; F. W. Simpson to W.E.D., n.d.

3. "Autobiographical Notes," 1933.

4. Philip Rahv (ed.), *Discovery of Europe* (Boston, 1947), p. xiv.

5. On this condition of *Lernfreiheit* or academic freedom and other qualities of German graduate education discussed in this chapter, see Richard Hofstadter and Walter P. Metzger, *The Development of Academic Freedom in the United States* (New York, 1955), chap. VIII and especially pp. 373, 383–391. Also see Friedrich Paulsen, *The German Universities* (New York, 1895); Jurgen Herbst, *The German Historical School in American Scholarship* (Ithaca, N.Y., 1965), chap. v and especially pp. 9, 19–22, 34–37. J. N. Bowman to L. P. Ware, March 31, 1955, in Ware, p. 14; W.E.D., "Autobiographical Notes," 1933; Newton Arvin (ed.), *The Selected Letters of Henry Adams* (New York, 1951), p. 9.

6. W.E.D., "Autobiographical Notes," 1933.

7. James W. Thompson, *A History of Historical Writing,* Vol. II (New York, 1942), pp. 422–428; G. P. Gooch, *History and Historians in the Nineteenth Century* (London, 1913), pp. 588–593.

8. This is the conclusion of both Thompson and Gooch.

9. W.E.D., "Karl Lamprecht and Kulturgeschichte," *Popular Science Monthly,* LXIII (September 1903), 419; W.E.D., "The German People," *The New York Times,* April 8, 1905; Thompson, pp. 427–428.

10. Hoetzsch later became a faculty member at the University of Berlin and won election to the Reichstag. Meyer was on the faculty of the University of Munich; and Laube joined the faculty at the University of Breslau.

"Autobiographical Notes," 1933. In his "Notes," Dodd cites 1899 as the year he took Marcks's seminar. His description of other events, however, persuades me that the date should be 1898.

11. As with so many other Americans, the German experience was to give Dodd little more than a technique. As Professor Laurence Veysey points out, "For the utility-minded..., Germany could at most confirm altruistic tendencies, spiritual gropings, or plain orthodoxies that had been nurtured on the western side of the ocean.... For Americans to whom morality rather than knowledge seemed the highest educational purpose, the source of their code lay deeply within them, and Germany could offer only a technique"—*The Emergence of the American University,* p. 132.

12. W.E.D. to Carl Becker, May 21, 1932; "Professor William E. Dodd's Diary, 1916–1920," p. 62; Ware, p. 15; "Autobiographical Notes," 1933; Elliott Goodwin to W.E.D., December 8, 1898, October 6, 1899, January 14 and 28, August 27, 1900; W.E.D. to Isabel Goodwin, February 19, 1931.

13. See "Autobiographical Notes," 1933; W.E.D., "Militarism in Germany," *Raleigh News and Observer,* November 12, 1899; W.E.D., "How Prussia Became Germany," *Raleigh News and Observer,* November 19, 1899; W.E.D., "German Politics and Art," *The New York Times,* July 2,

1904; W.E.D. to Walter Clark, September 7, 1906, in *The Papers of Walter Clark*, ed. Aubrey L. Brooks and Hugh T. Lefler (Chapel Hill, N.C., 1950), p. 79; W.E.D. to "Editors of The New Republic," October 18, 1930; Ware, pp. 12–15.

For a discussion of opposition to foreign students in German universities, see Roy T. House, "Foreigners in German Universities," *The Nation*, XCVI (March 6, 1913), 230.

14. "Autobiographical Notes," 1933. Dodd's debate with Goodwin was similar to those going on between Democrats and Republicans in the United States, and they also stimulated interest in Jeffersonian democracy. See Merrill D. Peterson, *The Jefferson Image in the American Mind* (New York, 1960), pp. 230, 266–271.

15. Calculated from the *Jahres-Verzeichnis der an den Deutschen Universitäten erschienenen Schriften* (Berlin, 1891 and 1907) for the period August 15, 1889–August 14, 1890, the average length of Ph.D. theses was 56 pages, and for the period August 15, 1905–August 14, 1906, the average length was 80 pages.

16. "Autobiographical Notes," 1933.

17. See W.E.D., *Thomas Jefferson's Rückkehr zur Politik 1796* (Leipzig, 1899). Joseph Charles, *The Origins of the American Party System* (New York, 1961), pp. 89–90. For a summary of the conventional picture of Jefferson's part in party organization, see Peterson, pp. 312–314. Other recent scholarship is in essential agreement with Dodd's account of Jefferson's part in party organization. See Noble E. Cunningham, Jr., *The Jeffersonian Republicans: The Formation of Party Organization, 1789–1801* (Chapel Hill, 1957); and Dumas Malone, *Jefferson and the Ordeal of Liberty* (Boston, 1962), especially pp. xvi–xvii and chaps. XVIII–XX.

18. "Autobiographical Notes," 1933; Herman Horne to W.E.D., February 27, 1898, January 24, and August 18, 1899; Ware, pp. 22–23; Josephus Daniels to W.E.D., May 16, 1900, and June 6, 1901. For Daniels' ties to Chapel Hill, see Josephus Daniels, *Editor in Politics* (Chapel Hill, 1941), chaps. XI–XII.

19. W.E.D., *Raleigh News and Observer*, November 12 and 19, 1899; Ware, p. 20; "Autobiographical Notes," 1933.

20. *Raleigh News and Observer*, December 24, 1899; Daniels, *Editor in Politics*, p. 232; W.E.D., "The Religion of Jefferson—He Was Not an Atheist as Charged," *Raleigh News and Observer*, January 28, 1900; "Autobiographical Notes," 1933; Ware, pp. 20–21.

21. "Autobiographical Notes," 1933. "My thesis," Dodd wrote Erich Marcks in 1927, "was a poor sort of thing"—March 5, 1927.

22. "Autobiographical Notes," 1933.

CHAPTER III SCIENTIFIC HISTORY

1. William L. Chenery, *So It Seemed* (New York, 1952), chaps. I and II and especially pp. 18–19. I am indebted to Dr. T. McNider Simpson for his reminiscences of Dodd, Randolph-Macon, and Ashland given in an interview on August 12, 1964. Stephenson, p. 33; Ware, p. 27; *Virginia: A Guide to the Old Dominion* (New York, 1940), pp. 354–355, 475; W.E.D. to William J. Peele, September 26, 1900, Peele MSS, Southern Historical Collection, University of North Carolina Library, Chapel Hill, N.C. (cited hereafter as Peele MSS, So. Hist. Coll.); Horne to W.E.D., November 21, 1900, and July 5, 1901; Sheib to W.E.D., December 11, 1900.

2. "Randolph-Macon College: Catalogue, 1900–1901," Randolph-Macon College Library, Ashland, Virginia; Stephenson, pp. 33–34; interview with Simpson, August 12, 1964; Ware, p. 26;

President J. M. McBryde to W.E.D., February 7, 1901; Edwin W. Bowen to J. D. Riggs, April 27, 1901; Daniels to W.E.D., June 6, 1901; Horne to W.E.D., July 4, 5, and August 6, 1901; "Autobiographical Notes," 1933; W.E.D. to Mrs. William E. Dodd, December 16, 1928.

3. Wood Gray, "Ulrich Bonnell Phillips," *The Marcus W. Jernegan Essays in American Historiography*, ed. William T. Hutchinson (Chicago, 1957), p. 354; Wendell H. Stephenson, "A Half Century of Southern Historical Scholarship," *The Journal of Southern History*, XI (February 1945), 4–5, 8–17.

4. Quoted in Ware, p. 55.

5. Quoted in Stephenson, *The South Lives in History*, p. 34.

6. See John P. Branch to W.E.D., May 8, 1905; Ware, pp. 33–34.

7. See *Annual Report of the American Historical Association*, 1901 (Washington, D.C., 1902), pp. 20, 31–32; W.E.D., "The Study of History in the South," *Raleigh News and Observer*, January 12, 1902; *American Historical Review*, VII (April 1902), 430–431; Ware, pp. 54–57; W.E.D., "The Status of History in Southern Education," *The Nation*, LXXV (August 7, 1902), 109–111.

8. See correspondence in *The Nation*, LXXV (August 21, 1902), 149–150; (August 28, 1902), 168–169; *American Historical Review*, VIII (April 1903), 419–420; W.E.D., "Some Difficulties of the History Teacher in the South," *The South Atlantic Quarterly*, III (April 1904), 117–122. Cf. *American Historical Review*, IX (April 1904), 443–444.

9. See W.E.D., "The Study of History in the South." For evidence of Dodd's early relations with these men, see Albert B. Hart, "Recommendation for William E. Dodd," April 19, 1902; Frederick J. Turner to W.E.D., April 21, 1902. W.E.D. to Charles F. Adams, Jr., July 3, 1902, Charles Francis Adams, Jr., MSS, Massachusetts Historical Society, Boston, Mass. (cited hereafter as Adams MSS). W.E.D., "The Place of Nathaniel Macon in Southern History," *American Historical Review*, VII (July 1902), 663–675; W.E.D., "North Carolina in the Revolution," *The South Atlantic Quarterly*, I (April 1902), 156–161.

10. W.E.D., *The Life of Nathaniel Macon* (Raleigh, 1903).

11. See Thomas J. Pressly, *Americans Interpret Their Civil War* (Princeton, 1954), chap. IV. See E. A. Dithmar to W.E.D., April 30, 1906; Ellis P. Oberholtzer to W.E.D., January 19, 1904; Ware, pp. 40–47, 50, 63–64; W.E.D. to Charles F. Adams, Jr., September 10, 1904, Adams MSS; Stephenson, *The South Lives in History*, p. 39; Peterson, chaps. V and VI.

12. "Randolph-Macon College: Catalogue, 1903–04," Randolph-Macon College Library; Ware, pp. 31, 47; W.E.D. to Mrs. William E. Dodd, March 9, 1929.

13. The emphasis on service and research in the universities at this time is best described in Veysey, chaps. II and III. See Bassett to W.E.D., November 24, 1903. On the Bassett controversy, see Hofstadter and Metzger, pp. 445–457.

14. *The New York Times*, November 21, December 12, 1903, January 16, March 12, March 19, 1904; "Correspondence of Leven Powell" and "Spencer Roane—Reprints from the Richmond *Enquirer*," *John P. Branch Historical Papers*, I, 217–256, 325–373; "Karl Lamprecht and Kulturgeschichte," *Popular Science Monthly*, LXIII (September 1903), 419–426; "Another View of Our Educational Progress," *The South Atlantic Quarterly*, II (October 1903), 325–333; "The United States Senate," *Biblical Recorder*, May 18, 1904; Ware, pp. 64–65.

15. Mrs. William E. Dodd to W.E.D., June 15, 23, 29, and July 1, 1904; *The New York Times*, July 2 and September 3, 1904.

16. "Autobiographical Notes," 1933; *The New York Times*, October 29, December 3, 10, and 31, 1904; W.E.D., "The Recent World Congress of Arts and Sciences at St. Louis," *Biblical Recorder*,

November 2, 1904; W.E.D. to George P. Brett, November 13, 1904. Cf. "In an evil moment I promised to write…a 'Life of Jefferson Davis'…collections of letters and papers seem to be scarce." W.E.D. to Charles F. Adams, Jr., September 18, 1904, Adams MSS. "Robert E. Lee and Reconstruction," *The South Atlantic Quarterly,* IV (January 1905), 63–70; *American Historical Review,* x (April 1905), 700–701; *The New York Times,* April 8, 1905; "The State Library as a Public Institution," *Richmond Times Dispatch,* May 4, 1905.

17. Mrs. William E. Dodd to W.E.D., May 18, 19, 1905; Ware, pp. 65–67.

18. "In disregard for the dictates of his scientific training, he [Dodd] did not defer writing until an exhaustive examination of all available materials could be made. Instead Dodd frequently relied upon his historical imagination and later journeyed to Richmond or Washington to seek proof of these surmises"—Ware, pp. 69–70. Stephenson contends that Dodd "ignored many available sources"—*South Lives in History,* p. 39.

19. W.E.D., *Jefferson Davis* (Philadelphia, 1907), pp. 2, 7, 15; W.E.D. to Charles F. Adams, Jr., September 18, 1904, Adams MSS; on the book's failings as a character portrait, see *The South Atlantic Quarterly,* VII (April 1908), 196–197.

20. *Davis,* pp. 7, 209–210. Cf. Pressly's discussion of the "liberal" historians' attitude toward the war, chaps. III, IV, and V passim.

21. *Davis,* chaps. XIII–XXI; W.E.D. to Charles F. Adams, Jr., June 26, 1906, Adams MSS. Cf. W.E.D. to Charles F. Adams, Jr., August 15, 1908, Adams MSS.

22. See a review of the book by Charles F. Adams, Jr., in *The American Historical Review,* XIII (July 1908), 878–880. Also see Lawrence Henry Gipson, "The Collapse of the Confederacy," *Mississippi Valley Historical Review,* IV (March 1918), 437–458, a paper written for a doctoral seminar taught by Dodd at the University of Chicago; James G. Randall and David Donald, *The Civil War and Reconstruction* (Boston, 1961), chaps. XIII and XIV and bibliographical notes on pp. 761–762.

23. See Thomas Johns to W.E.D., July 2, 1905.

CHAPTER IV TOWARD A DOUBLE LIFE

1. On southern progressivism, see Woodward, chap. XIV; Arthur Link, "The Progressive Movement in the South, 1870–1914," *North Carolina Historical Review,* XXIII (April 1946), 172–195; C. Vann Woodward, *Tom Watson* (New York, 1938); Dewey W. Grantham, Jr., *Hoke Smith and the Politics of the New South* (Baton Rouge, 1958).

2. On the progressive movement in Virginia, see Ralph C. McDanel, "The Virginia Constitutional Convention of 1901–02," *The Johns Hopkins Studies in Historical and Political Science,* Vol. XLVI, No. 3 (Baltimore, 1928); Robert C. Glass and Carter Glass, Jr., *Virginia Democracy,* Vol. I (Richmond, 1937); Allen Moger, *The Rebuilding of the Old Dominion* (New York, 1940); William E. Larsen, "Governor Andrew Jackson Montague of Virginia, 1862–1937: The Making of a Southern Progressive" (unpubl. Ph.D. diss., Department of History, University of Virginia, 1961); for a biographical sketch of Montague, see *Dictionary of American Biography,* Vol. XXII, Supplement Two (New York, 1958), pp. 467–468; clipping from the *Columbia* (S.C.) *State,* August 14, 1905, in Dodd's papers.

3. Quoted in Larsen, pp. 530–531.

4. On the ties between university professors and progressivism, see Frederick Rudolph, *The American College and University: A History* (New York, 1962), chap. 17. In this, Dodd neatly illustrates

what Professor Richard Hofstadter calls "the Protestant personality" in the progressive movement and "its ethos of personal responsibility" or "citizenlike civic consciousness"—*The Age of Reform* (New York, 1956), pp. 203–204.

5. W.E.D. to Andrew J. Montague, October 14, 1904, Andrew Jackson Montague MSS, Virginia State Library, Richmond, Va. (cited hereafter as Montague MSS); Larsen, p. 534; Montague to W.E.D., October 19, 1904. W.E.D. to Montague, March 13, June 15, 1905, Montague MSS. Montague to W.E.D., November 9, 1904, January 14, February 24, and June 16, 1905. W.E.D. to Montague, July 14, 22, 1905, and clipping from *The Hanover* (Va.) *Herald*, July 21, 1905, Montague MSS.

6. W.E.D. to Montague, August 24, 1905, Montague MSS.

7. W.E.D. to Theodore Roosevelt, March 12, 1907; W.E.D. to "Mr. Slemp," n.d.; William Loeb, Jr., to W.E.D., October 14, 1905, and February 13, 1906; W.E.D. to Henry Cabot Lodge, March 30, 1906; Elliott Goodwin to W.E.D., May 15, 1906; W.E.D. to Theodore Roosevelt, May 15, 1906; William Loeb, Jr., to W.E.D., May 15, 1906. W.E.D. to Montague, May 16, 1906, Montague MSS. On the Post Office scandal, see George E. Mowry, *The Era of Theodore Roosevelt* (New York, 1962), pp. 170–171; Albert B. Hart to W.E.D., June 2, 1906; W.E.D. to Judge Walter Clark, September 7, 1906, *The Papers of Walter Clark*, II, 80. Woodward, *Origins of the New South*, p. 371; Grantham, chap. IX; W.E.D. to Theodore Roosevelt, n.d., though probably October 5, 1906; William Loeb, Jr., to W.E.D., October 26, 1906.

8. "Virginia's Opposition to Chief Justice Marshall—Reprints from the Richmond *Enquirer*, 1821," *John P. Branch Historical Papers*, II, 78–183; *The New York Times*, December 1, 1906; "Chief Justice Marshall and Virginia, 1813–1821," *American Historical Review*, XII (July 1907); Hodder to W.E.D., January 17, 1907; Hart to W.E.D., February 8, 1907.

9. Woodward, *Origins of the New South*, pp. 402–406. This movement for educational reform was part of the larger struggle for southern progress. In Lawrence A. Cremin's words, it was a many-sided effort to use the school to realize the promise of American life—*The Transformation of the School* (New York, 1961), pp. viii, 88. W.E.D., "Freedom of Speech in the South," *The Nation*, LXXXIV (April 24, 1907), 383; Edwin Mims to W.E.D., June 15, October 20, 1907.

10. On these points, see Woodward, *Origins of the New South*, pp. 443–446; Veysey, pp. 346–356, 388–397, 414–418; Hofstadter, *Age of Reform*, pp. 153–155.

11. See Veysey, pp. 317–318. Woodrow Wilson's departure from Princeton in 1910 for a political career offers a good example. See Arthur Walworth, *Woodrow Wilson* (Boston, 1965), I, chap. IX.

12. W.E.D. to "Editor," *Hanover Herald*, March 15, 1907.

13. Gravatt to W.E.D., June 3, August 28, 1907. See numerous other Gravatt letters to Dodd for the period of the campaign, March–August 1907, in Box 6 of the Dodd MSS.

14. See the correspondence in Box 7 of the Dodd MSS. Also see Ware, pp. 93–94.

15. Montague to W.E.D., November 20, 1907, Montague MSS; W.E.D. to Charles F. Adams, Jr., April 26, 1906, Adams MSS. For Dodd's aid to Baker, see Ray S. Baker to W.E.D., November 20, 1907; Dewey W. Grantham, Jr., Introduction to Ray S. Baker, *Following the Color Line* (New York, 1964), p. vi.

16. W.E.D. to Mrs. William E. Dodd, January 26, 1908; *The Letters of Theodore Roosevelt*, ed. Elting E. Morison (Cambridge, Mass., 1952), v, 225; W.E.D., "Memorandum," March 5, 1908; Stephenson, *The South Lives in History*, pp. 49–50.

17. A.F. Thomas to W.E.D., August 30, September 4, 1907, May 21, 1908; John A. McNeill to W.E.D., April 2, June 1, 1908; A.H. Sands to W.E.D., April 23, 1908.

18. W.E.D. to Montague, August 10, 1907, Montague MSS; W.E.D. to Albert B. Hart, December 10, 1907, Andrew C. McLaughlin MSS, University of Chicago Library, Chicago, Ill. (cited hereafter as McLaughlin MSS). McLaughlin to W.E.D., January 31, February 7, 1908. McLaughlin had been particularly interested in Dodd's work on John Marshall. At McLaughlin's request, Dodd joined him in a session on constitutional history at the Madison meeting of the association. See McLaughlin to W.E.D., August 3, 1907.

19. Edwin E. Slosson, "University of Chicago," *The Independent,* LXVIII (January 6, 1910), 38; W.E.D. to Mrs. William E. Dodd, April 12, 1908; McLaughlin to W.E.D., June 6 and July 9, 1908. W.E.D. to Montague, July 27, 1908, Montague MSS. University of Chicago Bulletins: "University Public Lectures: Summer Quarter, 1908"; "Information Concerning Railroad Rates, Schedules and Special Parties from the South: Summer Quarter, 1908," University of Chicago Library (cited hereafter as U.C.L.). W.E.D. to McLaughlin, August 13, 1908, McLaughlin MSS.

20. McLaughlin to W.E.D., December 2, 1908, McLaughlin MSS. H. Morse Stephens to W.E.D., November 5, 1908.

21. See Frederic Bancroft to W.E.D., October 2, 12, 15, 16, 18, 21, 26, 1908. W.E.D. to Bancroft, September 28, October 3 and 14, 1908, Frederic Bancroft MSS, Columbia University Library, New York (cited hereafter as Bancroft MSS). W.E.D. to Charles F. Adams, Jr., September 3, November 3, 1908.

CHAPTER V SOMEWHAT OF A JEFFERSONIAN

1. John Spencer Bassett to W.E.D., January 10, 1909.

2. Thomas W. Goodspeed, *A History of the University of Chicago* (Chicago, 1916), pp. 421, 470; Edwin E. Slosson, *Great American Universities* (New York, 1910), pp. x, 409–410, 425–428, 430–432, 434; Veysey, pp. 322–323, 356–360, 368, 377–379; *The University of Chicago Survey,* Vol. I: *Trends in University Growth* (Chicago, 1933), pp. 137, 228–229.

3. For faculty members and course offerings, see "The University of Chicago: Circular of the Departments of Political Economy, Political Science, History, Sociology and Anthropology, 1909," pp. 26–32, U.C.L. Certainly in variety of courses taught, numbers of graduate instructors, and faculty teaching-load, the Chicago department compared favorably with those at Harvard, Yale, Columbia, Michigan, Wisconsin, Stanford, and Berkeley. My conclusion is based on a reading of the 1909–1910 catalogues and bulletins from the archives of each of these schools.

The other members of the Department in 1909–10 were: Dodd, of course; Benjamin Terry, Professor of Medieval and English History; Francis W. Shepardson, Associate Professor of American History; Joseph P. Warren, Assistant Professor of History, a modern European and English specialist; Marcus W. Jernegan and Dice R. Anderson, instructors in American history. See "Announcements: Register of Doctors of Philosophy, June 1893–June 1927," *The University of Chicago,* XXVIII, No. 4 (September 10, 1927), 23–24.

4. Stephenson, *The South Lives in History,* pp. 4–6, 20–21, 36; Wendell Holmes Stephenson, *Southern History in the Making* (Baton Rouge, 1964), pp. 8–10; Ware, pp. 112–113; W.E.D. to Montague, November 4, 1909; Montague to W.E.D., November 8, 1909, Montague MSS; W.E.D. to Victor Yarros, May 13, 1913; "University of Chicago: Circular...1909," pp. 31–32, U.C.L.; W.E.D. to H. Morse Stephens, April 20, 1909.

5. Slosson, *Great American Universities,* p. 436; Andrew C. McLaughlin, *Report on the Diplomatic Archives of the Department of State,* 1789–1840 (Washington, 1906); Herbst,

pp. 154–161; Ware, pp. 325–326; W.E.D., "Democracy and Learning," *The Nation*, LXXXIX (November 4, 1909), 430–431.

6. W.E.D. to Frederick Jackson Turner, February 3 and April 8, 1909, Frederick Jackson Turner MSS, Henry E. Huntington Library, San Marino, Calif. (cited hereafter as Turner MSS); W.E.D. to Montague, May 3, 1909, Montague MSS; W.E.D. to William K. Boyd, May 10, 1909, William K. Boyd MSS, Duke University Library, Durham, N.C. (cited hereafter as Boyd MSS). Boyd was Bassett's successor at Trinity. W.E.D. to H. Morse Stephens, April 20, 1909.

7. See "University of Chicago: Circular . . . 1909," pp. 31–32, U.C.L.

8. "The substance of the following papers," Dodd wrote in the preface to his book, "has been presented in the form of popular lectures at the University of California, the University of Indiana, the University of Chicago, Richmond and Randolph-Macon Colleges. . . ."—*Statesmen of the Old South, or From Radicalism to Conservative Revolt* (New York, 1911); W.E.D. to W. W. Cook, March 22, 1912; W.E.D. to Albert Beveridge, May 5, 1913.

9. *Statesmen of the Old South*, pp. 9, 12, 23, 32–33, 53–54, 103, 108–111, 114–115, 133–134, 166–167.

10. For a summary of critical reaction to Dodd's book, see Ware, pp. 163–166. Also see Stephenson, *South Lives in History*, p. 39; and more generally, Clement Eaton, *The Freedom-of-Thought Struggle in the Old South* (New York, 1964).

11. See John Higham, Leonard Krieger, and Felix Gilbert, *History* (Englewood Cliffs, N.J., 1965), pp. 171–177. Turner's comment is in Stephenson, *South Lives in History*, p. 41; W.E.D. to Turner, October 17, 1911, Turner MSS.

12. *American Historical Review*, XVI (July 1911), 774–788; Charles Beard to W.E.D., September 27, 1911.

13. On the influence of the Jefferson essay and its decline in relevance, see Peterson, pp. 279–280; Ware, p. 159; Richard Hofstadter, *The American Political Tradition* (New York, 1948), chap. 2; Leonard W. Levy, *Jefferson and Civil Liberties, the Darker Side* (Cambridge, Mass., 1963); Jefferson's complexity is most fully stated in Dumas Malone, *Jefferson and His Times* (3 vols.; Boston, 1948–62).

14. For conflicting interpretations of Calhoun, see Eaton, *Freedom-of-Thought Struggle*, pp. 146–147; Charles M. Wiltse, *John C. Calhoun* (3 vols.; Indianapolis, 1944–51); Gerald M. Capers, *John C. Calhoun—Opportunist: A Reappraisal* (Gainesville, 1960). The quotes are from Dodd's *Statesmen*, pp. 110–111, 133–134.

15. *Outlook*, c (January 13, 1912), 99. Cf. Theodore Roosevelt to W.E.D., February 13, 1912, William E. Dodd MSS, #225, So. Hist. Coll. On this aspect of progressive history, see John Higham, "Beyond Consensus," *American Historical Review*, LXVII (April 1962), 611, 618; Cushing Strout, *The Pragmatic Revolt in American History: Carl Becker and Charles Beard* (New Haven, 1958); Morton G. White, *Social Thought in America: The Revolt Against Formalism* (New York, 1949), chap. IV. On Beard, see Strout, pp. 92–93; White, pp. 109–110, 125; and Herbst, pp. 221–224.

Since both writers addressed themselves to central issues in America's history, it is interesting to compare the receptions given in progressive circles to Dodd's *Statesmen* and Beard's *Constitution*: where Dodd's book aroused limited interest, Beard's stirred a controversy in which progressives eagerly fought. What seems most important in explaining the difference was the fact that progressives could not use Dodd's book to argue their case; it was too partisan to make it an effective weapon in political debate. Beard's work, on the other hand, could be cited as evidence gathered by a "detached" observer. That there were other things making for greater interest in Beard's study goes without saying; but it was the tone of "scientific objectivity," the very quality absent from Dodd's book, which goes a long way toward explaining its greater popularity. It is also interesting to note that Algie Simons' *Social Forces in American History,* which Carl Becker called "a handbook for doctrinaire socialists," had more appeal for Dodd than Walter Weyl's *The New Democracy,* which was of great interest to Progressives. See Dodd's remarks in *The Dial,* LII (May 16, 1912), 396–397.

16. On the role of the scholar-expert in politics, see Richard Hofstadter, *Anti-intellectualism in American Life* (New York, 1963), pp. 197–214. Hofstadter's comparison of the attitudes of Woodrow Wilson and Theodore Roosevelt toward the "expert" is particularly revealing: "Unlike T.R...., he [Wilson] did not conceive of experts as likely agents or administrators of reform, but rather as hirelings available only to big business and special interests. Whereas most Progressive thinkers contrasted government by big business with a popular government that would employ experts to regulate unacceptable business practices, Wilson thought of big business, vested interests, and experts as a solid combine that could be beaten only by returning government to 'the people'"—p. 209. Cf. Herbst, chap. 7.

17. See Edgar Lee Masters, *The Tale of Chicago* (New York, 1933), pp. 280–282; W.E.D. to Montague, January 5, 1911, Montague MSS; Henry J. Smith, *Chicago: A Portrait* (New York, 1931), p. 99; Lloyd Lewis, *Chicago: The History of Its Reputation* (New York, 1929), pp. 295, 343; Charles Merriam, *Chicago: A More Intimate View of Urban Politics* (New York, 1929), pp. 94–98, 223, 268–273, 281–287; Charles Merriam, "Report on the Municipal Revenues of Chicago," *City Club of Chicago,* No. 2 (January 2, 1906); *Outlook,* XCIX (March 11, 1911), 524–525; Graham Taylor to W.E.D., August 16, 1910; Elliott Goodwin to W.E.D., March 7, 1911; Carter H. Harrison, II, *Stormy Years: The Autobiography of Carter H. Harrison* (Indianapolis, 1935), chaps. XXV–XXVII; Louise C. Wade, *Graham Taylor: Pioneer for Social Justice* (Chicago, 1964), p. 191; W.E.D. to Montague, May 18, 1909, Montague MSS.

18. W.E.D. to Montague, May 18, September 19, November 14, 1909, Montague MSS; W.E.D. to Walter Clark, June 4, 1911, *The Papers of Walter Clark,* II, 116–117.

19. W.E.D. to Frederic Bancroft, November 2 and 25, 1910, Bancroft MSS. Wilson's comment is in Arthur S. Link, *Wilson,* Vol. I: *The Road to the White House* (Princeton, 1947), pp. 315–316. On Dodd's efforts for Wilson in Virginia, see W.E.D. to Montague, January 1 and 5, February 15, May 8, 1911, Montague MSS; W.E.D. to Frederic Bancroft, April 30, 1911, Bancroft MSS; Larsen, pp. 601–607.

20. Garnett to W.E.D., June 15, July 22, 1911; Richmond *Times-Dispatch,* July 5, 6, 14, August 8, 12, and 18, 1911; Richmond *News Leader,* July 5, 6, 12, 19, 1911; Editor, Richmond *Evening Journal* to W.E.D., July 6, 1911; George H. Denny to W.E.D., July 15, 1911; William Jones to W.E.D., July 15, 1911. Montague to W.E.D., July 12 and September 8, 1911; W.E.D. to Montague, July 14, 17, August 19, 26, 1911; W.E.D. to the Press of Richmond, July 14, 1911, Montague MSS; Link, *Wilson,* I, 339–341.

21. For the background, see Link, *Wilson,* I, 335, 344–345, 409–412, 422–423, 429–430. For Dodd's activities, see Wilson to W.E.D., September 12, 1911; "Autobiographical Notes," 1933; T. R. Sullivan to W.E.D., December 23, 1911; Byron R. Newton to W.E.D., February 13, 1912; L. S. Bornemann to W.E.D., March 12 and 28, 1912; Elliott Goodwin to W.E.D., March 15, 1912. W.E.D. to Walter Clark, March 26, 1912, *The Papers of Walter Clark,* II, 146–147; University of Chicago, *The Daily Maroon,* February 21, 22, March 2, 7, 8, 9, 1912; Wilson to W.E.D., April 1, 1912, Ray

S. Baker MSS, Library of Congress, Washington, D.C. (cited hereafter as R. S. Baker MSS). William F. McCombs to W.E.D., April 4, 16, 1912; W.E.D. to McCombs, April 11, 1912; Theodore Jervey to W.E.D., May 16, 1912; Senator Charles Culberson to W.E.D., May 16, 1912; W.E.D., Theodore L. Neff, A. H. Salmon, William L. Chenery to Josephus Daniels, June 26, 1912.

22. W.E.D. to Henry Ellis, December 14, 1912; W.E.D., "The Social and Economic Background of Woodrow Wilson," *Journal of Political Economy,* xxv (March 1917), 279. For a critique of Dodd's view, a summary of the forces at work in making Wilson the nominee, and the Progressives' response to the nomination, see Link, *Wilson,* I, 463–465, 468–469. For a list of the leading progressives at the University of Chicago who supported Roosevelt, see Chicago *Daily Tribune,* November 1, 1912, p. 1.

23. W.E.D. to Julian S. Mason, October 31, 1912. Cf. W.E.D. to Bancroft, September 18 and October 27, 1912, Bancroft MSS. Dodd's description of himself as "somewhat of a Jeffersonian" is in W.E.D. to "Dear Sir," October 26, 1919.

For a summary of the differences between Roosevelt's New Nationalism and Wilson's New Freedom, see Arthur Link, *Woodrow Wilson and the Progressive Era,* 1910–1917 (New York, 1963), pp. 18–22.

24. For a picture of Dodd's activities, see Frank B. Lord to W.E.D., October 18, 1912; Erving Winslow to W.E.D., October 22, 1912; Chicago *Evening Post,* October 28, 29, 1912. For the quotes, see W.E.D. to Bancroft, September 18, 1912, Bancroft MSS; and W.E.D. to Henry Ellis, December 14, 1912.

CHAPTER VI THE ONLY THING WORTH FIGHTING FOR

1. W.E.D. to Ashley Horne, November 23, 1912; W.E.D. to Henry Ellis, December 14, 1912; W.E.D. to Daniels, December 17, 1912; Daniels to W.E.D., January 2, 1913; Arthur S. Link, *Wilson,* Vol. II: *The New Freedom* (Princeton, 1956), pp. 23–26, 157, 161–162; W.E.D. to Congressman William Jones, March 15, 1913. W.E.D. to Clark, April 21, 1913, *The Papers of Walter Clark,* II, 198. Cf. W.E.D. to William J. Bryan, March 6 and April 20, 1913; W.E.D. to ? in the Department of State, February 26, 1913; Link, *Wilson and the Progressive Era,* p. 29; Larsen, pp. 629–633; W.E.D. to Daniels, April 21, 1913.

2. See *Annual Report of the American Historical Association,* 1912 (Washington, 1914), pp. 27–28, 37–39; for a discussion of the impact of the New History on the profession, see Higham, *History,* pp. 104–116, 177; Dodd's paper is printed in *American Historical Review,* XVIII (April 1913), 522–536; W.E.D. to James Shotwell, January 18, 1913; W.E.D. to J. Franklin Jameson, February 7, 1913.

3. Ware, pp. 229–230, 235; on Dodd's trip, see W.E.D. to William K. Boyd, January 5 and February 17, 1913, Boyd MSS; for his speech, see W.E.D., "History and Patriotism," *The South Atlantic Quarterly,* XII (April 1913), 109–121.

4. The quote is from Strout, p. 24. Robinson's aim was to enable men to keep their thinking abreast of changes in their environment. See Higham, *History,* p. 112.

5. *The South Atlantic Quarterly,* XII, 118, 120.

6. The idea for the series actually dated back to the spring of 1912. But a formal agreement was not made until December and concentrated work on the project was not undertaken by Dodd until March 1913. The correspondence about the series can be found in Box 9 of Dodd's MSS.

7. See W.E.D. to William H. Glasson, May 10, 1913, William Henry Glasson MSS, Duke University Library, Durham, N.C. (cited hereafter as Glasson MSS). Glasson was professor of

economics at Trinity College in North Carolina. "Completed and published doctoral dissertations" and "Dissertations in Progress," 1914, Department of History MSS, University of Chicago Library, Chicago, Ill. (cited hereafter as Dept. of History MSS).

8. For the location and description of the farm, see *Virginia: A Guide to the Old Dominion,* pp. 524, 527; "Professor Dodd's Diary," pp. 9, 12; W.E.D., "Autobiographical Notes," 1933; W.E.D. to F. H. O'Hara, March 18, 1931. William T. Hutchinson to author, July 28, 1964. W.E.D. to McLaughlin, October 18, 1913, Dept. of History MSS.

9. *Robert J. Walker: Imperialist* (Chicago, 1914). For the value of Dodd's paper, see James P. Shenton, *Robert John Walker: A Politician from Jackson to Lincoln* (New York, 1961), p. xv. For Dodd's review, see *American Historical Review,* XIX (October 1913), 162–163. W.E.D. to McLaughlin, October 18, 1913, Dept. of History MSS. Cf. W.E.D. to McLaughlin, August 30, 1913, ibid.

10. W.E.D., *Expansion and Conflict* (Boston, 1915).

11. See Higham, *American Historical Review,* LXVII, 611.

12. *Expansion and Conflict,* p. vii. Turner's response to the work was: "I appreciate the fact that the Riverside series has not only furnished a very useful manual of history, but has also made inroads into the unconquered historical lands, your own volume not the least by any means in this respect. Sometimes I think you a bit too bold in your conclusions, sometimes I disagree, but always I see an illuminative piece of work, one based on independent research"—Turner to W.E.D., n.d. (but probably January 1916). For Dodd's answer, in which he wrote, "You will have seen at many points how much I am indebted to your work and I think my bibliographies indicate the fact," see February 6, 1916, Turner MSS.

13. See Ware, pp. 172–173, 237–238. For Dodd's courses, see "The University of Chicago: Circular of the Departments of Political Economy, Political Science, History, Sociology and Anthropology, 1913–1914," U.C.L. W.E.D. to Bancroft, March 14, 1914, Bancroft MSS.

14. W.E.D. to Arthur O. Lovejoy, January 31, 1914; W.E.D. to John Dewey, March 31, 1914; Dewey to W.E.D., November 15 and 18, 1914; W.E.D. to Dewey, June 20, 1915; Hofstadter and Metzger, p. 478.

15. W.E.D. to Bancroft, March 14, 1915. W.E.D. to Boyd, October 10, 1914, Boyd MSS. W.E.D. to Erich Marcks, October 11, 1914; Franklin Hoyt to W.E.D., October 26 and December 12, 1914; W.E.D. to "My Dear Brother," February 3, 1915; W.E.D. to Hoyt, February 12, 1915; W.E.D. to H. H. Webster, February 13, 1915; W.E.D. to Marcks, April 27, 1915.

16. W.E.D. to Mrs. William E. Dodd, August 25, 1914; W.E.D. to Daniels, January 6, 1915. The descriptions of preparedness advocates, southern and western progressive sentiment, and the Wilson-Daniels response are in Link, *Wilson and the Progressive Era,* pp. 180–181, 177–178; Lawrence W. Levine, *Defender of the Faith: William Jennings Bryan: The Last Decade, 1915–1925* (New York, 1965), pp. 48–49; W.E.D. to "Dear Sir," February 16, 1915.

17. Jacob E. Cooke, *Frederic Bancroft: Historian* (Norman, Okla., 1957), pp. 98–102; W.E.D. to Bancroft, March 14, 1915; Bancroft to W.E.D., December 24, 1914, March 10, April 9, 1915; Dice Anderson to W.E.D., April 25, 1915; W.E.D. to Bancroft, April 25, 1915; W.E.D. to Charles Ambler, May 17, 1915. W.E.D. to Boyd, May 21, 1915, Boyd MSS.

18. For Dodd's continuing detachment from the A.H.A. fight, see the correspondence in Box 11 of the Dodd MSS. For Dodd's role in the Chicago Literary Club, see W. N.C. Carlton to W.E.D., June 19, 1915. For Dodd's interest in the A.A.U.P., see W.E.D. to John Dewey, June 20, 1915; Dewey to W.E.D., June 23, 1915; Arthur O. Lovejoy to W.E.D., June 25, 1915; W.E.D.,

"Democracy and the University," *The Nation*, CI (October 14, 1915), 463–465. For a summary of the response of the A.A.U.P. to these cases, see Hofstadter and Metzger, pp. 478–482.

19. Link, *Wilson and the Progressive Era*, p. 165; typed statement, n.d., in Box 11 of the Dodd MSS; W.E.D. to Professor Lavisse, July 8, 1915. The article can be found under the title "Should We Build a Big Army and a Big Navy?," n.d., in Box 11. For one response to the article, see Edgar A. Bancroft to W.E.D., June 2, 1915. W.E.D. to Josephus Daniels, May 15, 1915; W.E.D. to George Trevelyan, May 19, 1915; W.E.D. to Walter Hines Page, July 15, 1915; W.E.D. to "Dear Sir," July 8, 1915; Link, *Wilson and the Progressive Era*, p. 179. For a discussion of Wilson's relations with "advanced progressives," see Link, *Wilson*, II, chap. VIII: "Reformers, Radicals, and the New Freedom."

20. "We expect to spend the fall in Loudoun. . . ," Dodd wrote Charles Ambler. "The little farm has been worth a mint to me in the way of nerve restorative. . . ."—W.E.D. to Ambler, July 9, 1915.

21. There is a substantial correspondence about these matters in Boxes 11 and 12 of the Dodd MSS. Perhaps the most successful scholarship Dodd undertook in the period after his *Riverside* work was his "valuable" criticism of Albert Beveridge's life of John Marshall. See Beveridge to W.E.D., July 17 and September 17, 1915, for just two samples of a vast correspondence.

22. W.E.D. to William H. Glasson, February 26, 1916, Glasson MSS; Albert Beveridge to W.E.D., February 28, 1916; Link, *Wilson and the Progressive Era*, pp. 179–182.

23. See Charles P. Janney to W.E.D., February 28, 1916; W.E.D. to Claude Kitchin, June 2, 1916. For criticism of Daniels at this time, see *The New York Times*, April 4, 9:1; April 7, 3:1; April 13, 5:2, 8. For Dodd's attempt to defend Daniels in the Chicago *Herald*, see W.E.D. to Keeley, April 20, 1916; Daniels to W.E.D., April 17, 1916.

24. W.E.D. to Bryan, May 17, 1916. On Bryan's opposition to Wilson and fears that he might split the Democratic party, see Levine, pp. 66–77. W.E.D. to Edward House, May 17, 1916. Dodd was introduced to House through Henry H. Childers of San Francisco. See Childers to W.E.D., April 26, 1916; and House to W.E.D., May 15, 1916.

25. For a discussion of provisions in the army bill applying to American colleges and universities, see Oswald G. Villard, "The Army Bill," *The Nation*, CII (June 1, 1916), 585. "Professor Dodd's Diary," p. 34. Cf. Dodd's five-page memorandum on military training at Chicago in Box 12 of his papers.

26. W.E.D. to Claude Kitchin, March 31, June 2, 1916, Claude Kitchin MSS, University of North Carolina Library, Chapel Hill, N.C. (cited hereafter as Kitchin MSS). On the tariff commission, see Arthur S. Link, *Wilson*, Vol. IV: *Confusions and Crises*, 1915–1916 (Princeton, 1964), pp. 341–344.

27. A copy of the contract is in Box 12 of Dodd's MSS. On his motives for agreeing to do the book, see "Professor Dodd's Diary," p. 30. W.E.D. to House, May 17, 1916. For a description of Beard's book, see Peterson, pp. 315–316. W.E.D., "Economic Interpretation of American History," *Journal of Political Economy*, XXIV (May 1916), 489–495. For Dodd's difficulties starting on the book, see Allen Johnson to W.E.D., June 13, 26, July 30, September 15 and November 7, 1916.

28. For the background, see Link, *Wilson and the Progressive Era*, pp. 233, 240–247. For the interview, see Post to W.E.D., August 15 and 25, 1916; Joseph Tumulty to W.E.D., August 17, 1916; "Professor Dodd's Diary," pp. 9–11. For Dodd's reaction to the conversation and the campaign, see W.E.D. to Oswald G. Villard, October 4, 1916, Oswald Garrison Villard MSS, Harvard University Library, Cambridge, Mass. (cited hereafter as Villard MSS). Ferdinand Schevill to W.E.D.,

October 15, 1916. W.E.D. to House, October 12, 1916, Edward M. House MSS, Yale University Library, New Haven, Conn. (cited hereafter as House MSS).

29. "Professor Dodd's Diary," pp. 13–20.

30. And this was Dodd's view despite the fact that he believed that Wilson's election was a victory for "the South and West…the farmers, small business men and perhaps a sprinkle of Union labor against the larger industrial, transportation and commercial interests"—W.E.D. to House, November 10, 1916, quoted in Link, *Wilson and the Progressive Era,* p. 250. For Dodd's most elaborate statement of this conclusion, see his "The Social and Economic Background of Woodrow Wilson," pp. 261–285.

31. For a description of American attitudes and policy in this period, see Link, *Wilson and the Progressive Era,* pp. 251–267. For Dodd's views, see "Professor Dodd's Diary," pp. 26–27.

32. See "Professor Dodd's Diary," pp. 26–27, 33; Baker to W.E.D., November 17 and December 20, 1916. Baker's letters were replies to notes of November 11 and December 6, 1916, from Dodd. W.E.D. to Kitchin, December 13, 1916; Kitchin to W.E.D., December 16, 1916, January 11, 1917, Kitchin MSS; W.E.D., "Classic Utterances of American Statesmen," *The Dial,* LXI (December 28, 1916), 578–579; W.E.D., "The United States of To-Morrow," *The Nation,* CIV (January 18, 1917), 74–75.

33. Wilson's comments to Cobb are quoted in Link, *Wilson and the Progressive Era,* p. 277. Dodd's statements are in "Professor Dodd's Diary," p. 39; and W.E.D. to Daniels, April 5, 1917, Josephus Daniels MSS, Library of Congress, Washington, D.C. (cited hereafter as Daniels MSS).

CHAPTER VII PUBLIC SERVICE

1. Carl Resek, ed., *War and the Intellectuals: Essays by Randolph S. Bourne,* 1915–1919 (New York, 1964), p. 3.

2. Levine, pp. 93–102; "Professor Dodd's Diary," pp. 43–44; W.E.D. to ?, May 20, 1917.

3. See Box 12 of Dodd's MSS for the many letters about his war work.

4. W.E.D. to Miller, April 16, 1917; Houston to W.E.D., May 4, 1917; "Professor Dodd's Diary," pp. 42, 46.

5. On the origins of the peace commission, see Lawrence E. Gelfand, *The Inquiry: American Preparations for Peace,* 1917–1919 (New Haven, 1963), chap. 1.

6. "Composite opinion of Professors Dunning, Robinson, Hazen, Shotwell, Hayes, Powell and Duggan": *William E. Dodd,* n.d.; James T. Shotwell to Sidney Mezes, December 3, 1917, Sidney E. Mezes MSS, Columbia University Library, New York (cited hereafter as Mezes MSS); House to W.E.D., October 14 and 17, 1917; Shotwell to W.E.D., November 9, 27, 30 and December 10, 18, 1917; "Professor Dodd's Diary," pp. 47–48, 50, 53–55; Evarts B. Greene to W.E.D., January 2, 1918; W.E.D. to Greene, January 18, 1918.

7. For Dodd's initial problems with the book, see Allen Johnson to W.E.D., January 22 and February 7, 1917. Apparently, Dodd returned to the manuscript about the beginning of December 1917, and sent it to the Yale press on February 1 or 2, 1918. See Johnson to W.E.D., January 27 and February 5, 1918. "That was a brief effort of mine, written in two months, albeit the result of a good many years general study and thought"—W.E.D. to Patteson, September 23, 1919. Cf. Dodd's comment to Carl Becker: "I am glad that you enjoyed my *Cotton Kingdom* written in six weeks and far too hasty. But I stand by the book as a key to future work, as correct diagnosis…."—October 21, 1921.

8. W.E.D., *The Cotton Kingdom* (New Haven, 1919), pp. 24–27, 30–34. Though later writers have challenged Dodd's case for planter domination of the economy, they have had little success in forging a new point of view. By contrast, Dodd's insights about the planters' social position have been accepted and expanded upon. See Randall and Donald, pp. 40–41.

9. *The Cotton Kingdom,* chap. 3, *passim.* For the continuing vitality of this argument, see Eaton, *The Freedom-of-Thought Struggle,* p. 27.

10. *The Cotton Kingdom,* pp. 62–63. Cf. Rollin G. Osterweis, *Romanticism and Nationalism in the Old South* (New Haven, 1949), p. 26.

11. *The Cotton Kingdom,* pp. 69–70; Eaton, *The Freedom-of-Thought Struggle,* p. 63. This theme, of course, is central to Eaton's entire story.

12. *The Cotton Kingdom,* pp. 71–79. For a summary of and a challenge to the stereotype, see Randall and Donald, chap. 2, esp. pp. 29–32.

13. *The Cotton Kingdom,* pp. 97–103, 111–115. Dodd's contentions about religion and education are borne out in Frank L. Owsley, *Plain Folk of the Old South* (Baton Rouge, 1949), pp. 96–104; Randall and Donald, p. 43.

14. For a summary of the stereotype, see Owsley, pp. 1–6; *The Cotton Kingdom,* p. 91; for evidence of the last, see Randall and Donald, pp. 30–31.

15. "Professor Dodd's Diary," p. 48; Gelfand, pp. 47–49, 70–71, 79–80.

16. Shotwell to Mezes, December 3, 1917, Mezes MSS. Mezes to W.E.D., October 31, 1917; John M. Redfall to W.E.D., November 13, 1917; Elliott Goodwin to W.E.D., November 7, 1917; Gelfand, p. 92. Shotwell to W.E.D., December 3, 1917, Mezes MSS. Shotwell to W.E.D., December 10, 18, 1917; W. G. Leland to W.E.D., December 20, 1917; "Professor Dodd's Diary," p. 55; Mezes to W.E.D., January 4, 1918, Mezes MSS; Gelfand, pp. 87–88.

17. "The Monroe Doctrine," February 2, 1918; "The Present Status of the Monroe Doctrine," February 7, 1918; W. A. Dunning, "Criticism of Dodd—The Present Status of the Monroe Doctrine," February 7, 1918; Shotwell to Mezes, February 6, 1918, Inquiry Document #135, Record Group #256, National Archives, Washington, D.C.

18. W.E.D. to Mezes, March 5, 1918; Mezes to W.E.D., March 8, 1918, Mezes MSS; Wallace Notestein to W.E.D., January 22, 1917 (should be 1918).

19. *The Dial,* LXIV (February 28, 1918), 198. Cf. W.E.D. to Kitchin, November 20, 1917, Kitchin MSS. W.E.D. to Kitchin, January 27, 1918. W.E.D. to House, February 26, 1918, House MSS; W.E.D. to Kitchin, January 28, February 26, 1918, Kitchin MSS. House to W.E.D., February 28, 1918; Kitchin to W.E.D., March 4, 1918.

20. Dodd, after all, had no expertise—the single most important qualification—to recommend him for appointment to either board. It is interesting to note that when Dodd recommended Charles Merriam, a man more readily recognized as an expert on government and economic affairs, for appointment to the Federal Trade Board in 1917, the Wilson administration offered him the post. See Ware, p. 135; Merriam, *Chicago,* p. 235.

21. On the lectures, see "Professor Dodd's Diary," pp. 56–57; and correspondence in Box 13 of Dodd's MSS.

22. W.E.D. to Mezes, March 5, 1918; Mezes to W.E.D., March 8 and April 12, 1918, Mezes MSS; Dodd published this survey under the title, "The Struggle for Democracy in the United States," *International Journal of Ethics,* XXVIII (July 1918), 465–484.

23. W.E.D. to House, May 1, 1918, House MSS; Mezes to W.E.D., May 6, 1918; House to W.E.D., May 3, 1918; Walworth, II, 161–162; Charles Forcey, *The Crossroads of Liberalism*

(New York, 1961), p. 284. On Bourne, LaFollette, and Villard, see Resek, chaps. 1–6; Belle C. LaFollette and Fola LaFollette, *Robert M. LaFollette,* Vol. II (New York, 1953), chaps. 46–52; Oswald Garrison Villard, *Fighting Years: Memoirs of a Liberal Editor* (New York, 1939), chaps. 18–29; on Bryan, see Levine, chap. 3 and pp. 147–152.

24. W.E.D. to Frederick Jackson Turner, August 23, 1930, Turner MSS; W.E.D., *Woodrow Wilson and His Work* (New York, 1921), p. xiv; "Professor Dodd's Diary," pp. 59, 60–66; W.E.D. to Kitchin, July 5, 1918, Kitchin MSS.

25. Joseph Tumulty to W.E.D., September 10, 1918; W.E.D. to Mrs. Woodrow Wilson, September 15, 1918; "Professor Dodd's Diary," pp. 68–78. For a discussion of Wilson's keen interest in combatting reaction and advancing domestic reform at home at this time, see Arno J. Mayer, "Historical Thought and American Foreign Policy in the Era of the First World War," *The Historian and the Diplomat,* ed. Francis J. Loewenheim (New York, 1967), pp. 73–90.

26. On Lodge, see John A. Garraty, *Henry Cabot Lodge: A Biography* (New York, 1953), pp. 340–342; for the response of the *New Republic,* see Forcey, pp. 285, 287–288; for Dodd's activities, see Frank Aydelotte to W.E.D., October 1 and 11, 1918. W.E.D. to Intercollegiate Menorah Assoc., November 12, 1918, Dept. of History MSS; "Professor Dodd's Diary," p. 78–79; *The Nation,* CVII (November 9, 1918), 557–558.

27. W.E.D. to House, October 22, 1918; W.E.D. to Wilson, November 19, 1918. Cf. "Professor Dodd's Diary," p. 80. W.E.D. to Henry R. Mussey, November 12, 1918; Walworth, II, 206–215.

28. W.E.D. to Herman Horne, December 3, 1918; W.E.D. to Moore, December 18, 1918; W.E.D. to Louis Post, December 6, 1918; Ruhl Bartlett, *The League to Enforce Peace* (Chapel Hill, 1944), pp. 113–119.

29. "Professor Dodd's Diary," p. 81; W.E.D. to Goodwin, December 10 and 29, 1918. *The New Republic,* XVII (December 21, 1918), 220–221, also found the meeting disquieting for its "reactionary" tone; W.E.D. to Editor, *Fortnightly Review,* December 19, 1918. The paper was published in *The Yale Review,* VIII (April 1919), 449–465.

30. W.E.D. to Professor Cross, January 25, 1919. For the House letter, see House to W.E.D., January 6, 1919, House MSS. W.E.D. to Jane Addams, January 29, 1919. W.E.D. to House, February 12, 1919, House MSS; W.E.D. to Dean Holgate, January 30, 1919. W.E.D. to Salomon O. Levinson, February 7, 1919, Salomon O. Levinson MSS, University of Chicago Library, Chicago, Ill. (cited hereafter as Levinson MSS). For the campaign put on by the League to Enforce Peace, see Bartlett, pp. 114–115. W.E.D. and S. O. Levinson to House, February 6, 1919, in both the Levinson and House MSS; Garraty, p. 350. W.E.D. to Prof. Elbert J. Benton, May 20, 1919; W.E.D. to Beveridge, May 26, 1919; W.E.D. to Tumulty, February 18, 1919.

31. Walworth, II, 276; Tumulty to W.E.D. February 27, 1919; "Professor Dodd's Diary, pp. 81–82.

32. W.E.D. to Prof. Stockton Axson, March 23, 1919; "University of Chicago: Circular of the Departments of…History…1919," U.C.L. W.E.D. to House, March 11, 1919; W.E.D. to Beveridge, March 19, 1919; on developments at the Conference, see Walworth, II, 292–300; Thomas A. Bailey, *Woodrow Wilson and the Lost Peace* (New York, 1945), p. 218; for Dodd's reaction, see W.E.D. to Axson, April 9, 1919; Editor, *The Round Table* to W.E.D., April 10, 1919; *The Round Table,* IX (June 1919), 532–544. The article is dated April 1919, p. 544. W.E.D. to Arthur Page, April 19, May 9, 1919; W.E.D. to J. Franklin Jameson, April 27, 1919; "The End of Europe as a Leader of Mankind," *The World's Work,* XXXVIII (July 1919), 254–257.

33. W.E.D. to Beveridge, May 26, 1919; W.E.D. to William J. Bryan, May 23, 1919; W.E.D. to Dr. Blackwell, May 24, 1919; W.E.D. to Mr. Brown of *The Nation,* May 24, 1919; for Wilson's attitude, see Arthur Link, *Wilson the Diplomatist* (Chicago, 1965), p. 133; for Dodd's efforts, see W.E.D. to New York *Evening Post,* May 19, 1919; W.E.D. to Editor of *The World,* May 23, 1919; W.E.D. to Mrs. George Bass, May 23, 1919; W.E.D. to Mr. Parks, June 1, 1919; W.E.D. to Edgar Hellweg, June 10, 1919; W.E.D. to Mr. Jameson, June 30, 1919.

34. W.E.D. to House, March 11, 1919. For Dodd's appeal to the German-Americans, see "Dilemma of German-Americans," *The Public,* XXII (August 2, 1919), 823–826. W.E.D. to Dr. Sibler, August 13, 1919; W.E.D. to Woodrow Wilson, July 7, 1919. Other Democrats were shortly advising the same thing. See Walworth, II, 360.

35. W.E.D. to Beveridge, August 7 and September 15, 1919; W.E.D. to Mr. Henderson, August 17, 1919; Levine, pp. 147–148; W.E.D. to Arthur Page, August 17, 1919.

36. *Wilson and His Work,* pp. 143, 247–248, 297, 355, 361; John Garraty, *Woodrow Wilson* (New York, 1956), pp. 200–201.

37. W.E.D. to Axson, August 13, 1919; W.E.D. to Beveridge, September 15, 1919; Secretary Houston's Secretary to W.E.D., September 18, 1919; W.E.D. to Arthur Page, October 15, 1919; W.E.D. to Beveridge, October 12, 1919; W.E.D. to Arthur Page, October 15, November 8, 1919; W.E.D. to Axson, November 23, 1919; W.E.D. to Erich Marcks, January 2, 1920; W.E.D. to James Winston, February 14, 1920; W.E.D. to Alvin Johnson, February 19, 1920; W.E.D. to J. Franklin Jameson, March 5, 1920.

CHAPTER VIII UNBROKEN HOPE

1. W.E.D. to Mr. Bowmar, December 17, 1919; W.E.D. to Erich Marcks, January 2, 1920. See the correspondence in Box 15 for Dodd's lecture schedule. W.E.D. to James G. McDonald, April 20, 1920; W.E.D. to Newton Baker, April 23, 1920; W.E.D. to Walter S. Rogers, April 7, 12, 1920.

2. See Levine, pp. 152–160; Arthur S. Link, *American Epoch: A History of the United States Since the 1890s* (New York, 1955), pp. 247–248; W.E.D. to Josephus Daniels, April 29, 1903, Daniels MSS; W.E.D. to H. H. Childers, April 26, 1920; W.E.D. to Louis Post, June 13, 1920.

3. For discussions of this split in the Democratic party in the twenties, see Arthur Link, "What Happened to the Progressive Movement in the 1920s," *The American Historical Review,* LXIV (July 1959), 833–851; Hofstadter, *The Age of Reform,* pp. 280–300; Frank Freidel, *Franklin D. Roosevelt: The Ordeal* (Boston, 1954), especially chap. X; Levine, chap. VIII.

4. W.E.D. to H. H. Childers, April 3, 1920; W.E.D. to Mr. Patteson, April 3, 1920; W.E.D. to "Dear Sir," April 4, 1920; Circular of "The Illinois Democratic Woman's Committee"; W.E.D. to Louis Post, May 24, 1920; W.E.D. to Mr. Everitt, June 15, 1920; W.E.D. to Senator Carter Glass, June 9, 1920; W.E.D. to C. H. Haskins, June 16, 1920; W.E.D. to Senator ?, June 13, 1920. Also see W.E.D. to Mr. Doubleday, May 2, 1920; as well as the *New York Times* story of June 6, 1920, v, 305, about his difficulties with his publishers.

5. "If I am any judge of American history and recent events, both in this country and in Europe," Dodd wrote McAdoo, "our country is now the land and the call for a true liberalism, such as Wilson represents, such as you represent.... If we take the opportunity and press aggressively the program that best fits our better economic and social thought, we shall develop a party that must not only win office but lead the world on that way which Wilson so appealingly pointed

out while in Paris." W.E.D. to Charles Ambler, June 18, 1920; W.E.D. to Louis Post, June 13, 1920; W.E.D. to William G. McAdoo, June 15, 1920.

6. On the 1920 Democratic convention, see Wesley Bagby, "The Road to Normalcy: The Presidential Campaign and Election of 1920," *The Johns Hopkins University Studies in Historical and Political Science,* Series LXXX (1962), No. 1, chaps. II and IV. W.E.D. to Mrs. Virginia LeRoy, June 20, 1920; on Bryan, see Levine, pp. 170–175; W.E.D. to Gov. J. W. Bickett of North Carolina, July 13, 1920; Freidel, pp. 72–74; W.E.D. to Edward House, July 15, 1920; James Cox to W.E.D., August 5, 1920.

7. See Hofstadter, *Anti-Intellectualism in American Life,* p. 213; William E. Leuchtenburg, *The Perils of Prosperity 1914–1932* (Chicago, 1958), pp. 123–125; W.E.D. to Carl Becker, July 15, 1920; W.E.D. to Alvin Johnson, August 29, 1920; W.E.D. to Albert Beveridge, August 27, 1920. On Beveridge's career, see Claude G. Bowers, *Beveridge and the Progressive Era* (Boston, 1932).

8. W.E.D. to James Cox, August 10, 1920; W.E.D. to Mrs. Slade, August ?, 1920; Pat Harrison to W.E.D., August 16, 1920; Desha Breckinridge to W.E.D., August 17, 22, 1920; W.E.D. to Desha Breckinridge, August 25, 26, 1920; "Professor Dodd's Diary," pp. 83–84; Freidel, chap. V; James M. Cox, *Journey Through My Years* (New York, 1946), chap. XXIV; W.E.D. to "Gentlemen," October 19, 1920.

9. W.E.D. to Mrs. Jeffrey, n.d.; W.E.D. to James Cox, November 4, 1920; "Professor Dodd's Diary," p. 84; for discussions of the Democracy's defeat in the 1920 election, see David Burner, "The Breakup of the Wilson Coalition of 1916," *Mid-America,* XLV (January 1963), 18–35; Bagby, "The Road to Normalcy," chap. V; W.E.D. to Miss Hearon, November 18, 1920; W.E.D. to Prof. Carruth, November 9, 1920. W.E.D. to Pres. Harry P. Judson, November 30, 1920; Judson to W.E.D., December 8, 1920, General Administrative File, University of Chicago MSS (cited hereafter as G.A.F., U.C. MSS); *Chicago Evening Post,* November 30 and December 1, 1920; *Chicago Tribune,* November 30, 1920.

10. W.E.D. to Newton Baker, November 10, 1920. Wilson, as Dodd soon found out, had no intention of undertaking an autobiographical work. See Gene Smith, *When the Cheering Stopped* (New York, 1964), pp. 194–195. Cf. Walworth, II, p. 412. "Professor Dodd's Diary," pp. 85–86; W.E.D. to Frederick J. Turner, February 15, 1921, Turner MSS; W.E.D. to Albert Beveridge, May 2, 1921.

11. See W.E.D. to Miss Hearon, November 18, 1920; W.E.D. to George Creel, April 17, 1921; W.E.D. to Mrs. William C. Storlie, December 6, 1921. W.E.D. to Newton Baker, June 11, 1921, Newton Baker MSS, Library of Congress, Washington, D.C. (cited hereafter as Newton Baker MSS). See *The Memoirs of Cordell Hull,* Vol. I (New York, 1948), pp. 112–113; Freidel, pp. 123–124. On Bryan's and Roosevelt's efforts to revive the Democratic party at this time, see Levine, chap. V *passim;* Freidel, chap. VII; W.E.D. to Cordell Hull, November 9, 1921; W.E.D. to Jouett Shouse, November 15, 1921; W.E.D. to Henry Morgenthau, December 21, 1921; Morgenthau to W.E.D., January 5, 1922.

12. W.E.D. to John R. Bolling, January 5, 1922, File IX, Woodrow Wilson MSS, Library of Congress, Washington, D.C. (cited hereafter as Wilson MSS); Bolling to W.E.D., January 8, 1922. On Dodd's failure to get the appointment, see W.E.D. to Daniel Roper, June 14, 1925. W.E.D. to Bolling, March 31, 1922, File IX, Wilson MSS; Bolling to W.E.D., April 9 and May 26, 1922.

13. W.E.D. to Baruch, May 6 and 22, 1922; Baruch to W.E.D., May 25, 1922. Cf. Cordell Hull to W.E.D., January 30 and May 17, 1922. W.E.D. to Woodrow Wilson, September 3, 1922; Wilson

to W.E.D., September 6, 1922, File IX, Wilson MSS. On Wilson's unwillingness to make public endorsements, see Smith, pp. 194–196.

14. On Wilson's efforts to draft a new reform program, see Link, "What Happened to the Progressive Movement in the 1920s," pp. 841–842; Smith, pp. 211–212. On Bryan's inability to lead the Democracy toward a new round of reform and his dependence on the churches to achieve his political goals, see Levine, chaps. V and VII. On the Conference for Progressive Political Action and the elections of 1922, see Kenneth C. MacKay, *The Progressive Movement of 1924* (New York, 1947), pp. 54–72; John D. Hicks, *Republican Ascendancy, 1921–1933* (New York, 1963), pp. 84–89. On Dodd's view of the Democracy at the end of 1922 and his attitude toward a third party, see W.E.D. to Woodrow Wilson, November 23, 1922; W.E.D., "The Democratic Party and the National Outlook," November 27, 1922, in *Addresses Before the Democratic Women's Luncheon Club of Philadelphia, 1922–1930* (Philadelphia, 1931).

15. For Dodd's schedule of talks in this period, see W.E.D. to Daniel Roper, February ? and April 13, 1923; W.E.D. to Angus W. McLean, April 9, 1923. W.E.D. to Brice Clagett, January 16, 1924, William G. McAdoo MSS, Library of Congress, Washington, D.C. (cited hereafter as McAdoo MSS). For the content of these speeches, see W.E.D., "The Democratic Party and the National Outlook," *loc. cit.;* W.E.D., "Democracy's Great Triumvirate," *The New York Times,* January 29, 1922, VIII, 16; W.E.D., "Wilsonism," *Political Science Quarterly,* 38 (March 1923), 115–132.

16. W.E.D. to Daniel Roper, December 23, 1922; W.E.D. to Angus W. McLean, April 9, 1923. Roper and McLean were representatives of South Carolina and North Carolina in the Democratic National Committee. See William G. McAdoo to W.E.D., February 28 and June 4, 1923; McAdoo to Roper, February 28 and April 7, 1923; W.E.D. to McAdoo, March 7, 1923; Roper to McAdoo, April 13, 1923, McAdoo MSS.

17. For Dodd's negative estimate of McAdoo, see W.E.D. to Roper, December 23, 1922. For Dodd's change of mood, see W.E.D. to McAdoo, June 18, 1923, McAdoo MSS; W.E.D. to Roper, June 30, 1923; Roper to W.E.D., July 13, 24, 1923; W.E.D. to Roper, August 27, 1923. McAdoo to W.E.D., July 12, 1923; McAdoo to Roper, August 2, 1923; W.E.D. to McAdoo, September 29 and November 18, 1923, McAdoo MSS; W.E.D. to Bolling, October 23, 1923, File IX, Wilson MSS.

18. McAdoo to W.E.D., November 12, 1923; W.E.D. to McAdoo, November 18, 1923; W.E.D. to Brice Clagett, January 16, 1924, McAdoo MSS; W.E.D. to Roper, December 17, 1923; Roper to W.E.D., December 31, 1923, and January 28, 1924. On Bryan's reluctance to support McAdoo in 1923, see Levine, pp. 295–303. On McAdoo's involvement in the Teapot Dome scandal, see Burl Noggle, *Teapot Dome: Oil and Politics in the 1920s* (Baton Rouge, 1962), pp. 99–105, 110–114. W.E.D. to McAdoo, February 8, 1924, McAdoo MSS; W.E.D. to Father, April 30. 1924; McAdoo to W.E.D., February 14, 1924, inviting Dodd to attend the February 19 meeting did not reach Dodd, who was out of town; David L. Rockwell to W.E.D., February 25, 1924. McAdoo to W.E.D., February 26, 1924, McAdoo MSS; W.E.D. to Bassett, March 9, 1924.

19. See MacKay, pp. 74–75; Freidel, pp. 166–167. W.E.D. to Louis Post, May 10, 1924; W.E.D. to Roper, April 25, 1924. Noggle, pp. 156–160; *The New Republic,* XXXIX (June 11, 1924), 63–64; W.E.D. to Charles Horne, June 7, 1924.

20. On Klan support of McAdoo and the Democratic convention, see Hicks, pp. 92–99, Freidel, pp. 166–169, Levine, pp. 307–316; MacKay, pp. 105–109. For Dodd's recognition that McAdoo's candidacy would split the party, see W.E.D. to Roper, June 16, 19, and 26, 1924.

21. W.E.D. to Claude Bowers, July 20, 1924. On the issue of party regularity, see MacKay, pp. 195–196; Levine, pp. 316–321. W.E.D. to Roper, August 24, 1924. Dodd offered no evidence to show that any substantial number of "Wilson Republicans and independents" had in fact announced for Davis.

22. For this campaign work, see the correspondence in Box 20 of the Dodd MSS. For analyses of the election results, see MacKay, chap. XI; Hicks, pp. 102–105.

23. W.E.D. to Daniels, March 30, April 7, 1925, Daniels MSS. W.E.D. to Roper, April 6, 1925. For Franklin Roosevelt's efforts both to revive the party and to aid Smith, see Freidel, chaps. XII–XIV.

24. On Lowden, see William T. Hutchinson, *Lowden of Illinois* (2 vols.: Chicago, 1957); the quote is from II, 558. W.E.D. to Lowden, April 24, 1926, Frank O. Lowden MSS, University of Chicago Library (cited hereafter as Lowden MSS). For Lowden's eagerness to have Dodd's ideas, see Lowden to W.E.D., March 30, April 19, May 17, 1926; W.E.D. to Lowden, April 8 and May 20, 1926, Lowden MSS. For Dodd's views on the farm problem, see "The Epic of the Embattled Farmer," *The New York Times,* July 24, 1927, IV, 1–2, 23.

25. W.E.D. to Roper, May 6, 1926; W.E.D. to Claude Bowers, August 4, 1926. W.E.D. to Lowden, May 7, 20, 1927, Lowden MSS; Hutchinson, II, 561–568. Dodd and Prof. Avery Craven of the University of Illinois spent a day in July at Lowden's farm discussing farm problems with him. See W.E.D. to Lowden, June 10, July 23, 1927; Lowden to W.E.D., June 20 and July 6, 1917, Lowden MSS; W.E.D. to Hugh McRae, August 4, 1927; W.E.D. to George F. Milton, August 4, 1927; W.E.D. to Senator Thomas Walsh, August 4, 1927.

26. Hutchinson, II, 568–574; for Lowden's coolness to Dodd, see W.E.D. to Lowden, August 4, October 26, and November 20, 1927; Lowden to W.E.D., August 9, October 29, November 25, 1927, Lowden MSS. On the primary, see W.E.D. to Lowden, April 11, 1928, Lowden MSS. For Dodd's speaking engagements on "The Devolution of the Farmer" and "Is There Any Help for the Farmer?," see W.E.D. to Roper, July 21, 1927. W.E.D. to Lowden, October 26, 1927, Lowden MSS; W.E.D., MS Diary, 1928, January 24, 30, February 2, 3, 1928. The quote is from W.E.D., "Shall Our Farmers Become Peasants," *The Century Magazine,* 116 (May 1928), 44.

27. On Lowden's defeat, see Hutchinson, II, chap. XXV. W.E.D. to Lowden, August 14, 1928, Lowden MSS; W.E.D. to Frank L. Polk, August 18, 1928.

CHAPTER IX AGAINST THE TIDE

1. For some of this material on Dodd's personal and professional life in the twenties, I have relied on interviews by correspondence gathered by Lowry P. Ware for use in chapter 3 of his thesis. To these, I have added the following pen and personal interviews: letters to me from: Henry Steele Commager, August 24, 1964; Philip Davidson, August 4, 1964; L. Ethan Ellis, August 27, 1964; Lawrence Henry Gipson, July 28, 1964; William T. Hutchinson, July 28, 1964; Saul K. Padover, August 18, 1964; J. Fred Rippy, August 3, 1964. Personal interviews: Avery O. Craven, August 21, 1964; Louis Gottschalk, August 20, 1964; Roy F. Nichols, August 3, 1964; Bessie L. Pierce, August 20, 1964; T. McNider Simpson, August 12, 1964. Other material for this description of Dodd has been drawn from Martha Dodd, *Through Embassy Eyes* (New York, 1939), pp. 4, 10; Ware, pp. 115–126, 133–136; Avery O. Craven, "William E. Dodd as Teacher," *The University of Chicago Magazine* (May 1940), pp. 7–8; "The University of Chicago: Circular of the Departments of Political Economy, Political Science, History, Sociology and Anthropology," for

the years after 1909 in the University of Chicago Archives; "Register of Doctors of Philosophy of the University of Chicago, June 1893–June 1927," *The University of Chicago Announcements,* XXVIII (September 10, 1927), 24–27; list of "Some Doctors Who have worked out their theses with W.E.D.," in Box 58 of the Dodd MSS.

The other five students who published their theses were Dice Anderson, Catherine Cleveland, Rachel C. Eaton, Cleo Hearon, and Theodore Jack. See "Writings on American History," *Annual Report of the American Historical Association* for the years 1913, 1914, 1916, and 1919. The quotes from Beard and Beveridge are from Beard to W.E.D., December 3, 1920; Beveridge to W.E.D., June 17, 1921. Dodd's complaint to his colleague is in W.E.D. to Max Farrand, January 25, 1921.

2. W.E.D. to Dice Anderson, January 18, 1921; W.E.D. to Margaret Wilson, January 20, 1921; W.E.D. to Woodrow Wilson, February 22, 1921; W.E.D. to Mrs. Wilson, May 10, 1921; Mrs. Wilson to W.E.D., May 22, 1921; W.E.D. to Frank Cobb, May 29, 1921.

3. Beard to W.E.D., December 3, 1920; Jameson to W.E.D., April 30, 1921; W.E.D. to Becker, October 21, 1921; Sandburg to W.E.D., December 31, 1923, and January 10, 1924; Beveridge to W.E.D., April 3 and 21, 1924; W.E.D. to Bowers, May 27, 1925; W.E.D. to Nichols, October 20, 1923, and February 1, 1924, letters in the possession of Professor Nichols. For Dodd's offices, see *Annual Report of the American Historical Association,* Vol. I for the years 1917 and 1920. For Dodd's editorship, see J. Franklin Jameson to W.E.D., February 6, 1922, September 24 and November 16, 1923.

4. Stephenson, *The South Lives in History,* p. 22; Gray, *Marcus W. Jernegan Essays,* pp. 354–355; Interview with Craven, August 21, 1964; list of "Some Doctors Who have worked out their theses with W.E.D." Reuben Frodin, "Very Simple, But Thoroughgoing," *The Idea and Practice of General Education: An Account of the College of The University of Chicago* (Chicago, 1950), pp. 35–38; *Trends in University Growth,* pp. 13–19; Charles Breasted, *Pioneer to the Past: The Story of James Henry Breasted* (New York, 1943), p. 236. For the History Department's attitude, see Dean David A. Robertson to Andrew C. McLaughlin, January 18, 1923; McLaughlin to Robertson, January 29, 1923; McLaughlin to Prof. H. C. Morrison, March 14, 1923, Dept. of History MSS.

5. W.E.D. to Bishop Atkins, December 25, 1921; W.E.D. to Yeomans, February 9, 1923; Daniel Roper to Edward House, March 28, 1924; Roper to W.E.D., April 4, 1924.

6. See Higham, *History,* pp. 68–82, 117–131, 183–211; Strout, chaps. 2–5; W.E.D. to Barnes, June 28, 1924; Lippmann is paraphrased in Arthur M. Schlesinger, Jr., *The Crisis of the Old Order* (Boston, 1957), pp. 150–151; W.E.D., "The University and the Nation," *A.A.U.P. Bulletin,* IX (March 1923), 23.

7. *The New York Times,* January 29, 1922, VII, 16:1; April 23, 1922, III, 1:1; November 21, 1926, IV, 1; December 5, 1926, IV, 3; April 17, 1927, IV, 6; *American Mercury,* IV (April 1925), 342–352; V (July 1925), 303–313; *The Century Magazine,* CXI (March 1926), 531–538; (April 1926), 734–745; CXIII (March 1927), 569–584; (April 1927), 661–673; CXIV (May 1927), 46–61; W.E.D., *Lincoln or Lee: Comparison and Contrast of the Two Greatest Leaders in the War Between the States; The Narrow and Accidental Margins of Success* (New York, 1928), pp. 3–4. On Dodd's style, cf. Stephenson, *Journal of Southern History,* XI (February 1945), 29–30. Quoted in Higham, *History,* p. 79.

8. Clipping from *Wilmington* (N.C.) *Morning Star,* December 29, 1926; clipping from *The Advance* (Baton Rouge, La.), July 23, 1926, in Box 23 of the Dodd MSS. The speeches can be found in Box 21.

9. W.E.D. to Bolling, January 20, 1924; Bolling to W.E.D., January 22, 1924; Claude Bowers to W.E.D., February 9, 1924; Mrs. Wilson to Mr. Wells of Harper and Brothers, February 26, 1924; Mrs. Wilson to W.E.D., March 3, 1924. W.E.D. to Daniel Roper, April 2, 1924; W.E.D. to Claude Bowers, April 3, 1924; W.E.D. to Axson, April 3, 1924; Mrs. Wilson to W.E.D., June 4, 1924.

10. On plans and problems Baker and Dodd faced in doing this work, see Baker to W.E.D., February 29, March 9, May 10, 1924. *The Public Papers of Woodrow Wilson: College and State: Educational, Literary and Political Papers* (1875–1913), Vol. I, eds. Ray Stannard Baker and William E. Dodd (New York, 1925), p. vi; Baker to W.E.D., June 17, 21, and 23, 1924; *The Papers of Woodrow Wilson,* Vol. 1: 1856–1880, ed. Arthur S. Link (Princeton, N.J., 1966), pp. x–xi.

11. W.E.D. to Erich Marcks, July 14, 1924; Frederick L. Allen to W.E.D., July 19, 25, 1924; W.E.D. to Albert Beveridge, November 7, 1924; William E. Dodd, Jr., to W.E.D., n.d., 1924. W.E.D. to President Burton, December 1, 1924, G.A.F., U.C. MSS. For Dodd's reaction to Mrs. Wilson's invitation to Baker to write an official life, see Baker to W.E.D., January 9, 1925; W.E.D. to Baker, January 18, 1925; W.E.D. to Claude Bowers, January 21, 1925.

12. On the A.H.A. program, see W.E.D. to Claude Bowers, May 27, 1925; *Annual Report of the American Historical Association for the Year* 1925 (Washington, 1929). For Dodd's views of the Chicago Forum, and his *Century* articles, see W.E.D. to Mrs. Langworthy, June 5, 1925; W.E.D. to H. H. Howland, November 22, 1925; for Dodd's idea of the university, see *A.A.U.P. Bulletin,* IX (March 1923), 16–24.

13. Roper to W.E.D., June 10, 1925; W.E.D. to Roper, June 14, 1925. W.E.D. to C. E. Ayers, June 16, 1925; W.E.D. to Laing, June 25, 1925; Frodin, *The Idea and Practice of General Education,* pp. 39–44. Cf. Chauncey S. Boucher, *The Chicago College Plan* (Chicago, 1935), p. 1. Later information in this chapter on Chicago's administrative problems and reforms is drawn from Frodin, pp. 44–54, 93, and Boucher, pp. 1–7.

14. W.E.D. to John S. Bassett, August 10, 1925; W.E.D. to J. Franklin Jameson, August 20, 1925. W.E.D. to Andrew C. McLaughlin, November 2, 1925, Dept. of History MSS.

15. The additions to the department were: Chauncey S. Boucher, Professor of American History, Samuel N. Harper, Associate Professor of Russian Language and Institutions, Bernadotte E. Schmitt, Professor of Modern History, Godfrey Davies, Assistant Professor of English History, Eugene N. Anderson, Instructor in European History, and William T. Hutchinson, Instructor in American History—drawn from the University of Chicago catalogues for these years. For this complaint, see "Summary Conclusion Based upon Appended Records of Registration in the Department of History," n.d., 1927, Dept. of History MSS. For changes in student-faculty ratios, see *Trends in University Growth,* pp. 118–121.

16. Carl Huth to Prof. Allee, January 19, 1927, Dept. of History MSS. On the split in the department, see W.E.D. to Josephus Daniels, October 30, 1926; interview with Bessie L. Pierce, August 20, 1964. The text was a co-operative effort with Professors Eugene C. Barker and Walter P. Webb. The publisher was Row, Peterson and Co.

17. For a discussion of what Dewey called "the adoption of the scientific habit of mind in application to social affairs" in the twenties, see White, chap. XII. W.E.D., MS Diary, January 7 and April 9, 1928. For Dodd's concern with both writing and administration, see W.E.D. to Carl Becker, May 15, 1928; W.E.D. to Daniel Roper, May 12 and 17, 1928.

18. See W.E.D., MS Diary, May 10, 14, 15, June 12, July 2, 9, and 24, 1928; W.E.D. to Laing, July 11, 1928; and a host of other letters about this business in Boxes 29, 30, and 31 of the Dodd MSS and in the Dept. of History MSS.

19. James W. Thompson to W.E.D., October 26, 1928; Einar Joranson to W.E.D., November 17, 1928, Dept. of History MSS; W.E.D. to Carl Becker, December 16, 1928; W.E.D. to Laing, December 17 and 20, 1928; W.E.D. to Raymond B. Fosdick, December 21, 1928.

20. Laing to W.E.D., December 13, 1928; Henry Gale to W.E.D., December 13, 1928; W.E.D. to Frederic Woodward, December 24, 1928; Woodward to W.E.D., December 27, 1928; M. L. Raney to W.E.D., December 26, 1928; W.E.D. to Laing, January 14, 1929; W.E.D. to Mrs. William E. Dodd, March 24 and April 15, 1929.

21. See Newton Baker to W.E.D., July 10 and September 12, 1929; W.E.D. to Baker, September 23, 1929; W.E.D. to Laing, January 8, March 22, April 9, 1930. Laing to W.E.D., January 11, 1930, Dept. of History MSS; Hutchins to W.E.D., January 3, 1930; Board of Trustees to W.E.D., June 3 and 5, 1930, Dept. of History MSS; W.E.D., "Memorandum," June 24, 1930, in Box 31 of the Dodd MSS; inscribed in a copy owned by Emma Beekmann, one of Dodd's masters' students in 1930, who gave me her recollections of Mr. Dodd.

22. W.E.D. to Hutchins, December 7, 1930, Dept. of History MSS. For Dodd's progress on his Old South study, see W.E.D. to Prof. J. M. Gambrill, January 10, 1931.

23. Hutchins to W.E.D., December 12, 1930. W.E.D. to Woodward, December 11, 1929, Dept. of History MSS; for information on Dodd's chairmanship, I have drawn on interviews with Craven, August 21, 1964, Pierce, August 20, 1964, and Gottschalk, August 20, 1964; Hutchinson to author, July 28, 1964; and Ware, pp. 143–144. For the History faculty in these years, see catalogues in the University of Chicago Library.

24. For Dodd's reaction to the reforms, see W.E.D. to Laing, November 26, 1930; W.E.D. MS Diary, 1928, January 23, February 6, 10, 21, and March 7, 9, 1931; the quotes from Hutchins are in Robert M. Hutchins, *No Friendly Voice* (Chicago, 1936), pp. 5–6, 9; in a "Budget Recommendation for the Year 1931–1932, Department of History (Social Sciences)," which I found in a small collection of Dodd papers in the Randolph-Macon Library, Ashland, Virginia, there is the following estimate of Dodd: "For various reasons, it would be desirable to increase Mr. Dodd's salary to $10,000....He is the most distinguished member of the Department....I think that such recognition would add greatly to his peace of mind." Dodd's letter to Hutchins is from March 10, 1931.

25. W.E.D. to Hutchins, June 5, 1931; Board of Trustees to W.E.D., July 16, 1931; on Dodd's involvement in departmental problems in this period, see the correspondence in the Dept. of History MSS; W.E.D. to Esther Aphelin, August 31, 1931; W.E.D. to Bernadotte Schmitt, December 16, 1931; W.E.D. to E. T. Filbey, April 25, 1932. W.E.D. to McLaughlin, June 17 and July 30, 1932, McLaughlin MSS. The quote is from W.E.D. to Ruml, June 13, 1932, Dept. of History MSS.

CHAPTER X AMBASSADOR BY DEFAULT

1. For background material in this chapter, I have relied primarily on Schlesinger, Jr., pp. 142–144, 161–162, 193–195, 273–278, 282–288, 393–395, 398–403, 450–452, 466–474, and, more generally, chap. 28; Frank Freidel, *Franklin D. Roosevelt: The Triumph* (Boston, 1956), pp. 84–88, 170–171, 175–176, 178–182, 201–205, 228–237, 248–256, 321, and, more generally, chaps. XII, XIV, XVI, XVIII, XIX, XX.

W.E.D. to Newton Baker, November 2, December 16, 1928, Newton Baker MSS; W.E.D., "The Passing of the Old United States," *The Century Magazine,* CXIX (October 1929), 39–51; W.E.D. to Roper, May 29, 1929; W.E.D. to Prof. C. D. Burns, October 30, 1929.

2. On Peek, see Gilbert C. Fite, *George N. Peek and the Fight for Farm Parity* (Norman, Okla., 1954); W.E.D., "The End of an Era," *Atlantic Monthly*, CXLIX (March 1932), 370.

3. For Peek's view, see Fite, pp. 43, 235–236; William E. Leuchtenburg, *Franklin D. Roosevelt and the New Deal, 1932–1940* (New York, 1963), p. 75. Dodd's attitude was expressed in W.E.D. to Frederick J. Turner, January 5, 1925, Turner MSS; W.E.D. to H. L. Mencken, n.d., 1925; W.E.D. to Franklin D. Roosevelt, April 24, 1932, Democratic National Committee, Virginia MSS, Franklin D. Roosevelt Library, Hyde Park, N.Y. (cited hereafter as D.N.C.); W.E.D., *Atlantic Monthly*, CXLIX (March 1932), 372–373; W.E.D. to Viscount Cecil, n.d., 1936.

4. W.E.D., "The University and the Public," November 1930, in Box 37 of the Dodd MSS; W.E.D. to Roper, December 29, 1931, January 2 and November 18, 1932; Fite, pp. 237–241.

5. W.E.D. to Frank Graham, June 19, 1930; W.E.D. to Josephus Daniels, November 5, 1930; W.E.D. to Mrs. Follansbee, November 28, 1930; W.E.D. to Robert Lathan, January 13, 1931; W.E.D. to Desha Breckinridge, January 27, 1931; W.E.D. to George Milton, January 27, 1931; W.E.D. to Newton Baker, March 13, 1931; W.E.D. to H. C. Nixon, March 11, April 13, 1931.

6. Baker to W.E.D., March 18, 1931; W.E.D. to House, November 10, 1930; W.E.D. to Mary Hinsdale, May 6, 1931; W.E.D. to Roper, June 9, 1931; unidentified newspaper clipping, August 4, 1931, on House's announcement for F.D.R., in Box 39 of the Dodd MSS.

7. W.E.D. to F.D.R., August 21, 1931, D.N.C., Virginia. With the letter, Dodd enclosed a copy of his 1929 article, "The Passing of the Old United States." On the Howe organization, see Lila Stiles, *The Man Behind Roosevelt* (New York, 1954), pp. 154–155; Leila Sussman, "Voices of the People—A Study of Political Mass Mail" (unpubl. Ph.D. diss., Dept. of Sociology, Columbia University, 1957). For evidence that the reply to Dodd was ghosted, see the original of Dodd's August 21 letter in the Hyde Park Library which has stamped at the top: "The Governor Has Not Seen." Moreover, the carbon of the answer to Dodd of August 26, 1931, bears the initials "G.E.F.": Gabrielle E. Forbush. Finally, for the fact that a good bit of Roosevelt's in-coming correspondence at this time was much like Dodd's and that Roosevelt spent his time writing almost exclusively to intimates, that is, men he knew and addressed by their first names, see Sussman, p. 255; Elliott Roosevelt (ed.), *FDR: His Personal Letters* (New York, 1947), III, *passim*.

8. W.E.D. to Jouett Shouse, October 28, December 1, 1931; W.E.D. to H. C. Nixon, December 17, 1931; W.E.D. to Roper, December 23, 1931, January 2, 5, 1932; Roper to W.E.D., December 29, 1931, January 7, 1932; House to W.E.D., December 30, 1931; W.E.D. to House, January 6, 1932.

9. For Lippmann's editorial and for Roosevelt's troubles with Hearst and then the Wilsonians, see Freidel, *The Triumph*, pp. 248–254. W.E.D. to F.D.R., February 8, 1932, D.N.C., Illinois. Roper to W.E.D., February 12, 1932; W.E.D. to Josephus Daniels, February 28, 1932. The Hull quote is in Freidel, *The Triumph*, p. 255.

10. W.E.D. to Newton Baker, March 24, 1932; W.E.D. to Josephus Daniels, April 13, 1932. W.E.D. to F.D.R., April 24, 1932, D.N.C., Virginia; W.E.D. to House, June 8, 1932; W.E.D. to Cyrus Eaton, June 7, 1932.

11. See, for example, W.E.D. to Daniels, April 13, 1932; W.E.D. to Hull, April 21, 1932; Hull to W.E.D., April 23, 1932. W.E.D. to Roper, April 29, 1932; Roper to W.E.D., May 18, 1932; W.E.D. to House, May 28, 1932; House to W.E.D., June 2, 1932; House to F.D.R., June 2, 1932, House MSS.

12. F.D.R. to W.E.D., March 23, 1932, D.N.C., Illinois. The carbon of this letter at Hyde Park is initialed "G.E.F.," while Dodd's letter to Roosevelt of February 8, 1932, also bears the stamp

"The Governor Has Not Seen." On F.D.R.'s conversations with university people, see Raymond Moley, *After Seven Years* (New York, 1939), pp. 20–21. W.E.D. to F.D.R., April 24 and June 7, 1932; F.D.R. to W.E.D., June 7, 1932, D.N.C., Virginia. Both of Dodd's letters again show the stamp "The Governor Has Not Seen." W.E.D. to House, July 3, 1932, House MSS; W.E.D. to Roper, June 23, 1932.

13. W.E.D. to Cyrus Eaton, June 7, 1932; W.E.D. to Judge Horner, June 27 and July 8, 1932; W.E.D., "To Members of the Illinois Delegation," July 1, 1932; W.E.D. to Ralph Hayes, July 23 and 30, 1932. W.E.D. to F.D.R., July 30, 1932, D.N.C., Illinois.

14. W.E.D. to Richard Crane, July 13 and August 2, 1932; Crane to W.E.D., July 21, 1932. W.E.D. to House, July 6, 1932, House MSS; W.E.D. to Robert Field, July 6, 1932; Field to W.E.D., July 11, 15, 1932; Richard Roper to W.E.D., July 20, 1932; W.E.D. to Richard Roper, July 22, 1932; W.E.D. to Daniel Roper, July 30, 1932; W.E.D. to F.D.R., July 30, 1932; W.E.D. to F.D.R., September 8, 1932; W.E.D. to Judge Horner, August 2, 1932; Daniel Roper to W.E.D., August 9, 1932; W.E.D. to Judge Bingham, August 11, 15, 1932; Robert Jackson to W.E.D., August 27, 1932; Daniel Roper to W.E.D., August 20, 29, September 7, 1932. W.E.D. to Newton Baker, July 19 and August 17, 1932, Newton Baker MSS; W.E.D. to Baker, September 11, 1932; Baker to W.E.D., September 13, 1932.

15. W.E.D. to Cyrus Eaton, October 4, 1932; W.E.D. to Daniel Roper, October 4, 1932; Daniel Roper to W.E.D., October 11, 21, 1932; W.E.D. to Richard Roper, October 5, 1932; W.E.D. to House, October 13, November 8, 16, 1932. W.E.D. to House, October 15 and November 1, 1932, House MSS; House to W.E.D., October 17 and November 6, 1932. W.E.D. to F.D.R., November 9, 1932, D.N.C., Illinois.

16. W.E.D. to Daniel Roper, November 18 and December 15, 23, 1932; W.E.D. to Richard Crane, November 25, 1932; Daniel Roper to W.E.D., December 21, 1932. For Roper's uncertainty, see Daniel Roper to House, January 24, 1933, House MSS. Howe to W.E.D., January 16, 1933; W.E.D. to Norman Davis, January 22, 1933. W.E.D. to President Hutchins, February 17, 1933, Dept. of History MSS.

17. W.E.D. to Hull, February 23, 1933; W.E.D. to House, February 25, March 4, 1933; Hull to W.E.D., February 27, 1933; House to W.E.D., February 27, 1933; W.E.D. to Roper, March 4, 1933; W.E.D. to Mrs. William E. Dodd, March 12, 1933.

18. House to W.E.D., March 7, 1933; Roper to W.E.D., March 22, 1933; cf. W.E.D. to Roper, March 15, 1933. On Dodd's role in naming an assistant director, see William L. Austin to W.E.D., April 25, May 5, 1933; W.E.D. to Mrs. William E. Dodd, March 20, 1933.

19. *F.D.R.: His Personal Letters,* III, 337–338; F.D.R. to Hull, April 20, 1933, President's Official File 198B, Franklin D. Roosevelt MSS, Hyde Park, N.Y. (cited hereafter as P.O.F.). Hull's response is written on Roosevelt's letter to him. Roper to House, June 10, 1933, House MSS.

20. Edward J. Flynn, *You're the Boss* (New York, 1947), pp. 146–148. Flynn's account is generally confirmed by Herbert Lehman to author, October 18, 1960.

21. Sumner Welles, *Seven Decisions That Shaped History* (New York, 1950), p. 216; William Langer and S. Everett Gleason, *The Challenge to Isolation, 1937–1940* (New York, 1952), p. 8. Cf. Robert Sherwood's comments: ". . . the State Department machinery was full of leaks.... That is why Roosevelt and Hopkins sent all their vital messages through military communications instead of through the regular diplomatic channels. . . ." ". . . the permanent career men . . . knew that they would still be there when the Franklin Roosevelt Administration had been replaced by another one, which might well be reactionary and isolationist . . . and they were determined to keep their

records clean of New Deal or one world taints against that highly possible day." *Roosevelt and Hopkins: An Intimate History* (New York, 1948), pp. 756–757.

22. William Phillips to F.D.R., May 18, 1933, P.O.F. 198B. For these pressures, see Hull, *Memoirs*, I, chap. 17; *Foreign Relations of the United States, 1933*, II (Washington, 1949), pp. 183–543 *passim*. (Hereafter all volumes in this series are identified by FR, year, and volume.)

23. Roper to House, June 10, 1933, House MSS. Cf. Roper to W.E.D., June 8, 1933. William E. Dodd, Jr., and Martha Dodd (eds.), *Ambassador Dodd's Diary, 1933–1938* (New York, 1941), p. 3.

Scholars have questioned the authenticity, accuracy, and value of the *Diary*. See, for example, Thomas A. Bailey's review in *The American Historical Review*, XLVII (January 1942), 390–392. Arthur M. Schlesinger has suggested that the *Diary* was the creation of Dodd's son and daughter. "Since he [Dodd] had expressly told me he was not finding leisure to keep a journal, the book took me by surprise, and I assumed, charitably, that the young people had pieced it together from the father's private letters to friends. When I suggested this in a letter to the son,...he made no reply. In any case passages in the book indicated that they could not have been set down at the time"—*In Retrospect: The History of a Historian* (New York, 1963), pp. 120–121.

Despite this, it seems to me that a journal or diary did exist. My conjecture is based on letters to Dodd from William L. Chenery, the editor of *Collier's* magazine, dated January 7, 11 and March 29, 1938, in which there are repeated references to Dodd's "diary of recent events in Germany" and the possibility of writing a series of articles or a book based on that material. Dodd's failure to prepare such articles or a book was explained by him in a letter of July 8, 1937, to Edward C. Aswell: "...a book about Germany, based upon my experience and contacts, would not be approved by the Government.... Therefore,... I shall not be able to submit a manuscript to you." Undoubtedly the fact that Dodd lived for only two years after his return from Berlin, during much of which time he was seriously ill, also helps explain his failure to turn the diary into articles or a book.

To this there can now be added a forthright letter of February 12, 1968, from Martha Dodd Stern to the present writer: "I would like to 'lay the ghost' about the matter of the *Diary* once and for all. It is absolutely authentic. Dodd had a couple of dozen of black shiny medium size notebooks in which he wrote every night he could possibly do so, in his Berlin study before going to bed, and at other times as well. Within the pages of these notebooks were also clipped newspaper articles, speeches, letters and occasional copies of reports he made. While he was very ill, he gave my brother and me permission to copy this *Diary* with a view to publication later.... We naturally edited it as carefully as we could, included some of the letters and reports, took out potentially dangerous material (such as references to German anti-Nazis...who might have suffered from his naming them) deleted some extraneous or repetitious confidential or other material. When the book was first brought into shape it was over 1200 pages. With the assistance of Joseph Barnes (whom the publishers, Harcourt Brace, brought in to help us on the job) we cut the book down to its present length. But we added absolutely *nothing* that was not in the notebooks, either hand-written, or included for reference by him. In other words, he did keep an extensive hand-written *Diary* the whole time he was in Berlin and we, his son and daughter, published it as it was, adding some of the material he had enclosed in it at the time, or later when he returned to the States, to make it into a book. The mistake we made was not to explain in a foreword exactly how the *Diary* came into being. One reviewer at the time said he doubted the existence of the *Diary*, in answer to which we put on display at Scribners bookstore on Fifth Ave, New York...one of the black notebooks, open at a page to show his writing and the exactitude of the printed work."

Although the *Diary* was partly drawn from other sources, and is consequently something other than what we usually think of as a diary, it has nevertheless proved to be of value. Arthur M. Schlesinger, Jr., for example, paraphrases Dodd's account of a dinner at Rexford G. Tugwell's home on February 1, 1935, citing the *Diary* as follows: "In view of manifest defects in editing, the Dodd *Diary* cannot be taken as an exclusive source. However, Tugwell was sufficiently impressed by the evening to get independent statements the next day from [Paul] Appleby and [John F.] Carter; and these along with Tugwell's own diary notations, support Dodd's general account." *The Politics of Upheaval* (Boston, 1960), p. 671.

In checking the *Diary* against both historical events and Dodd's letters and diplomatic reports, I found the *Diary* to be generally accurate.

A new edition of the *Diary* was recently published in East Germany. *Tagebuch des USA-Botschafters William E. Dodd in Berlin, 1933–1938.* Aus d. Engl. 3 Aufl., Berlin, 1964.

24. Dodd's appointment provoked an interesting aftermath of controversy. One group of writers argues that Roosevelt selected Dodd because of his superior qualifications. In their opinion, Dodd's Ph.D. from Leipzig and his knowledge of German made him a worthy successor to those American scholars—George Bancroft and Andrew D. White—who had served as ambassadors to Berlin. Further, Dodd's Jeffersonianism made him a standing example of American liberalism to Germans. See *The New York Times*, June 11, 1933, 12:1; June 13, 1933, 18:2; April 15, 1934, IX, 2:1; Martha Dodd, *Through Embassy Eyes*, p. 11; *Ambassador Dodd's Diary*, p. 3; Daniel Roper, *Fifty Years of Public Life* (Durham, N. C., 1941), pp. 334–335; Charles Thayer, *Diplomat* (New York, 1959), p. 256.

Conversely, we find in Ed Flynn's memoirs an anecdote to the effect that Roosevelt meant to appoint Walter F. Dodd, a former law professor at the University of Illinois and at Yale, and in the rush to get someone, appointed William E. Dodd by mistake. See Flynn, p. 148. *The New York Times* of November 2, 1947, 29:3, carries Flynn's retraction of this story.

Franklin L. Ford—"Three Observers in Berlin: Rumbold, Dodd and François-Poncet," in *The Diplomats*, ed. Gordon A. Craig and Felix Gilbert, Vol. II (New York, 1963), pp. 447–448—and Charles C. Tansill—*Back Door to War* (Chicago, 1952), pp. 45–46—come closer to the truth in suggesting that Roper and House were instrumental in arranging Dodd's appointment, though I have been unable to find any evidence that House played a part. Nor for that matter apparently did Cordell Hull, who was in London at the time.

25. *Ambassador Dodd's Diary*, pp. 3–4; William T. Hutchinson to author, July 28, 1964. W.E.D. to F.D.R., June 7, 1932, D.N.C., Virginia; W.E.D. to Norman Davis, January 22, 1933; W.E.D. to Hull, February 23, 1933.

26. Jay Pierrepont Moffat MS Diary, June 10, 1933, Harvard University Library, Cambridge, Mass. (cited hereafter as Moffat MS Diary); *Ambassador Dodd's Diary*, p. 6; FR, 1933, II, 209, 338, 216–220.

27. On developments in Germany, see Alan Bullock, *Hitler: A Study in Tyranny* (New York, 1961), pp. 213–242, 267–277; Gordon A. Craig, "The German Foreign Office from Neurath to Ribbentrop," in *The Diplomats*, II, 406–413. For German-American developments, see FR, 1933, II, 352–354, 432–444.

28. The meeting is described in *Ambassador Dodd's Diary*, pp. 4–6. For Roosevelt's attitude toward the London Economic Conference and international economic matters in general, see Arthur M. Schlesinger, Jr., *The Coming of the New Deal* (Boston, 1959), chaps. 12 and 13; Leuchtenburg, *Roosevelt and the New Deal*, pp. 199–203.

29. Moffat MS Diary, June 13, 15, 23, 27, and 29, 1933; *Ambassador Dodd's Diary*, pp. 6–10; Roper to House, July 10, 1933, House MSS; Martha Dodd, *Through Embassy Eyes*, pp. 12, 15–17.

CHAPTER XI PEACEFUL NEGOTIATIONS

1. Martha Dodd, *Through Embassy Eyes*, pp. 20–24; *Ambassador Dodd's Diary*, pp. 12–16; W.E.D. to Hull, July 22, 1933, Cordell Hull MSS, Library of Congress, Washington, D.C. (cited hereafter as Hull MSS); *Register of the Department of State, July 1, 1933* (Washington, 1933), pp. 45, 177–178, 221; FR, 1933, II, 381–385, 277–280; Bullock, pp. 238–241.

2. On these debt matters, see Joachim Remak, "Germany and the United States, 1933–1939" (unpubl. Ph.D. diss., History Dept., Stanford University, 1955), pp. 132–134; FR, 1933, II, 442–445; *United States Tariff Commission,* "Foreign-Trade and Exchange Controls in Germany" (No. 150, second series, 1942), pp. 61–62; W.E.D. to F.D.R., July 30, 1933, Official File 523, Roosevelt MSS (cited hereafter as O.F. 523).

3. W.E.D. to Hull, July 22, 1933, Hull MSS; FR, 1933, II, 248–252, 281–283; W.E.D. to F.D.R., July 30, August 12, 1933, O.F. 523; W.E.D. to Baker, August 12, 1933, Newton Baker MSS; *Ambassador Dodd's Diary*, pp. 20–21; Craig, in *The Diplomats*, II, 406–409; Bullock, pp. 276–277; William Shirer, *The Rise and Fall of the Third Reich* (New York, 1963), pp. 290–291.

4. FR, 1933, II, 403–405, 385–386, 255–258; *Ambassador Dodd's Diary*, pp. 24, 26; Martha Dodd, *Through Embassy Eyes*, p. 39; Moffat MS Diary, November 4, 1933; Nancy H. Hooker (ed.), *The Moffat Papers, 1919–1943* (Cambridge, Mass., 1956), pp. 97–98.

5. FR, 1933, II, 259; W.E.D. to House, August 25, 1933, House MSS; W.E.D., 862.00/3076, August 26, 1933, Department of State MSS, National Archives, Washington, D.C. (cited hereafter as State Dept. MSS); *Ambassador Dodd's Diary*, pp. 27–35. For the general accuracy of von Wiegand's information about Hindenburg's will, see Shirer, pp. 315–317.

6. FR, 1933, II, 390; 123 Dodd, William E./46, 47, 48, 56, September 14, 26, 27, October 4, 1933, State Dept. MSS; Hull to W.E.D., October 5, 1933; W.E.D. to Hull, October 4, 1933.

7. Moffat MS Diary, September 20, 1933; W.E.D. to F.D.R., July 30, 1933, O.F. 523; House to W.E.D., August 30, September 11 and 26, 1933; Katharine Crane, *Mr. Carr of State* (New York, 1960), pp. 314–317; *Ambassador Dodd's Diary*, pp. 33–34; W.E.D. to Hull, October 4, 1933.

8. Messersmith, George S., 862.00/3097 1/2, September 29, 1933, State Dept. MSS. For the accuracy of Messersmith's picture of the Foreign Office and Neurath, see Paul Seabury, *The Wilhelmstrasse* (Berkeley, 1954), pp. 90–91. F.D.R. to W.E.D., September 13, 1933, O.F. 523. For Roosevelt's general concern with the success of the disarmament negotiations, see FR, 1933, I, 208–211.

9. FR, 1933, II, 478–483, 450–453; *Ambassador Dodd's Diary*, pp. 41–42; W.E.D., 862.51/3716, October 13, 1933, State Dept. MSS; *U.S. Tariff Commission,* 1942, pp. 62–63.

10. For the fact that Germany's actions, particularly in leaving the disarmament conference, were viewed by many both in and out of Germany at the time as no more than expressions of more or less justifiable nationalism, see Bullock, pp. 277–279; Craig, in *The Diplomats,* II, 409–415. For a more recent statement of this view, see A. J. P. Taylor, *The Origins of the Second World War* (New York, 1966), pp. 69–79. For Dodd's attitude, see *Ambassador Dodd's Diary*, pp. 41–42, 47–50; W.E.D. to Hull, October 19, 1933, Hull MSS.

11. FR, 1933, II, 392, 394–397; *Ambassador Dodd's Diary*, p. 47; W.E.D., 862.51/3716, October 13, 1933, State Dept MSS.

12. For the speech, see 123 Dodd, William E./51, October 13, 1933, State Dept. MSS; *The New York Times,* October 13, 1:6; October 14, 14:4. For the response, see W.E.D. to F.D.R., October 13, 1933, President's Secretary's File (cited hereafter as P.S.F.); W.E.D. to Hull, October 19, 1933, Hull MSS; W.E.D. to House, October 20, 24, 1933, House MSS; W.E.D. to Baker, October 28, 1933, Newton Baker MSS; *Ambassador Dodd's Diary,* pp. 46–47, 50–51.

13. Messersmith, George, 862.00/3128, October 28, 1933, State Dept. MSS; *The New York Times,* April 15, 1934, IX, 2:1; Thomas Wolfe to Maxwell Perkins, May 23, 1935, *The Letters of Thomas Wolfe,* ed. Elizabeth Nowell (New York, 1956), pp. 459–463.

14. W.E.D. to F.D.R., October 13, 1933, P.S.F.; W.E.D. to Hull, October 19, 1933, Hull MSS; Messersmith, George, 862.00/3128, October 28, 1933, State Dept. MSS. Cf. W.E.D. to William Phillips, November 17, 1933, House MSS. Moffat MS Diary, October 12, 1933; House to W.E.D., October 21, 1933.

15. FR, 1933, II, 452–453; *Documents on British Foreign Policy,* 1919–1939, Second Series, Vol. V, 1933 (London, 1956), pp. 680–682 (cited hereafter by series and volume); *The New York Times,* October 15, 1933, 1:5; W.E.D. to Hull, October 19, 1933, Hull MSS.

16. W.E.D. to F.D.R., October 28, 1933, President's Personal File 1043 (cited hereafter as P.P.F.); FR, 1933, II, 397–398, 260–268, 454–456, 360–365; 301–307; *Ambassador Dodd's Diary,* pp. 55–56, 62; W.E.D., 862.404/35, November 8, 1933; Messersmith, George, 862.00/3128, October 28, 1933, State Dept. MSS.

17. W.E.D. to House, November 21, 1933, House MSS. On the German-Polish discussions, see Bullock, pp. 280–281. For the disarmament discussions, see *Documents on German Foreign Policy,* 1918–1945, Series C (1933–1937), II (Washington, 1959), pp. 39, 152–153 (cited hereafter by series and volume); *British Documents,* Second Series, Vol. V, 707–708, 711–713; André François-Poncet, *The Fateful Years* (New York, 1949), pp. 116–118; W.E.D. to F.D.R., November 27, 1933, P.S.F.; *Peace and War: United States Foreign Policy, 1931–1941* (Washington, 1943), pp. 194–195.

18. For a general statement about the British attitude toward continued talks, see Taylor, pp. 74–75. For Dodd's attitude, see *Ambassador Dodd's Diary,* pp. 63–64; FR, 1933, I, 327–328, 330.

19. FR, 1933, I, 330–332; Moffat MS Diary, December 10, 11, and 26, 1933; William Phillips MS Diary, December 10, 11, 1933, Harvard University Library, Cambridge, Mass. (cited hereafter as Phillips MS Diary). On the Far Eastern policy of the United States, see Dorothy Borg, *The United States and the Far Eastern Crisis of 1933–1938* (Cambridge, Mass., 1964), chap. II.

20. FR, 1933, I, 335–336; *Ambassador Dodd's Diary,* pp. 64–66; W.E.D. to Phillips, December 14, 1933, House MSS; W.E.D. to Josephus Daniels, December 26, 1933, Daniels MSS; W.E.D. to F.D.R., December 28, 1933, P.S.F.; FR, 1933, I, 353–355; W.E.D. to F.D.R., January 3, 1934, O.F., 523.

21. W.E.D. to House, January 8, 1934. W.E.D. to R. Walton Moore, January 18, 1934, R. Walton Moore MSS, Franklin D. Roosevelt Library, Hyde Park, New York (cited hereafter as Moore MSS).

22. FR, 1933, II, 454–460; FR, 1934, II, 331–338, 340, 342–346; *Ambassador Dodd's Diary,* pp. 69–70, 73–74; *German Documents,* Series C, II, 280–283, 443–444. E. David Cronon, *Josephus Daniels in Mexico* (Madison, 1960), pp. 115–119.

23. W.E.D. to F.D.R., February 8, 1934, P.S.F. On Roosevelt and the reciprocal trade agreements act, see Schlesinger, Jr., *Coming of the New Deal,* pp. 253–260.

24. For the German trade offensive, see *German Documents,* Series C, II, 537–539, 551–552; FR, 1934, II, 406–417; W.E.D., 662.1115/60, February 21, 1934, State Dept. MSS; Konrad Heiden, *Der Fuehrer* (Boston, 1944), p. 717; Bullock, p. 310; *Ambassador Dodd's Diary,* pp. 80–81, 83, 87–88.

25. FR, 1934, II, 526–528, 530–531, 509–516; *German Documents,* Series C, II, 556–557; *Ambassador Dodd's Diary,* pp. 86–87; Moffat MS Diary, March 6, 1934.

26. FR, 1934, II, 218–221; *Ambassador Dodd's Diary,* pp. 88–89; Ernst Hanfstaengl, *Unheard Witness* (Philadelphia, 1957), pp. 197, 214. Cf. Hitler's comment on Dodd in 1941 in *Hitler's Secret Conversations, 1941–1944,* trans. Norman Cameron and R. H. Stevens, with an introductory essay by H. R. Trevor-Roper (New York, 1953), p. 84: "To think that there was nobody in all the Ministry [the Foreign Office] who could get his clutches on the daughter of the former American ambassador, Dodd...," Hitler rambled. "Old Dodd, who was an imbecile, we'd have got him through his daughter." Gerhard L. Weinberg, "Hitler's Image of the United States," *American Historical Review,* LXIX (July 1964), 1010–1011. Cf. James V. Compton, *The Swastika and the Eagle* (Boston, 1967), chaps. 1–2.

27. *Ambassador Dodd's Diary,* pp. 93, 95, 100–101; *German Documents,* Series C, II, 597, 611; *The New York Times,* March 24, 1934, 17:4; W.E.D. to House, March 24, April 10, 11, 1934, House MSS; House to W.E.D., March 25, 31, April 14, 1934; Leo F. Wormser to W.E.D., March 28, 1934; W.E.D. to Mrs. William E. Dodd, March 28, 1934; Max Epstein to W.E.D., April 19, 1934; George F. Bauer to W.E.D., April 3, 23, 24, 1934.

28. George Messersmith to W.E.D., April 3, 1934, George S. Messersmith MSS, University of Delaware, Newark, Del. (cited hereafter as Messersmith MSS); Moffat MS Diary, March 24, 28, April 25, 1934. W.E.D. to Mrs. William E. Dodd, March 28, 1934; W.E.D., "Memorandum as to Existing World Complex," n.d., in Box 45 of the Dodd MSS; *Ambassador Dodd's Diary,* pp. 97–98.

29. For Dodd's picture of Roosevelt, see his penciled comment on scrap paper dated April 27, 1934, in Box 43 of his papers: "The President's one fixed purpose is to prevent minority groups from exploiting the masses, to enable common folk to enjoy the fruits of their own toil and to stop the drift toward war. In these things all men everywhere ought to support him." On the attitudes of Roosevelt and Hull toward international economics, see Julius W. Pratt, *The American Secretaries of State and Their Diplomacy,* Vol. XII: *Cordell Hull* (New York, 1964), pp. 107–117. On Hull's more conservative approach to international politics, compared to F.D.R.'s, see Donald F. Drummond, "Cordell Hull," *An Uncertain Tradition: American Secretaries of State in the Twentieth Century,* ed. Norman Graebner (New York, 1961), pp. 199–201. On the Foreign Service, see Sherwood, p. 757.

30. *Ambassador Dodd's Diary,* pp. 92–94; W.E.D. to F.D.R., January 3, 1934, O.F. 523; cf. W.E.D. to F.D.R., December 28, 1933, P.S.F., and W.E.D. to R. Walton Moore, January 18, 1934, Moore MSS; also see Moffat MS Diary, March 27 and May 5, 1934; Phillips MS Diary, June 25, 1934; Wilbur J. Carr MS Diary, March 26, 28, June 28, 1934, Wilbur J. Carr MSS, Library of Congress, Washington, D.C. (cited hereafter as Carr MS Diary); Cronon, pp. 64–67; Crane, pp. 314–317.

31. For Dodd's feeling that Roosevelt shared his opposition to isolationism, see W.E.D. to House, May 12, 1934, House MSS. For the results of his conversations with Jewish leaders and his luncheon with the editors, see *Ambassador Dodd's Diary,* pp. 95, 98–100; W.E.D. to R. Walton Moore, May 15, 1934, Moore MSS.

CHAPTER XII WAR AND NOT PEACE

1. W.E.D. to House, May 23, June 4, 1934, House MSS; House to W.E.D., May 25 and June 7, 1934; *Ambassador Dodd's Diary,* pp. 101–106, 108–113; W.E.D. to F.D.R., August 15, 1934, P.P.F. 1043; FR,

1934, II, 424–426, 364–368; W.E.D., 500A15A4/2544, May 28, 1934; W.E.D., 762.65/103, June 16, 1934, State Dept. MSS; W.E.D., "Memorandum," June 1, 1934, in Box 44 of the Dodd MSS.

2. François-Poncet, p. 130; Messersmith to W.E.D., June 2, 1934, Messersmith MSS. FR, 1934, II, 216–217, 224–229; W.E.D., 862.00/3276, June 27, 1934; 123 Dodd, William E./93, June 27, 1934, State Dept. MSS; Bullock, pp. 254–265.

3. FR, 1934, II, 229–237. Dodd has been sharply criticized for his reporting of the June 30 events. Moffat and Phillips at the time complained that Dodd was "shockingly lax" or slow in providing them with information about developments. Moreover, historians have tended to suggest that Dodd was either inaccurate or without objectivity in his analysis of these events: Moffat MS Diary, July 2 and 5, 1934; Phillips MS Diary, July 5, 1934; Tansill, p. 289, Ford, in *The Diplomats,* II, 451. Yet compared with the published reports of the British Ambassador and with what we know today about the purge, Dodd seems to have sorted out in a reasonably short time what was an almost impossibly complicated affair. Cf. for example, Phipps' comment of July 2 that "Sudden disappearance of S.A. uniforms and fast cars has today restored pre-Nazi aspect of Germany." Also, see Phipps' report of July 1 which was much less to the point than the one Dodd wrote on the following day. *British Documents,* Second Series, VI, 1933–1934, pp. 780–782.

4. *Ambassador Dodd's Diary,* pp. 118–119, 123, 126.

5. W.E.D. to Moore, May 15, June 21, 1934, Moore MSS; W.E.D. to Wilbur J. Carr, May 30, 1934; W.E.D. to Moore, June 8, 1934; Moore to W.E.D., June 19, 30, 1934; Herbert S. Houston to W.E.D., June 19 and 22, 1934; W.E.D. to F.D.R., June 27, 1934; *The New York Times,* July 1, 1934, IV, 2:2; *Ambassador Dodd's Diary,* p. 128.

6. FR, 1934, II, 376–380; W.E.D. to Hull, June 19, 1934, Hull MSS; Phillips MS Diary, June 5, 1934; Moffat MS Diary, July 7, 11, and 14, 1934; *Ambassador Dodd's Diary,* pp. 119–120, 122, 126–132.

7. FR, 1934, II, 240–243; François-Poncet, p. 154; Bullock, pp. 281–284; G. M. Gathorne-Hardy, *A Short History of International Affairs,* 1920–1939 (London, 1952), pp. 370–373, 388–391; FR, 1934, I, 489–490, 493–494, 498–499; *Ambassador Dodd's Diary,* pp. 132–135; W.E.D., 862.00/3341, July 26, 1934, State Dept. MSS; W.E.D. to Hull, August 2, 1934, Hull MSS.

8. FR, 1934, II, 243–247, 273–274; *Ambassador Dodd's Diary,* pp. 137–139, 157–158; W.E.D. to Roper, August 14, 1934, O.F., 523; W.E.D., 862.00/3378, August 15, 1934, State Dept. MSS; W.E.D. to House, September 1, 1934, House MSS; Bullock, pp. 266–267.

9. W.E.D. to F.D.R., August 15, 1934, P.P.F. 1043; W.E.D. to Roper, August 14, 1934, O.F. 523; *Ambassador Dodd's Diary,* pp. 141–144, 148–149, 152, 159. On François-Poncet, see Ford, in *The Diplomats,* II, 463–464.

10. *Ambassador Dodd's Diary,* pp. 159–161; *The New York Times,* September 10, 1934, 8:2; clipping from *The New York Sun,* September 11, 1934, in Box 44 of the Dodd MSS.

11. F.D.R. to W.E.D., August 25, 1934, P.P.F. 1043; *Ambassador Dodd's Diary,* pp. 162–167. On the Nye investigation, see Leuchtenburg, *Franklin Roosevelt and the New Deal,* pp. 217–218.

12. *Ambassador Dodd's Diary,* p. 171; FR, 1934, II, 262–263, 300–301; W.E.D., 862.404/79, September 21, 1934; W.E.D., 862.20/700, September 24, 1934, State Dept. MSS.

13. *Ambassador Dodd's Diary,* pp. 170–177; FR, 1934, I, 442–443; FR, 1934, II, 275–278, 385–386; W.E.D. to Moore, October 5, 1934, Moore MSS.

14. W.E.D. to Moore, November 5, 1934, Moore MSS; W.E.D., 862.404/92, November 2, 1934, State Dept. MSS; *Foreign Affairs,* XIII (October 1934), 1–5; Earl R. Beck, *Verdict on Schacht* (Tallahassee, Fla., 1955), p. 75; *Ambassador Dodd's Diary,* pp. 180–182.

15. FR, 1934, II, 251–253; W.E.D., 862.404/94, November 19, 1934; W.E.D., 862.00/3477, December 5, 1934, State Dept. MSS; *Ambassador Dodd's Diary*, pp. 184–185, 188, 192–193. Cf. William Shirer, *Berlin Diary*, 1934–1941 (New York, 1941), p. 24.

16. *Ambassador Dodd's Diary*, pp. 184, 192, 197–198; *German Documents*, Series C, III, 366–367, 682–685, 674–678, 680–682; W.E.D. to Moore, November 30, 1934, Moore MSS; W.E.D., 862.00/3477, December 5, 1934, State Dept. MSS; Shirer, *Berlin Diary*, p. 25.

17. W.E.D. to Michael Williams, January 3, 1935; W.E.D. to House, January 3, 1935; Carrie Chapman Catt to W.E.D., January 8, 1935; Abraham Flexner to W.E.D., January 17, 1935; Raymond L. Buell to W.E.D., January 21, 1935. W.E.D. to Moore, January 22, 1935, Moore MSS; *Ambassador Dodd's Diary*, pp. 207–210; F.D.R. to W.E.D. February 2, 1935, P.P.F. 1043. For the background on the World Court and Roosevelt's attitude toward the League, see Leuchtenburg, *Franklin Roosevelt and the New Deal*, pp. 215–217; Hull, *Memoirs*, I, 386–389.

18. W.E.D. to F.D.R., January 30, 1935, P.P.F., 1043; *Ambassador Dodd's Diary*, pp. 210–212; W.E.D. to Josephus Daniels, February 13, 1935, Daniels MSS.

19. On Beard, see Strout, pp. 115–116 and chap. 7; Higham, History, pp. 123–129. For Beard's address, see *American Historical Review*, XXXIX (January 1934), 219–229.

The fact that Dodd was somewhat out of step with the majority of professional historians did not bar him from the presidency of the association. Having continued to take a leading part in association affairs in the late twenties and early thirties—including continued service as an editor of the *Review*, a member of the committee on publications, an association delegate to the Social Science Research Council, a chairman or participant at annual meetings in sessions on southern history, agricultural history, and social studies in the schools, and as a second and then first vice-president—Dodd was a logical choice for election to the association's highest office.

For Dodd's views, see *Ambassador Dodd's Diary*, pp. 171–172, 174; *American Historical Review*, XL (January 1935), 217–231; (April 1935), 437.

20. *Ambassador Dodd's Diary*, pp. 212–213. Cf. Arthur M. Schlesinger, Jr., *The Politics of Upheaval* (Boston, 1960), pp. 67, 141–142.

21. *Ambassador Dodd's Diary*, pp. 213–214. Roosevelt's view of Long was shared by others at this time. See Schlesinger, Jr., *Politics of Upheaval*, pp. 66–68. Dodd's impression of the President's response to his defeat on the World Court does not square with other accounts. See ibid., p. 5; Leuchtenburg, *Franklin Roosevelt and the New Deal*, pp. 216–217.

22. See W.E.D. to Miss Smithies, June 9, 1924; W.E.D. to Dr. Wilbur Post, November 15, 1925; W.E.D. to "Wife and Children," February 8, 1928; Dr. Thomas R. Brown to W.E.D., February 9 and March 7, 1935. W.E.D. to Mr. Meyer, February 4, 1935; *Ambassador Dodd's Diary*, pp. 214–215.

23. "Confidential Memorandum," February 7, 1935; Moffat MS Diary, December 6 and 28, 1934; Phillips MS Diary, November 28, 1934; Carr MS Diary, November 5, 6, 1934. W.E.D. to F.D.R., January 30, 1935, P.P.F. 1043.

CHAPTER XIII ROOSEVELT'S AMBASSADOR

1. W.E.D. to Moore, February 22, 1935, P.S.F.; *Ambassador Dodd's Diary*, pp. 216–17; W.E.D. to House, March 3, 1935, House MSS; W.E.D. to Moore, March 11, 1935, Moore MSS; FR, 1935, II, 343–5.

2. Bullock, pp. 286–8; FR, 1935, II, 294–7, 300–301, 306–9; *Ambassador Dodd's Diary*, pp. 222–3; François-Poncet, pp. 169–73; Shirer, *Berlin Diary*, pp. 28–33; *Peace and War*, pp. 255–6.

3. FR, 1935, II, 315–17, 319; FR, 1935, I, 208–9; on Hitler and the army, see Gordon A. Craig, *The Politics of the Prussian Army* (New York, 1955), chap. XII.

4. FR, 1935, II, 257–8, 392–5, 320–1. For the Danzig elections, see Gathorne-Hardy, pp. 384–7; for Dodd's dispatch, see W.E.D., 862.20/850, April 10, 1935, State Dept. MSS.

5. FR, 1935, I, 244–6, 280–83; FR, 1935, II, 331–2, 266–70; *Ambassador Dodd's Diary*, pp. 242–3, 245–6; *The New York Times*, May 20, 1935, 8:6. For Hitler's speech, see Bullock, pp. 289–91; for Dodd's impressions, see W.E.D., 611.6231/627, May 7, 1935, State Dept. MSS; W.E.D. to F.D.R., May 9, 1935, P.S.F.; W.E.D. to Phillips, May 29, 1935.

6. Taylor, pp. 87, 110; Bullock, pp. 291–3; W.E.D. to Moore, June 6 and 27, 1935, Moore MSS; FR, 1935, II, 337–9; W.E.D. to F.D.R., July 29, 1935, P.S.F.; *Ambassador Dodd's Diary*, pp. 252–9.

7. FR, 1935, II, 350–58, 401–3; W.E.D., 862.00 P.R./179, July 5, 1935; W.E.D., 862.00/3539, July 17, 1935; W.E.D., 862.404/130, July 24, 1935; W.E.D., 862.00/3523, August 1, 1935, State Dept. MSS; *The New York Times*, July 21, 1935, IV, 3:7, 4:1; July 31, 1935, 2:6; August 1, 1935, 1:3; August 4, 1935, IV, 5:1; *Ambassador Dodd's Diary*, pp. 263–4.

8. *Ambassador Dodd's Diary*, 261–2; W.E.D. to Moore, July 18, 1935, Moore MSS; Dr. T. R. Brown to W.E.D., July 1, 1935. For a discussion of the neutrality campaign in America at this time, see Robert A. Divine, *The Illusion of Neutrality* (Chicago, 1962), chap. 4.

9. *Ambassador Dodd's Diary*, pp. 255, 265–6; W.E.D. to F.D.R., May 9, 1935, P.S.F.; W.E.D., 862.404/141, September 5, 1935; W.E.D., 862.4016/1550, September 7, 1935, State Dept. MSS; FR, 1935, II, 278–81.

10. *Ambassador Dodd's Diary*, pp. 266–8; W.E.D., 765.84/916, August 22, 1935, State Dept. MSS.

11. W.E.D. to Messersmith, October 7, 1935, P.S.F.; FR, 1935, II, 287–9, 365–76, 387–90; W.E.D., 862.00/3544, October 5, 1935; W.E.D., 862.00/3551, October 21, 1935; W.E.D., 862.20/1082, November 4, 1935; W.E.D., 862.00/3565, December 21, 1935, State Dept. MSS; W.E.D. to Moore, October 29 and November 27, 1935, Moore MSS; *The New York Times*, November 24, 1935, IV, 5:3; *Ambassador Dodd's Diary*, pp. 280–81, 283–5.

12. W.E.D. to F.D.R., October 31, 1935, P.S.F.; W.E.D. to House, 711.00/11, October 27, 1935, State Dept. MSS. On Roosevelt's neutrality policy, see Divine, pp. 122–134. W.E.D. to Moore, November 17 and 27, 1935, Moore MSS.

13. For Moore's attitude, see Divine, pp. 101–2, 122–3. Moffat MS Diary, March 16, 1934; Carr MS Diary, April 19, 1935; Phillips MS Diary, December 30, 31, 1935, January 1, 2, 29, 1936; Ford, in *The Diplomats*, II, 469–70; *Ambassador Dodd's Diary*, pp. 291–2; W.E.D. to Moore, October 17, 1935, Moore MSS.

14. *Ambassador Dodd's Diary*, pp. 291–3; FR, 1936, I, 165–6; W.E.D. to Moore, January 2, 1936, Moore MSS, in which Dodd mentions a telegram on the neutrality question sent to Hull on December 30.

15. W.E.D. to F.D.R., October 31, 1935; F.D.R. to W.E.D., December. 2, 1935; W.E.D. to F.D.R., December 15, 1935, January 4, 1936; F.D.R. to W.E.D., January 6, 1936, P.S.F. For Roosevelt's speech, see Franklin D. Roosevelt, *Public Papers and Addresses*, Vol. 5, comp. S. I. Rosenman (New York, 1938), pp. 8–18. F.D.R. to Moore, September 11, 1935, O.F. 523; Carr MS Diary, April 19, 1935; Phillips MS Diary, January 29, 1936.

16. FR, 1936, II, 160–62, 197–9, 178–9; *Ambassador Dodd's Diary,* 295–7; W.E.D., 765.84/3575, January 29, 1936, State Dept. MSS; W.E.D. to Josephus Daniels, February 8, 1936, Daniels MSS.

17. On the reoccupation of the Rhineland, see Bullock, pp. 295–300; Taylor, pp. 96–101. For Dodd's views, see FR, 1936, I, 188–96; *Ambassador Dodd's Diary,* pp. 312–16; W.E.D., 762.65/176, February 28, 1936; W.E.D. 762.00/110, February 29, 1936, State Dept. MSS; W.E.D. to F.D.R., March 3, 1936, P.S.F.

18. FR, 1936, I, 207–9, 214–16, 218–19, 233–4, 237–8, 245–6; Gathorne-Hardy, pp. 419–26; W.E.D. to F.D.R., April 1, 1936, P.S.F.

19. FR, 1936, I, 249–55, 263–4, 278; W.E.D. to Josephus Daniels, March 26, 1936, Daniels MSS; *Ambassador Dodd's Diary,* pp. 323–4.

20. F.D.R. to W.E.D., March 16, 1936, P.P.F., 1043; W.E.D. to F.D.R., April 1, 1936, P.S.F.; FR, 1936, I, 219–27; *Ambassador Dodd's Diary,* pp. 328–32.

21. 123 Dodd, William E./139, April 17, 1936, State Dept. MSS; *The New York Times,* April 17, 1936, 44:3; clipping from *The Chicago Daily News,* April 17, 1936, in Box 45 of the Dodd MSS.

22. W.E.D. to Moore, April 18, 1936, O.F. 523; *Ambassador Dodd's Diary,* pp. 332–3; Shirer, *Berlin Diary,* p. 60; *The New York Times,* April 25, 1936, 9:2; May 11, 1:1; May 12, 18:3; May 13, 14:3.

23. W.E.D. to Moore, June 6, July 18, October 29, 1935, Moore MSS; *Ambassador Dodd's Diary,* p. 261; W.E.D. to F.D.R., January 4 and 7, 1936, P.S.F.; Schlesinger, Jr., *Politics of Upheaval,* pp. 494–5, 502–3.

24. W.E.D. to "Family," April 19, 1936; W.E.D. to Mrs. Dodd, June 11, 1936; Dr. T. R. Brown to W.E.D., May 2, 15, and 20, 1936; *Ambassador Dodd's Diary,* p. 334.

25. Moore to W.E.D., May 6, 1936. W.E.D. to Moore, May 20, 1936, Moore MSS; W.E.D. to Mrs. Dodd, June 3, 1936; W.E.D. to House, July 18, 1936; *Ambassador Dodd's Diary,* pp. 334–7. The phrase "mere technical academies" is drawn from a report to Dodd on the state of Germany's universities written in the summer of 1936 by Prof. Wolfgang Windleband of the University of Berlin, in Box 44 of the Dodd MSS.

26. Schlesinger, Jr., *Politics of Upheaval,* pp. 586–7; W.E.D. to Josephus Daniels, June 2, 1936, Daniels MSS; W.E.D. to Moore, June 5, 1936, Moore MSS; W.E.D. to Mrs. Dodd, June 19, 28, 1936; *The New York Times,* July 1, 1936, 10:4; July 9, 1936, 16:3; *Ambassador Dodd's Diary,* pp. 336–7.

27. For an excellent analysis of progressive opposition to F.D.R., see Otis L. Graham, Jr., *An Encore for Reform: The Old Progressives and the New Deal* (New York, 1967), especially chap. II. W.E.D. to Baker, July 28, 1936; Baker to W.E.D., September 10, 1936; W.E.D. to William A. White, August. 26, 1936, Newton Baker MSS.

28. For Dodd's ideas, see, as just a few examples, W.E.D. to F.D.R., December 15, 1935, P.S.F.; W.E.D. to Fred Sayre, February 18, 1936; W.E.D. to Viscount Cecil, n.d., 1936, in Box 46 of the Dodd MSS; *The New York Times,* July 1, 1936, 10:4. On Roosevelt's eagerness for government economies, see Schlesinger, Jr., *Politics of Upheaval,* pp. 510–12; and, more specifically, W.E.D. to Moore, February 18, April 14, 1936; Moore to W.E.D., April 1, 1936, Moore MSS.

CHAPTER XIV FOUR YEARS' SERVICE IS ENOUGH

1. *Ambassador Dodd's Diary,* pp. 341, 347, 349; W.E.D. to Moore, August 17, 1936, Moore MSS. By the time Dodd returned to Berlin, it was already public knowledge that Mussolini was sending material to Franco and that the French, at least, were sharply divided over aiding the Republic. See Hugh Thomas, *The Spanish Civil War* (Middlesex, Eng., 1965), chaps. 24–26.

2. F.D.R. to W.E.D., August 5, 1936, P.S.F.; FR, 1936, I, 335; FR, 1936, II, 227 ff; Beck, pp. 84–85; John Morton Blum, *From the Morgenthau Diaries: Years of Crisis, 1928–1938* (Boston, 1959), pp. 149–155; W.E.D. to F.D.R., August 19, 1936, P.S.F.; *Ambassador Dodd's Diary,* pp. 344–345, 351–353.

3. François-Poncet, pp. 203–207; *Ambassador Dodd's Diary,* pp. 340–344, 347–348; FR, 1936, II, 198–199; W.E.D. to Moore, August 17, 1936, Moore MSS; W.E.D. to Moore, n.d. (but probably early September), in Box 46 of the Dodd MSS; W.E.D. to F.D.R., August 19, 1936, P.S.F.; on the press corps in Berlin, see Martha Dodd, *Through Embassy Eyes,* chap. V.

4. FR, 1936, II, 201–202, 171–173, 480–481, 493–494, 509–510; W.E.D., 852.00/2526, August 11, 1936; W.E.D., 852.00/2860, August 28, 1936, State Dept. MSS.

5. FR, 1936, I, 335–338, 350–353, 355–356; FR, 1936, II, 148–152, 154–155; W.E.D. to Moore, October 8, 1936, Moore MSS; W.E.D. to F.D.R., October 19, 1936, P.S.F.

6. FR, 1936, I, 370–374, 396–397; FR, 1936, II, 549–550, 560–562, 571; *Ambassador Dodd's Diary,* pp. 359, 363–366. On Roosevelt's response to the Spanish Civil War, see F. Jay Taylor, *The United States and the Spanish Civil War* (New York, 1956), chap. III. F.D.R. to W.E.D., November 9, 1936, P.S.F.

7. There is an excellent discussion of Roosevelt's interest at this time in heading off a war through some kind of conference and the part of the Buenos Aires meeting in this in Borg, pp. 369 ff. For Dodd's views, see W.E.D. to Moore, November 9, 25, 1936, Moore MSS; W.E.D. to F.D.R., December 7, 1936, P.S.F.; FR, 1936, II, 586–587, 591–592, 594, 612, 617, 621–622; *Ambassador Dodd's Diary,* pp. 362–363, 367–369, 376–377. For the fact that the Foreign Office and high command were eager to reduce European tensions over the Spanish Civil War through international co-operation, see Craig, in *The Diplomats,* I, 429–431.

8. W.E.D. to Moore, December 19, 26, 1936, Moore MSS; *Ambassador Dodd's Diary,* pp. 371–372; 123 Dodd, William E./155, December 24, 1936, State Dept. MSS; Moore to W.E.D., December 26, 1936, Moore MSS; Waldo Heinrichs, Jr., *American Ambassador: Joseph C. Grew and the Development of the United States Diplomatic Tradition* (Boston, 1966), p. 233.

9. On the Spanish Arms Embargo and opposition to it, see Divine, pp. 168–172; for Dodd's reaction, see W.E.D., 852.00/4281, January 6, 1937, State Dept. MSS; for Cudahy's view, see FR, 1937, I, 24–26; for Roosevelt's, see F.D.R. to W.E.D., January 9, 1937, P.S.F. W.E.D., 852.00/4281, January 6, 1937, State Dept. MSS; *Ambassador Dodd's Diary,* pp. 377–378, 380–381; for Schacht's proposal, see also FR, 1937, I, 29–31.

10. W.E.D. to Moore, February 17, 1937, Moore MSS. For domestic developments in the United States at this time, see Leuchtenburg, *Franklin Roosevelt and the New Deal,* pp. 231 ff.

11. *Ambassador Dodd's Diary,* pp. 374–375, 382–387; FR, 1936, II, 155–160; W.E.D., 852.00/4286, January 6, 1937; W.E.D., 862.00/3639, January 12, 1937; W.E.D., 862.00P.R./213, January 18, 1937; W.E.D., 862.00/296, January 25, 1937; W.E.D., 862.00/3641, February 3, 1937; W.E.D., 862.00/3644, February 26, 1937, State Dept. MSS.

12. *Ambassador Dodd's Diary*, pp. 382, 386–389, 393–395; W.E.D., 500.A19/58, March 4, 1937, State Dept. MSS; W.E.D. to Hull, April 5, 1937, in the Daniels MSS; FR, 1937, II, 367–375.

13. Moore to W.E.D., April 3, 1937; F.D.R. to Moore, April 5, 1937; T.M. Wilson to Moore, April 6, 1937; Moore to W.E.D., April 8, 1937; Moore to F.D.R., April 9, 1937, Moore MSS. Most of this correspondence can also be found in the Roosevelt MSS, P.S.F.

14. FR, 1937, II, 320–322; FR, 1937, I, 82–83; W.E.D. to F.D.R., April 13, 1937, P.S.F.; W.E.D., 762.63/352, April 27, 1937, State Dept. MSS. For Dodd's trip, see *Ambassador Dodd's Diary*, pp. 404–406.

15. Moore to W.E.D., April 27, May 11, 1937; Moore, "Memorandum," May 12, 1937, Moore MSS; *The New York Times*, May 12, 1937, 4:3; May 13, 1937, 8:4; May 14, 1937, 22:5; Cincinnati *Times and Star* clipping, May 18, 1937, in Box 47 of the Dodd MSS.

16. On the fear of fascism in America, see Leuchtenburg, *Franklin Roosevelt and the New Deal*, chap. 12; "Roosevelt's Virginia Reel Rehearsal," May 16, 1937, Raymond Clapper MS Diary, Library of Congress, Washington, D.C. (cited hereafter as Clapper MS Diary); F.D.R. to W.E.D., May 25, 1937, P.S.F.; reports of dissatisfaction with Dodd in the State Department were recorded in Arthur Krock's column in *The New York Times*, May 14, 1937, 22:5; Roosevelt's estimate of Dodd's performance was made in his conversation with Clapper on May 16.

17. Dodd's comment was made to Professor Eugene Anderson, a colleague of Dodd's at the University of Chicago, who was in Germany in 1937. The comment is recorded in a long letter Professor Anderson wrote after leaving Germany and which he was kind enough to let me read. W.E.D. to Moore, May 14, 1937, Moore MSS.

18. FR, 1937, II, 395–405; *Ambassador Dodd's Diary*, pp. 403–404, 410–414.

19. FR, 1937, I, 92–93, 322, 336–337, 341, 343, 352–353; W.E.D. to Moore, June 3, 1937, Moore MSS; W.E.D. to F.D.R., June 12, 1937, P.S.F.; W.E.D. to Hull, June 21, 1937; *Ambassador Dodd's Diary*, pp. 412–413, 416–421; W.E.D. to Sir Eric Phipps, July 1, 1937.

20. W.E.D. to Moore, May 14, July 6, 1937; Moore to W.E.D., May 15, 1937, Moore MSS; F.D.R. to Hull, June 17, July 23, 1937, O.F. 523; W.E.D. to House, June 5, 1937; *Ambassador Dodd's Diary*, pp. 408–409, 421–422; Moore to F.D.R., July 17, 1937, O.F. 523. For the fact that Roosevelt did invite Davies to take over Dodd's post toward the end of the year, see Joseph E. Davies, *Mission to Moscow* (New York, 1941), pp. 139–146; Carr MS Diary, June 1, 1937; Clapper MS Diary, June 10, 1937.

21. *The New York Times*, August 5, 1937, 3:3; *Ambassador Dodd's Diary*, pp. 423–427; W.E.D. to Senator Burke, August 15, 1937; W.E.D. to F.D.R., August 26, 1937, P.S.F.; Borg, chaps. X and XIII; F.D.R. to W.E.D., August 30, 1937, P.P.F. 1043.

22. Spencer Miller, Jr., to W.E.D., September 2 and 3, 1937. W.E.D. to Hull, September 6, 1937; "Memo," September 10, 1937, O.F. 198; Messersmith to W.E.D., September 17, 20, 1937; Fred W. Wile to W.E.D., October 5, 1937; Gerhard Ritter, *Carl Goerdeler und Die Deutsche Widerstandsbewegung* (Stuttgart, 1954), pp. 160–161; *The New York Times*, September 4, 1937, 13:4; W.E.D. to Hull, September 23, October 28, 1937, Hull MSS; 123 Dodd, William E./188, October 7, 1937, State Dept. MSS; W.E.D. to Moore, July 6, September 13, 1937, Moore MSS.

23. FR, 1937, II, 377–383; *German Documents* Series D, I, 627–632; 862.00/3664, August 11, 1937, State Dept. MSS; *The New York Times*, August 26, 1937, 4:2; September 4, 1937, 1:4; September 5, 1937, 11:1; Moffat MS Diary, September 16, 18, 1937; *Ambassador Dodd's Diary*, p. 427.

24. W.E.D. to Josephus Daniels, October 5, 1937, Daniels MSS; W.E.D. to Moore, October 20, December 2, 1937, Moore MSS; *Ambassador Dodd's Diary*, pp. 428–430; Schlesinger, Jr., *Coming of the New Deal*, chap. 35, especially pp. 583–587.

25. FR, 1937, II, 383; 123 Dodd, William E./218, November 27, 1937, State Dept. MSS; W.E.D. to Moore, December 2, 1937, Moore MSS; *Ambassador Dodd's Diary*, pp. 433–435, 443; Clapper MS Diary, December 21, 1937. On Roosevelt's decision to appoint a career diplomat whose presence "would have no special political significance," see Davies, pp. 254–256.

26. W.E.D. to Senator LaFollette, November 15, 1937; FR, 1937, I, 154–155; *Ambassador Dodd's Diary*, pp. 431–433. Roosevelt's letter is in FR, 1937, I, 154.

27. *Ambassador Dodd's Diary*, pp. 446–447.

28. Felix Gilbert, "Two British Ambassadors: Perth and Henderson," in *The Diplomats*, II, 541–543, 552–553; Ford, in *The Diplomats*, II, 463–464, 468–471; Ford and Carl Schorske, "The Voice in the Wilderness: Robert Coulondre," in *The Diplomats*, II, 569, 572–573, 576–578.

CHAPTER XV   REAPING THE WHIRLWIND

1. For Dodd's schedule of talks during his first three months back in the United States, see the voluminous correspondence in Boxes 48, 49, and 50 of his papers. Also see W.E.D. to Daniels, January 20, 1938, Daniels MSS. For the content of these speeches, see *The New York Times*, January 14, 1938, 1:2; January 31, 1938, 6:1; February 22, 1938, 15:8; February 23, 1938, 19:4; *The Washington Star*, January 24, 1938, clipping in Box 48; *The Chicago Daily News*, March 1, 1938, clipping in Box 49 of the Dodd MSS.

2. I have gathered the reactions to Dodd's speeches from *The New York Herald Tribune*, January 14, 1938, pp. 1, 18; *The New York Times*, January 16, 1938, 9:1; *The Washington Post*, January 24, 1938, pp. 1, 9; *The Detroit News*, January 26, 1938, pp. 1, 13; *The Milwaukee Journal*, March 2, 1938, p. 1; *The Chicago Tribune*, March 1, 1938, p. 4; *The St. Louis Post-Dispatch*, March 1, 1938, p. 3; March 2, 1938, p. 2; March 4, 1938, IV, 1, 5; *The Dayton Journal*, March 9, 1938, p. 5; March 11, 1938, p. 1; *The Cleveland Plain Dealer*, March 10, 1938, pp. 1, 5; *The Chattanooga Times*, March 30, 1938, pp. 1, 5. For the German-Italian reaction to Dodd's speeches, see *German Documents* Series D, I, 682, 685; T. Ogeltree to W.E.D., (?) 1938; *The New York Times*, January 15, 1938, 1:2; February 25, 1938, 3:3; September 11, 1938, 31:1.

3. W.E.D. to McIntyre, February 16, 1938, P.P.F. 1043; "Memo for the President," April 6, 1938, O.F. 523; W.E.D. to Moore, April 26, 1938; Moore to W.E.D., April 27, 1938, Moore MSS; F. H. Mueller to W.E.D., February 7, 1938; Hull to W.E.D., March 24, May 13, 24, June 11, 1938; W.E.D. to Herman Reissig, May 23, 1938.

4. For these background events, see Pratt, XII, 286–289; Hull, *Memoirs*, I, 572–575; Leuchtenburg, *Franklin Roosevelt and the New Deal*, pp. 284–285, 261, 266–267. For Dodd's opinion, see W.E.D. to Herman Reissig, May 23, 1938.

5. *Ambassador Dodd's Diary*, p. 446; Martha Dodd, *Through Embassy Eyes*, pp. 370–371; W.E.D. to Daniels, May 30, August 14, 1938, Daniels MSS; W.E.D. to Moore, July 21, 1938, Moore MSS.

6. For Dodd's schedule of speeches in this period, see Boxes 50 and 51 of his MSS. For the speech itself, see W.E.D., "The University and the Totalitarian State," *The Educational Record*, XIX (July 1938), 319–322. Cf. W.E.D., "The Bible of a Political Church: A Commentary on the Nazi Primer," *The Nazi Primer*, ed. Harwood L. Childs (New York, 1938), pp. 256–280.

7. A copy of Dodd's address can be found in Box 50 of his papers. Cf. Dodd's earlier statement on Nazi propaganda in untitled Washington press clipping, January 15, 1938, and untitled Detroit press clipping, January 28, 1938, in Box 48. For the A.C.L.U. pamphlet, see U.S. Congress,

House, Committee on Un-American Activities, *Hearings, Un-American Propaganda in the United States,* 75th Cong., 3rd Sess., 1938, p. 1469. On the Dies Committee, see Leuchtenburg, *Franklin Roosevelt and the New Deal,* pp. 280–281.

8. Gerhart Seger to W.E.D., April 25, 1938; W.E.D. to Robert G. Sproul, October 1, 1938; Frank B. Hanson to W.E.D., September 9, 1938; Messersmith to W.E.D., April 23, June 21, 23, 1938; Ralph C. Busser to W.E.D., January 20, 1938. These are just a few samples of letters written by and to Dodd about refugees. Many more can be found in Boxes 49–52.

9. William E. Dodd, Jr., to W.E.D., January 22, 1938. W.E.D. to Moore, July 21, 1938, Moore MSS; Dodd's speech "Virginia's Opportunity" is in Box 51 of the Dodd MSS; on the fate of the Roosevelt candidates, see Leuchtenburg, *Franklin Roosevelt and the New Deal,* pp. 266–268; on Dodd's difficulties arranging an appointment, see W.E.D. to F.D.R., August 7, September 29, 1938; McIntyre to W.E.D., September 1, 1938, P.P.F. 1043; M. H. Carter to W.E.D., August 17, 1938; W.E.D. to Moore, August 20, 1938; Moore to W.E.D., August 22, 1938, Moore MSS; W.E.D. to Hull, September 24, 1938, Hull MSS.

10. Early to W.E.D., October 5, 1938, P.P.F. 1043; for Dodd's schedule of talks, see Boxes 50–51 of his papers; for the speeches themselves, see "Our Democratic Hopes and Disappointments" in Box 51; *The New York Times,* December 10, 1938, 1:3.

11. I am indebted to Martha Dodd Stern for information about her father's medical problems: letter to author, February 12, 1968. W.E.D. to Moore, December 10, 1938, Moore MSS; *The New York Times,* January 10, 1939, 11:4; January 17, 1939, 12:6.

12. For Dodd's speaking engagements in November, December, and January, see Box 52 of his papers; on Dodd's illness, see William E. Dodd, Jr., to Moore, January 31, 1939, Moore MSS; Hamilton Holt to W.E.D., February 7, 1939. W.E.D. to Daniels, February 13, 1939, Daniels MSS; on Roosevelt's activities, see Langer and Gleason, pp. 45–50; W.E.D. to F.D.R., January 28, 1939, O.F. 523.

13. F.D.R. to W.E.D., February 7, 1939, O.F. 523; Daniels to W.E.D., February 20, 1939, Daniels MSS; W.E.D. to Moore, February 28, 1939, Moore MSS; *The New York Times,* March 3, 1939, 25:7.

14. See William Buttrick, Dodd's secretary, to Mrs. H. C. Barrow, March 9, 1939; Buttrick to Claude Bowers, March 15, 1939; for details about Dodd's talks on the West Coast, see Box 52 of his papers; for his condition, see W.E.D. to Moore, March 21, 1939, Moore MSS.

15. ". . . My physicians have urged no lectures in six months," Dodd wrote on a letter of March 20, 1939, from George Knapp. W.E.D. to F.D.R., April 28, 1939, P.P.F. 1043; W.E.D. to Daniels, May 9, 1939, Daniels MSS; W.E.D. to Moore, June 7, 1939, Moore MSS; Saul K. Padover to author, August 18, 1964; William E. Dodd, Jr., to Moore, May 25, 1939, Moore MSS.

16. *The New York Times,* July 10, 1939, 21:7; July 11, 1939, 4:2; July 13, 1939, 3:3; Memorandum for F.D.R., n.d., 1939; F.D.R. to W.E.D., July 10, 1939; Martha Dodd Stern to F.D.R., July 21, 1939, P.P.F. 1043; C. D. Johns to W.E.D., July 21, 29, 1939.

17. Dodd's condition is described in several letters in Boxes 53–54 of his papers. W.E.D. to F.D.R., September 18, 1939, P.P.F. 1043; W.E.D. to Daniels, January 1, 1940, Daniels MSS.

18. *The New York Times,* February 9, 1940, 21:3; February 10, 1940, 15:1; eulogies by Avery Craven, Charles Merriam, and Marcus W. Jernegan in *The University of Chicago Magazine* (May 1940), pp. 6–10, 20–21, 27; F.D.R. to William E. Dodd, Jr., February 9, 1940, P.P.F. 1043.

19. The quotation is from Charles Beard's introduction to *Ambassador Dodd's Diary,* p. xvi.

BIBLIOGRAPHICAL NOTE

Any study of William E. Dodd must begin with the more than twenty thousand items in his collection of papers at the Library of Congress, Washington, D.C. These include letters, diaries, and typescript copies of his writings from the turn of the century to his death in 1940. While there are some items from the 1890s, manuscripts relating to his earliest years are almost nonexistent. In addition to this principal collection of Dodd papers, there is a small body of his manuscripts at the Randolph-Macon College Library in Ashland, Virginia. For the most part, though, these are copies of letters in the Library of Congress collection. The most significant item in the Randolph-Macon holdings is "Professor Dodd's Diary, 1916–1920," which has been reproduced with only limited omissions by W. Alexander Mabry in *The John P. Branch Historical Papers of Randolph-Macon College*, New Series, II (March 1953). There is also a very small collection of Dodd letters in the Southern Historical Collection in the University of North Carolina Library at Chapel Hill. Again, though, these are chiefly items found in the principal collection.

There are a number of other manuscript collections which greatly help to fill out a study of Dodd. For his earliest years as a historian and reformer, these are the William J. Peele MSS in the Southern Historical Collection of the University of North Carolina Library; the William K. Boyd and the William Henry Glasson MSS in the Duke University Library at Durham, N.C.; the Charles Francis Adams, Jr., MSS in the Massachusetts Historical Society in Boston; the Andrew Jackson Montague MSS in the Virginia State Library, Richmond; the Andrew C. McLaughlin MSS, the Department of History MSS, and the General Administrative Files of the University of Chicago in the University of Chicago Library; the

Frederic Bancroft MSS in the Columbia University Library, New York City; the Frederick Jackson Turner MSS in the Henry E. Huntington Library, San Marino, Calif.; and the Ray Stannard Baker MSS in the Library of Congress.

For the period 1913–1932 a number of the collections mentioned above were useful as well as the following: the Claude Kitchin MSS in the University of North Carolina Library; the Oswald Garrison Villard MSS in the Harvard University Library, Cambridge, Mass.; the Edward M. House MSS in the Yale University Library, New Haven, Conn.; the Josephus Daniels MSS, the Newton Baker MSS, the Woodrow Wilson MSS, and the William G. McAdoo MSS in the Library of Congress; the Sidney E. Mezes MSS in the Columbia University Library; the Inquiry Document #135 which is part of the Record Group #256 in the National Archives, Washington, D.C.; the Salomon O. Levinson MSS and the Frank O. Lowden MSS in the University of Chicago Library.

For the last eight years of Dodd's life, the following, again in addition to several manuscripts already mentioned, proved to be of value: the Democratic National Committee MSS for Virginia and Illinois, 1932, the R. Walton Moore and the Franklin D. Roosevelt MSS in the Franklin D. Roosevelt Library, Hyde Park, New York; the Jay Pierrepont Moffat and the William Phillips MSS in the Harvard Library; the Cordell Hull, the Wilbur J. Carr, and the Raymond Clapper MSS in the Library of Congress; the George S. Messersmith MSS in the University of Delaware Library, Newark, Del.; and the Department of State MSS relating to Dodd and Germany, 1933–38, in the National Archives.

This study of Dodd's life required much reading in a variety of books, articles, memoirs, and printed documents, all of which are cited in the footnotes and will not be repeated here. Of these, however, a small number were primarily or substantially about Dodd: Wendell Holmes Stephenson, "A Half Century of Southern Historical Scholarship," *Journal of Southern History*, XI (February 1945), pp. 3–32, and *The South Lives in History* (Baton Rouge, 1955) are fine general discussions of Dodd's career as a historian, though they fail to distinguish between Dodd's contribution to southern history and his shortcomings as a progressive writer. Lowry Price Ware, "The Academic Career of William E. Dodd" (unpubl. Ph.D. diss., Dept. of History, University of South Carolina, 1956), contains some useful information, especially about the early years. Jack K. Williams, "A Bibliography of the Printed Writings of William E. Dodd," *North Carolina Historical Review*, xxx (January 1953), pp. 72–85, was helpful. The recollections of Dodd by Avery Craven ("As Teacher"), Charles Merriam ("As Statesman"), and Marcus Jernegan ("As Historian") in the *University of Chicago Magazine* (May 1940), pp. 7–10, 27, were useful, especially the piece by Craven.

The one widely read work on Dodd's ambassadorial career is Franklin L. Ford, "Three Observers in Berlin: Rumbold, Dodd, and François Poncet," in Gordon Craig and Felix Gilbert (eds.), *The Diplomats, 1919–1939* (Princeton, N.J., 1953). My evaluation of Dodd's performance as an ambassador differs markedly from Mr. Ford's. For a brief statement of my view, see Robert Dallek, "Beyond Tradition: The Diplomatic Careers of William E. Dodd and George S. Messersmith, 1933–1938," *The South Atlantic Quarterly*, LXVI (Spring 1967), pp. 233–44. Charles Beard has written a sympathetic appraisal of Dodd the man and the ambassador in the form of an introduction to Dodd's diary: William E. Dodd, Jr., and Martha Dodd (eds.), *Ambassador Dodd's Diary, 1933–1938* (New York, 1941). Dodd's ambassadorial career is also discussed at length in Martha Dodd, *Through Embassy Eyes* (New York, 1939).

While a great many newspapers, especially during and after his diplomatic career, carried stories about Dodd, the most useful were: *The New York Times, Raleigh News and Observer,* Richmond *Times-Dispatch,* Chicago *Evening Post,* and *Chicago Tribune.*

A number of Dodd's friends, colleagues, and students have shared their recollections with me. All of these interviews and letters are cited in the narrative, especially in Chapter IX, and I will not repeat them here.

Dodd himself, of course, was a prolific writer. Most of his writings have been either discussed or noted in the course of this study. With the exception of book reviews and encyclopedia articles, the following is a list of those which do not appear in the text or did not receive a full citation.

"The Principle of Instructing United States Senators," *The South Atlantic Quarterly,* I (1902), 326–332.

"Some Blemishes of the Southern People," *Raleigh News and Observer,* November 5, 1902.

"The South and Education," Richmond *Times-Dispatch,* November 6, 1902.

"The Effect of the Adoption of the Constitution upon the Finances of Virginia," *Virginia Magazine of History and Biography,* x (1903), 360–370.

"Carnegie Library in Richmond," Richmond *Times-Dispatch,* April 20, 1906.

"The President's Gridiron Speech," Richmond *Times-Dispatch,* February 8, 1907.

"John Taylor of Caroline," *The Nation,* XCII (1911), 316.

"The West and the War with Mexico," *Illinois State Historical Review,* v (1911), 159–172.

"Greenback Finance," *The Public,* XX (1917), 1220–1222.

"President Wilson and the World Peace," *The Nation,* CVII (1918), 557–558.

"The Slavery Problem," *Source Problems in United States History,* Andrew C. McLaughlin and others (New York, 1918), 369–437.

"Social Philosophy of the Old South," *American Journal of Sociology,* XXIV (1918), 735–746.

"The Great Loyalty in America," *Historical Outlook,* X (1919), 363–367.

"Roosevelt," *The Public,* XXII (1919), 1140–1141.

"Nationalism in American History," *Texas History Teacher's Bulletin,* VIII (1920), 55–66.

"President Wilson, His Treaty and His Reward," *World's Work,* XXXIX (1920), 440–447.

"Responsibility of the Senate Majority," *New Republic,* XXIII (1920), 58–59.

"Wilson and the American Tradition," *Pacific Review,* I (1921), 576–581.

"The Dilemma of Democracy in the United States," *Virginia Quarterly Review,* I (1925), 350–363.

"Andrew Jackson and His Enemies, and the Great Noise They Made in the World," *Century Magazine,* CXI (1926), 734–745.

"The Declaration of Independence," *Virginia Quarterly Review,* II (1926), 334–349.

"The Making of Andrew Jackson: All Things Worked Together for Good to Old Hickory," *Century Magazine,* CXI (1926), 531–538.

"Lincoln's Last Struggle—Victory?," *Lincoln Centennial Association Papers,* Springfield, Illinois, 1927, 49–98.

"Virginia Takes the Road to Revolution," in *The Spirit of '76 and Other Essays,* Carl Becker and others (Washington, 1927), 101–135.

The Growth of a Nation, with Eugene C. Barker and Walter P. Webb (New York, 1928).

"Our Ingrowing Habit of Lawlessness," *Century Magazine,* CXVI (1928), 691–698.

"The Habit of Crime in the United States," *Rice Institute Pamphlet,* XVI (1929), 143–151.

"Have the Scientists Done a Better Job?" *Christian Century,* XLVI (1929), 138–141.

The Story of Our Nation, with Eugene C. Barker and Walter P. Webb (New York, 1929).

"Woodrow Wilson—Ten Years After," *Contemporary Review,* CXXXV (1929), 26–38.

"Tom Paine," *American Mercury,* XXI (1930), 477–483.

"Basic Causes of the Great Depression," *University of Chicago Magazine,* New Series, XXIV (1932), 353–355.

"Historical Appeal of the Democratic Party," *Chicago Daily News,* February 12, 1932.

"Pseudo-Sovereignty as Depression's Root," *Baltimore Sun,* April 29, 1932.

"Something Less than a Revolution," *University of Chicago Magazine,* New Series, XXIV (1932), 401–403.

"Tariff and Debt Policies and Problems," *Chicago Daily News,* February 19, 1932.

"The Federal Constitution and Its Application, 1789 to 1933," *Bulletin, College of William and Mary,* XXVII (1933), 69 pp.

Our Nation Begins, with Eugene C. Barker and Walter P. Webb (New York, 1933).

Our Nation Grows Up, with Eugene C. Barker and Walter P. Webb (New York, 1933).

Our Nation's Development, with Eugene C. Barker and Henry S. Commager (New York, 1934).

"Abraham Lincoln and His Problem, 1861," *Research and Progress,* I (1935), 106–110.

"Lincoln's Dilemma," in *If Lincoln Had Lived,* M. L. Raney and others (Chicago, 1935), 43–58.

"Dilemma of Modern Civilization," in *Neutrality and Collective Security,* ed. Quincy Wright (Chicago, 1936), 93–106.

"Woodrow Wilson, 1918–1920, and the World Situation, 1938." A Pamphlet of the Democratic Women's Luncheon Club of Philadelphia, 1938, 28 pp.

Larson, Erik. *In the Garden of Beasts: Love, Terror, and an American Family in Hitler's Berlin* (New York, Random House, 2011).

Weinstein, Allen, and Alexander Vassiliev. *The Haunted Wood* (New York, Modern Library, 1999), p. 62.